FROM THIS VERSE

365 INSPIRING STORIES ABOUT THE POWER OF GOD'S WORD

ROBERT J. MORGAN

THOMAS NELSON PUBLISHERS
NASHVILLE

The Author and Publisher sincerely appreciate all the writers who are quoted in *From This Verse*. We have made every attempt to contact each one and secure permission before including their work. Unfortunately, we were not able to locate a few people, whose work is included here with our heartfelt thanks.

Published in Nashville, Tennessee, by Thomas Nelson, Inc.

ISBN 0-7852-1393-7

Printed in the United States of America

Dedication

Here are 366 Bible verses that altered lives and changed history. In this book, you'll learn amazing and inspiring stories about specific verses of Scripture that . . .

- *Kept a missionary off the* Titanic
- *Led to the widespread use of anesthesia during surgery*
- *Inaugurated the era of global communications*
- *Persuaded President Harry Truman to recognize the modern state of Israel*
- *Sparked the greatest revival in American history, the Great Awakening*
- *Motivated a famous Olympic athlete to "go for the gold"*
- *Prepared the residents of Concord, Massachusetts for the "Shot Heard 'Round the World"*
- *Inspired the Christmas carol* Joy To The World
- *Saved a teenager from being tortured to death by the Cherokees*
- *Led reformer Martin Luther to Christ*
- *Led Augustine to the Lord*
- *Brought Charles Wesley to Christ*
- *Sparked the development of the largest missionary force in history, the Wycliffe Bible translators*
- *Seared the heart of an international smuggler who literally tried to smoke the Bible*
- *Empowered Franklin Graham to break his addiction to cigarettes*
- *Enabled a man to forgive his son's murderer*
- *Facilitated the collapse of Communism in Russia during the 1989 coup attempt against Mikhail Gorbachev*
- *and 349 more!*

Of course, Bible verses are not magic wands to wave over our troubles, making them disappear like rabbits down a hat. But the Word of God *is* a two-edged sword, alive and powerful, "piercing even to the division of soul and spirit, and of joints and marrow, and is a discerner of the thoughts and intents of the heart" (Hebrews 4:12). It is inspired, infallible, inerrant, and packed with authority. And yields its secrets through daily study and meditation, bringing us into intimate fellowship with its divine author, and making us like fruit-bearing trees whose leaves remain green, even in drought.

Many of the following 366 verses are promises, for we never face any life-situation for which God has not supplied specific promises that give us "mercy and grace to help in time of need." The stories in this book, in fact, are merely illustrations of the efficacy of God's promises in meeting all the challenges, big and small, we face in life. Peter said we have been given "exceedingly great and precious promises, that through these you may be partakers of the divine nature, having escaped the corruption that is in the world through lust" (2 Peter 1:4).

The old Puritan Thomas Watson put it very quaintly in a sermon to his little congregation in England on Sunday, August 17, 1662:

> *Trade much in the promises. The promises are great supports to faith. Faith lives in a promise, as the fish lives in the water. The promises are both comforting and quickening, the very breast of the gospel; as the child by sucking the breasts gets strength, so faith by sucking the breast of a promise gets strength and revives. The promises of God are bladders [flotation devices] to keep us from sinking when we come to the waters of affliction. O! trade much in the promises, there is no condition that you can be in, but you have a promise.*

J. I. Packer comes round to the same point (minus the breasts and bladders) in his book *Knowing God:*

> *In the days when the Bible was universally acknowledged in the churches as "God's Word written," it was clearly understood that the promises recorded in Scripture were the proper, God-given basis for all our life of faith, and that the way to strengthen one's faith was to focus it upon particular promises that spoke to one's condition.**

Here, then, are 366 promises, commands, prayers, truths, and precepts that have made a difference on this planet. I hope they make a difference in your life too.

My deepest respect and appreciation go to Phil Stoner and Teri Wilhelms of Thomas Nelson Publishers who have given me superb backing, encouragement, and advice. Thanks, also, to Nelson's Jonathan Merkh, Beverly Riggs, Blythe McIntosh, and Kristin Trimpe for their support, and especially for their smiles.

I appreciate the staff and members of my church, The Donelson Fellowship, for listening to these stories on Sunday mornings and for allowing me time to compile them into this volume.

Special thanks, too, to my daughter Hannah, a student at the University of Tennessee, for her editorial assistance.

Most of all, I want to say a heartfelt word to my dear wife, Katrina Polvinen Morgan, a daily student of the Scripture and a gifted Bible teacher, for her love, insight, companionship, and encouragement.

To her this book is affectionately dedicated.

*J. I. Packer, *Knowing God* (Downers Grove, IL: InterVarsity Press, 1973), p. 103.

January

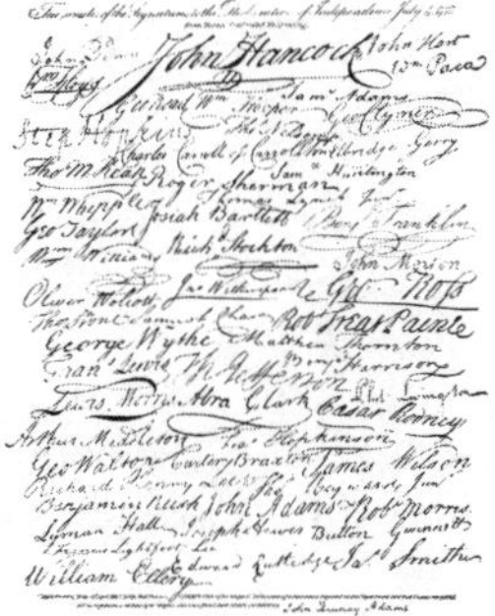

Teach Them Diligently

Leaning

abcdefghij
klmnopqr
stuvwxyz

"Here I Am, Mother!"

Infinite Consolation

To Their Descendants

January **1**

Infinite Consolation

After long years of ministry, the venerable Charles Simeon of Cambridge came to his deathbed. As his friends gathered about, he smiled, asking them, "Do you know the text that comforts me just now?"

"No," they replied. "Tell us."

"I find infinite consolation in the fact," he said, "that in the beginning God created the heavens and the earth."

Intimate comfort in an infinite God.

Yet the creating power of God not only gives us *dying* comfort, but *daily* comfort. One night during a particularly full moon, I sat on the back porch a long time, gazing through binoculars at God's "lesser light." I could even detect the rough edges of mountains and jagged peaks, and I considered again the wisdom of God in designing the universe with rings and orbs, thus giving us endless opportunities for new beginnings.

The earth, being a sphere, spins on its axis. The sun, being round, provides on orbit for the earth. The result? Every 60 seconds, we have a new minute. Every 60 minutes, we have a new hour. Every 24 hours, we have a new day. And every 365 days, we have a new January 1, a new beginning.

This is why hymnist Frances Ridley Havergal so loved New Year's Day and often devoted it to greeting her friends with special poems. At the beginning of 1874, for example, Frances, 36, printed the following poem on a specially designed greeting card and sent it out under the title "A Happy New Year! Ever such may it be!

It's too good to sing but once a year, so I've recently taken to singing it during devotions on my birthday as well.

Another year is dawning, Dear Master, let it be,
In working or in waiting, Another year for Thee.
Another year of progress, Another year of praise,
Another year of proving, Thy presence all the days.

Today's Suggested Reading

Genesis 1:1–10

In the beginning, God created the heavens and the earth. Genesis 1:1

"Here I Am, Mother!" January **2**

All three of the Wesley brothers started life curiously. John was rescued from a blazing house, a "brand plucked from the fire." Charles, born prematurely, was tightly bound for days in swaddling clothes. And Samuel?

Samuel, born February 10, 1690, worried his parents from the beginning by refusing to utter sounds. As he grew, no amount of coaxing would draw from him even one word. Friends feared he was dumb. But one day when five, Samuel hid under a table. His mother, Susanna, became alarmed when she couldn't find him, and that prompted Samuel to speak his first sentence: "Here I am, Mother!"

After that, there was no stopping him. Susanna soon realized Samuel was a precocious child. She taught him the alphabet in a snap, then she proceeded to teach him to read. What textbook did she choose? Genesis.

In short order, Samuel read all of Genesis 1:1 by himself. Then the first ten verses. Then he memorized the whole chapter, ending with the last verse: "Then God saw everything that He had made, and indeed it was very good. So the evening and the morning were the sixth day."

It was a firm foundation. Samuel became a clergyman, poet, and educator who exerted a lasting impact on many—including his younger brothers Charles and John (though he objected to their Methodism).

But Samuel's life was cut short. He went to bed in apparent health on November 5, 1739, age 49, only to awaken at three in the morning, ill. By seven, he was dead. His influence, however, outlived him and on his tombstone are the words:

Here lye interred
the remains of Rev. Mr. Samuel Wesley, A. M.
A man, for his uncommon wit and learning, esteemed by all
An excellent preacher:
But whose best sermon
was the constant example of an edifying life.

Today's Suggested Reading
Genesis 1:27–31

Then God saw everything that He had made, and indeed it was very good. So the evening and the morning were the sixth day.
Genesis 1:31

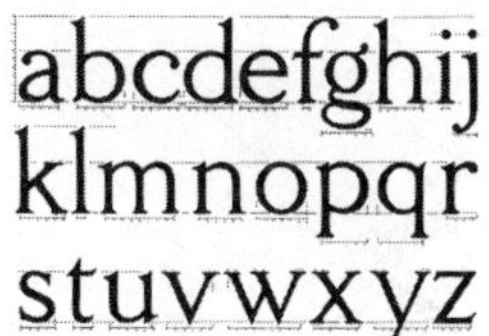

January **3**

Chloroform

Imagine surgery before the day of anesthesia. Patients were strapped down while scalpel and saw cut through tissue and bone, every slice and turn of the knife causing unimaginable pain.

One Christian physician determined to do something about it. Sir James Young Simpson (1811–1870) practiced medicine in Scotland. He became senior president of the Royal Medical Society of Edinburgh when only twenty-four, and in time received virtually every possible honor and position. He dreamed of finding a way of putting patients to sleep during surgery. On Monday evenings, Simpson periodically invited small groups of physicians to his home to experiment with chemicals, crystals, and powders, which were placed over a burning brazier while the doctors inhaled the fumes. Nothing worked until November 4, 1847. One of the men had purchased a crystal called chloroform in Paris. As the doctors sniffed the burning substance, they fell to the floor unconscious.

Simpson had his answer, but he soon encountered another problem. He was attacked by fellow Christians who claimed that pain was a God-ordained part of life. Freedom from pain comes only in heaven, and it is immoral to devise dangerous ways of escaping it on earth.

Sir James went to the Scriptures, seeking answers. He no sooner opened his Bible than he came to this verse: "And the Lord God caused a deep sleep to fall on Adam, and he slept; and He took one of his ribs, and closed up the flesh in its place." Carefully studying the text, Simpson wrote an article entitled, "Answer to the Religious Objections Advanced Against the Employment of Anesthetic Agents in Midwifery and Surgery." He ended his paper saying, "We may rest fully assured that whatever is true on point of fact or humane and merciful in point of practice, will find no condemnation in the Word of God."

His critics were silenced, and a new day dawned in medical science.

Today's Suggested Reading
Genesis 2:18–24

And the Lord God caused a deep sleep to fall on Adam, and he slept; and He took one of his ribs, and closed up the flesh in its place. Genesis 2:21

Chain Reaction

The oddly-shaped, world-famous All Souls' Church of London sits on Regent Street next to the BBC. Its esteemed pastor, Richard Bewes, credits his faith to Genesis 3:9, as spoken long ago by evangelist D. L. Moody.

In 1882, Moody, 45, conducted a whirlwind campaign through England. On Tuesday evening, September 26, he preached from this verse. In the audience, 14-year-old Tommy Bewes, youngest of 12 children in a lawyer's family, sat in rapt attention. Three days later, Tommy wrote to his sister, Evie: *I am writing to tell you some good news which you will be glad to hear. I went to one of Moody's and Sankey's meetings on Tuesday and there I was saved. He spoke from the ninth verse of the third of Genesis. It is, "Where art thou?" He said that was the first question God ever asked man in the Bible, and that is the first question that people ought to ask themselves. . . .*

Tommy's life was permanently changed, and he later became a prominent evangelical clergyman. His son, Cecil, by and by, was also led into ministry and spent over 20 years in missionary service in Kenya before returning to head up England's largest missionary society.

Cecil, in turn, had four children. One became a missionary surgeon in Africa. Another, a Christian businessman in London. A daughter became wife of an evangelical clergyman. And the fourth, Richard Bewes, is today the vicar of All Souls' Church in London.

Altogether, over 100 children, grandchildren, and great-grandchildren flow from Tommy's life, almost all of them involved in some aspect of Christian service. "Our family is today, several generations on," says Richard, "still feeling the reverberations of a single message. To God be all the glory; the credit must be his. And I'm sure that's the way Moody would have had it!"*

Today's Suggested Reading

Genesis 3:1–15

Then the Lord God called to Adam and said to him, "Where are you?" *Genesis 3:9*

---

*Adapted from Richard Thomas Bewes, "Three Generations: The Testimony of a Family," in *Decision Magazine,* September, 1982, p. 3.

Failure?

Dwight L. Moody never imagined the chain reaction produced by his sermon as described on the previous page. In this life, Christian workers seldom see more than a splinter of their success. Many preachers thrash about in apparent failure, not realizing that some word or verse or sermon or deed, like a well-buried seed, will eventually bring forth a mighty harvest. Even Moody himself occasionally succumbed to discouragement. According to his son, William Moody, he once said:

One Sunday I had preached and there did not seem to be any result. On the Monday I was very much cast down. I was sitting in my study, brooding over my want of success, when a young man who conducted a Bible class called upon me. As he came in I could see he was away up on the mountain top, while I was down in the valley. Said he: "What kind of day did you have yesterday?"

"Very poor; I had no success, and I feel quite cast down. How did you get on?"

"Oh, grandly! I never had a better day."

"What was your subject?"

"I had the life and character of Noah. Did you ever preach on Noah? Did you ever study his life? You had better do it now. It will do you good."

When the young man went away, I got out my Bible and some other books and read all I could find about Noah. I had not been reading long before the thought came stealing over me: Here is a man who toiled on for 120 years and never had a single convert outside his own family. Yet he did not get discouraged.

"I closed my Bible," said Moody. "The cloud had gone; I have never hung my harp on the willows since that day."

Today's Suggested Reading
Genesis 6:9–22

Thus Noah did; according to all that God commanded him, so he did. Genesis 6:22

Sodom Converted

January **6**

While studying law in Adams, New York, Charles Finney purchased a Bible and, for two or three years, weighed its message. One fall morning in 1821, walking to his office, he suddenly detoured to a nearby forest and ventured into the woods. There between fallen trees, he tried to pray. At first, he was troubled that someone might see him. But finally *an overwhelming sense of my wickedness in being ashamed to have a human being see me on my knees took such possession of me that I cried to the top of my voice that I would not leave that place if all the men of earth and all the devils in hell surrounded me.*

Finney prayed until the peace of Christ filled his heart.

In the days following, almost everyone Finney met was stricken with conviction of sin and converted. A revival swept through Adams, and soon Finney found himself preparing for the ministry.

One of his more unusual sermons was preached some time later in a village near Evans Mills, New York. During the service, Finney, who seldom prepared his sermons in advance, asked God to give him a text. Suddenly he remembered the story of Sodom, city of Lot. Genesis 19:14 rushed to mind: "Get up, get out of this place; for the Lord will destroy this city!"

In his sermon, Finney painted the condition of Sodom before God destroyed it. *I had not spoken in this strain more than a quarter hour when an awful solemnity seemed to settle upon them; the congregation began to fall from their seats in every direction and cried for mercy. If I had had a sword in each hand, I could not have cut them down as fast as they fell. Everyone prayed who was able to speak at all.*

Only afterward Finney learned the village where he preached was known as Sodom, and the man who had invited him was called Lot.

Today's Suggested Reading

Genesis 19:12–25

Get up, get out of this place; for the Lord will destroy this city! Genesis 19:14

Letters of Gold

Young Miss Laura Belle Barnard, deeply southern and very proper, shocked family and friends when she declared she was going to India as a missionary. Even her denomination, the Free Will Baptists, were shocked, for they had no missions program as yet.

But Laura Belle, as good as her word, did go to India. Her first furlough approached just as World War II erupted. She was troubled about leaving and about her prospects for returning. But . . . *God gave me a word and confirmed it twice. I had been reading from a certain devotional book, and that morning I was especially asking God to give me clear understanding as to whether or not I should leave India at that time. This was the verse for the day in that devotional book: "And, behold, I am with thee, and will keep thee in all places whither thou goest, and will bring thee again into this land; for I will not leave thee, until I have done that which I have spoken to thee of" (Genesis 28:15).**

Shortly after, a friend unexpectedly urged the same verse on her. Then another friend sent her an envelope marked, "To be opened as you leave the shores of India." Aboard ship, Laura Belle opened the letter and read these words: *I asked the Lord to give me a word of encouragement for you as my farewell message. This passage, as I was reading my Bible this morning, seemed meant for you. I pass it on with the confidence that it is the Lord's word to you now."*

It was Genesis 28:15.

The war delayed Laura Belle Barnard's return for five long years. But she never lost confidence that God would keep his thrice-given promise, to watch over her and bring her again into this land.

Today's Suggested Reading
Genesis 28:10–22

Behold, I am with you and will keep you wherever you go, and will bring you back to this land; for I will not leave you until I have done what I have spoken to you. Genesis 28:15

---

*King James Version

Beat-Up or Up-Beat? January **8**

Problems don't always come in threes. Sometimes they come in fours, fives, or sixes. Consider the patriarch Jacob. He had lost one son. Another had been accused of espionage and was imprisoned. Now his beloved Benjamin was in danger. Family problems multiplied, a famine struck, and the whole family teetered on the edge of starvation. Jacob, aged and defeated, complained, "All these things are against me."

His attitude was understandable, but he badly underestimated God's care. He didn't realize the truth of Hudson Taylor's little poem:

Ill that God blesses is our good
And unblest good is ill;
And all is right that seems most wrong
If it be his sweet will.

In *A Turtle on a Fencepost,* Allan Emery tells of accompanying businessman Ken Hansen to visit a hospitalized employee. The patient lay very still, his eyes conveying anguish. His operation had taken eight hours, and recovery was long and uncertain.

"Alex," said Ken quietly, "you know I have had a number of serious operations. I know the pain of trying to talk. I think I know what questions you're asking. There are two verses I want to give you—Genesis 42:36 and Romans 8:28. We have the option of these two attitudes. We need the perspective of the latter."

Hansen turned to the passages, read them, then prayed and left. The young man, Alex Balc, took the message to heart. He later enjoyed full recovery.

Every day we choose one of these attitudes amid life's difficulties—to be beat-up, or to be up-beat. To say with Jacob in Genesis 42:36: *All these things are against me.*

Or to say with Paul in Romans 8:28: *All these things are working together for good to those who love the Lord. . . .**

Today's Suggested Reading
Genesis 42:29–36

All these things are against me. Genesis 42:36

---

*Adapted from Allan Emery, *Turtle on a Fencepost* (Word Books, 1979).

Helps to Holiness

Jacob may not have known Romans 8:28, but his son did. At least, Joseph's words in Genesis 50:20 are the Old Testament's counterpart to Romans 8:28. And those are the very words that comforted Samuel Logan Brengle when his head was bashed in.

Brengle, whose father was killed in the Civil War, was raised by his mother on an Indiana farm. Under her guidance, he became a Christian, and after her death, selling the farm to finance his education, he prepared for ministry. Brengle ached for the hungry and homeless, and he traveled to London to join the Salvation Army.

There Brengle met General William Booth, founder of the Army, who eyed the young American and said ominously, "Brengle, I don't think you will want to submit to Salvation Army discipline. We are an Army, and we demand obedience."

"I have received the Holy Spirit as my sanctifier and guide," replied Brengle. "He has led me to offer myself to you. Give me a chance."

He got his chance, and he excelled in humility and service. It was some time later in Boston that the attack came. He was ministering in skid row, and a drunk aimed a brick at his skull. It nearly killed him. But while recovering, Brengle devoted himself to writing articles for the Salvation Army's magazine, *War Cry*. His columns became so popular they were collected and published as *Helps to Holiness*. Afterward many people told Brengle how much his little book had meant to them. His invariable reply was, "Well, if there had been no little brick, there would have been no little book."

His wife kept the offending brick, and on it she painted Genesis 50:20 as their testimony: "As for you, you thought evil against me; but God meant it unto good. . . ."*

Today's Suggested Reading
Genesis 50:15–26

But as for you, you meant evil against me; but God meant it for good, in order to bring it about as it is this day, to save many people alive. Genesis 50:20

---

*King James Version

God's Payroll

Samuel Logan Brengle and Billy Sunday had much in common. Both were raised by godly mothers on Midwestern farms after their fathers had perished in the Civil War. Both became famous preachers who gave the credit to their Lord and to their mothers. And both were very familiar with skid row. Brengle preached there. Sunday lived there awhile.

Billy Sunday initially gained fame as an outfielder for the Chicago White Sox, but his career was marred by drinking. One night, staggering down the street, he heard a Salvation Army group singing a song his mother used to sing: "Where Is My Wandering Boy Tonight?" Later that evening at the Pacific Garden Mission, Sunday gave his life to Christ. He soon left the baseball diamond for the pulpit.

Among his inimitable, bombastic sermons is one from Exodus 2:9 about Moses' mother: "Take this child away and nurse him for me, and I will give you your wages." Thinking of his own mother, Sunday said: *Being a king, emperor, or president is mighty small potatoes compared to being a mother. Commanding an army is little more than sweeping a street compared with training a boy or girl. The mother of Moses did more for the world than all the kings that Egypt ever had. Oh, you wait until you reach the mountains of eternity, then read the mothers' names in God's Hall of Fame. I tell you women: Fooling away your time, hugging and kissing a poodle dog, drinking a cocktail, and playing cards is mighty small business compared to molding the life of a child.*

"Take this child away and nurse it for me, and I will give thee thy wages." God pays in joy that is fireproof, famine-proof, and devil-proof.

"Take this child away and nurse it for me, and I will give thee thy wages." If you haven't been doing that, then get your name on God's payroll.

Today's Suggested Reading

Exodus 2:1–10

Take this child away and nurse him for me, and I will give you your wages. Exodus 2:9

Touchdown

Brian Pruitt always kneels in the end zone after scoring—and he scores as fast as anyone in football. On the first drive of a recent game at Central Michigan University, for example, Brian scored on a 66-yard run before ninety ticks of the play clock had elapsed. That's typical. "You can't say enough good things about Brian Pruitt," said one coach. "Power, strength, and speed in a compact body. He's just a complete package."

If so, it took awhile for the package to develop. During Brian's senior year of high school, he grew empty and depressed. He was contemplating suicide one day when fellow player Jeff Mostek offered him a ride home. Jeff witnessed to Brian and invited him to an evangelistic meeting. When the altar call was given, Brian raced forward as though rushing for a touchdown.

But Brian's new faith was quickly put to the test. His dream of playing collegiate football faded when he was disqualified during his first year at Central Michigan because of low grades. During those days, Brian drew strength in Exodus 4, noticing how God told Moses to cast down his staff. When Moses later retrieved it, it possessed new strength.

It was my talent, but that year God said, "Lay it all down," to the point where I didn't even care if I played anymore. I was like, "God, whatever you want for my life." When I picked it back up, it wasn't my talent anymore, it was God's talent. Even though I got discouraged, God took that year, and he prepared me for what was going to come. I don't think I could have handled the publicity and all those things if I wouldn't have spent that year in preparation.

I'm not a football player, Brian Pruitt now says. *I'm a Christian who plays football.**

Today's Suggested Reading
Exodus 4:1–12

Then the Lord said to Moses, "Reach out your hand and take it by the tail" (and he reached out his hand and caught it, and it became a rod in his hand), that they may believe that the Lord God of their fathers . . . has appeared to you." Exodus 4:4–5

*Adapted from "A Mt. Pleasant Surprise," by Karen Foulke in *Sports Spectrum,* March, 1995, p. 11.

New Year's Sermon

Time has forgotten quaint Roland Hill, but in eighteenth-century England he was dearly loved. He founded and built London's famous Surrey Chapel with his own inheritance, and there he preached to immense audiences from 1773 until his death fifty years later. When he grew so old his voice barely carried across the pews, his people said, "But it does us good if we can only see him!"

On his last New Year's Day, Roland Hill chose Exodus 12:2 as the text for his sermon. He was 89 years old and would be dead by mid-April. But his sermon was clear and deep and powerful. Its point was simple: Just as the slaying of the Passover Lamb in Exodus 12 served as the beginning of the Hebrew calendar, so our experience with the Lamb of God, Jesus Christ, begins a new life for each of us. Here are a few sentences from his message on the first Sunday of 1833:

> *Brethren, time passes very quickly. We are now beginning a new year—which of us will be alive when the year is concluded? The days of my pilgrimage must be nearly ended. . . . But my dear brethren, we never begin to live till we live to God. I remember once seeing an old man, I suppose he must have been 70 or 80 years of age; and I asked him how old he was. He looked at me for a time, and faltered in his voice, the tears trickling down his cheeks; says he, "I am two years old." "Two years old?" "Ah, sir," says he, "till a little time ago I lived the life of a dead man; and I never knew what life was till I met with the life which is 'hid with Christ in God.'"*

Today's Suggested Reading
Exodus 12:1–11

This month shall be your beginning of months; it shall be the first month of the year to you. Exodus 12:2

Elim House

Carey Falwell grew up running bootleg whiskey during Prohibition, aided by his beloved younger brother Garland, a likable chap with a grin that could melt an iceberg. But the brothers were star-crossed. Garland was wild and careless, flying along mountain roads in a black roadster, drinking heavily, causing trouble. One day Garland armed himself with two pistols and aimed them at Carey in a drunken rage. A dangerous cat-and-mouse game ensued, but Carey finally fired a shotgun in self-defense, instantly killing his younger sibling.

Carey never reconciled himself with the tragedy. Morning after morning, he visited Garland's grave, staring down, hat gripped in hand. Night after night, unable to sleep, he brooded at the table or in the barn, nursing a whiskey, trying to forget. Dark moods seized him and his drinking increased. Time passed, and he grew embittered. He eventually succumbed to cirrhosis of the liver.

Against all odds, Carey's son Jerry grew up to be a minister. And it was Jerry Falwell who led his Thomas Road Baptist Church to purchase a farm and establish there a treatment center for alcoholics. The first man to enroll was Earl Thompson, who had once helped Carey Falwell smuggle his booze.

But what should the new center be called? As Jerry studied Exodus 15, he read of the Israelites going from the Red Sea to the waters of Marah to the wells of Elim. There were lessons at every stop, and along the way the Lord replaced bitterness with blessings. The center was named Elim House, a place of blessing. Soon other Elim Houses popped up around the nation, modeled after the one in Lynchburg.

One day, when Jerry Falwell took his mother to see Elim House, she laid her hand on his arm, and, eyes moist, said, "Do you know, Jerry, if your father hadn't died you might not have cared enough about the others to build this place."

Today's Suggested Reading

Exodus 15:22–27

Then they came to Elim, where there were twelve wells of water and seventy palm trees; so they camped there by the waters. Exodus 15:27

Resting on That Word

January **14**

Among the lesser-known heroes of the church is a man with the unlikely name of Ebenezer Erskine, who first fell in love with Exodus 20:2 at age ten when his father, Rev. Henry Erskine, was teaching on the Shorter Catechism. The forty-third question asks: "What is the preface to the Ten Commandments?" The answer: "The preface to the Ten Commandments is: 'I am the Lord thy God which have brought thee out of the land of Egypt. . . .'" Young Ebenezer learned the whole Catechism, but this question took central place in his thoughts.

Eighteen years later he followed his father's steps into the pastorate. *But I began my ministry without much zeal, mechanically, being swallowed up in unbelief.* One day his wife grew fevered, and in her delirium, she cried out about her husband's cold heart. Ebenezer, sitting by her, was pierced, and the old text came back to him: *I am the Lord your God.* Shortly after, he offered himself up, *soul and body, unto God the Father, Son, and Holy Ghost. I flee for shelter to the blood of Jesus. I will live to him; I will die to him.*

Ten years later, now a 38-year-old pastor, he preached a powerful sermon on his old text: *I am the Lord thy God.* It made a lasting impression on his congregation and swept over Scotland in printed form.

More years passed, and Erskine gave out at age 73. One of his elders, visiting his bedside, said, "You have often given us good advice, Mr. Erskine, as to what we should do with our souls in death; may I ask what you are now doing with your own?"

"I am doing what I did forty years ago," replied the old preacher. "I am resting on that word, 'I am the Lord thy God.'"

Today's Suggested Reading
Exodus 20:1–11

I am the Lord your God, who brought you out of the land of Egypt, out of the house of bondage. Exodus 20:2

Candles

On August 19, 1991, Communist hardliners in Moscow, angry with their loss of Eastern Europe, seized control of the Soviet government while Mikhail Gorbachev was in the Crimea. Boris Yeltsin and the Russian parliament were trapped in the parliament building as thousands of brave citizens gathered outside, forming a human barricade. Tanks and troops ringed the building, and the world held its breath.

Here's what the newspapers didn't report. According to Barbara Von Der Heydt in her book *Candles Behind the Wall,* when news of the coup broke, Iven Kharlanov and Anatoly Rudenko of the Bible Society in Moscow discussed how to persuade the troops not to fire on protesters. They called Bible societies around the world asking prayer, then plotted a bold scheme.

Just as the storming of parliament appeared imminent, they showed up with a truck loaded with New Testaments. Christians went from soldier to soldier and from tank to tank, handing out the Scripture and quoting Exodus 20:13. One woman, Shirinai Dossova, walked over to one of the tanks and knocked loudly on its side with her knuckles. She continued until the baffled driver opened the hatch and appeared. "It says in this book that you shouldn't kill," she said, thrusting a Bible at him. "Are you going to kill us?"

The young soldier looked confused. He took the Bible, saying, "We're not intending to kill anybody."

Almost all the soldiers accepted the proffered Testaments. Some tucked them in their pockets while others began reading at once. Many had always wanted a Bible but had never seen one. And with each Bible came the question, "You're not really going to kill us, are you? This book says, 'Thou shalt not kill.'"

The coup collapsed, the Communist empire crashed to the ground—and historians are still pondering why the expected attack on the parliament building never materialized.**

Today's Suggested Reading
Exodus 20:12–17

*Thou shalt not kill. Exodus 20:13**

*King James Version

**Adapted from *Candles Behind the Wall* by Barbara Von Der Heydt (Grand Rapids, MI: Eerdmans Publishing Co., 1993).

An Unexpected Verse January **16**

Jim Elliot was unsure what to do after graduating from Wheaton College in 1949. He spent the summer praying for guidance, and on October 29 received a letter about the need for workers in Ecuador. Jim felt a "simple urge" in that direction. On November 25, his diary records interest in Peru and India. On December 1, British Guiana entered the picture. Four days later he wrote, *Stirred for work among the Ecuadorian Quichuas again.*

On December 17, his missionary plans narrowed to either India or Ecuador. On December 31, he wrote: *O Lord, if you see anything in me holding back the revelation of Your will about Ecuador, uncover it. Had a letter from India today which ended, "I would rejoice to think the New Year would find you here." Still I am waiting.*

Early in 1950, he received acceptance from Wycliffe Bible Translator's study camp in Oklahoma. *Feel as though the Lord would have me there, whether I go to India or South America.* Elliot arrived at the camp, still torn between two nations. The tutor assigned him was a missionary from Ecuador, and from him Jim first learned of the savage Aucas.

But India still burned within him. On July 4, Jim set aside ten days for prayer. On July 14 he wrote, *I asked for some word from God ten days ago, which would encourage my going to Ecuador. It came this morning in an unexpected place. I was reading in Exodus 23 when verse 20 came out vividly. "Behold I send an angel before thee to keep thee by the way and to bring thee into the place which I have prepared."* Coming as it did, with such preceding feelings and simple believing for some promise, I take this as leading . . . to Ecuador.*

This is the verse that sent Jim Elliot to his death, to his martyrdom, and to his glory—and that brought the Aucas, in God's timing, to faith in Jesus Christ.

Today's Suggested Reading
Exodus 23:20–33

Behold, I send an Angel before you to keep you in the way and to bring you into the place which I have prepared. Exodus 23:20

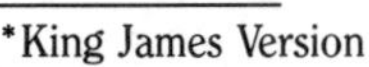

*King James Version

January **17** Urim and Thummim

Harry A. Ironside was an exacting Bible student who took painstaking care in correctly interpreting and teaching the Word of God. Usually. There was one occasion, however, when, using a story, he stretched the meaning of a text to the breaking point. But even then, he got it right.

It was in a sermon from Leviticus 8:8 about the Urim and Thummim. This mysterious device was attached to the priest's breastplate and somehow served to reveal God's will in certain matters. Some believe it was a pouch containing two stones, one indicating "Yes" and the other signifying "No." Others believe it was composed of jewels attached to the priest's breastplate and which somehow indicated God's will in various matters.

Ironside gave it all a different twist as he told of a young British minister well-versed in all matter of theology. In his church sat a poor cobbler who, though uneducated, knew the Bible through and through. One day the minister, wanting to impress the cobbler, asked, "Can you tell me what the Urim and the Thummim were?"

"I don't know exactly," replied the cobbler at length. "I understand that the words apply to something that was on the breastplate of the high priest. I know that through the Urim and Thummim the high priest was able to discern the mind of God. But I find that I can get the mind of the Lord nowadays just by changing two letters."

"By changing two letters?" asked the minister.

"Yes. I take this blessed book, and just by usin' and thummin' I get the mind of the Lord."

Ironside, laughing, endorsed the cobbler's view. Use the Word of God daily, he told his audience. Thumb through it frequently, for it reveals the mind of Christ.

Today's Suggested Reading
Leviticus 8:1–9

Then he put the breastplate on him, and he put the Urim and the Thummim in the breastplate.
Leviticus 8:8

Ten to Two

January **18**

Several years ago a group of fledging students sat around the old oak table in Ruth Bell Graham's kitchen, listening to her stories. They were lonely and homesick. College life had been ruder than expected. Ruth's eyes glowed as she told of her own bouts with loneliness while a boarding student in Korea, and again during her husband's extended absences while preaching. But the joy of God's presence during Bible study helped ease the pain, she said. "Bible students are wide-eyed travelers in the midst of wonders."

She showed them her little notebook, one she had worn out several times. "I've found a leather craftsman who rebinds it for me when necessary," she explained. "Here I jot journal entries, stories I hear, and spiritual lessons God teaches me. As you record your Bible studies, over the years you'll actually be compiling your own personal Bible commentary."

The next day, one of the students opened his heart to her in private, admitting defeat in his Christian life. The depth of her wisdom was veiled only by the simplicity of her response. She told him of the twelve spies in Numbers 13. They were sent by Moses to scrutinize the Promised Land. It was theirs for the taking, for God had assured them of his presence and of his conquering power. But ten of the spies lost their nerve, seeing only giants, walled cities, and strong defenses. Joshua and Caleb, on the other hand, were undaunted and full of faith. "Let us go up at once and possess the land," they said, "for the Lord our God is with us."

"Now," asked Ruth, "what was the difference between the two sets of spies? Just this . . ." She paused for effect. "The ten compared themselves to their problems, but the two compared their problems with God!"

And I will never forget her words that day, or the discerning smile that punched them home.

Today's Suggested Reading

Numbers 13:26–33

Then Caleb quieted the people before Moses, and said, "Let us go up at once and take possession, for we are well able to overcome it." Numbers 13:30

Look and Live

The saintly Robert Murray McCheyne, who died at 29, lives on through his matchless sermons and letters. One of those letters, dated March 20, 1840, begins like this: *I do not even know your name, but I think I know something of the state of your soul. Your friend has told me a little of your mind; and I write a few lines just to bid you look to Jesus and live. Look at Numbers 21:9, and you will see your disease and your remedy. You have been bitten by the great serpent. The poison of sin is through and through your whole heart, but Christ has been lifted up on the cross that you may look and live.*

D. L. Moody bore the same message. During the Battle of Murfreesboro, he visited the bedside of a dying soldier. Moody shared the gospel, but the man shook his head saying, "He can't save me. I've sinned all my life." Moody tried verse after verse, but nothing worked until *I read from the third chapter of John. As I read on, his eyes became riveted upon me, and he seemed to drink every syllable. When I came to the words, "As Moses lifted up the serpent in the wilderness, even so must the Son of Man be lifted up: that whosoever believeth in him should not perish but have eternal life," he stopped me and asked: "Is that there?"*

"Yes," I said.

"Well, I never knew that was in the Bible. Read it again." Moody read it over and over, explaining how the brass snake in Numbers 13 foreshadowed Christ's death on Calvary.

Early next morning I came to his cot, but it was empty. The attendant told me the young man had died peacefully, repeating to himself that glorious proclamation: "Whosoever believeth in him should not perish, but have eternal life."

Today's Suggested Reading
Numbers 21:4–9

So Moses made a bronze serpent, and put it on a pole; and so it was, if a serpent had bitten anyone, when he looked at the bronze serpent, he lived. Numbers 21:9

Has He Said?

The Protestant Reformation, which began in 1517, produced virtually no church-sent missionaries until two Moravians, Leonard Dober and David Nitschmann, left the warmth of their community of Herrnhut and ventured to St. Croix in 1732.

It was Herrnhut's leader, Count Nicholaus Ludwig von Zinzendorf, who spurred their going. Zinzendorf had visited Copenhagen the previous year on political business. While there, he had met a black man from St. Thomas, who pleaded with him to send someone to share the gospel with his enslaved family members in the Danish West Indies.

Back at Herrnhut, Zinzendorf shared this burden, and it took root. A year later, on August 18, 1732, two young men were commissioned as missionaries in an unforgettable service in which a hundred hymns were sung. Leonard Dober and David Nitschmann soon left Herrnhut for Copenhagen, seeking passage to the islands.

But Copenhagen proved unfriendly, and the two men were pelted with obstacles. One disappointment followed another, and much opposition arose to their mission. No one would help them. No ship would take them. Their hearts sank.

At that critical moment, Numbers 23:19 turned up in their daily devotional book: *Has He said, and will He not do? Or has He spoken, and will He not make it good?* Inspired by these words, Dober and Nitschmann determined to persevere, believing that God would fulfill what he had started through them.

A handful of people in Copenhagen began helping them, and the tide of public opinion turned. Two royal chaplains lent their support, and even the Queen of Denmark encouraged them. Princess Charlotte contributed financially. A court official secured passage for them on a Dutch ship, and on October 8, 1732, they sailed for the West Indies, opening the modern era of missions.

The Lord had spoken to them, and He had made it good.

Today's Suggested Reading

Numbers 23:11–19

God is not a man, that He should lie, nor a son of man, that He should repent. Has He said, and will He not do? Or has He spoken, and will He not make it good? Numbers 23:19

January **21**

Morse Code

Today's "Global Village" and "Information Superhighway" began with a young artist named Samuel Morse. The son of a minister, Morse sailed to London at age 19 to study art. He was acutely homesick. "I wish that in one instant I could tell you of my safe arrival," he wrote, "but we are 3000 miles apart and must wait four weeks to hear from each other."

Morse became a respected artist and portrait painter, but his life took a sudden turn in 1832 as he traveled back to America aboard the *Sully.* One night the conversation at his dinner table turned to the sending of electric messages along a length of wire. Morse was seized by the idea, and, arriving home, took a room atop his brother's newspaper building and spent every spare moment slaving over his "Tele-Graph."

After years of trial and error, Morse prepared a dramatic demonstration. He laid two miles of waterproofed wire under New York Harbor. Unfortunately, a ship's anchor caught the wire and destroyed it, and the crowds left, muttering.

But Morse planned an even more dramatic demonstration for the United States Congress. On May 24, 1844, before assembled dignitaries, he sent a message from the U.S. Capitol to the railroad depot in Baltimore. The first telegraph message consisted of four words from Numbers 23:23: *"What Hath God Wrought!"*

All America and Europe were soon linked by telegraph poles and wires.

"It is all of God," Morse later said. "He used me as His hand in all this. I am not indifferent to the rewards of earth and the praise of my fellow men, but I am more pleased with the fact that my Father in heaven has allowed me to do something for Him and for His world. Not unto us, but unto God be all the glory. Not what hath man, but what hath God wrought!"

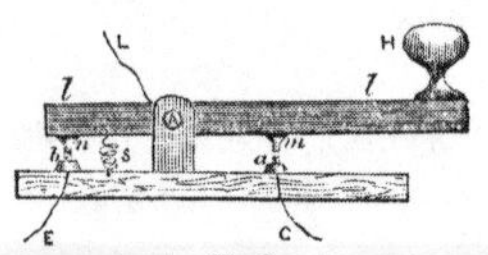

Today's Suggested Reading
Numbers 23:19–23

*What hath God wrought! Numbers 23:23**

---

*King James Version

To Their Descendants

January **22**

For a hundred years before the establishment of the modern state of Israel, Christians worked alongside Jews in advancing Zionism, but nothing created more sympathy for the rebirth of the Jewish nation than reports emerging after World War II of the Holocaust. Still, President Harry Truman, aware of impending Arab-Israeli conflict, was reluctant to recognize the new state. On May 12, 1948, several advisors gathered with him to discuss the issue. Secretary of State George C. Marshall was against recognition, warning that the Jews faced war on every side. But to Marshall's dismay, Clark Clifford, Truman's political advisor, urged the president to recognize Israel at once.

"I don't even know why Clifford is here," Marshall grumbled. "This is not a political meeting."

"He is here," Truman said, "because I asked him."

Clifford made his case calmly and persuasively. He reminded the men of the 6 million Jews murdered by the Nazis, and of the survivors with nowhere to go. A separate Jewish state was inevitable, Clifford said. And then he quoted Deuteronomy 1:8—*See, I have set the land before you; go in and possess the land which the Lord swore to your fathers—to Abraham, Isaac, and Jacob—to give to them and their descendants after them.*

Marshall became so angry he threatened to vote against Truman in the next election, bringing the meeting to an icy close. But two days later, the nation of Israel was born, and President Harry Truman became the first head of state to afford it official recognition.

Later, when Israel's Chief Rabbi, Isaac Herzog, visited the White House, he told Truman, "God put you in your mother's womb so that you would be the instrument to bring the rebirth of Israel after 2000 years."

"I thought he was overdoing things," said an observer, "but when I looked over at the president, tears were running down his cheeks."

Today's Suggested Reading

Deuteronomy 1:1–8

See, I have set the land before you; go in and possess the land which the Lord swore to your fathers—to Abraham, Isaac, and Jacob—to give to them and their descendants after them.
Deuteronomy 1:8

Solomon's Wisdom

Solomon Ginsburg seemed destined to follow in his father's footsteps as a rabbi to the oppressed community of Polish Jews. But during his early manhood, to his father's horror, Solomon became a Christian.

His conversion brought him intense persecution. On one occasion he was beaten unmercifully, kicked till unconscious, and left for dead in a garbage box, bones broken, clothing soaked with blood. "Oh, but those were glorious times," he later said.

Solomon became a fiery evangelist across both Europe and South America. In 1911, needing rest, he decided to head to America on furlough. His route took him to Lisbon where he planned to cross the Bay of Biscay to London, then on to the States.

Arriving in Lisbon, Ginsburg found the bulletin boards plastered with weather telegrams warning of terrific storms raging on the Bay of Biscay. It was dangerous sailing, and he was advised to delay his trip a week. His ticket allowed him to do that, and he prayed about it earnestly.

But as he prayed, he turned to his W.M.U. prayer calendar and found the text for that day was Deuteronomy 2:7—"For the Lord your God has blessed you in all the work of your hand. He knows your trudging through this great wilderness. These forty years the Lord your God has been with you; you have lacked nothing." The Lord seemed to assure him that his long, worldwide travels were under divine protection. Ginsburg boarded ship at once, crossed without incident, and caught the *Majestic* in London. His transatlantic voyage was smooth and restful.

Only after arriving in the United States did Solomon learn that had he delayed his trip in Lisbon, he would have arrived in London just in time . . .

. . . just in time to board the *Titanic*.

Today's Suggested Reading

Deuteronomy 2:1–7

For the Lord your God has blessed you in all the work of your hand. He knows your trudging through this great wilderness. These forty years the Lord your God has been with you; you have lacked nothing. Deuteronomy 2:7

Teach Them Diligently

Deuteronomy 6 contains God's three best ideas for raising children. As parents, we should: (1) Love the Lord our God with all our hearts—verse 5; (2) Let the Word of God dwell richly in our hearts—verse 6; and (3) Teach the Word diligently to our children—verse 7. If I could start the parenting years over again, I would lead my children to memorize more Scripture.

So would Mayo Mathers.

Mayo is a wife, mother, writer, and co-owner of a business in Oregon. When son Tyler was in the fifth grade, he was given a two-week assignment to memorize part of the Declaration of Independence. Mayo drilled him diligently, printing words onto cards and taping them around the house, even to the headboard of his bed. They reviewed the project morning and evening, and by the end of the period, everyone in the family knew the assignment perfectly.

At the same time, Tyler had been given a memory verse to learn for his Sunday school class. But Mayo waited until the following Sunday morning, as they drove to church, to cram the verse into his brain.

The next day in her devotions, Mayo came across Deuteronomy 6:7—You shall teach [God's Scriptures] diligently to your children, and shall talk of them when you sit in your house, when you walk by the way, when you lie down, and when you rise up.

*I realized that that was what I had done with memorizing part of the Declaration of Independence, but not with memorizing the Bible verse. And having emphasized Tyler's school assignment over his Sunday school assignment, I was teaching him to seek the rewards of this world over the rewards of heaven.**

It's very easy to neglect Bible memory, but nothing is more important for our children. And no time is better for beginning than today!

Today's Suggested Reading
Deuteronomy 6:1–9

You shall teach them diligently to your children, and shall talk of them when you sit in your house, when you walk by the way, when you lie down, and when you rise up. Deuteronomy 6:7

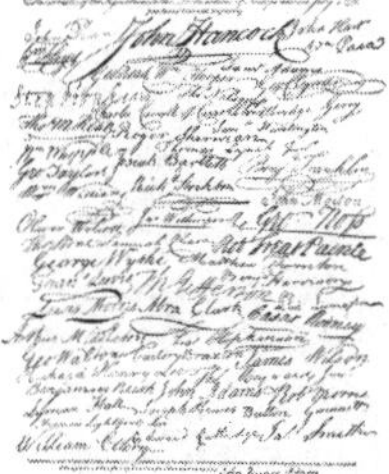

---

*Adapted from "Good Enough for a Piece of Candy," by Mayo Mathers in *Decision*, December, 1997, p. 33, © 1997; published by the Billy Graham Evangelistic Association.

Remembering

On a recent trip to London, I searched out a little church sitting quietly amid the bustling, towering buildings of London's financial district. The door was unlocked, and I ventured into the dimly-lit chapel, with its high pulpit and handful of pews. On the left wall was the plaque I sought, a tribute to the church's former pastor whose remains were buried beneath my feet in the church vault. I read the words aloud, my voice bouncing against the stone walls: *John Newton, clerk, once an infidel and libertine, a servant of slaves in Africa, was, by the rich mercy of our Lord and Saviour Jesus Christ, preserved, restored, pardoned, and appointed to preach the faith he had long labored to destroy.*

As a young man, Newton had been a seaman and slave trader whose mouth was a cesspool of profanity, and who liberally helped himself to the female slaves he transported. But he also became a deserter, flogged by the British Navy, who was reduced to being the slave of a sadistic woman, herself a slave, in Africa.

Out of all this he was saved. And he became one of England's greatest preachers, the author of the beloved hymn *Amazing Grace.*

When he entered the ministry, he printed Deuteronomy 15:15 in bold letters on a plaque and fastened it across the wall over his study mantle, and in the sight of this verse he prepared every sermon: *Thou shalt remember that thou wast a bondsman in the land of Egypt, and the Lord thy God redeemed thee.**

Late in life, when his mind began failing, he told his friend William Jay, "My memory is nearly gone; but I remember two things, that I am a great sinner and that Christ is a Great Savior."

Thou shalt remember, the Lord had said.

I remember, said Newton. *I once was lost, but now I'm found, was blind but now I see.*

Today's Suggested Reading

Deuteronomy 15:1–15

You shall remember that you were a slave in the land of Egypt, and the Lord your God redeemed you. . . . Deuteronomy 15:15

---

*King James Version

The Ridderhofs had little money, but they were rich in singing, worshiping, and love. Their daughter, Joy, knew the gospel from infancy, and at age 13, she gave her heart to the Lord Jesus. She went on to study at the University of Los Angeles, preparing to be a teacher. At the same time, Joy kept busy leading Bible clubs, witnessing to neighbors, and singing in a quartet. Her friends didn't dream she secretly battled anxiety. Yet exams, public speaking, and the uncertainty of the future kept her spinning from one state of worry to the next, all of it well-hidden but inwardly crippling.

Then she attended a Victorious Christian Life Conference at her church. The speaker, Robert C. McQuilkin, declared, "Worry is a sin. It amounts to a grievous lack of faith in the Father's care." That week changed Joy's attitude, and soon she found herself enrolling in McQuilkin's Bible School in South Carolina.

Four years later, she was back in Los Angeles, well-trained for missionary service, but unsure of her next step. "Lord, whatever door you open, I'll go there," she prayed. Soon a mission board approached her about Honduras. Joy, wanting to serve God in Africa, was hesitant. But while lunching at a friend's house, she picked a card at random from a little box of Bible verses. It was Deuteronomy 28:8—"The Lord will command the blessing on you in your storehouses and in all to which you set your hand, and He will bless you in the land which the Lord your God is giving you."

The verse spoke directly to her in an undeniable way, and Joy sensed God's directing her to Honduras. As it turned out, Honduras became but the first stop on a lifelong, worldwide ministry for Joy Ridderhof, founder of Gospel Recordings, Inc., an enterprise that has blanketed the earth with recordings of the gospel in nearly 5,000 languages.

Today's Suggested Reading
Deuteronomy 28:1–8

The Lord will command the blessing on you in your storehouses and in all to which you set your hand, and He will bless you in the land which the Lord your God is giving you. Deuteronomy 28:8

A Novel Sight

For over 200 years Sunday schools have gathered the people together, millions of men, women, and children, hearing and learning and observing the words of God's law. Much of the credit goes to Robert Raikes, an eighteenth-century newspaper publisher in Gloucester, England. Raikes was a prosperous and pompous man with a soft spot for ragamuffins. He determined to begin a school for them in the slums of Gloucester. Since children worked Mondays through Saturdays, he selected Sundays, and in 1780 his first Sunday school began in Mrs. Meredith's kitchen on Sooty Alley. The children learned reading and writing, using the Bible as a textbook. After several years, Raikes's experiment was working well enough to publicize in his newspaper.

Then he had another idea. An annual festival was held near Gloucester, and it was always packed with hard-drinking, rabble-rousing crowds. Raikes distributed curious leaflets inviting the people to the festival to witness "a novel sight." On Sunday, September 24, 1786, the crowds flocked in. There, standing before the church, were 331 clean, well-dressed Sunday school children. Many in the crowd had never before seen a clean, well-dressed child.

Raikes had persuaded his friend, Dr. Samuel Glasse, to prepare a special address. Glasse rose, looked at the throng, and preached a sermon from Deuteronomy 31:12–13—"Gather the people together, men and women and little ones, and the stranger who is within your gates, that they may hear and that they may learn to fear the Lord your God and carefully observe all the words of this law, and that their children, who have not known it, may hear and learn to fear the Lord your God as long as you live. . . ."

Dr. Glasse's sermon swept across England in printed form under the title, "The Piety, Wisdom, and Policy of Promoting Sunday Schools." And the Sunday school movement was soon established.

Today's Suggested Reading
Deuteronomy 31:7–13

Gather the people together, men and women and little ones, and the stranger who is within your gates, that they may hear and that they may learn to fear the Lord your God and carefully observe all the words of this law, and that their children, who have not known it, may hear and learn to fear the Lord your God as long as you live. . . . Deuteronomy 31:12–13

The Wrath to Come

Today's ominous verse of Scripture is one of the most famous in Western history, for it sparked the Great Awakening that brought revival to colonial America. On a July Sunday in 1741, Jonathan Edwards stood to preach in Enfield, Connecticut. During the previous night, a group of godly women had spent the entire evening praying for God's visitation on their town. Using this text, Edwards quietly spoke these words: *In this verse is threatened the vengeance of God on the wicked unbelieving Israelites, who were God's visible people, and who lived under the means of grace; but who, notwithstanding all God's wonderful works towards them, remained void of counsel, having no understanding in them.*

Edwards went on to say, *Unconverted men walk over the pit of hell on a rotten covering, and there are innumerable places in this covering so weak that they will not bear their weight, and these places are not seen. The arrows of death fly unseen at noon-day; the sharpest sight cannot discern them. God has so many different unsearchable ways of taking wicked men out of the world and sending them to hell . . . they have deserved the fiery pit, and are already sentenced to it . . . the devil is waiting for them, hell is gaping for them, the flames gather and flash about them. . . .*

As Edwards preached, the audience was seized by a tidal wave of fear. Strong men gripped their seats, shaking, crying. Women fell to the floor. Many in the crowd begged God's forgiveness, and by the end of the day, 500 people in the village were converted. The revival swept to nearby towns, then from city to city. Under the preaching of Edwards and George Whitefield and others, thousands entered the kingdom, transforming the moral and spiritual complexion of America.

Therefore, Edwards said at the conclusion of his famous sermon, *let everyone that is out of Christ now awake and fly from the wrath to come.*

Today's Suggested Reading
Deuteronomy 32:28–35

Vengeance is Mine, and recompense;
Their foot shall slip in due time;
For the day of their calamity is at hand,
And the things to come hasten upon them.
Deuteronomy 32:35

Leaning

I grew up in the Appalachian Mountains, in a church that loved the old hymns and gospel songs. Among our favorites was this one, based on Deuteronomy 33:27:

What a fellowship, what a joy divine,
Leaning on the everlasting arms;
What a blessedness, what a peace is mine,
Leaning on the everlasting arms.

I only recently learned the simple story behind the song. A. J. Showalter was a professor of music with a deep love for hymnology and an even deeper love for his students. He frequently kept up with his pupils for years afterward, writing letters of comfort and counsel. One evening in 1887, he was in Hartselle, Alabama, leading a singing school in a local church. He dismissed his students for the evening, collected his precious hymnbooks, and returned to his boardinghouse.

Two letters had arrived, both from former pupils. Each of the young men was heartbroken, having just lost his wife. Professor Showalter went to the Bible, looking for a verse to comfort them. He selected Deuteronomy 33:27—"The eternal God is your refuge, And underneath are the everlasting arms. . . ." As he pondered that verse, these words came to mind:

Leaning, leaning, Safe and secure from all alarms;
Leaning, leaning, Leaning on the everlasting arms.

He scribbled replies to his bereaved friends, then reached for another piece of paper. He wrote to hymnist Elisha Hoffman. "Here is the chorus for a good hymn from Deuteronomy 33:27," his letter said in gist, "but I can't come up with any verses." Hoffman wrote three stanzas, sent them back, Showalter set it all to music, and ever since, these words have cheered us in our adversity:

What have I to dread, what have I to fear,
Leaning on the everlasting arms.
I have blessed peace with my Lord so near,
Leaning on the everlasting arms.

Today's Suggested Reading
Deuteronomy 33:26–29

The eternal God is your refuge,
And underneath are the everlasting arms. . . .
Deuteronomy 33:27

Even on the Golf Course

Those needing strength often turn to Joshua 1:1–11, a potent passage given to Joshua as he assumed the leadership of Israel: *Moses My servant is dead. Now therefore, arise, go over this Jordan, you and all this people. . . . As I was with Moses, so I will be with you. . . . Be strong and of good courage. . . .*

Tom Lehman, PGA Tour Player of the Year in 1996, has often spoken of this verse. He came to Christ in high school when a friend invited him to a Fellowship of Christian Athletes meeting. After playing golf in college, he joined the PGA Tour briefly but didn't play well enough to continue. In 1991 he won three tournaments on the Ben Hogan Tour and was named Player of the Year, qualifying him again for the PGA Tour.

Then in 1995, he got a scare. Doctors discovered precancerous colon polyps. Tom and his wife got down on their knees and committed the matter to God. Joshua 1:9 sustained him: *Be strong and of good courage; do not be afraid, nor be dismayed, for the Lord your God is with you wherever you go.* Surgery was successful, and Lehman resumed his golf.

The following year, he and Steve Jones were playing the 18th hole during the final round of the U.S. Open. Both men longed to win their first major championship, and they were tied for the lead. The situation was tense, but the men calmed themselves by quoting Scripture to each other, Lehman reminding Jones of Joshua 1:9.

Jones won out by one stroke. But, remembering his verse, Tom shook off the discouragement and entered the British Open. He arrived in England quoting Joshua 1:9 to himself. This time, he won a two-stroke victory.

"In every difficult situation," he said, "even on the golf course, I remember Joshua 1:9."

*Be strong and of good courage; do not be afraid, nor be dismayed, for the Lord your God is with you wherever you go.**

Today's Suggested Reading
Joshua 1:1–11

Be strong and of good courage; do not be afraid, nor be dismayed, for the Lord your God is with you wherever you go. Joshua 1:9

*Adapted from "Being Strong and Courageous," by Tom Lehman, as told to Jim Adair, in *Decision*, June 1997, p. 11, © 1997; published by the Billy Graham Evangelistic Association.

January **31** Encircling the Walls

Here is another Joy Ridderhof story.

Joy, born in 1903, started an organization called Gospel Recordings, Inc. to record the gospel for every language group on earth. It is now approaching five thousand languages, and millions around the world have heard of Christ through GR recordings.

But it wasn't easy. Joy, a single career woman, faced loneliness, sickness, dangerous travels, foreign intrigue, and financial crises at every step. One year, Gospel Recordings badly needed more room at its Los Angeles base. Joy and her staff prayed about it for months, and suddenly a large site became available. It seemed ideal, and the board authorized a $6,000 deposit. The property cost ten times that much, but Joy refused to publicly appeal for funds.

She was in Wheaton, Illinois, as the deadline approached. If $60,000 didn't materialize within a week, the property would be lost along with the $6,000 deposit. Only half the amount was on hand, and Joy's staff called her in crisis. Her laconic instructions were to claim Joshua 3:5 and to *follow the Jericho pattern for the remaining seven days. And cable the branch offices to join us.*

No other explanation was given, but none was needed. The staff understood. Cables flew around the world: BUILDING DEADLINE OCTOBER NINTH FOLLOW JERICHO PATTERN NEXT SEVEN DAYS JOSHUA 3:5.

The walls of Jericho had fallen after the Israelites had circled them for seven days. In the same way, the staff of Gospel Recordings encircled the problem with prayer, two hours a day for seven days.

The walls fell. In an overseas call from London, a British GR staffer announced an unexpected legacy had just arrived for the ministry, and it was exactly enough to complete the building's purchase.

The home staff burst into the Doxology, and Joy Ridderhof continued her speaking tour through Illinois with a new story of God's faithfulness.

Today's Suggested Reading
Joshua 3:1–5

Sanctify yourselves, for tomorrow the Lord will do wonders among you. Joshua 3:5

February

Those Precious Words

What Those Oats Can Do

Is It Well With the Child?

Dying Pleas

If My People

February **1**

As for Me

In the 1700s, a young man named James Taylor proposed marriage to his girlfriend, and a wedding date was set. Neither of them were Christians. James, in fact, so detested itinerant preachers that he often pelted them with rotten tomatoes or eggs.

Shortly before his wedding, one of John Wesley's circuit riders entered town, and James, hearing of it, wanted to disrupt the meeting. But as James listened in the fringes of the crowd, the preacher quoted Joshua 24:15: *But as for me and my house, we will serve the Lord.*

The words stuck James like an arrow.

When the day of his wedding arrived, the verse was still lodged in his thoughts. That morning James retired to the fields to think. He was about to take a wife, to establish a home, but he wasn't serving the Lord. He knelt in the grass and earnestly asked Christ to be his Savior. By the time he finished praying, he was alarmed to discover it was time for the wedding.

Rushing to the chapel, he apologized for being late, and the ceremony proceeded. Then he shocked his bride and guests, by announcing he had become a Christian. He soon began witnessing to his new wife, but she remained resistant. Finally one day James came home so burdened for her that he picked her up and carried her to the bedroom. There with a forceful hand he made her kneel beside him. Soon both were weeping, and there she, too, became a Christian.

Eight generations have since passed, each filled with Christian workers serving the Lord. Included among them is James Taylor's great-grandson, Hudson Taylor, founder of the China Inland Mission, who opened the interior of China to the gospel of Jesus Christ.

Today's Suggested Reading

Joshua 24:14–25

But as for me and my house, we will serve the Lord. Joshua 24:15

While Barak Trembled . . .

February **2**

There have been many Deborahs since the original one, women strong and wise, effective leaders among God's people. The first Deborah created a precedent that has often shielded the others from criticism. Consider, for example, Paula, born into a wealthy family in Rome in A.D. 347. She grew up aristocratic and respected, but at age 33 she encountered Jesus Christ in a way that changed her life.

She became friends with the great Bible translator Jerome and eventually left her family in Rome to settle near him in Bethlehem. Jerome was crusty and impatient, but Paula got on with him splendidly and aided him in his work. She established a nearby monastery where she and her co-workers ministered to the poor and hungry. "What poor man, as he lay dying, was not wrapped in blankets given by Paula?" wrote Jerome. "What bedridden person was not supported by money from her purse?"

Jerome and Paula worked side-by-side, unmarried, as brother and sister. As Jerome labored to exhaustion, translating the Bible into Latin, Paula paid his expenses from her family inheritance and gathered supplies for his work. She copied his manuscripts. She studied Greek and Hebrew and critiqued his work. Jerome, who needed intellectual and critical stimulation, found her conversations invaluable. She was strong, astute, kind, and committed.

When Jerome finished his translations of Job, Isaiah, Samuel, Kings, Esther, Galatians, Philemon, Titus, and the prophets, he dedicated them all to Paula. Almost at once, his reading public was offended. "Dedicating these books to a woman? What's the meaning of this?"

But Jerome had a ready response: *These people do not know that while Barak trembled, Deborah saved Israel.*

And for that his critics had no reply.

Today's Suggested Reading
Judges 4:4–10

Now Deborah, a prophetess, the wife of Lapidoth, was judging Israel at that time. Judges 4:4

Death by Tent Peg

For over a hundred years, ministers around the world have marveled over the sermons of Charles Haddon Spurgeon. He didn't prepare manuscripts in advance, seldom knowing on Friday what he would speak about on Sunday. Yet when he stood to preach, audiences were entranced by his eloquence, insight, and authority. I've often been impressed, moreover, by his bluntness. The modern American pulpit seldom speaks of "hell, fire, and brimstone." But Spurgeon had no qualms about it. He often used the starkest illustrations imaginable to press home the need for repentance. One Sunday as he waxed eloquent on this theme, his mind flew to the story of Deborah in Judges 4.

In that chapter, Deborah's ragged army routed the forces of Sisera, the Canaanite king. Sisera escaped and ran for his life until he was exhausted. Coming to a friendly village, he sought refuge in the tent of a woman named Jael. She welcomed him, gave him nourishment, showed him where to lay his head, and promised to divert those seeking him.

Then while he slept, she took a hammer and drove a tent peg through his temple into the ground. "So he died," says the Bible laconically. Spurgeon saw here a powerful warning to the unrepentant.

Such are many of you, sleeping in jeopardy of your souls; Satan is standing, the law is ready, vengeance is eager, and all saying, "Shall I smite him? I will smite him this once, and he shall never wake again." Like Sisera, I tell thee, sinner, thou art sleeping in the tent of the destroyer; thou mayst have eaten butter and honey out of a goodly dish; but thou art sleeping on the doorstep of hell: even now the enemy is lifting up the hammer and the nail to smite thee through the temples and fasten thee to the earth, that there thou mayst lie forever in the death of everlasting torment. . . .

As usual, Charles Spurgeon had hit the nail on the head.

Today's Suggested Reading

Judges 4:12–21

Then Jael, Heber's wife, took a tent peg and took a hammer in her hand, and went softly to him and drove the peg into his temple, and it went down into the ground; for he was fast asleep and weary. So he died. Judges 4:21

Samuel and Hannah

The story of Hannah and her son Samuel has a modern counterpart in Adjai Samuel Crowther and his mother. Adjai, eleven years old, was seized by slavers near his village in West Africa about 1820. The terrified boy was thrown in a crowded slave pen, then chained aboard a slave ship. He suffered untold panic and pain until the ship was captured by a British steamer. Adjai was rescued and placed under the care of missionaries at Sierra Leone. There he was enrolled in school and heard of the Lord Jesus Christ. A benevolent clergyman, Samuel Crowther, financed his education. Adjai was baptized at age 16, and he took the name of his benefactor: Adjai Samuel Crowther.

By and by, Samuel, as he was called, traveled to England to further his studies. His keen mind quickly grasped languages and academics, as well as practical skills such as carpentry. When he returned as a minister to Africa, he settled near the Niger River, married, preached, began a boarding school for African children, and worked ceaselessly for the gospel.

Years passed, and one day Samuel was preaching at Freetown, not far from the spot of his kidnapping. In the corner of his eye, he saw an old woman, bowed and depressed. She appeared to have borne a heavy sorrow. As he talked with her, she opened her heart, telling him of her hard life and of the loss of all her children. "But the worst of all," she wailed, "was losing my little boy Adjai."

Samuel gazed into her eyes and recognized his own mother. Under his tender ministry, she shortly afterward became a Christian herself, and at her baptism she, too, took a Christian name. She chose Hannah—the mother of Samuel, the man of God.

Today's Suggested Reading

1 Samuel 1:1–20

So it came to pass in the process of time that Hannah conceived and bore a son, and called his name Samuel, saying, "Because I have asked for him from the Lord." 1 Samuel 1:20

Chariot of Fire

Leaving his young son in boarding school in Great Britain was the hardest thing Rev. James Dunlop Liddell, Scottish missionary to China, had ever done. But Eric thrived like a hare in the highlands. He studied hard. He loved sports, particularly rugby. He joined a Bible study, attended church regularly, and became a member of the Crusader Christian Union. He also began his lifelong habit of early morning Bible reading and prayer.

Eric advanced to the university, joined the track team, and won races like a thoroughbred. Every week he brought home more prizes and trophies until he soon ran out of storage space. His legs became a Scottish national treasure, and all the world followed him to the 1924 Olympics.

All the while, Eric's Christian life continued on the fast track as well, and his newly-found fame gave opportunities for preaching and witnessing. At the Paris Olympics, his faith was put to the test when his chosen venue, the 100 meter race, was scheduled for Sunday. Eric, who didn't believe in competing on the Lord's Day, opted out. He entered the 400 meter run instead as the world watched and wondered.

In his dressing room just before the race, Eric unfolded a small bit of paper that had been given to him by the team masseur. It read: "In the old book it says 'He that honors me I will honor.' Wishing you the best of success always." Eric knew the verse well. It was 1 Samuel 2:30. He smiled and made up his mind that, win or lose, he would honor God.

His time that day was 47.6 seconds. He won. He set a new world record. He and the Lord had honored each other.

Today's Suggested Reading
1 Samuel 2:26–36

. . . those who honor Me I will honor, and those who despise Me shall be lightly esteemed. 1 Samuel 2:30

Resignation

Whenever our wishes contradict the Father's will, it is wise to yield.

> *. . . nevertheless, not as I will, but as you will—Matthew 26:39*
>
> *. . . we ceased, saying, "The will of the Lord be done"—Acts 21:14*
>
> *. . . and if I perish, I perish—Esther 4:16*
>
> *Though He slay me, yet will I trust him—Job 14:15*
>
> *Teach me to do your will—Psalm 143:10*
>
> *I do not seek my own will but the will of the Father—John 5:30*

Consider also Eli's words in 1 Samuel 3:18, for they once helped Robert Moffat through a bitter disappointment. He had fallen in love with his employer's daughter, Mary Smith. He wanted to propose, and she wanted to accept. They dreamed of serving the Lord together in South Africa. But they lived in the days when missionaries regularly fell in distant, unmarked graves. Robert's parents, though apprehensive, were willing to let him go. But Mary's parents refused. They could not relinquish their daughter, they said, nor bring themselves to give consent.

Robert's heart was rent. Should he marry his beloved and remain in Scotland? Or should he surrender to God's will? He wrote his parents with the answer: *From the clearest indications of His Providence, He bids me go out alone, and He who appoints crosses and disappointments also imparts resignation and grace sufficient unto the day. So I am bold to adopt the language of Eli and say, "It is the Lord, let Him do what seemeth Him good."** So on October 18, 1816, Robert and Mary tore themselves apart, and Robert boarded ship, alone and grief-stricken.

But the story ends happily. Three years later, Mary's parents surrendered her to the Lord's keeping and allowed her to join Robert in Africa. The two were married at last, and walked hand-in-hand in remarkable missionary service for the next fifty years.

Today's Suggested Reading

1 Samuel 3:1–19

And he said, "It is the Lord. Let Him do what seems good to Him."
1 Samuel 3:18

---

*King James Version

The Oxen Option

God is an animal lover. He created animals, He saved them during the flood, and He often used them in the Bible. Remember Balaam's donkey? Peter's rooster? Elijah's ravens? And in 1 Samuel 6, the Lord used two milk cows. The Philistines had seized Israel's Ark of the Covenant and had suffered grievously. Wanting to return it, they placed it in a cart drawn by two cows and sent it randomly on its way. The Lord, it seems, held the reins, for the ark traveled straightway back to Israel.

Barnabas Shaw, a colleague of Robert Moffat's in South Africa, had a similar experience. Shaw was a Methodist missionary from England who journeyed to Capetown to preach the gospel, only to be forbidden from doing so by the governor. Not knowing how to proceed, Shaw purchased a yoke of oxen and a cart and put his goods in the back. Shaw and his wife, taking their seat, gave the Lord the reins.

The oxen rambled into the interior, lowing, trudging ahead day after day, covering 200 miles in just under a month. One evening while camping in the bush, Shaw heard noises nearby. Upon investigation, he found a tribe of Hottentots led by its chief, Little Namaqualand. They had left their homes and village to travel to Capetown in search of a missionary to teach them "the Great Word."

Had either party started a half-day sooner or later, or veered a half-mile this way or that, they would never have met. But as it was, Barnabas Shaw established a thriving work among them, spending eleven years before returning to England for furlough.

All in all, he devoted over forty years to advancing the gospel in South Africa.

Today's Suggested Reading
1 Samuel 6:1–15

Then the cows headed straight for the road to Beth Shemesh, and went along the highway, lowing as they went, and did not turn aside to the right hand or the left. 1 Samuel 6:12

Ebenezer

Witty, warm, full of wisdom, F. W. Boreham's books are collectors' items. In *The Other Side of the Hill,* Boreham, who pastored in New Zealand and Australia, tells of growing up in England.

In the dear old home at Tunbridge Wells, there hangs a text. It is only a scrap of paper, cut from the corner of a penny almanac; and yet, if something had to go, I fancy the finest pictures in the house would be sacrificed to save it. It reads:

Hitherto
Hath
The Lord
*Helped Us**

It has been there for more than thirty years; but I remember, as though yesterday, the day it appeared. We boys had a dim consciousness that things were going hardly with father and mother. He looked anxious and worried; her eyes were often red and swollen. Then one day the newly framed text made its appearance on the wall. It was as if the weather had cleared up; the fog had lifted; father and mother were happier. We mustered courage to ask some explanation.

[*Mother said:*] *"You know your father and I had a great trouble, and we feared a much heavier one. On Tuesday of last week, I had to drop my work, pick up the baby, and walk up and down the kitchen feeling I could endure it no longer. In pacing up and down, I paused in front of the sheet-almanac on the wall. The only thing I saw was the text in the corner. It was as if someone had spoken the words: "Hitherto hath the Lord helped us." I was so overcome I sat down and had a good cry; and then I began again with a fresh heart and trust. When father came home, I told him about it, and he cut out the text with his penknife and hung it where you now see it.***

As long as he lived, F. W. Boreham never forgot the power of that lesson.

Today's Suggested Reading
1 Samuel 7:5–12

Then Samuel took a stone and set it up between Mizpah and Shen, and called its name Ebenezer, saying, "Thus far the Lord has helped us."
1 Samuel 7:12

---

*King James Version
**F. W. Boreham, *The Other Side of the Hill.*

February 9 Those Precious Words

On my bookshelf sits an old volume with a mile-long title: *Autobiography of Lemuel Norton: Including His Early Life—Two Years in a Printing Office—Eleven Years at Sea, in which he was Twice Shipwrecked, and Experienced Several Narrow Escapes From Death. Also His Christian Experience and Labors in the Gospel Ministry.*

Once, returning home between voyages, Norton, then an infidel, shared a bedroom with Deacon Weed, who prayed upon retiring, "Lord, I am going to bed with this impenitent sinner." Norton later recalled:

The next morning, I awoke with a most singular groan, which surprised me not a little. In a few minutes, the old gentleman arose and went to where my mother was getting breakfast, and said, "That son of yours is going to be a Christian." Mother replied, "What makes you think so, Deacon Weed?" Said he, "I asked the Lord if he would make him a Christian to make him groan; and he immediately groaned out."

Sure enough, Norton was soon converted and began devouring the Scripture.

In 1817, Thanksgiving Day was the first time I took a text and tried to explain it to the church. The day previous while traveling along the road, these words pressed through my mind: "Only fear the Lord and serve him in truth, with all your heart; for consider what great things he hath done for you." These words, so full of encouragement, looked to me very suitable for the foundation of a discourse the next day. On being assembled, the acting deacon passed the Bible to my hand. I turned to the text named above, and read with much solemnity those precious words which had been food to my soul the day before. And if ever words found place in every heart, these did, for the attention given them was profound.*

I spoke just twenty minutes with much freedom, when all at once I found nothing further to say, and took my seat. From this day forward it was understood that I had commenced preaching the gospel. . . .

Today's Suggested Reading

1 Samuel 12:20–25

Only fear the Lord, and serve Him in truth with all your heart; for consider what great things He has done for you. 1 Samuel 12:23

---

*King James Version

Staying by the Stuff

February **10**

David's army had plunged into battle, but the more exhausted soldiers stayed behind to guard the camp. Afterward, the combatants refused to share the booty with those left behind. But King David issued this rule: "As his part is who goes down to the battle, so shall his part be who stays by the supplies." Those words hold a special memory for businessman Allan Emery.

Emery's dad shared a story with his family at supper one night, having just returned from a business trip. As he had left the train that afternoon, Mr. Emery, whose Christianity was well-known, was approached by a porter. He drew aside and listened to the man's story.

"There were two boys in my family," said the porter. "My mother worked hard to see we had the best education available. I was a good student. When I graduated from high school, my desire was to fulfill my mother's wish that I become a preacher. Well, while I was doing this, my younger brother went in a different direction. He drank and partied and nearly killed himself by living for the devil. About the time I was accepted for college, my brother was converted.

"He had nothing, so he asked me to provide his education. I was so happy to see this great change in his life, I agreed and today my brother is a nationally known preacher. You may have heard him on the radio. He has led thousands to Christ. So, you see, I couldn't go into the ministry and I am too old now. Mr. Emery, do you suppose the Lord will give me credit for the souls my brother led to Him?"

That evening at the dinner table, Mr. Emery nearly broke down as he told his family that story and as he shared his answer. Young Allen, all ears, never forgot the principle of 1 Samuel 30:24, or his father's wisdom in sharing it.

Today's Suggested Reading

1 Samuel 30:21–31

But as his part is who goes down to the battle, so shall his part be who stays by the supplies; they shall share alike. 1 Samuel 30:24

"Murder! Murder!"

George Whitefield, the fiery evangelist with a voice that could be heard a mile away, came to Plymouth, England, for a crusade, but a motley crew threatened him harm. His room was burgled, and Whitefield moved to an undisclosed address. The young thugs set another trap for him, but Whitefield, smelling a rat, didn't show. The indignant conspirators resolved to murder him that night.

As Whitefield, exhausted, returned to his room and dressed for bed, a knock sounded. A well-dressed gentleman wished to speak with him, he was told. Whitefield seldom refused a nocturnal "Nicodemus" who came wanting to be born again. He admitted the man who was dressed as a lieutenant from a man 'o war. They chatted a moment, but when Whitefield asked his name, the young man gave a false name, that of another officer. "That's impossible," said Whitefield, "I met that officer two weeks ago."

The man suddenly sprang up and slammed his cane across Whitefield's head, commencing the attack. "Murder! Murder!" screamed the terrified evangelist. "Murder! Murder!" Another thug joined the attack, throwing the landlady violently down the stairs. Neighbors, hearing the screams, drove away the attackers, but news of the attempt flashed abroad like lightning, and the next time he rose to preach, Whitefield faced an innumerable mass. He began preaching, unaware that another attacker had slipped into the crowd. Harry Tanner, a young thug, planned the evangelist harm.

But as Tanner watched in horror, George Whitefield suddenly turned toward him, looked him in the eye, squinted, and thundered Nathan's famous words to David, "Thou art the man!" Tanner was shaken to the depths of his soul. The next day he returned to the crusade, and this time he gave his life to Christ.

Today's Suggested Reading

2 Samuel 12:1–13

Then Nathan said to David, "You are the man!" 2 Samuel 12:7

Dying Pleas

It took his parents' dying words to lead Sam Jones to Christ.

His mother's last words, modeled after 2 Samuel 12:23, were: "Sam, I will never be able to return to you, but you can come to me."

But Sam became instead a hopeless alcoholic. Then, during a binge, he learned his father was dying. He rushed to the bedside, and his dad moaned, "My poor, wicked, wayward, reckless son. You have brought me down in sorrow to my grave. Promise, my boy, to meet me in heaven."

Overwhelmed, Sam fell to his knees and cried, "I promise, I'll quit drinking. I'll meet you and Mother in heaven."

I went to the bar and begged for a glass of liquor and looked in the mirror. I saw my hair matted, the filth and vomit on my clothes, one of my eyes closed, and my lips swollen. I said, "Is that all that is left of the proud and brilliant lawyer, Sam Jones?" I smashed the glass on the floor, fell to my knees and cried, "Oh God! Oh God, have mercy!" The bartender ran to my side and thought I was dying. I staggered to my cheap rooming house and asked for black coffee. I went through three days and nights of hell, but when the morning came, something happened to old Sam Jones. I went to the clothing store and said, "I want you to give me a new suit. I got saved last night." I went to the barber for I had not had a shave in a month. I left to go to my wife whom I had beaten till she was black and blue. She didn't even recognize her own husband. I said, "Honey, God has given you a new husband and the children a new daddy, and I wonder if you will forgive me and start all over."

I have been going round the country bragging about Jesus ever since.

Today's Suggested Reading
2 Samuel 12:15–25

I shall go to him, but he shall not return to me.
2 Samuel 12:23

So Great a People

At 5 P.M. on April 12, 1945, Vice President Harry Truman, wearied by his afternoon in the United States Senate, ducked into Sam Rayburn's private office in the Capitol. Someone mentioned to him that the White House had called. Harry picked up the phone and dialed the number, National 1414. Press Secretary Steve Early came on, voice tense, asking Truman to come to the White House "quickly and quietly." He was to enter the main entrance on Pennsylvania Avenue.

Harry exited the room alone, then began racing through the ornate halls of the Capitol, shoes pounding marble. He jumped in his old Mercury and sped through the traffic. At 5:25, he pulled under the north portico. Two ushers took his hat and escorted him to the small elevator. Waiting for him upstairs was Eleanor Roosevelt. "Harry," she said, "the president is dead."

Truman groped for words. "Is there anything I can do for you?" he asked at length.

"Is there anything *we* can do for *you?*" Eleanor replied. "You are the one in trouble now."

That night, Truman took the oath of office as president of the United States, his hand resting on an inexpensive Gideon Bible grabbed from the desk of the White House's head usher. The following Monday, Truman addressed a joint session of Congress. His speech lasted but fifteen minutes. Most of it had been written by presidential speechwriters, but the conclusion he had added himself. The Congress was hushed and the nation spellbound by their radios as he said: *At this moment I have in my heart a prayer. As I have assumed my duties, I humbly pray Almighty God, in the words of King Solomon: "Give therefore Thy servant an understanding heart to judge Thy people, that I may discern between good and bad: for who is able to judge this Thy so great a people?"* I ask only to be a good and faithful servant of my Lord and my people.*

Today's Suggested Reading
1 Kings 3:1–10

Therefore give to Your servant an understanding heart to judge Your people, that I may discern between good and evil. For who is able to judge this great people of Yours?
1 Kings 3:9

---

*King James Version

Chickens and Spiders and Dogs

February **14**

John Brenz, friend of Martin Luther, remembered this verse from 1 Kings while hiding from the Spanish Cavalry. Emperor Charles V repeatedly tried to assassinate him, and on one occasion Brenz barely heard of the plot in time to grab a loaf of bread and duck into his neighbor's hayloft. There he hid fourteen days. The bread was quickly gone, but the Lord sent a hen who showed up and laid an egg each day for fourteen days. In this way, Brenz was kept alive. On the fifteenth day the chicken didn't come, and the reformer wondered what he would do. But from the street below came the cries, "The cavalrymen are gone at last."

In a similar way, a dog provided for the needs of another reformer, John Craig, who was arrested during the Inquisition. On the eve of his scheduled execution, Craig escaped, but while fleeing through the Italian backcountry, he ran out of food and money. Suddenly a dog approached him, a purse in its mouth. Craig tried to drive the animal away, but the dog persisted in bringing the purse to Craig. In it was enough money to take him to freedom.

Here's one more story. Robert Bruce of Scotland was running for his life, fleeing persecutors. He ducked into a small cave, and a spider immediately appeared and spun a web over the opening. Bruce's pursuers fanned across the landscape, knowing he was near. Two of them approached the cave, and one of the men started to go in. The other one stopped him, saying, "He could never have gotten in there without breaking that spider's web."

Bruce breathed this prayer, "O God, I thank Thee that in the tiny bowels of a spider you can place for me a shelter."

Ravens, chickens, dogs, spiders, and creatures great and small—as Jesus once said of a donkey, the Master has need of them.

Today's Suggested Reading
1 Kings 17:1–7

The ravens brought him bread and meat in the morning, and bread and meat in the evening; and he drank from the brook. 1 Kings 17:6

February **15**

Dried-Up Brooks

Allan Emery arrived at his hotel after midnight. It had been a long day, and he brooded over his meeting next morning with a customer. He expected to lose the account and be displaced as the firm's supplier.

From his father, Allan had inherited the family wool business, carefully tended and passed down, father-to-son. But every year saw fewer customers, for wool was being replaced with synthetic fibers.

Allan laid his Bible on the nightstand, tempted to go to bed without reading it. But while saying his prayers, he pled, "Lord, if you have something to say to me, some encouragement, let me have it now." Opening the book, he read 1 Kings 17. Elijah had felt secure by the brook Cherith, but one day the little stream dried up. God had allowed it, for he had other places for Elijah to go, other things for him to do, other ways of meeting his needs. The dried-up brook was a guidepost telling Elijah it was time to move on.

Allan recognized that his brook, too, was drying up. Soon he decided to liquidate the wool business. He helped employees find other jobs, then wondered what he himself should do.

One night at a dinner, Allan met Ken Hansen of Service-Master Industries. The two hit it off, and soon Emery was with the firm. In time, he became a director, and he was also able to devote himself to many evangelical causes, serving as president of the Billy Graham Association and a trustee of Wheaton College and Gordon-Conwell Theological Seminary. For many years, he and his wife hosted a Bible study in their expansive home, attended by 100 young people.

"I thought back to my questioning God's wisdom and faithfulness," he said. "I saw why it was necessary for my brook to dry up to make me leave its security to begin a new and wonderful ministry."*

Today's Suggested Reading

1 Kings 17:6–16

And it happened after a while that the brook dried up. . . . 1 Kings 17:7

*Adapted from Allan Emery, *Turtle on a Fencepost* (Word Books, 1979).

Payday Someday

February **16**

The following verse from 1 Kings became the basis of the most famous sermon ever delivered by Robert G. Lee. Lee, who grew up dirt poor, began preaching in rural South Carolina, and ended up as pastor of the Bellevue Baptist Church in Memphis, where over 24,000 people joined during his long ministry there (1927–1960). Though he prepared and preached thousands of sermons, he is best remembered for his famous "Payday Someday," which he preached over 1200 times around the world. People drove thousands of miles to hear it. Recordings of it are collectors' items, and it still flourishes in printed form.

Lee, who was gifted with elastic vocal cords and a keen sense of drama, told the story of Ahab and Jezebel through the eyes of the different participants, using different voices for each character. After vividly telling the story, he described the grisly death scene of Jezebel: *The men put their strong fingers into her soft feminine flesh and picked her up, painted face and all, bejeweled fingers and all—and threw her down. Her body hit the street and burst open. Some of her blood splattered on the walls of the city, disgracing them. There she lies, twisting in death agony in the street.*

Then Lee thundered:

"Payday—Someday!" God said it—and it was done! Yes, and from this we learn the power and certainty of God in carrying out His own retributive providence, that men might know that His justice slumbereth not. Even though the mill of God grinds slowly, it grinds to powder. And the only way I know for any man or woman on earth to escape the sinner's payday on earth and the sinner's hell beyond is through Jesus Christ, who took the sinner's place upon the cross, becoming for all sinners all that God must judge, that sinners through faith in Christ Jesus might become all that God cannot judge.

Today's Suggested Reading

1 Kings 21:1–24

And concerning Jezebel the Lord also spoke, saying, "The dogs shall eat Jezebel by the wall of Jezreel." 1 Kings 21:23

Is It Well with the Child?

Marcus and Narcissa Whitman crossed the Continental Divide on July 4, 1836, en route to Oregon to evangelize the Northwest. Narcissa was beautiful, blue eyes, radiant face, hair "like the gold of the sunset." Her diary records their adventures as they forded swollen streams, climbed steep mountains, clung to narrow paths, bounced over rough trails, and evaded warring Indians. Reaching Oregon at last, they built a primitive hut and began their mission.

On her twenty-first birthday, Narcissa gave birth to a daughter, and little Alice Clarissa soon became the joy of her life. "My Clarissa is my own little companion," she wrote, "and dear daughter."

On Sunday, June 23, 1839, Marcus took little Clarissa into the garden after church services. They cut a rhubarb stalk, and shortly afterward the little girl ran to the kitchen for drinking cups. Marcus, meanwhile, had settled down to read. Suddenly they grew aware that Clarissa was missing. They raced to the river where others joined the search. An old Indian swam into the water to look among the tree roots and emerged with her body.

They buried Clarissa in a peaceful spot just north of the compound. A friend preached the funeral service from 2 Kings 4:26, a text often used at the funerals of children, for the child in this Scripture had also died, but was soon to be raised: " 'Is it well with the child?' And she answered, 'It is well.' "

"Lord, it is right; it is right," Narcissa wrote. "She is not mine, but Thine; she has only been lent to me for a little season, and now, dearest Savior, Thy will be done."

Marcus and Narcissa were separated from their little girl for only eight years. In 1847, a band of hostile Indians attacked the compound, and the little family was reunited in heaven.

Today's Suggested Reading
2 Kings 4:17–37

Please run now to meet her, and say to her, "Is it well with you? Is it well with your husband? Is it well with the child?" And she answered, "It is well." 2 Kings 4:26

If My People

Shortly after the 1952 Republican Convention, General Dwight D. Eisenhower asked Billy Graham to meet him in Chicago to suggest "a religious note" of some sort for some of his campaign speeches. Graham told the general he would be glad to help privately. Accordingly, Graham and Eisenhower met shortly thereafter at the Brown Palace Hotel in Denver, and Graham shared Bible verses appropriate to the needs of the United States.

The evangelist also took the opportunity to give the general a red leather Bible and to urge him to personally consider the gospel of Jesus Christ. Eisenhower listened respectfully.

Later, five days before his inauguration, Eisenhower invited Graham to the Commodore Hotel in New York. "I'd like to quote one or two passages from the Bible in my inaugural speech," he said. Gazing out the window, Eisenhower told Graham that he felt one of the reasons he was elected was to help set the moral and spiritual climate of America. Graham suggested several verses, among them Psalm 33:12 and 2 Chronicles 7:14.

Over the next several days, Eisenhower prepared a speech that opened in prayer and that spoke repeatedly of spiritual things. "In the swift rush of great events," he scribbled in his final draft, "we find ourselves groping to know the full meaning of these times in which we live. In our quest for understanding, we beseech God's guidance."

On Tuesday, January 30, 1953, Dwight D. Eisenhower was sworn into office as his hand rested on two Bibles, both opened to 2 Chronicles 7:14: "If My people who are called by My name will humble themselves, and pray and seek My face, and turn from their wicked ways, then I will hear from heaven, and will forgive their sin and heal their land."

Today's Suggested Reading
2 Chronicles 7:1–18

. . . if My people who are called by My name will humble themselves, and pray and seek My face, and turn from their wicked ways, then I will hear from heaven, and will forgive their sin and heal their land.
2 Chronicles 7:14

Heard 'Round the World

God providentially sets crucial men in critical eras, and there uses them to make a difference. William Emerson, for example, was a 32-year-old minister in Concord, New Hampshire, who apprehensively watched his flock slide toward revolutionary war against England. He studied the Scriptures and prayed for wisdom in knowing what to say.

Ministers were the orators of the day, the shapers of the public mood. Many colonial preachers held a high view of God's providence, and thought of colonists as having been placed on the new continent for a divine purpose. The role of preaching thus proved more influential in the American Revolution than many historians realize.

In the spring of 1775, Concord feared an attack by British General Thomas Gage. A militia was formed, and on March 13, Emerson addressed the soldiers. What should he say? His words would have profound impact—toward either pacifism or war. He chose 2 Chronicles 13:12 as his text: "And behold, God Himself is with us for our captain. . . ."*

For my part, the more I reflect upon the movements of the British nation, the more satisfied I am that our military preparation here for our own defense is justified in the eyes of the impartial world. Nay, for should we neglect to defend ourselves by military preparation, we never could answer it to God and to our own consciences.

He told the soldiers that their strength lay not in their weaponry but in their moral and spiritual resolve. *The Lord will cover your head in the day of battle and carry you on from victory to victory.*

Shortly afterward, British troops marched on Concord, but Emerson and the militia, bolstered by these things and alerted by Paul Revere, rallied to meet them. A shot was fired "heard 'round the world."

Today's Suggested Reading
2 Chronicles 13:1–12

God Himself is with us as our head, and His priests with sounding trumpets to sound the alarm. . . . 2 Chronicles 13:12

*King James Version

Much More

In 1865, when Hudson Taylor founded the China Inland Mission (now Overseas Missionary Fellowship), he determined to depend on God alone for the needed finances. From that day no direct solicitation of funds has occurred, yet the Mission's needs have been continuously met from unexpected sources at critical times, in answer to prayer.

Several years ago, Phyllis Thompson chronicled many stories of God's faithfulness to CIM in her little book, *Proving God*. "Through the ninety and more years of its history," she wrote, "although no public or private appeal for funds has ever been authorized, its work and workers have been sustained by an unfailing supply."

For example, Thompson recalls that in December, 1954, when funds were especially low, Mission personnel heard of a gift coming their way from a wealthy American lady. Nobody at CIM remembered having met the lady, but she had sometimes sent small donations to the Mission's London office. Now she had apparently included CIM in her will to the tune of $5,500.

As it turned out, however, the money was not for the China Inland Mission. It went instead to a Bible school organized by Chinese in the Far East. While the CIM personnel were glad for their Chinese brothers, they naturally felt a bit disappointed. But their attention was soon drawn to 2 Chronicles 25:9, and they claimed the verse as their own: "The Lord is able to give you much more than this."

Within days another communication came from the woman's estate. She had indeed remembered the mission, but not for $5,500. The amount being sent was $75,000, with an additional $60,000 coming later! Mission directors met for prayer with overflowing and humbled hearts. They sang the Doxology and thanked the Lord for his goodness in sending them "much more than this."

Today's Suggested Reading
2 Chronicles 25:5–13

Then Amaziah said to the man of God, "But what shall we do about the hundred talents which I have given to the troops of Israel?" And the man of God answered, "The Lord is able to give you much more than this." 2 Chronicles 25:9

Good Habits

Once when I was a student contemplating ministry, I asked Ruth Bell Graham if she had any advice about preaching. Her three simple rules have shaped my pulpit ministry far more than all the homiletics books I've ever read. She said, "Preach expository sermons, keep them short, and use a lot of illustrations." She went on to suggest Ezra as a role model. Ezra 7:10 gives us his *preparation* for preaching: he prepared his heart to seek the Law of God, then to obey it, and then to teach it. Nehemiah 8:8 gives us his *procedure* in preaching: He read from the book of the law distinctly, gave the sense, and caused the people to understand the reading.

When asked for advice about ministry, evangelist D. L. Moody gave his workers several rules, and they, too, included the Ezra model. Moody said, in summary:

1. Have for constant use a portable reference Bible, a concordance, and a topical textbook.
2. Always carry a Bible or Testament in your pocket.
3. Do not be afraid of marking it or making marginal notes.
4. Set apart time each day for study and meditation.
5. Always ask God to open the eyes of your understanding.
6. Cast every burden of doubt upon the Lord.
7. Believe in the Bible as God's revelation to you, and act accordingly. Reverence all Scripture.
8. Learn at least one verse of Scripture each day. Verses committed to memory will be wonderfully useful in your daily life.
9. Try at any cost to master the Bible. You ought to know it better than anyone in your congregation or class. Adopt a systematic plan for Bible study, and strive to be exact in quoting Scripture.
10. Always practice Ezra 7:10: Prepare your heart to study and obey the way of the Lord.

Today's Suggested Reading
Ezra 7:1–10

For Ezra had prepared his heart to seek the Law of the Lord, and to do it, and to teach statutes and ordinances in Israel. Ezra 7:10

Lifted to Safety

In January, 1963, Ralph Borthwick, missionary pilot with JAARS, prepared to transport two Wycliffe Bible translators, Stan and Junia Schauer, to their base with the Yucuna tribe. They took off about noon, hoping to easily find their little landing strip on the uncharted Miritiparana River. Everything went well at first, but soon the sky darkened and a tropical storm engulfed them. Rain struck the windshield like bullets, and the plane heaved violently.

They emerged from the storm, north of their intended path, far from known checkpoints. Ralph flew aimlessly for hours, his fuel growing lower. The jungle below was thick and endless, and Ralph knew it would swallow them up like green quicksand. He found an uncharted river and followed it, desperately seeking a sandbar on which to land, but the river dwindled and disappeared, and Ralph had no choice but to turn back. Sharply banking the Helio 457, he headed downstream. The gas gauge registered empty.

He looked over to Stan. "How about leading us in prayer?" Stan asked God to lead them directly to a sandbar that would offer a safe landing. Then he pulled a small Bible from his shirt pocket and read Job 5:8–9—*But as for me, I would seek God, and to God I would commit my cause—who does great things, and unsearchable, marvelous things without number. . . . Those who mourn are lifted to safety.*

A huge sandbar suddenly appeared before them in the river. All three missionaries saw it at once, though none had spotted it earlier while flying upstream. It appeared free of obstructions and seemed newly formed, smooth and hard and long. Ralph touched down safely, and that evening the missionaries slept under a star-splashed sky.

It took three days for rescuers to find them, but two camouflaged Colombian Air Force planes finally landed with fuel. Ralph studied his charts, took off again, and one hour later touched down safely at his intended destination.

Today's Suggested Reading

Job 5:1–16

But as for me, I would seek God, and to God I would commit my cause—Who does great things, and unsearchable, marvelous things without number. . . . Those who mourn are lifted to safety. Job 5:8–11

What Those Oats Can Do

When Henry Crowell was nine, his father died from tuberculosis, and when he was seventeen, Henry himself contracted the disease. He appeared to be dying as he attended D. L. Moody's campaign in Cleveland, Ohio. He listened carefully as Moody thundered: "The world has yet to see what God can do through a man fully dedicated to him."

Crowell determined to be God's man. *To be sure, I would never preach like Moody. But I could make money and support the labors of men like Moody. I resolved, "Oh God, if you preserve my life and allow me to make money to be used in your service, I will keep my name out of it so you will have the glory."*

Shortly thereafter Henry found Job 5:19: "He shall deliver you in six troubles, yes, in seven no evil shall touch you." The Lord seemed to assure him of healing through that verse.

Henry grew stronger and began honing his business instincts, shrewdly investing his family's wealth. He started companies, purchased properties, and introduced innovations to the marketplace. When a mill owned by nearby Quakers became available, Henry purchased it and began dreaming of modern cereal products for American homes. Thus Quaker Oats Company was born.

The money rolled in—and it rolled out. Henry consistently gave 65 to 70 percent of his income to Christian causes. Millions of dollars flowed to churches, schools, and missions. He worked tirelessly for the new, fledgling Moody Bible Institute of Chicago. Under his vision, MBI escaped financial ruin and became a powerful training center. He helped start Moody Press, Moody Magazine, and Moody radio ministries.

And he was still dreaming at age 89. Shortly before his death, he spoke to the board of Moody Bible Institute, complimenting them for their vision but telling them to *think in terms of still greater things for the glory of Christ.*

Today's Suggested Reading

Job 5:17–27

He shall deliver you in six troubles, yes, in seven no evil shall touch you. Job 5:19

Point of No Return

Shortly after the death of their daughter Robin, Roy Rogers and Dale Evans met a pale little boy who stuck out his hand and said, "Howdy, pahtnah!" He had been abandoned in a Kentucky motel, and was physically and mentally disabled.

Roy and Dale adopted him, calling him Sandy in honor of his hair. He was bright-eyed and good-natured. He had trouble riding tricycles, he often fell, and he proved emotionally fragile. But they gave him medical attention, good food, and lots of love. During a Billy Graham Crusade, Sandy made a decision for Christ and grew quickly in the Lord.

As Sandy grew older, Roy and Dale enrolled him in military school and he loved it. At seventeen, he enlisted in the army "to prove myself." Sandy worked hard and won respect. He was sent to Germany, then volunteered for Vietnam. "Put your faith in the Lord," he wrote home, "because (as I have found out) He's always around when you need Him. All He asks in return is your devotion."

Then one day Dale Evans, returning from a trip, was met at the airport. "It's Sandy, Mom. He's dead." The news hit her hard, and it grew worse. Sandy had returned from 26 days of maneuvers, dog tired. His buddies had taken him out for the night, needling him to "prove you're a man." Sandy, who couldn't tolerate alcohol, had given in. They fed him hard liquor until he collapsed. He was found next morning dead in his bunk.

Dale Evans survived the sorrow only by drawing strength from Scripture, particularly from Job 13:15. "Tragedy in a Christian's life is a refiner," she wrote. "God has not promised an easy way, but peace at the center of the hard way. The clouds of sorrow have been heavy, but I have reached the point of no return in my Christian experience, and with Job I can cry, 'Though He slay me, yet will I trust Him.' "

Today's Suggested Reading

Job 13:13–19

Though He slay me, yet will I trust Him. Job 13:15

The Grammy Awards

Charles," said Grandfather Spurgeon, "I have nothing to leave you but rheumatic gout; and I have left you a great deal of that."

But Rev. James Spurgeon left his grandson a great deal more than that.

Charles went to live with his grandparents at age one. James, pastor of an Independent church, had a "large head and large voice." He wore breeches, buckled shoes, and silk stockings. He was a great preacher, and under his tutelage young Charles fell in love with the message and the ministry of preaching.

As a teenager, Charles was once asked to preach at a church in Suffolk. His train being delayed, James began a sermon for him. When the old man saw Charles enter, he interrupted himself. "Here comes my grandson," he said. "He may preach the gospel better than I can, but he cannot preach a better gospel; can you, Charles?" Young Charles took up the sermon from Ephesians 2, right where his grandfather had left off.

Nor did Charles ever forget Grandmother Spurgeon, sitting by the fire, an open Bible on her lap, speaking of the Lord. She taught him many lessons, and she was goodhearted and kind. She kept a little shelf over the kneading trough where she placed bits of sweet pastry, low enough for the boy's plump fingers.

The old couple's grandparenting ministry became the most important thing they ever did for the Lord, for it produced England's greatest preacher.

One Sunday morning, Grandmother Spurgeon told her husband she did not feel well. She would stay home, read her Bible, and pray while he preached. When the old man returned to the manse at noon, there she was, sitting in her old armchair by the fire, her Bible on her lap, her head quietly bowed.

She was with the Lord. Her finger, cold and stilled in death, rested on Job 19:21: "The hand of God hath touched me."

Today's Suggested Reading
Job 19:21–29

*The hand of God hath touched me. Job 19:21**

*King James Version

Sweet Dreams

We've been working with a high school student named Eric whose newfound Christianity is . . . well, under construction. The other day, for example, he told me of sharing Christ to friends at school.

"How did it go?" I asked.

"Not so well," replied Eric. "When my friend didn't listen to me, we got into an argument, and I slapped him across the face."

"Eric," I moaned, "We've got to work on your witnessing techniques."

We've also had to work on his dreams. Shortly after his conversion, Eric complained of vivid, recurring nightmares. "I'm clinging to a cliff," he told us, "about to drop. A friend is gripping me by the arm, and I'm screaming for her to pull me up. But a dark figure whispers in her ear. She lets go of me, and I plunge into the chasm and wake up in terror."

"When I finally go back to sleep, I dream I'm in a boat. Another friend smiles at me, but then pushes me into the water. When I scream for help, she runs over me with the boat. I start sinking, going down and down and down until I descend into a ring of fire. Then a black figure approaches me, saying, 'This is where you belong and this is where you will stay.' Fire explodes all around me, and I wake up drenched in sweat."

"How can I get rid of these dreams?" Eric asked.

We offered a simple suggestion: "Try memorizing Psalm 4:8 and fall asleep quoting it. Ask the Lord to use it to drive away the nightmares."

Eric took our advice. He memorized the verse before bedtime one evening, and now he falls asleep meditating on it.

It has proved effective.

"I have never had the nightmares since," said Eric, grinning. "I lie down now, and I sleep in peace, because the Lord alone makes me dwell in safety."

Today's Suggested Reading

Psalm 4:1–8

I will both lie down in peace, and sleep; for You alone, O Lord, make me dwell in safety. Psalm 4:8

Mastering Midlife

Just as he reached midlife, Jim Conway fell into vicious depression. *Repeatedly, I had fantasies of getting on a sailboat and sailing off to some unknown destination.* He was a pastor, a husband, a father, and an author. But he wanted to run away like a prodigal and start a new life. He later wrote:

The midlife crisis is a time of high risk for marriages. It's a time of possible career disruption and extramarital affairs. There is depression, anger, frustration, and rebellion.

At midlife, a man begins to realize his body is not as strong as it used to be, nor his wife as young. He often feels like a failure at work because his accomplishments fall short of previous expectations. He's caught between generations, having to care for aged parents just as his children are lurching through the teen years. When the kids graduate and fly the coop, it sometimes hits the father harder than the mother. Then come the college bills. All of this hit Conway like a sucker punch.

I had literally come to the end of my rope. I was ready to leave everything and run away. I crawled into bed that November night and hardly slept as I made my plans. I was awake through most of the night, detailing specific steps I would take as I left my present life and ran away to start another life. . . .

But the next morning, as he starting reading his Bible where he had left off the day before, in Psalm 18, he found these words (or they found him): "In my distress I called upon the Lord, and cried out to my God; He heard my voice from His temple. . . . He drew me out of many waters. . . . You will light my lamp; the Lord my God will enlighten my darkness."

He closed his Bible.

The healing had begun.*

Today's Suggested Reading

Psalm 18:1–16

In my distress I called upon the Lord, and cried out to my God; He heard my voice from His temple, and my cry came before Him, even to His ears. Psalm 18:6

---

*Adapted from Jim Conway, *Men in Midlife Crisis* (Elgin, IL: David C. Cook Publishing Co., 1986).

Misplaced Buts

Robert C. McQuilkin established a great Bible conference in Asheville, North Carolina, called Ben Lippen, and years later Vance Havner preached there. Both men came away with the same lesson from Psalm 23:1.

In the early days of Ben Lippen, McQuilkin gave a breakfast devotion one morning, saying: "Is the Lord meeting all your needs or isn't he? Now, most Christians will say, 'Why certainly the Lord is meeting all my needs, but . . .'—and then follow that 'but' with all the things that are troubling them. 'The Lord is my Shepherd, but I have not a gift for personal work. The Lord is my Shepherd, but I don't have a job. The Lord is my Shepherd, but my child is sick.' You see? You have the *but* in the wrong place. And so I would say, 'We have tremendous deficits, but the Lord is my Shepherd. I'm not very strong, but the Lord is my Shepherd. I'm all confused, but the Lord is my Shepherd . . . .'"

Years later, evangelist Vance Havner came to preach at Ben Lippen. He was worried about his wife, Sara, who had contracted a rare and deadly disease. Her life was ebbing away, and doubt and dread overwhelmed him.

While there he began thinking of Psalm 23. The Lord impressed him that he was acting more like a billy goat than a sheep—always butting. "Yes, I know that the Lord is my Shepherd BUT . . . I'm growing old and who is going to care for me? What if I get sick and my helpmeet cannot come to my aid?"

Havner climbed the nearby mountaintop to pray, and there the Lord restored his soul. *Surely He who has brought me through nearly seventy-two years of dangers, toils, and snares will see that I finish the journey. Surely goodness and mercy shall follow me the rest of the way and I shall dwell in the house of the Lord forever.*

"Lord," he said, "help me be a lamb and not a billy goat!"

Today's Suggested Reading
Psalm 23:1–3

The Lord is my Shepherd; I shall not want.
Psalm 23:1

The Frostbitten Shepherd

In my hometown of Elizabethton, Tennessee, lived an aged schoolteacher named Beula Thomas, who was raised on the Colorado prairie. Before her death, she recorded her childhood recollections, including the vivid incident that brought her to faith in Jesus Christ.

An early blizzard hit the Rockies during the winter of 1912, and a local shepherd, Mr. Woods, was caught with his flock in the mountains near the Thomas homestead. He desperately tried to herd his sheep into a hollow space close together so they could keep warm. Woods knew the thick snow would provide a protective covering for his sheep, saving them from the bitter wind; and the warm breath from the sheep would melt the snow near their faces, allowing them to breathe.

But instead of listening to their shepherd, the sheep bolted after the lead sheep and ran into a thick snowdrift where they perished. The despondent, half-frozen shepherd showed up at the Thomas house, seeking refuge from the storm. Mrs. Thomas heated water for the poor man's hands and feet while her husband rubbed them vigorously to ward off frostbite. Over a supper of salmon patties, the man told his sad story.

"I'll come back after the blizzard and skin the sheep," said Mr. Woods. "The birds and coyotes will take care of the meat."

The three Thomas children were gripped by this unexpected visitor. Shortly afterward, while they discussed it all with their mother, she quoted Psalm 23, explaining that Jesus is the Good Shepherd who cares for us, though all we like sheep have gone astray. "Some people are stubborn and refuse to follow Christ and are lost forever. But Jesus came to lead his sheep to eternal safety."

As she used that story to explain the gospel, her words spoke to the children, and that day both Beula and sister Pearl chose to follow the Master's voice.

Today's Suggested Reading
Psalm 23:4–6

Surely goodness and mercy shall follow me all the days of my life. . . . Psalm 23:6

March

The Secret of Revival

That Palace

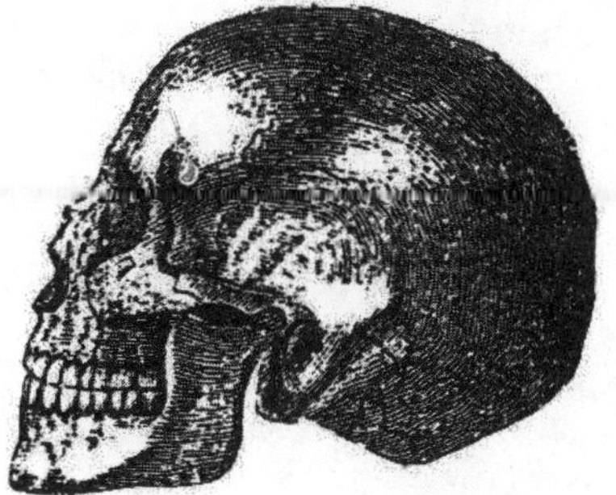

Its Thin Gray Hair

Refuge

Cheju-do

March **1**

The Secret of Revival

Duncan Campbell grew up harnessed to a set of bagpipes, and he eventually became a sought-after entertainer in his Scottish village. But one night during a concert, he suddenly asked himself, "Is this all life offers a young man like me?" Excusing himself, he hurried home where his mother led him to Christ. He served the Lord in churches in his native highlands until age 50 when he left as a missionary to the Outer Hebrides Islands.

A mission church had already been established on Lewis Island, and several of its members had been pleading for revival. One night in a prayer meeting, a young man rose and read Psalm 24: "Who may ascend into the hill of the Lord? Or who may stand in His holy place? He who has clean hands and a pure heart. . . ."

"Brethren," the man said, "it seems just so much humbug to be waiting and praying as we are, if we ourselves are not rightly related to God." Instantly the Christians began confessing their sins to God and to one another.

When Duncan Campbell arrived soon afterward, he went straight to the church and preached, then dismissed the service. The crowd filed from the building; but instead of going home, they stood under the stars, weeping, praying and confessing their sins. The number soon swelled to 600, and all night the Holy Spirit moved through the village. Hundreds trusted Christ as Savior.

The revival spread to nearby villages, and Duncan traveled for three years, strengthening the converts. Night after night, churches were filled with worshipers, often until five o'clock the following morning. Duncan later said that during those days he could stop any passerby on the island and find him thinking about his soul.

Duncan Campbell lived until 1971, and he preached until the last week of his life. But the Lewis Revival proved the most fruitful period of his ministry.

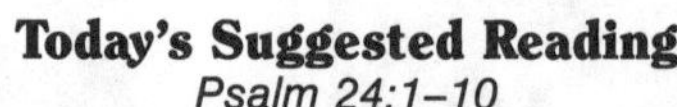

Today's Suggested Reading

Psalm 24:1–10

Who may ascend into the hill of the Lord? Or who may stand in His holy place? He who has clean hands and a pure heart. Psalm 24:3–4

The Three Margarets

Three Margarets stood trial April 13, 1685, ready to suffer for their faith in Christ. They were Scottish Covenanters, and their crime consisted chiefly of attending field meetings and unauthorized preaching services on the highlands. They were declared guilty, and the prosecutor demanded they kneel to receive sentence. When the women refused, they were brutally shoved to the floor. Margaret MacLachlan, a widow of seventy, was to die by drowning. Margaret Wilson, an 18-year-old farmer's daughter, would also drown. Margaret Maxwell, a 20-year-old maid, was sentenced to be flogged.

Maxwell was publicly whipped three days successively—and she lived to talk about it to old age. The other two Margarets were taken to an abysmal inlet by the sea and tied to long, wooden stakes. There the advancing surf climbed their bodies in fits and jerks, rising to their waists, to their necks, then to their faces.

The older Margaret, tied further out, uttered nothing but quiet prayers to God. Her body struggled in the chilling tide and went limp. The soldiers yelled to Margaret Wilson, "Don't you see her? Won't you recant?"

"No," she shouted, "I do not see her. I see only Jesus Christ." Then she began singing the Scottish version of Psalm 25:8–9, asking God to guide her to Himself, to make His path known.

God good and upright is:
The way He'll sinners show;
The meek in judgment He will guide
And make His path to know.

Then as the sea filled her lungs and swept over her head, the 18-year-old uttered her ten last words: "We are more than conquerers through Him that loved us!"

Today's Suggested Reading

Psalm 25:1–15

Good and upright is the Lord; therefore He teaches sinners in the way. The humble He guides in justice, and the humbled He teaches His way. Psalm 25:8–9

Four Days' Journey

Margaret Wilson was far from the only Covenanter who died while singing the Scottish Psalms. Hugh M'Kail, a brilliant young man, was born about 1640 and educated at the University of Edinburgh. He entered the ministry, but was expelled from the state church at age 20 after signing the Presbyterian Covenant, which the Scottish Crown considered treasonous. Royal troops pursued him, and he escaped time and again by the skin of his teeth.

Hiding near his father's farmhouse, M'Kail often withdrew into the mountains and prayed in nooks and hollows and caves. But at length he was caught. In Edinburgh, he was intensely questioned, but said little. A device called the boot was then placed around his leg, into which staves and wedges were driven an inch at a time until his bones were crushed. Still he said nothing.

He was condemned to be hanged in four days, and his sole comment was, "O how good news, to be within four days' journey of enjoying the sight of Jesus Christ!" He spent the time in praise and prayer, meeting with his friends and aged father, his cheerfulness never forsaking him.

On the day of his execution, he was up at five, waking his companions and quoting Scripture. He prayed a final time with his father, then spent the morning encouraging his friends. At mid afternoon, he was brought to the scaffold, his young face strong and unworried. Looking out at the crowd, he lifted his voice and sang Psalm 31:

In you, O Lord, I put my trust;
Let me never be ashamed;
Deliver me in Your righteousness . . .

And thus, at 26 years of age, he died as he had lived, for the Lord.

Today's Suggested Reading
Psalm 31:1–5

In You, O Lord, I put my trust;
Let me never be ashamed;
Deliver me in Your righteousness. Psalm 31:1

God's Man Now

Thirty-year-old George W. Truett had just been named pastor of the First Baptist Church of Dallas, and some of his men, wanting to get to know him, took him quail hunting. Among them was Jim Arnold, the city's Chief of Police. Another of the men later recounted what happened: *At 3:30, just as we were starting home, George Truett accidentally shot Capt. Arnold in the right leg, below knee, making an awful wound. I succeeded in stopping the blood by using my suspenders as a tourniquet. Brother Truett was in agony unspeakable. Never saw the like. Arnold suffers much. Fainted several times.*

The following Sunday, Arnold died. All Dallas was stunned and Truett was devastated. He paced the floor day and night, unable to eat or sleep, muttering, "I will never preach again. I could never again stand in the pulpit."

Finally this verse came to mind, and his words began changing. As he paced, he mumbled, "My times are in thy hand. My times are in thy hand." Finally he collapsed in sheer exhaustion.

That night he vividly dreamed of Jesus standing by his bed. The Lord said, "Be not afraid. You are My man from now on." Later the dream came again, then a third time. At length it was announced that Truett was returning to the pulpit. Churches across Dallas dismissed services and gathered at First Baptist in support.

"When Brother Truett came into the pulpit," a member later said, "he looked terrible, his face drawn, his eyes sad. He remained silent for a long moment. You could have heard a pin drop. When he began, somehow he sounded different. His voice! I shall never forget his voice that morning. . . ."

Truett remained at the First Baptist Church until his death in 1944. During his tenure, membership increased from 700 to over 7,000, with a total of 19,531 new members received and over 5,000 baptisms recorded.

He was God's man now.

Today's Suggested Reading

Psalm 31:15–24

*My times are in thy hand. . . . Psalm 31:15**

---

*King James Version

Tramp for the Lord

At their wedding, Corrie ten Boom's parents adopted this verse as their life text: "I will instruct you and teach you in the way you should go; I will guide you with My eye." Later, during the Nazi reign of terror, the entire family remained faithful to God even while interred in the death camps. Sadly, only Corrie survived.

After the war, invitations came for her to tell her story and share the gospel. She adopted her parents' verse as her own and began speaking throughout Western Europe. Then she was invited to America; but when she applied for her traveling documents, she was refused. The Dutch official was hard as flint and unwilling to process her request. One day while again waiting in line, Corrie claimed Psalm 32:8, asking God to help her. Suddenly a man passed by, stopped, smiled, and said, "Don't we know each other? You're a cousin of mine. We've not seen each other for years!"

"Are you going to America too?" asked Corrie.

"Not at all. My office is in this building. If you have trouble, ring up. Here's my number."

When at last Corrie came to the window, the Dutch official was curt and coarse as always. Corrie slid the phone number across to him. "Will you please call this number?" The man looked at the paper, his eyes growing wider. Dialing the number, he spoke a few words, listened to the response, hung up—and promptly issued Corrie her traveling papers.

For the rest of her life, Corrie constantly bumped into the right people at just the right times to pave her way around the globe as "a tramp for the Lord." She considered this verse her personal assurance from the Master: "I will instruct you and teach you in the way you should go; I will guide you with My eye."

Today's Suggested Reading
Psalm 32:1–11

I will instruct you and teach you in the way you should go; I will guide you with My eye. Psalm 32:8

Staying Single

In 1 Corinthians 7, the Bible recommends the single life, for unmarried people have more time for the Lord and fewer burdens to distract from His work. But it isn't an easy road, and remaining single requires special grace, as Amy Carmichael found out.

Amy Wilson Carmichael (1867–1951) was born in Northern Ireland and educated in a Wesleyan Methodist boarding school. Having a heart for missions, she spent fifteen months in Japan, but suffered there physically and emotionally. She traveled on to Ceylon, then to England, then to India where she found her niche at last, working with girls whom she rescued from slavery and prostitution, raising them in her Dohnavur Fellowship. Her life touched thousands, her books have blessed millions, and her work remains to this day.

Like most young ladies, Amy, attractive and radiant, wanted to be married. But her great work would have been impossible as a married woman, and God gave her Psalm 34:22 as a special promise. Amy's struggle with this issue was deeply personal, one she was unable to share for more than forty years, when at last she said this to one of her "children" who was facing a similar dilemma:

On this day many years ago, I went away alone to a cave in the mountain called Arima. I had feelings of fear about the future. That is why I went there—to be alone with God. The devil kept on whispering, "It's all right now, but what about afterwards? You are going to be very lonely." And he painted pictures of loneliness—I can see them still. And I turned to my God in a kind of desperation and said, "Lord, what can I do? How can I go on to the end?" And He said, "None of them that trust in Me shall be desolate" (Psalm 34:22). That word has been with me ever since.

Today's Suggested Reading

Psalm 34:17–22

*The Lord redeemeth the soul of his servants: and none of them that trust in him shall be desolate. Psalm 34:22**

---

*King James Version

March 7 Cleared for Take-Off

Cameron Townsend, founder of Wycliffe Bible Translators, nearly lost his life in a plane crash at the hands of an inexperienced Mexican pilot. That's when he conceived the idea of an efficient aviation program to serve his jungle-based translators, and thus was born JAARS—Jungle Aviation and Radio Service. But planes are expensive, and acquiring them was slow going in the early days.

On one occasion, JAARS' Bernie May envisioned adding a DC-3 to the mission's small fleet. The DC-3 was versatile, easy to fly, safe, and able to carry almost anything in its enormous belly. Bernie prayed earnestly for such a plane, but in keeping with Wycliffe practice, he seldom said anything about it. One day, Bernie spoke at Pittsburgh's First Presbyterian Church, telling stories of God's faithfulness. Afterward he was approached by Paul Duke.

"I'm chief pilot for the Blaw-Knox Steel Corporation," said Duke. "I don't know anything about your needs in South America, but my company has a DC-3 which they are getting ready to dispose of. Are you interested?"

Bernie was very interested. But initial contacts with the company went badly, for the plane had already been promised to others. Bernie boarded his flight in Pittsburgh with a sense of disappointment. As he fastened his seatbelt and pulled his Bible from his briefcase, it opened to Psalm 37: "Delight yourself also in the Lord, And he shall give you the desires of your heart." The words struck with such force that Bernie startled his fellow passengers by exclaiming, "Wow!" It was as though God were promising him that DC-3.

It took months for the pieces to fall together, but eventually Bernie May had his plane. As he taxied it toward the runway on his way to the JAARS base in South America, his headset crackled with some of the sweetest words he had ever heard, a voice from the control tower: "DC-3 two thousand Lima, cleared for takeoff—and may the Lord bless you, sir."

Today's Suggested Reading
Psalm 37:1–8

Delight yourself also in the Lord, And He shall give you the desires of your heart. Psalm 37:4

Talking to Yourself

Several years ago, I lapsed into prolonged discouragement. I was hitting thirty-five, and my accomplishments seemed meager. Fears and disappointments cropped up like so many weeds. One day I booked a room at a nearby resort and, needing a good counselor, invited the British expositor Martyn Lloyd-Jones to join me. He fit nicely into my backpack in the form of his book *Spiritual Depression,* and that week the Lord used his words to restore my soul. The opening chapter struck me forcibly. Lloyd-Jones observed that the Psalmist was talking to himself when he said, "Why are you cast down, O my soul?"

I say we must talk to ourselves instead of allowing "ourselves" to talk to us! Do you realize what that means? I suggest that the main trouble in this whole matter of spiritual depression is that we allow our self to talk to us instead of talking to our self. This is the very essence of wisdom in the matter. Have you realized that most of your unhappiness in life is due to the fact that you are listening to yourself instead of talking to yourself?

*The main art in the matter of spiritual living is to know how to handle yourself. You have to take yourself in hand, you have to address yourself, preach to yourself, question yourself. You must say to your soul: "Why art thou cast down"—what business have you to be disquieted? You must turn on yourself and say to yourself: "Hope thou in God"—instead of muttering in this depressed, unhappy way. Then you must go on to remind yourself of who God is, and what God has done, and what God has pledged to do.**

I took Lloyd-Jones' counsel to heart, and I left my retreat quoting another verse, Psalm 103:1: "Bless the Lord, O my soul; and all that is within me, bless His holy name."

I've been talking to myself ever since.

Today's Suggested Reading
Psalm 42:1–11

Why are you cast down, O my soul? And why are you disquieted within me? Hope in God, for I shall yet praise Him for the help of His countenance. Psalm 42:5

---

*D. Martyn Lloyd-Jones, *Spiritual Depression* (Grand Rapids: Wm. B. Eerdmans Co., 1965), pp. 20–21.

A Mighty Fortress

In 1947, missionaries Dick and Margaret Hillis settled with their four children by the Mule River in the Honan province of China. Nearby, a mission church swelled with nearly a thousand Chinese every Sunday. It would have been a happy time but for the impending war between Chiang kai-Shek and the forces of Mao Tse-tung.

One day, Nationalist Captain Hwang urgently told Dick, "The Communists are marching on Mule River Market. You had better take your family and flee." But it was too late. The Communists had blown up all railroad bridges. That evening the Hillises heard the first shots, and soon the battle raged around them. There was no sleep as they spent that night in prayer. The city soon fell, and the streets filled with Communist troops.

Then a new danger arose. Captain Hwang, outside the city walls, was lobbing shells at the Communists. The bombing reached a crescendo one night as each shell dropped closer to the Hillis home. The house next door exploded, killing all the inhabitants, and it appeared the Hillis home would be next. The family huddled in the corner as another shell exploded, sending dirt, glass, and bricks through windows and walls. The house quaked. The children screamed, momentarily deafened. The family prepared for death. But the shelling abruptly stopped, and the Hillises cautiously emerged from their corner. The room was filled with debris, but no one was hurt.

By and by, as Dick tucked each child into bed, he knelt beside Margaret Anne and noticed a dirty scrap of paper stuffed under her pillow. On it was printed in big, childlike letters these words: "God is our refuge and strength, a very present help in trouble."

During the Chinese nights of terror, little Margaret Anne had been resting on a very big verse from a very faithful God.*

Today's Suggested Reading
Psalm 46:1–7

God is our refuge and strength, a very present help in trouble. Psalm 46:1

---

*Adapted from Jan Winebrenner, *Steel in His Soul: The Dick Hillis Story* (Chicago: Moody Press, 1985), pp. 105–114.

Like an Envelope

Brenda Ludwig was away at a conference when the call came. Her son had been badly injured in a terrible wreck and was being airlifted to a hospital, just clinging to life. He had been drinking. He wasn't expected to live. Would she wait for her husband, who would be there in an hour to pick her up?

It was the longest hour of Brenda's life, but this verse flashed to her mind: "Be still, and know that I am God." In that hour, and during the weeks and months that followed as her son made a slow recovery, the verse never left her. "I could feel God like an envelope around me," she said.

The students at Wheaton College felt the same presence on September 22, 1967. They had assembled for chapel that morning, excited that their beloved chancellor, Dr. V. Raymond Edman, would be back in the pulpit after recovering from his heart attack.

They reached for their Bibles as Edman rose to speak: *This will be the first time in more than ten months that I have attempted to speak in public. But I want you to consider with me an invitation to visit a king.*

After describing the majesty of meeting the King of Ethiopia, Edman said, *But I speak primarily of another King. This chapel is the house of the King. . . . Chapel is a time of worship, a time of meeting the King. Come in, sit down and wait in silence before the Lord. Your heart will learn to cultivate what the Scripture says, "Be still and know that I am God." Over these years I have learned the immense value of that deep, inner silence as David, the king, sat in God's presence to hear from Him. . . .*

And with those words, Edman slumped forward and, as the students watched in shock, he entered the presence of the King.

Today's Suggested Reading

Psalm 46:8–11

Be still, and know that I am God. I will be exalted among the nations, I will be exalted in the earth! Psalm 46:10

March 11 Fever, Filth, and Fetters

America's first foreign missionary, Adoniram Judson, shared the spotlight with a striking woman—his wife Ann. She was beautiful, intelligent, and brave. Her commitment to Christ was expressed in her diary: *Whether I spend my days in India or America, I desire to spend them in the service of God. I am quite willing to give up temporal comforts and live a life of hardship and trial, if it be the will of God.*

As it turned out, it was. In Burma, Ann suffered disease, poverty, and the death of her children. She and Adoniram labored six years before baptizing their first convert. She translated Scripture, opened a school, and worked side-by-side with her devoted husband, enduring unspeakable agony during his seventeen months of cruel imprisonment. His feet and hands were tied to bamboo poles for months at a time, and he was suspended in painful positions for hours. He suffered galloping dysentery, vermin, fever, filth, and fetters.

Ann was always nearby, sneaking him food, bribing his guards, whispering words of hope, racking her brain for ways to save his Bible translations. She badgered governmental officials on his behalf and tracked him down when he was relocated. But her health finally broke, and she collapsed on the mat floor of a wretched bamboo hut. There she lay, emaciated, shaven, suffering from smallpox, able to do little more than cry. In her distress, she remembered Psalm 50: *If I ever felt the value and efficacy of prayer, I did at this time. I could make no efforts to secure my husband. I could only plead with that great and powerful Being who has said, "Call upon Me in the time of trouble and I will hear, and thou shalt glorify Me." God made me at this time feel so powerfully this promise, that I became quite composed, feeling assured that my prayers would be answered.*

Today's Suggested Reading
Psalm 50:1–15

Call upon Me in the day of trouble; I will deliver you, and you shall glorify Me. Psalm 50:15

Matthew Henry's Diary

Matthew Henry's name is forever linked to his famous Bible commentary that has blessed millions of students since it was published in the early 1700s under the title *Exposition of the Old and New Testaments.* Popularly called *Matthew Henry's Commentary,* it is usually considered the greatest devotional commentary ever written in the English language.

Matthew, who had practiced law before entering the ministry, began his commentary in November, 1704, and the first volume was finished four years later. By his death at age 52 in 1714, he had finished his work through the Gospel of John. A group of thirteen noted ministers, using his notes, completed his commentary through Revelation.

Matthew was born in 1662, the son of Rev. Philip Henry. His devotion to Christ is seen by this remarkable diary entry made on October 18, 1675, when he was only 13 years old. The boy compiled a thanksgiving list in which he credits his salvation to a sermon from Psalm 51:

For Spiritual Mercies; for the Lord Jesus Christ, his incarnation, Life, Death, Resurrection, Ascension and Intercession, for Grace, Pardon, Peace, for the Word, the means of Grace, for Prayer, for good Instructions, for the Good I have got at any time under the Word, for any Succour and Help from God under Temptation, for Brokenness of Heart, for an Enlightening. Lord Jesus, I bless thee for thy Word, for good Parents, for good Education, that I was taken into Baptism; and, Lord, I give thee thanks, that I am thine and will be thine.

I think it was three years ago that I began to be convinced, hearing a Sermon by my Father on Psalm 51:17: "The Sacrifices of God are a broken Spirit; a broken and a contrite Heart, O God, thou wilt not despise." I think it was that melted me, afterwards I began to enquire after Christ.

Today's Suggested Reading

Psalm 51:1–17

*The sacrifices of God are a broken spirit: a broken and a contrite heart, O God, thou wilt not despise. Psalm 51:17**

---

*King James Version

Scalded and Saved

For many years John Fletcher shied away from the Lord, feeling unworthy of the gospel. He joined the army and accepted a commission to fight for Portugal against Brazil. But in his hotel room waiting for his ship to board, Fletcher ordered some tea. The maid spilled the boiling water on his leg, scalding him so badly he couldn't sail. From his window, he sadly watched the ship vanish beyond the horizon.

It was never heard from again. Fletcher, meanwhile, recovered enough to travel to England, where one night he had a terrifying dream that woke him to his backslidden condition. Shortly afterward he listened attentively to a Methodist evangelist, and the Lord began working on his heart. Fletcher, who later became one of John Wesley's closest associates, described his conversion in 1755 like this:

On January 21, I began to write a confession of my sins, together with a resolution to seek Christ even unto death; but, my business calling me away, I had no heart to go on with it. (Two days later) having continued my supplication till near one in the morning, I then opened my Bible, and fell on these words, "Cast thy burden on the Lord, and He shall sustain thee. He will not suffer the righteous to be moved." Filled with joy, I fell again on my knees to beg of God that I might always cast my burden upon him. My hope was now greatly increased, and I thought I saw myself conqueror over sin, hell, and all manner of affliction.

I shut my Bible, and as I shut it, I cast my eye on the words, "Whatsoever ye shall ask in my name, I will do it." So having asked perseverance and grace to serve God till death, I went cheerfully to take my rest.

Today's Suggested Reading
Psalm 55:16–23

Cast your burden on the Lord, and He shall sustain you; He shall never permit the righteous to be moved. Psalm 55:22

Vows Spoken in Trouble

In his 1906 book *Method in Soul-Winning,* Henry Mabie tells of preaching one night from Psalm 66:13–14. Afterward, a brickmaker asked him home. *We entered the house in perfect silence. He stirred up the fire, drew up some chairs, and said: "Now we'll just sit down and have a talk. Your words tonight compel me to tell you what I have never told anyone before."*

The man had vowed upon his mother's death to live for the Lord, but he hadn't followed through. Moving to Illinois, he intended to give his life to Christ, but had not done so. When gold fever broke in California in 1849, he had rushed westward. Near St. Louis, cholera broke out on his riverboat, and men died at intervals through the night. Every half hour the steamer drew to shore to bury a victim in the sand. "Lord, if you will spare my life," the brickmaker prayed, "I'll serve you."

Traveling across the plains, he was endangered by Indians. He made constant vows to the Lord, pleading for safety. Arriving in California, he promised to serve God, "if you will prosper me in my finds." These vows too went unpaid. Later, traveling abroad with his gold, his ship was gripped by scurvy. The brickmaker himself grew ill, and he again made vows to God. The pattern had continued unabated all this life.

The old man looked up from the fire and said, "Now I'm ready to pay my neglected vows. I'm ready to confess Christ before these neighbors of mine and before the church."

"Suffice it to say," wrote Mabie, "the man and his wife came out, throwing their whole souls into their new life in Christ. It was one of the most thrilling narratives ever told me; and the whole event was so unexpected by the entire neighborhood that it was the talk of the place for years."

Today's Suggested Reading

Psalm 66:1–15

I will go into Your house with burnt offerings; I will pay You my vows, which my lips have uttered and my mouth has spoken when I was in trouble. Psalm 66:13–14

March **15** Inventory of Blessings

Almost everyone is familiar with John Newton's famous hymn *Amazing Grace,* and many know its story. But few know that Newton was not only a poet and preacher, he was a prodigious letter writer. Among his correspondents was a wealthy nobleman to whom Newton wrote 26 letters. In the 15th, written on April 20, 1774, Newton describes the joy of being a Christian, quoting from and elaborating on Psalm 73:24:

What a comfort, what an honour is this, that worms have liberty to look up to God, and that He, the high and holy One who inhabiteth eternity, is pleased to look down upon us, to maintain our peace, to supply our wants, to guide us with His eye, to inspire us with wisdom and grace suitable to our occasions! Those who profess to know something of this fellowship and to depend upon it, are by the world accounted enthusiasts who know not what they mean, or perhaps hypocrites who pretend to what they have not in order to cover some base designs. But we have reason to bear their reproaches with patience.

Let them rage, let them, if they please, point at me for a fool as I walk the streets; if I do but take up the Bible, or run over in my mind the inventory of the blessings with which the Lord has enriched me, I have sufficient amends. Jesus is mine; in Him I have wisdom, righteousness, sanctification, and redemption,—an interest in all the promises and in all the perfections of God.

He will guide me by His counsel, support me by His power, comfort me with His presence, while I am here; and afterwards, when flesh and heart fail, He will receive me to His glory.

Today's Suggested Reading
Psalm 73:21–28

You will guide me with Your counsel, and afterward receive me to glory. Psalm 73:24

Cheju-do

The Far East Broadcasting Company was founded to take "Christ to the World by Radio," and today it beams forth in 150 languages to Asia, the Middle East, and Africa. But the early years were marked by struggle. For example, in 1969 when Okinawa reverted to Japanese control, FEBC lost its access to broadcast from the island. Mission officials frantically sought a place for an even larger station to reach China.

While traveling with U.S. military personnel, FEBC's George Littman looked out his plane window and saw a beautiful volcanic piece of land lying in the Yellow Sea off the Korean Peninsula. It was the island of Cheju-do, 400 miles closer to China than Okinawa. FEBC officials approached the Korean government for permission to build a quarter-million-watt station for international broadcasting. After months of negotiations, the Koreans appeared ready to grant permission.

FEBC's president, Robert Bowman received a call from his Asian staff: "Mr. Bowman, if the government says 'yes,' we must move quickly. It's going to take a lot of money."

"I don't have a dollar of it right now," replied Bob. "If God gives an affirmative answer from the government, He will provide."

But in the wee hours, Bob woke in a panic, worried about generating the funds. He rose, reached for his Bible, and began to pray. He turned to Psalm 78, and the Lord gave him verse 53: "He led them on safely, so that they did not fear. . . ." Bob continued reading and came to verse 72: "So He shepherded them according to the integrity of his heart, and guided them by the skillfulness of His hands." Bob's heart was stilled and strengthened.

The story of how the Lord provided for the project is too long to tell here. Suffice to say that on June 30, 1973, the new Cheju-do transmitting site was dedicated to the glory of God, and untold millions behind the Bamboo Curtain have since heard the message of Jesus Christ.

Today's Suggested Reading
Psalm 78:40–55

And He led them on safely, so that they did not fear; but the sea overwhelmed their enemies. Psalm 78:53

March **17**

How Should We Then Die?

The Far East Broadcasting Company was but one of a galaxy of ministries springing up at the end of World War II to alter the Christian landscape of the world. During the same period, for example, Francis and Edith Schaeffer set out as missionaries to Switzerland where they founded a study center for European students searching for truth. They called it "L'Abri," a French word meaning "Shelter." Through their hospitality at L'Abri and through their books and seminars, the Schaeffers helped thousands of young people find Christ.

Then, during a 1978 visit to Mayo Clinic in Rochester, Minnesota, Francis was diagnosed with an advanced case of lymphoma and told he had only six to eight weeks to live. His cancer went into remission twice, and his life was extended five more years, during which he ministered on both sides of the Atlantic with unusual power.

Nearing death, he said, "By God's grace, I have been able to do more in these last five years than in all the years before I had cancer." He continued taking his treatments, praying for healing, and speaking quietly for the Lord; but it became clear he was dying.

As was his custom, he met this final challenge by turning to the Scriptures, and the Lord gave him Psalm 84:5–7: "Blessed is the man whose strength is in You, whose heart is set on pilgrimage. As they pass through the Valley of Baca [Valley of Weeping], they make it a spring; the rain also covers it with pools. They go from strength to strength; each one appears before God in Zion."

Those words became a constant comfort to Francis. The Lord gave him strength. His valley of weeping became a spring from which others found the Lord. And finally, early on May 15, 1984, he appeared before God in Zion.

Today's Suggested Reading
Psalm 84:1–7

Blessed is the man whose strength is in You, whose heart is set on pilgrimage. Psalm 84:5

That Palace

Brutal, bare-fisted political scandals are nothing new to American politics. Andrew and Rachel Jackson were vilified by their critics and the press during his presidential campaigns. Rachel had previously married Army Captain Lewis Robards, but he proved an abusive husband and the marriage was unhappy. She separated from him and believed she had successfully obtained a divorce. The Jacksons were married in Natchez, Mississippi, only to learn two years later that Rachel's divorce was not properly processed. Andrew and Rachel were remarried on January 17, 1794, in Nashville.

In the 1828 campaign, Jackson's opponents dug all this up and used it against him, making it one of the bitterest contests in American history. Andrew was called a "paramour husband," and Rachel was labeled a "convicted adulteress." Jackson, deeply devoted to his wife, lashed back in anger, while Rachel suffered inwardly and withdrew to their home, the Hermitage, outside Nashville. Being a devout Christian, she turned to her Bible for comfort.

Jackson won the election and rejoined Rachel at the Hermitage to prepare for their move to Washington. But it wasn't to be. On December 22, 1828, on the eve of their much heralded departure for the nation's capital, Rachel wasn't feeling well. She dreaded their move to the White House. As her maid Hannah helped her to a chair by the fire, Rachel remarked, "I would rather be a door-keeper in the house of God than to live in that palace."

Twenty minutes later Rachel cried, "I am fainting!" and collapsed in Hannah's arms. The servant's screams brought Andrew bursting into the room, followed by doctors and friends. Rachel was lifted into bed as the doctors listened for her heartbeat. There was none. Andrew was so ravaged in grief that friends feared he, too, might succumb.

But a few days later, having buried his beloved, the grim but determined President-elect left alone for "that palace" at 1600 Pennsylvania Avenue.

Today's Suggested Reading
Psalm 84:8–12

For a day in Your courts is better than a thousand. I would rather be a doorkeeper in the house of my God than dwell in the tents of wickedness.
Psalm 84:10

You Come Too!

"In October, 1969, what I had feared most happened without warning," wrote homemaker Phyllis Cochran. "Our middle child, seven-year-old Suzy, was diagnosed as having a brain tumor. The neurologist's words cut deeply: 'Your daughter may die.'"

Phyllis felt her world toppling down, and even the beautiful fall colors seemed dark and grim. Questions flew to her mind: "Is this all there is to life—to be born, live, and die? Is there a purpose in life? Have I missed something?" Though she didn't know God, she cried to Him, asking help.

Suzy survived her surgery with her right side impaired, and she began trying to learn to sit, stand, and walk again. But a second operation left her hovering near death.

That night was the darkest yet of my life. While Phil and our two other children slept, I sat alone crying to God. I felt as though I were in an inky dark tunnel. God waited at the other end, and I needed desperately to reach Him, but I couldn't find my way.

Phyllis thumbed through her grandmother's old Bible, and her eyes fell on Psalm 88:1—"O Lord, God of my salvation, I have cried out day and night before You. Let my prayer come before You; incline Your ear to my cry." Those words proved a sudden shaft of light, and Phyllis continued reading through the night.

Suzy slowly recovered, and when a neighbor invited them to a Bible study, both Phyllis and Suzy attended. There they heard the plainspoken gospel, and soon both were born again.

Suzy died soon afterward, but her last words were, "When they take me out of here, make sure you come too." In keeping with that simple request, every member of the family has found Jesus Christ as Lord and Savior, along with many friends and relatives.

"And one day," says Phyllis, "our family will be complete again to walk together on streets of gold."*

Today's Suggested Reading
Psalm 88:1–18

O Lord, God of my salvation, I have cried out day and night before You. Psalm 88:1

---

*Adapted from "I Cried, 'Where Are You God?'" by Phyllis Cochran in *Decision*, pp. 4–5.

A New Psalm

March **20**

High in spirits and eager for home, D. L. Moody boarded ship in Southampton for New York. *We were about three days on our voyage. I was on my couch, feeling thankful to God, for in all my travels by land and sea, I had never been in any accident of a serious nature. While engaged with these thoughts, I was startled by a crash and shock, as if the vessel had been driven on a rock. My son jumped from his berth and rushed on deck. He was back again in a few minutes, exclaiming the vessel was sinking. I did not believe it, but concluded to dress and go on deck. The report was true. Other passengers rushed on deck declaring their cabins were filling with water. The ship was helpless. The passengers could only stand still on the poor drifting, sinking ship and look into our watery graves. The night closed in without a sign of a sail.*

That was an awful night, the darkest in all our lives—several hundred men, women, and children waiting for doom. No one dared sleep. We were all together in the saloon. The agony and suspense were too great for words. Sunday morning dawned without help or hope. With one arm clasping a pillar to steady myself, I read Psalm 91, and we prayed that God would still the raging sea and bring us to our desired haven. It was a new psalm to me from that hour. The eleventh verse touched me deeply, like the voice of divine assurance. One lady thought those words must have been written for the occasion, and afterwards asked to see the book for herself.

The second night enveloped them, but at 3 A.M. they were accosted by the *Lake Huron,* bound from Montreal to Liverpool. The angels had a busy time of it, but in the end all were saved.

Today's Suggested Reading
Psalm 91:1–11

For He shall give His angels charge over you, to keep you in all your ways. Psalm 91:11

Refuge

The doctor's words were a slap in the face. As Don and Sharon Kiser sat in stunned silence, the physician explained that Don's kidneys were working at only twenty-five percent.

That night, Sharon slept only fitfully, hearing the words "kidney failure" reverberate in her mind like an unending echo. *At 6:00 A.M. the next morning, I felt exhausted. I looked out at my favorite spot, the pond and the tall pine trees that stretch behind our house. But this morning, with just a faint flicker of light left from the moon, the trees looked grotesque and eerie. The pond looked like a murky abyss waiting to swallow me and my frightening thoughts.*

Sharon dropped into a chair, Bible in hand. "Jesus," she cried, "I'm desperate. I need something from your Word." But no verse would come to her, and in her despair she couldn't even think where to turn in the Scriptures for comfort. She opened her Bible at random and suddenly saw these words: "When my anxious thoughts multiply within me, thy consolations delight my soul."*

That was it! My anxious thoughts were not just adding to one another—they were multiplying faster than I could count. God was acknowledging that I was human. He told me that He would delight my soul in the midst of turmoil.

Reading the verse until she had memorized it, Sharon closed her Bible and rested in the calm of those words. Her husband's condition worsened, but at every point Sharon found the steadiness and strength to deal with it.

*We are still dealing with Don's serious kidney condition, and I dare not just quote a Bible verse and go skipping on my merry way. But I am grateful for experiencing the comfort of God's Word. I have taken refuge there. God's Word is the unchanging element in a swirling, difficult situation. I have put my trust in Him, and I know that He is sufficient.***

Today's Suggested Reading

Psalm 94:16–23

In the multitude of my anxieties within me, your comforts delight my soul. Psalm 94:19

---

*New American Standard Version

**Adapted from "When My Anxious Thoughts Multiply" by Sharon Schuller Kiser, in *Decision*, August, 1996, pp. 7–8.

A 36-Year Visit

Isaac Watts was an odd little eighteenth-century Christian whose classic poems like *O God Our Help in Ages Past, I Sing the Mighty Power of God, When I Survey the Wondrous Cross, At the Cross* (and 600 others!) have earned him the title the "Father of English Hymns." He was born amid persecution. His father was a nonconformist deacon who was sometimes jailed for his faith, and one such incident caused Mrs. Watts to prematurely give birth to stunted little Isaac.

But young Watts developed a strong spirit. When as a teenager he grumbled about the music in his church, his father told him to write his own songs if he thought he could do better than King David. So he did. His new-fangled hymns were met with resistance, but he pressed on.

In 1712, some friends invited him to spend several weeks in their home, recovering from an illness. He stayed with them 36 years, during which he devoted himself to publishing a volume of hymns based on the biblical Psalms. He studied each psalm, then prepared his poetic version in the light of the New Testament, thus giving David's psalms a decidedly Christian slant.

As Watts studied Psalm 98, he thought of the Christmas story. Verse 4 seemed to beautifully describe the joy that engulfed the world on the night Christ was born. Verse 6 spoke of the Lord as a King. Verse 7 exhorted all nature to sing. Verses 8 and 9 spoke of his coming to rule the earth with truth and grace.

Out of his enraptured meditation came Watts' version of Psalm 98, ringing with these words:

Joy to the world! The Lord is come;
Let earth receive her King;
Let every heart prepare him room,
And heaven and nature sing.

Today's Suggested Reading

Psalm 98:1–9

Shout joyfully to the Lord, all the earth; break forth in song, rejoice, and sing praises. Psalm 98:4

March **23** The Old Hundredth

An old divine once said that Psalm 100, known affectionately as the "Old Hundredth," brings heaven down to earth and raises earth to heaven. In Wesley's day, it once drew multitudes to hear heaven's gospel.

In his delightful book, *My Dear Sister: John Wesley and the Women in His Life,* Maldwyn Edwards tells of Lady Huntingdon's spurring Wesley to undertake a preaching tour of the north. She offered him her manservant John Taylor as his assistant. Accordingly, the two headed upland and soon arrived at Wesley's village of Epworth where he should have enjoyed a hometown hero's welcome. He had grown up in this dull little town, and his father had pastored there for many years.

But on Sunday morning, Wesley was not asked to speak in the old church, and the current pastor took the opportunity of blasting him as an "enthusiast."

After the service, Taylor stood in the churchyard and announced, "Mr. Wesley, not being permitted to preach in the church, will preach here at six o'clock." A great multitude showed up, and Wesley, standing atop his father's tomb, preached for three hours from Romans 14:17—". . . for the kingdom of God is not eating and drinking, but righteousness and peace and joy in the Holy Spirit."

From Epworth the two men trudged on to Newcastle, arriving late in the day. They were shocked by the drunkenness, cursing and swearing that filled the streets. Even the smallest children were vulgar. Wesley ventured into the worst part of town, and John Taylor began singing the words of Psalm 100. Two or three people turned aside to listen. Others soon drew up, and the crowd swelled to five hundred, and then to a thousand. Wesley began preaching, and the number rose to fifteen hundred.

Newcastle was deeply touched, and later became a main power center for early Methodism.

Today's Suggested Reading
Psalm 100:1–5

Enter into His gates with thanksgiving, and into His courts with praise. Be thankful to Him, and bless His name. Psalm 100:4

Beneath His Underwear March **24**

The man glared at the book on the table. He hated it, but it tenaciously nipped at him like a dog that wouldn't be shaken.

Ronnie Byers had grown up an indulged child. As a teen, he became self-centered and oblivious to the needs of others. He married, fathered two children, bought a nice house, and purchased the most expensive bass boat in Kentucky. But he soon wanted to flee all his responsibilities. Telling his wife he no longer loved her or the children, he moved into a motel.

There he found a Gideon Bible open on the nightstand. He promptly closed it. The next day he returned to his room to discover the Bible open again. This time he threw it on a lower shelf. The next day it was back by his bed. He buried it under the mattress, but next afternoon there it was on the nightstand. He next hid it in a drawer beneath his underwear, but the next day it was open in its rightful place.

In the meantime, Ronnie's wife had begun meeting with four of her friends at five o'clock each morning to pray for him. "Every time he sees a Bible," they prayed, "may he feel convicted."

At length, Ronnie decided to kill himself with the gun he kept in the nightstand drawer. But as he reached for the gun, he again spied the Bible. It was open to Psalm 103:12—"As far as the east is from the west, so far has He removed our transgressions from us."

"God spoke to my heart through that verse," he later said, "and I repented of my sins." He quickly found his wife and told her what had happened. His home was restored, and Ronnie Byers eventually became a minister of the very gospel that he had once buried beneath his underwear.*

Today's Suggested Reading
Psalm 103:1–12

As far as the east is from the west, so far has He removed our transgressions from us.
Psalm 103:12

*Adapted from "That Book Was Cramping My Style" by Rev. Ronnie Byers, in *Converted and Called* (Nashville: The Gideons International, n.d.), pp. 14–15.

March **25** Pavilioned in Splendor

Sir Robert Grant knew all about kings, pomp, ceremony, and the trappings of power. He was born about 1785 while his father was in India as chairman of the famous East India Company. Later his father became a member of the British Parliament, and some years later Robert followed in his footsteps—both as a politician and as a Christian.

Robert became a member of Parliament, then a director of the East India Company. At age 50, he was named Governor of Bombay. Deeply devoted to missions, Robert lent his support and encouragement to missionaries in India, and he even sometimes wrote hymns for them to sing.

One day as he studied Psalm 104, he compared the greatness of the King of kings with the comparatively pallid splendor he had so often witnessed of British royalty. Verse 1 says of God: "O Lord my God, You are very great: You are clothed with honor and majesty." Verses 2–3 add that God covers Himself "with light as with a garment" and "makes the clouds His chariot." Verse 5 reminds us that God "laid the foundations of the earth." All of creation reflects God's greatness, verse 24 proclaiming, "O Lord, how manifold are Your works!" Verse 31 says, "May the glory of the Lord endure forever."

Sir Robert Grant filled his heart with these verses, and from his pen came one of the most magnificent hymns in Christendom:

O worship the King, all glorious above,
And gratefully sing His power and His love;
Our Shield and Defender, the Ancient of Days,
Pavilioned in splendor and girded with praise.

O tell of His might and sing of His grace,
Whose robe is the light, whose canopy space;
His chariots of wrath the deep thunderclouds form,
And dark is His path on the wings of a storm.

Today's Suggested Reading

Psalm 104:1–9

Bless the Lord, O my soul! O Lord my God, You are very great: You are clothed with honor and majesty. Psalm 104:1

Shipwrecked

Alexander Duff, first foreign missionary of the Church of Scotland, got off to a rough start. He was young, only 23, and bright and innovative. But on his way to India in 1829 with his new wife, he was shipwrecked—not once but twice! The most serious wreck occurred when his ship, the *Lady Holland,* was within a few miles of India.

At 10 o'clock at night, Duff was half-undressed when a shock and shudder ran through the vessel. He rushed to the deck where the captain met him with terrifying words, "Oh, she's gone! She's gone!" The ship split apart, but a portion clung precariously to a reef. Through the night the passengers huddled in terror in the surviving portion, expecting every moment to be swept away. They were saved the next day, but their clothes and prized possessions were lost, including Duff's entire library of eight hundred volumes.

Later, standing on the shore and looking sadly toward the reef, Duff saw a small package bobbing atop the water. He watched and waited as it floated close enough for him to wade out and retrieve.

It was his Bible. Of all his precious books, it alone survived. His heart soared, for he took it as a sign from the Lord that this one Book alone was worth more than all the others put together.

He assembled his fellow survivors and read Psalm 107, the Traveler's Psalm. Soon, using the same Bible, he began his first class with a little group of five boys under a banyan tree. Within a week the class had grown to three hundred, and it soon became a school that evangelized and educated the higher classes in India, producing a qualified generation of leaders for the nation's young church.

Today's Suggested Reading
Psalm 107:23–31

Then they cry out to the Lord in their trouble, and He brings them out of their distresses. He calms the storm, so that its waves are still. Psalm 107:28–29

Especially for Me

Robert Schumacher was exhausted when he flopped into his bunk and lit a cigarette. It was the first week of the Allied invasion of North Africa, and he had spent the day unloading his ship. Suddenly the loudspeakers blared: "Now hear this! All hands. Man your battle stations."

Men scattered like mice. Robert jumped up and started toward the deck when a deafening explosion knocked him to the floor. Regaining consciousness, he found his face pressed to the floor and his nose full of acrid smoke. His hair was ablaze, and men were walking over him. Cries and moans filled the air. Robert lunged toward the deck, pushed a rubber life raft over the side, and clambered aboard.

Just as he made it to shore, the *USS Bliss* exploded with tremendous force. Robert watched it burn and sink, weeping for his friends still aboard. Issues of life and death haunted him, and he soon began reading his Bible. Alone one evening in his pup tent, he found Christ as his Savior.

As the invasion pushed on, Schumacher faced new dangers. In January, 1944, a hail of bombs fell around him. He jumped under his truck, fingers digging into the ground, and prayed. Nearby buildings exploded with blinding flashes of red light and deafening roars.

The bombs continued raining down the next day. It was there, near Anzio, Italy, that Robert burrowed into his foxhole and found Psalm 118: "Oh, give thanks to the Lord, for He is good. . . . I called to the Lord in my distress; the Lord answered me. . . . The Lord is on my side; I will not fear. . . . All nations surrounded me. . . . But the Lord helped me. The Lord is my strength and song. And He has become my salvation."

"It seemed written especially for me," Robert later wrote.

It was.*

Today's Suggested Reading

Psalm 118:1–14

The Lord is on my side; I will not fear. What can man do to me? Psalm 118:6

---

*Adapted from "Peace in the Midst of War" by Robert W. Schumacher in *Moody Magazine*, November, 1989, pp. 95–96.

Its Thin Gray Hair

For many years, the bleached skull of James Guthrie looked down on the crowds at Netherbow Port, horrifying the little boy who sometimes couldn't keep from glancing up at his father's head. Guthrie's head and hands had been nailed there by Scottish authorities following his execution.

In life, Guthrie had been unflappable and self-possessed, having a knack for stilling arguments and making peace. He taught philosophy at the University of St. Andrews and preached the gospel in the Scottish town of Stirling. But he believed that Christ—not the Scottish king—should rule the church, and for that he was eventually arrested on charges of treason.

At his trial, Guthrie assured the crown that, while he respected its civil authority, he didn't believe the king should control church affairs. For that, he was sentenced to die. On the day of his execution, June 1, 1661, he rose about four A.M. for worship, as unflappable as ever. Psalm 118 was on his mind, and when someone asked how he felt, he replied with the words of verse 24: "Very well. This is the day the Lord has made; we will rejoice and be glad in it."

His five-year-old son was brought to him, and, taking the boy on his knee, he imparted final expressions of fatherly love and counsel (which must have been effective, for young William later became a minister himself). Guthrie was then hanged and his head affixed on Netherbow Port. He was later immortalized in this old Covenanter poem:

They have set his head on the Netherbow,
To scorch in the summer air;
And months go by, and the winter's snow
Falls white on its thin gray hair.
And still that same look that in death he wore
Is sealed on the solemn brow—
A look of one who has travailed sore,
But whose pangs were ended now.

Today's Suggested Reading
Psalm 118:21–29

This is the day the Lord has made; we will rejoice and be glad in it. Psalm 118:24

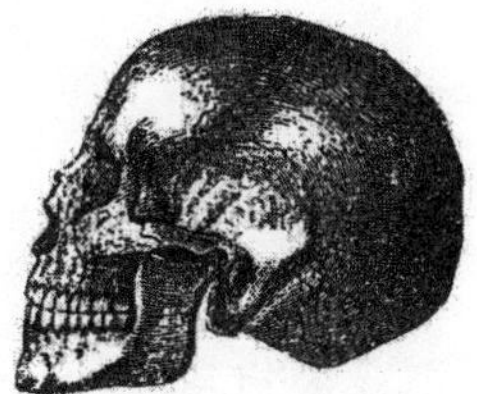

March 29 Rebuilding the Bible

If I could start over, I would have my children hide more of God's Word in their hearts. Scriptures memorized in childhood are potent, time-released capsules that can save and salvage many a situation, and many a life.

When Howard Rutledge's plane was shot down over Vietnam, he parachuted into a little village and was immediately attacked, stripped naked, and imprisoned. For the next seven years, he endured brutal treatment. His food was little more than a bowl of rotting soup with a glob of pig fat—skin, hair, and all. Rats the size of cats and spiders as big as fists scurried around him. He was frequently cold, alone, and often tortured. He was sometimes shackled in excruciating positions and left for days in his own waste with carnivorous insects boring through his oozing sores. How did he keep his sanity?

It took prison to show me how empty life is without God, and so I had to go back in my memory to those Sunday school days in Tulsa, Oklahoma. If I couldn't have a Bible and hymnbook, I would try to rebuild them in my mind. I tried desperately to recall snatches of Scripture, sermons, gospel choruses from childhood, and hymns we sang in church.

How I struggled to recall those Scriptures and hymns! I had spent my first eighteen years in Sunday school, and I was amazed at how much I could recall; regrettably, I had not seen then the importance of memorizing verses from the Bible. Now, when I needed them, it was too late. I never dreamed that I would spend almost seven years in a prison in North Vietnam or that thinking about one memorized verse could have made the whole day bearable.

*One portion of a verse I did remember was, "Thy word have I hid in my heart." How often I wished I had really worked to hide God's Word in my heart. . . .***

Today's Suggested Reading

Psalm 119:1–11

*Thy word have I hid in mine heart, that I might not sin against thee. Psalm 119:11**

---

*King James Version

**Adapted from Howard and Phyllis Rutledge with Mel and Lyla White: *In the Presence of Mine Enemies* (Grand Rapids, MI: Fleming H. Revell, Co., a division of Baker Book House, copyright © 1973), passim.

Strays

Psalm 119, the longest chapter in the Bible, isn't beyond memorizing. In my first pastorate in the Tennessee mountains, an old lady rose one Sunday in Sunday school and quoted all 176 verses without missing a word. She had learned it in childhood.

William Grimshaw (1708–1763) also occasionally employed this psalm during his long and fruitful ministry in Haworth, England. He was a powerful preacher, nevertheless not everyone in town showed up every Sunday to hear him.

"It was his frequent custom," wrote John Newton, "to leave the church at Haworth while the psalm before the sermon was singing, to see if any were absent from worship and idling their time in the churchyard, the street, or the ale-houses; and many of these whom he so found he would drive into the church before him."

Newton continues, "A friend of mine, passing a public-house in Haworth on a Lord's day morning, saw several persons making their escape out of it, some jumping out of the lower windows, and some over a low wall. He was at first alarmed, fearing the house was on fire; but upon inquiring what was the cause of the commotion, he was only told that they saw the parson coming. They were more afraid of the parson than of a justice of the peace. His reproof was so authoritative, and yet so mild and friendly, that the stoutest sinner could not stand before it."

What does all this have to do with Psalm 119?

On particularly sparse Sundays, according to a village tradition, Grimshaw would announce the 119th Psalm would be sung by the congregation. All 176 verses would be sung, giving the parson plenty of time to round up the strays and assemble a sizable congregation to hear the preached Word.

Today's Suggested Reading
Psalm 119:169–176

I have gone astray like a lost sheep; seek Your servant, for I do not forget Your commandments. Psalm 119:176

Missing the Soup

In *The Power of Positive Thinking,* Norman Vincent Peale tells of traveling to a certain city one day to lecture. He was met at the train station by a committee who rushed him to a bookstore for an autographing party, then to another. Then he was whisked to a restaurant for a luncheon, then to a hotel with just time to change clothes before flying to another reception where he chatted with VIPs, addressed several hundred listeners, and drank three glasses of fruit punch. He rushed back to his hotel, being told he had twenty minutes before dinner. As he dressed, the phone rang. "Hurry, hurry," said the voice, "we must rush down to dinner."

Excitedly, Norman chattered, "I will rush right down." He flew from the room so rattled he could hardly lock the door. As he rushed toward the elevator, he suddenly stopped, out of breath, and said, "What is this all about? What is the meaning of this ceaseless rush?" He marched back to his room, saying to himself, "I do not care if I go to dinner. I do not care whether I make a talk." He phoned his host, saying, "If you want to save a place for me, I will be down after a while, but I'm not going to rush any more."

Peale sat down, opened his Bible, and read slowly aloud Psalm 121, ending with the words: "The Lord shall preserve your going out and your coming in from this time forth, and even forevermore." Closing his Bible, he spent time meditating on those words, breathing deeply, and praying. Twenty minutes later when he walked into the dining room, he felt like a new man. "And all I missed was the soup," he said, "which by general consent was no great loss."

Today's Suggested Reading
Psalm 121:1–8

The Lord shall preserve your going out and your coming in from this time forth, and even forevermore. Psalm 121:8

April

You Know
I Mean You

Good Interest

That Soul-Refreshing Text

One Plus One

Poles Apart

Precious Seed

Del Tarr grew up in parsonages in Minnesota and South Dakota, and most of his friends lived on farms. Crops were sown, cultivated, and harvested, but never once did he see farmers weeping over the seed. Later, as a Bible student, he was perplexed by Psalm 126. Why did the sower go forth with weeping?

Later, Del served as missionary just below the Sahara Desert in West Africa, where the climate is similar to that of Bible lands. The rainfall comes in May through August. The other eight months are bitterly hot and bone dry, dust from the Sahara getting inside of everything—mouths, houses, even wristwatches.

No farming is possible those eight months. Everything must be grown May through August. In the fall, granaries are full and so are stomachs. The people seem happy, their lives overflowing in song and dance and fellowship. By December supplies begin to recede and families begin eating but one meal a day. By February, people feel hungry. By March, food is rationed to one-half meal a day, and the children cry from hunger.

April is the month that haunts my memory. The dust filters down through the air, and sounds carry for long distances. April is the month you hear the babies crying at twilight. Their mother's milk is now stopped. . . .

Then, inevitably, it happens. A six- or seven-year-old boy comes running to his father one day with sudden excitement. "Daddy! Daddy! We've got grain! Out in the hut where we keep the goats—there's a leather sack hanging on the wall—Daddy, there's grain in there."

The father stands motionless. "Son, we can't do that," he softly explains. "That's next year's seed grain. It's the only thing between us and starvation. We're waiting for the rains, and then we must use it."

Instead of feeding his desperately weakened family, he goes to the field and—I've seen it—with tears streaming down his face, he takes the precious seed and throws it away. He scatters it in the dirt!

*Why? Because he believes in the harvest.**

Today's Suggested Reading
Psalm 126:1–6

He who continually goes forth weeping, bearing seed for sowing, shall doubtless come again with rejoicing, bringing his sheaves with him. Psalm 126:6

---

*Del Tarr, "Making Truth Memorable" in *Leadership Journal*, Spring, 1983, Vol. IV, Num. 2, pp. 66–67.

For Those at Sea

Archibald Gracie relished his swim on April 14, 1912. The ship's pool was a "six-foot tank of salt water, heated to a refreshing temperature. In no swimming bath had I ever enjoyed such pleasure before." But his account went on to say, "How near it was to being my last plunge. Before dawn of another day, I would be swimming for my life in midocean in a temperature of 28 degrees!"

After his swim that Sunday night aboard ship, Colonel Archibald Gracie retired to his cabin and fell asleep, only to be awakened by "a sudden shock and noise." Dressing quickly, he ascended to the deck and learned the ship had collided with an iceberg.

During the same moments in New York, his wife's sleep was also disturbed. Seized by sudden anxiety, she sank to her knees holding her prayerbook, "which by chance opened to the prayer 'For Those at Sea.'" She prayed earnestly until about 5 A.M. when the burden lifted. She rested quietly until eight when her sister "came softly to the door, newspaper in hand, to gently break the tragic news that the *Titanic* had sunk."

What had happened meantime to her husband? *I was in a whirlpool, swirling round and round, as I still tried to cling to the railing as the ship plunged to the depths below. Down, down, I went: it seemed a great distance . . . [Ascending back to the surface] I could see no* Titanic. *She had entirely disappeared beneath the surface of the ocean without a sign of any wave. A thin light-gray smoky vapor hung like a pall a few feet above the sea. There arose the most horrible sounds ever heard by mortal man, the agonizing cries of death from over a thousand throats. . . .*

Col. Archibald Gracie, pulled into a lifeboat, later shared his testimony, basing it on Psalm 130:1—"Out of the depths I have cried to You, O Lord." *I know of no recorded instance of Providential deliverance,* he wrote, *more directly attributable to . . . prayer.*

Today's Suggested Reading
Psalm 130:1–8

Out of the depths I have cried to You, O Lord. Psalm 130:1

April **3**

Poles Apart

Two men lived poles apart, literally. Sir John Franklin (1786–1847) explored the Arctic, finding there the famous Northwest Passage. Fifty years later Sir Ernest Shackleton (1874–1922) became the greatest of all Antarctic explorers. Oddly, both claimed the same verse of Scripture.

Shackleton once said he took with him to the South Pole one passage of Scripture, Psalm 139:9–10—"If I take the wings of the morning, and dwell in the uttermost parts of the sea, even there Your hand shall lead me, and Your right hand shall hold me." In 1907, spurred on by that verse, he pushed to within 97 miles of the polar cap, closer than anyone else of his time. In 1914, he tried again. His ship *Endurance* was crushed in the ice, but he managed to lead his men back to safety in an epic journey.

Franklin, however, devoted himself to the opposite end of the world. Explorers had been searching for 300 years for the elusive Northwest Passage, a sea route linking the Atlantic and Pacific oceans through the icy north waters. Franklin found it. He was a worldwide hero, and all the world followed his fourth expedition when, in 1845, his two ships and 129 men left England. Sir John was a dedicated Christian who served his men like a pastor, teaching them the Word of God.

But they were never heard from again. A total of 39 expeditions sought them as the world held its breath. Reports and rumors slowly told of abandoned ships and frozen bodies. Finally two skeletons were found. Alongside them was Sir John Franklin's Bible, with these words underlined: "If I take the wings of the morning, and dwell in the uttermost parts of the sea, even there Your hand shall lead me, and Your right hand shall hold me."

Today's Suggested Reading
Psalm 139:1–12

If I take the wings of the morning, and dwell in the uttermost parts of the sea, even there Your hand shall lead me, and Your right hand shall hold me. Psalm 139:9–10

The Boy in the Rafters

April **4**

From the time he was a child, Harry Ironside read the Bible through at least once a year. By age 14, he had read it 14 times. In 1888, he attended D. L. Moody's campaign in Los Angeles. Hazzard's Pavilion was packed, so Harry clambered up the girders and sat in the rafters. "Lord," he prayed, moved by the thousands below, "help me some day to preach to crowds like this, and lead souls to Christ."

But Harry had never given his own heart to Christ, and his ardor quickly cooled. Soon he was dabbling in "the devil's blandishments" and indulging in "the follies of the world." On a Thursday night in February, 1890, he attended a loud party. As he moved toward the drinks, he felt uncomfortable with himself. Suddenly a Scripture passage flashed to his mind—Proverbs 1:23: "Turn at my rebuke; surely I will pour out my spirit on you; I will make my words known to you."

It was a sword through his soul, and he instantly saw himself as a guilty, self-willed rebel. The friends surrounding him seemed suddenly different, like people laughing at the edge of a precipice, their eyes closed, just a step from eternal death in the chasm below.

Harry hurried home. It was past midnight, and he removed his shoes, thinking he could slip in quietly; but his worried mother was not asleep. He whispered an apology, then rushed to his room and fell on his knees crying, "Lord, save me!" He turned in his Bible to Romans 3, then to John 3, poring over each verse. "God," he prayed at last, "I take Thee at Thy Word. I believe that Thou dost now save my soul because I trust in the Lord Jesus Christ."

In later years, Harry became a well-known Bible teacher and the pastor of the church established by the man he had watched from the rafters—the Moody Memorial Church of Chicago.

Today's Suggested Reading

Proverbs 1:23–28

Turn at my rebuke; surely I will pour out my spirit on you; I will make my words known to you. Proverbs 1:23

April **5**

The Timberwolf

Nothing takes the wind from our sails like disappointment, as 6′11″ NBA force Andrew Lang learned in 1996. He had been playing well for the Atlanta Hawks, who were barreling toward the play-offs. But he was abruptly traded late in the season to the fledgling Minnesota Timberwolves. Lang suddenly exchanged his warm, peachy life in Georgia for the cold winter of Minnesota, and a tear in his left calf muscle slowed him further.

But Lang had given his life to Jesus Christ as a 13-year-old in Pine Bluff, Arkansas; and as a devoted follower, he determined to view things through the lens of Scripture. He was upbeat, and he attributed his buoyancy to one of his favorite passages, Proverbs 3:1–2—"My son, do not forget My law, but let your heart keep My commands; for length of days and long life and peace they will add to you."

"On my own," Lang said, "I don't know what each day brings. That's God's business. There are so many things out of our control. Those are the things God oversees. The negatives reinforce my faith. I don't know what is ahead. But I have faith in God. I was raised to fear the Lord. I wouldn't be here if it weren't for God's blessings."

One of the advantages of his next NBA move, from Minnesota to Milwaukee, he soon learned, was the number of solid Christians who played for the Bucks. The fellowship and camaraderie were bracing. "I can't tell you how thankful I am for this opportunity. You can't ask for a better core of positives."

During the off-season, Lang enjoys time with his family, conducts basketball camps for young people, and shares the gospel through personal interaction and public ministry. When his professional career winds down, he hopes to attend seminary to prepare for Christian work. Andrew Lang is committed to remember and keep God's commands, knowing they bring length of days, long life, and peace.*

Today's Suggested Reading
Proverbs 3:1–4

My son, do not forget My law, but let your heart keep My commands; for length of days and long life and peace they will add to you. Proverbs 3:1–2

---

*Adapted from "The Buck Stops Here" by Glen Geigler in "Sports Spectrum", March, 1997, pp. 16–21.

The Packer

Mike Holmgren is another athlete who learned that disappointments are God's appointments. He was raised in a churchgoing, Swedish-American family, in a second-floor flat above his grandfather's bakery, a stone's throw from the San Francisco 49ers football stadium. At an early age he caught football fever. In high school, Mike was chosen all-American quarterback. In college, he played for UCLA, dreaming of a career in the NFL. His excitement was unbounded in 1970 when he was drafted by the St. Louis Cardinals. But he was cut during the preseason. Then the New York Jets considered him as Joe Namath's backup, but later went with another player.

I was crushed. All that had mattered to me was playing pro football, and now that would never happen. The flight home from New York was the longest five hours of my life. I felt like a failure.

Returning home, Mike retreated to his bedroom in depression, but there found his old, dust-covered Bible. He had become a Christian at age 11, but in his intense pursuit of football, he had forgotten the Lord. Now as he thumbed through the Bible, he found a verse he had once memorized in Sunday school: "Trust in the Lord with all your heart, and lean not on your own understanding; in all your ways acknowledge Him, and He shall direct your paths."

Mike recommitted his life to Jesus Christ. Shortly afterward, he fell in love with a girl who had just returned from a missionary stint in Zaire. They were married, and Mike began coaching at his high school alma mater. He has been coaching ever since, becoming one of the most successful NFL coaches in America as head coach of the Green Bay Packers.

*Win or lose, I now realize what really matters: It's not the Super Bowl rings—it's the crown of eternal life that Jesus Christ has won for us through His victory on the cross.**

Today's Suggested Reading

Proverbs 3:5–10

Trust in the Lord with all your heart, and lean not on your own understanding; in all your ways acknowledge Him, and He shall direct your paths. Proverbs 3:5-6

---

*Adapted from "What Matters Most in My Life" by Mike Holmgren as told to Greg Asimakoupoulos, in *Decision,* October, 1997, pp. 8–9, © 1997; published by the Billy Graham Evangelistic Association.

Six Dollars

The young man had never dreamed of earning so much money. What would his father say now? What would his friends think? How proud his mother would be.

But Robert Nicholas's parents back in Ontario were concerned. Six dollars for a sixty-hour week was too much for a young man on his own in Chicago in 1900. Could he handle it, or would it ruin him? His father wrote him a lengthy letter, warning of the dangers of money. Be cautious and wise, he said. Give to the Lord. Some people are financially blessed so as to be generous in the Lord's work. And don't forget Proverbs 11:24, a verse Mr. Nicholas prominently quoted in his letter to Robert: "There is one who scatters, yet increases more; and there is one who withholds more than is right, but it leads to poverty."

The verse had its intended effect. Robert began giving his tithes and offerings to the Lord. Joining a nearby Methodist church, he worked in the Sunday school and witnessed to friends.

Within five years, he purchased his own hardware store in nearby Oak Park and soon built it into one of the strongest businesses in Illinois. His leadership in Oak Park brought in department stores, banks, and schools. He advised and aided nearby Christian colleges, and helped finance many projects for the Kingdom. Selling his hardware store in 1929, he opened a lending institution that went through the darkness of the Great Depression without a single default. Homes and homeowners were saved by his counsel and patience. Many missionaries and mission boards, churches, and students received aid from him, the gifts often coming anonymously.

His life overflowed because he never forgot his father's counsel: Scattering leads to increasing more, but withholding brings poverty.

Today's Suggested Reading
Proverbs 11:16–24

There is one who scatters, yet increases more; and there is one who withholds more than is right, but it leads to poverty. Proverbs 11:24

You Know I Mean You

Colonial New England preachers were plainspoken men who often found Scripture texts that were appropriate for the occasion. One minister, whose son had been born the night before, preached from Isaiah 9:6: "For unto us a Child is born, unto us a Son is given." Another minister, Dr. Mather Byles, was once upset at the nonappearance of a minister named Prince, who was to bring the sermon that day. Byles mounted the pulpit himself, preaching from Psalm 118:9: "It is better to trust in the Lord than to put confidence in princes."

In another church, a man named Ephraim showed serious signs of backsliding. The next Sunday, the minister chose for his text Hosea 4:17: "Ephraim is joined to idols, let him alone."

After Mary Prescott and John Physick were married in Portland, Maine, on July 4, 1770, their pastor (at the bride's request) preached from Luke 10:42: "Mary has chosen that good part."

Another bride married a man named John against her parents' wishes. The next Sunday at her request, the minister preached a sizzling sermon from Matthew 11:18: "John came neither eating nor drinking, and they say, 'He has a demon.'" (The John in question later became the second president of the United States—John Adams).

On another Sunday in colonial America, in a village suffering from a shortage of food, the congregation gathered on the Lord's day. Among them was a Colonel Ingraham, who was hoarding a reserve of corn, hoping for a better price. The parson bellowed forth from Proverbs 11:26: "The people will curse him who withholds grain, but blessing will be on the head of him who sells it." But the offender sat stiff and unmoved. At last the minister, provoked to anger, shouted, "Colonel Ingraham, Colonel Ingraham! You know I mean you. Why don't you hang down your head?"

There is no record of the results.

Today's Suggested Reading
Proverbs 11:25–31

The people will curse him who withholds grain, but blessing will be on the head of him who sells it. Proverbs 11:26

April 9 A Pail of Blackberries

While family devotions are important, the most effective sharing is spontaneous. Children learn best when parents convey the Scriptures naturally and frequently, "when you sit in your house, when you walk by the way, when you lie down, and when you rise up" (Deuteronomy 6:7).

For example, Robert Webber, a professor of theology, grew up on the mission field where his parents served the Africa Inland Mission. Once on furlough, the young family settled in Montgomery, Pennsylvania, in a small home near a farm. Robert was nine, and he loved blackberries. One day he grabbed a bucket and started picking blackberries on nearby bushes. Without thinking, he strayed onto the neighbor's property and started picking the farmer's crop.

Suddenly, the neighbor burst out the front door, waving his fist. "Get out of my field!" he shouted. "And don't let me catch you on my property ever again! Do you understand me?"

Robert was terrified, and he quickly ran to tell his father. Mr. Webber said, "Give me that pail of blackberries. We're going next door to talk to that man." The two marched across the yard, Robert thinking to himself, "Good! My dad will show him a thing or two!"

"Mr. Farmer," said Robert's dad. "I'm sorry my son was on your property. Here, I want you to have these blackberries."

The neighbor was completely disarmed. "Hey," he said, "I'm sorry I yelled at the boy. I don't want the blackberries. I don't even like blackberries. You keep them. And you can pick all the berries you want from my field."

*As we walked back home, Dad turned to me and said, "The Scripture says, 'A soft answer turns away wrath.' Remember that, Robert." I've not always lived up to that Scripture, or to the example of my father, but I've never forgotten those words or my dad's action that gave those words meaning.**

Today's Suggested Reading
Proverbs 15:1–9

A soft answer turns away wrath, but a harsh word stirs up anger. Proverbs 15:1

---

*Adapted from "A Father's Influence," by Dr. Robert Webber in *What My Parents Did Right,* compiled and edited by Gloria Gaither (Nashville: Star Song Publishing Group, 1991), pp. 207–208.

A Still, Small Voice

The cold, hard eyes of Adolf Hitler locked onto Martin Neimoller, but the courageous clergyman didn't flinch. "We, too, as Christians and churchmen, have a responsibility to the German people," said Neimoller. "That responsibility was entrusted to us by God, and neither you nor anyone in this world has the power to take it from us." The Fuhrer angrily turned away. That evening Neimoller's rectory was ransacked, and a bomb later went off in his hall. Shortly after, Neimoller mounted the pulpit of his church in Berlin, saying, "It is a testing time, and God is giving Satan a free hand."

In June, 1937, Neimoller was seized by the Gestapo and held in solitary confinement until his trial the following February. His situation was perilous, for the indictment against him comprised fourteen typewritten pages. On the morning of his trial, he was led from his cell by a green-uniformed official. Through eerie underground passageways they went, the two of them, from the prison to the Nazi court. A sense of terror overwhelmed Neimoller, a dread for himself, his family, his church. He feared the death camps.

The maze of tunnels was dark and silent but for the echoes of their footsteps. As the two men ascended their last flight of stairs, Neimoller seemed to hear a voice, hushed and whispered, repeating some words. He strained to listen, and they came again more clearly. "The name of the Lord is a strong tower," said the voice. "The righteous run to it and are safe."

It was the guard, speaking under his breath. Neimoller gave no sign of hearing the words, but from that moment his fear was gone, replaced by an indescribable peace and assurance that never left him, even during the next seven years of suffering, even through his darkest days at Dachau.

Today's Suggested Reading

Proverbs 18:1–11

The name of the Lord is a strong tower; the righteous run to it and are safe. Proverbs 18:10

Planned in Heaven

Here is one of the tender love letters of our time, a husband to his wife, written from Los Angeles on August 11, 1963, two days before the couple's twentieth wedding anniversary:

How can I find words to express my appreciation for all you have meant to me. Your love and patience with me in my ups and downs . . . have meant more to me than you will ever know. Your counsel, advice, encouragement and prayer have been my mainstay—and at times I have almost clung to you in my weakness, in hours of obsession, problems and difficulties. "Whoso findeth a wife findeth a good thing, and obtaineth favour from the Lord." One reason that in spite of my own lack of spirituality, discipline and consecration I have found favor of the Lord is because of you. I found a good wife and as a result have found favor with God. . . . It seems that in the recent months my capacity to love you has been increased—I did not think that age would bring greater and deeper love—but it has and is. I love the wife of my youth more every day! When we are apart, I miss you so much more than I used to. A week seems like a month. Yes, I am thankful to God for you. What a wonderful helpmeet He provided—certainly our marriage was planned in heaven. I am thankful for the five precious children you bore me—each one a bundle of joy. And what a wonderful mother you have been to them! No child ever had a greater mother than our children. You may compare yourself to Susanna Wesley and think you are a failure—but she did not rear her family in a modern, secular society. For our generation you are near perfection.

The letter was addressed to Ruth Bell Graham from her husband, Billy.**

Today's Suggested Reading

Proverbs 18:18–24

*Whoso findeth a wife findeth a good thing, and obtaineth favour of the Lord. Proverbs 18:22**

---

*King James Version

**Quoted in Patricia Daniels Cornwell, *A Time for Remembering* (Minneapolis: Grason, 1983), p. 149.

Good Interest

April **12**

The China Inland Mission was founded by Hudson Taylor with the understanding it would never solicit funds, but trust God alone for provision. It was a lesson borne of Taylor's own experiences. When he first sensed God's calling him to missions, Hudson left his family's beautiful home and moved to the ghetto of Drainside, so named for the stench of its sewers. His purpose was to "endure hardness" and to "help those in need."

Near midnight one Sunday, he was called to the bedside of a sick woman and her starving children, who desperately needed financial help. Hudson tried to pray, but words wouldn't come, for he knew he had a silver coin that would alleviate this suffering and hunger. It was his last cent. Finally he capitulated, dug it from his pocket and reluctantly gave it to them. Returning home, he found only one bowl of porridge.

I reminded the Lord as I knelt at my bedside of His own Word, that he who giveth to the poor lendeth to the Lord: I asked Him not to let my loan be a long one, or I should have no dinner next day.

Next morning for breakfast my plate of porridge remained, and before it was consumed the postman's knock was heard at the door. I was not in the habit of receiving letters on Monday. On opening the envelope, I found nothing written within; but a pair of kid gloves from which, as I opened them in astonishment, halt a sovereign fell to the ground. "Praise the Lord!" I exclaimed. "400 percent for twelve hours' investment; that is good interest."

I cannot tell you how often my mind has recurred to this incident, or all the help it has been to me in circumstances of difficulty. If we are faithful to God in little things, we shall gain experience and strength that will be helpful to us in the more serious trials of life.

Today's Suggested Reading
Proverbs 19:10–17

He who has pity on the poor lends to the Lord, and He will pay back what he has given.
Proverbs 19:17

Polio

Once while Francis and Edith Schaeffer returned from America to their Swiss home, young Franky grew ill and lost his ability to walk. The doctor diagnosed polio, and Edith devoted her waking hours to caring for him.

Francis was in Italy when Franky suffered another attack. The local doctor arrived, begging to inject the child with a virtually untested serum he had invented. "Please let me use it. Don't deny the boy the possibility of help. He may never walk again otherwise."

Edith, sick with panic, silently cried, "Oh Father, show me what is best. I'll go with the doctor unless you stop me, God. I don't know what else to do." Meanwhile the doctor paced the floor, saying, "Hurry, hurry . . . no time to lose." Jumping in the car, they raced to the little hospital. The ether mask was affixed over Franky's screaming face, and the injection given, with another scheduled for the morning.

I became increasingly frightened about it. But in the early morning as I was reading my Bible beside Franky, a verse in Proverbs suddenly hit me. "The king's heart is in the hand of the Lord, as the rivers of water: he turneth it whithersoever he will." I thought, "If God can turn a king's heart the way He can turn the course of a river, surely God can turn the decision of this doctor in the direction best for Franky"; and as I asked God to do this, I stopped trembling. The doctor walked in with a nurse and as she started to pull the cot towards the operation room, the doctor put up his hand and said sharply, "Wait." Then he gazed at Franky a few minutes and finally said, "I've changed my mind. We won't do it." The second injection was never given.

*Whatever that injection did, Franky did not have any paralysis, and the day came when he could sit up, then stand, and finally walk.***

Today's Suggested Reading
Proverbs 21:1–12

*The king's heart is in the hand of the Lord, as the rivers of water: he turneth it whithersoever he will. Proverbs 21:1**

---

*King James Version

**From *L'Abri,* by Edith Schaeffer, copyright © 1969, pp. 65–71. Used by permission of Good News Publishers/Crossway Books, Wheaton, Illinois 60187.

Blood, Sweat, and Prayers

Today's verses changed the life of a rich young ruler. William Borden grew up with a family fortune that included the Borden milk company. He was handsome, extremely bright, a gifted athlete. From his family's mansion on Chicago's Gold Coast, he cast a maturing eye over fame and power.

But he primarily focused on Jesus Christ. In 1906, as a freshman at Yale, he traveled to Nashville to attend a convention of the Student Volunteer Movement, devoted to overseas missions. Samuel Zwemer, missionary statesman, was there with his maps, and his message melted Borden's heart regarding the Islamic world. Zwemer proclaimed:

Shall we stand by and allow these millions to continue under the curse and snare of a false religion, with no knowledge of the saving love and power of Christ? Of course it will cost life. It is not an expedition of ease nor a picnic excursion to which we are called. . . . It is going to cost many a life, and not lives only, but prayers and tears and blood. We do not plead for missions. We simply bring the facts before you and ask for a verdict. "If thou forebear to deliver them that are drawn unto death, and those that are ready to be slain; if thou sayest, Behold we knew it not; doth not he that pondereth the heart consider it? and he that keepeth thy soul, doth not he know it? and shall not he render to every man according to his works?"

Borden returned to Yale committed to Muslim missions. In time, he gave his fortune to Christian causes and left the shores of America for China, dying en route of spinal meningitis. Under his pillow was stuffed a last message: "No Reserve! No Retreat! No Regrets!" His story was broadcast in newspapers across America, and his biography by Mrs. Howard Taylor resulted in numbers of young people offering themselves to missions.

Today's Suggested Reading
Proverbs 24:10–16

*If thou forbear to deliver them that are drawn unto death, and those that are ready to be slain; if thou sayest, Behold, we knew it not; doth not he that pondereth the heart consider it? and he that keepeth thy soul, doth not he know it? and shall not he render to every man according to his works? Proverbs 24:11–12**

*King James Version

Wonderful Things

Rev. Charles Bowles, an African-American, fought for the colonies in the Revolutionary War, then settled down in New Hampshire where he became a Christian. When he felt God calling him to ministry, he initially fled to the sea like a modern Jonah, but eventually yielded and was ordained by the Free Will Baptists. Despite some opposition because of his skin color, Charles became a prolific evangelist and church planter until his death at age 82.

In an 1852 biography, we find this story: *On one occasion, Charles had an appointment to preach near a tavern in which a gentleman from New York put up for the night. In the evening the landlord informed the guest that a colored man was to preach near by, and invited him to attend; but he indignantly refused, alleging that the sermon was probably borrowed; but being urged again, consented on condition that the landlord give Charles the following text, and he would preach from it that evening. They went to the house, laid the text on the desk, and took their seats. It was Proverbs, 30th chap., 19th verse. At first Charles thought of declining; it was a new and difficult subject; one which he had never studied and upon which he was unprepared to preach. Elder Nathaniel Bowles, a white man who had labored much with him, was present with him, and they consulted for some time upon it. At last Charles determined that brother Nathaniel should read a long hymn to be sung, then make a long prayer, then read another long hymn, so as to give Elder Charles time to prepare his subject. When the last hymn was being sung, the text appeared clear in his mind, and after speaking for a few moments upon the literal meaning, he began to make a spiritual application of the subject. The gentleman who gave the text was cut to the heart, and soon after converted to God.*

Today's Suggested Reading

Proverbs 30:11–19

There are three things which are too wonderful for me, yes, four which I do not understand: the way of an eagle in the air, the way of a serpent on a rock, the way of a ship in the midst of the sea, and the way of a man with a virgin. Proverbs 30:18–19

A Time to Fight

April **16**

Today's text is widely remembered as President John F. Kennedy's favorite passage of Scripture, but he is far from the first American leader who appreciated its value. Peter Muhlenberg once used it with powerful effect.

Muhlenberg was a native of Pennsylvania, where his parents had settled as Lutheran missionaries from Germany to the American colonies. Much of Peter's youth, however, was spent in Europe, for his father had wanted him educated in Germany (just as many American missionaries today send their children back to the States for boarding school). Young Peter, however, wasn't good educational material, and he spent most of his teen years working in a grocery store and serving in the army.

He returned to Pennsylvania in 1767, wanting to follow his father's footsteps into the ministry. He was ordained by the Anglicans, and began pastoring a church among German people in Virginia. In 1774 he was elected to the Virginia Legislature and was present at St. John's Church in Richmond when Patrick Henry proclaimed, "Give me liberty or give me death!" Peter was so moved that he promptly joined George Washington's army.

He resigned from his church, and on a bitterly sad Sunday preached his farewell sermon. He read Ecclesiastes 3:1, "To everything there is a season, a time for every purpose under heaven." Looking up, he said, "There is a time to preach and a time to pray, but there is also a time to fight, and that time has now come." Then to the shock of his congregation, he suddenly flung off his ministerial robe to reveal underneath the uniform of a militia colonel.

He recruited other men in his church, and they became known as the "German Regiment" under the command of Peter Muhlenberg, who achieved the rank of major general. After the war, Peter returned to Philadelphia a hero and spent his remaining days serving in local and national government.*

Today's Suggested Reading
Ecclesiastes 3:1–8

To everything there is a season, a time for every purpose under heaven.
Ecclesiastes 3:1

---

*Adapted from "Fighting Words" by Mark Couvillon in *Christian History*, Issue 50 (Vol. XV, No. 2), p. 13.

One Plus One

Often in my ministry I'm asked to prepare marriage ceremonies from today's passage, for it tells us that one plus one equals more than two. A good marriage exceeds the sum of its partners.

Charles Wesley thought so, too. Charles isn't as famous as his brother John Wesley, the founder of Methodism; yet Charles' hymns are far better known than John's sermons. All over the world, Christians still sing, *O, For a Thousand Tongues; Christ the Lord Is Risen Today; Hark, the Herald Angels Sing;* and *Jesus, Lover of My Soul.*

Charles wrote hymns day and night, sometimes jumping off his horse and running into nearby houses, shouting, "Pen and ink! Pen and ink!" He reportedly composed 8,989 hymns during his lifetime, an average of ten poetic lines every day for fifty years. He was still writing hymns on his deathbed.

When Charles fell in love, he wrote his love letters in the form of hymns, composing forty of them, right up to his wedding day. He was forty years old and had met Sally Gwynne, who was half his age, while on a preaching trip in Wales. Sally's father, a wealthy landowner and magistrate, had initially opposed the Methodist movement, but he came to be one of the Wesleys' most enthusiastic supporters.

As Charles pondered his love for Sally, and as he studied Ecclesiastes 4, he brought the two subjects together in a hymn that began:

Two are better far than one
For counsel or to fight
How can one be warm alone
Or serve his God aright?

The couple was married on August 3, 1749, at Garth, Wales, with John officiating. Charles preached at their honeymoon spot for two weeks, then left for an evangelistic tour. Their marriage, however, was a happy one, and Charles soon cut back on his journeys, deciding that two, after all, are better far than one.

Today's Suggested Reading
Ecclesiastes 4:9–12

Two are better than one, because they have a good reward for their labor. Ecclesiastes 4:9

The Whiteskin Cries

April **18**

Bob and Carolyn Thomas, friends of mine who served in Papua New Guinea, once sent me this letter with Ecclesiastes 7:2 printed across the top:

It was Sunday morning in the village. I started a fire in the fireplace while Carolyn fixed cheese omelets. As soon as I finished breakfast, I turned on our shortwave and picked up the Kentucky Derby on a U.S. station. It was exciting to hear, but afterwards I was flooded with homesick memories of our springtime family ritual of watching the Derby together. I was surprised when the tears came.

Looking back, I realize the Lord was preparing my heart for another sorrow. A village leader had just died. I planned to spend Sunday on the mountain where my village friends were mourning, so I hiked to the top of the mountain and joined my adopted village brothers. In this area of New Guinea, people kick the bamboo-woven walls off the house of someone who dies. It is a release for their enormous grief. The walls of this dead man's house had already been kicked off and nailed back three times.

I felt so sorry for them. I thought again how I missed my family back home. I couldn't hold them back, so a few tears trickled down. Then I heard whispers through the crowd, "Lala siacma" ("The Whiteskin cries!"). Suddenly two men leapt on top of me, knocking my glasses off. They held me tightly and the whole crowd wailed.

Afterwards they told me they didn't think Whiteskins cried. In their culture, if someone is sad and only cries a little, they jump on him to help the mourner cry hard and get it all out. They say it is no good if the sorrow stays inside you and kills you. I thought, "Wow, they are wiser than we are about mourning."

So the story went out over the mountains that the Whiteskins really love us, they share our deep sorrow.

*It was good to be in the house of mourning.**

Today's Suggested Reading

Ecclesiastes 7:1–7

Better to go to the house of mourning than to go to the house of feasting. Ecclesiastes 7:2

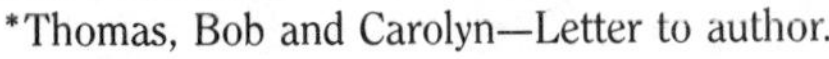

*Thomas, Bob and Carolyn—Letter to author.

April **19** 8 O'Clock Each Evening

Never stop praying for "hopeless" cases; the example of E. Howard Cadle teaches us there are none. Cadle's mother was a Christian, but his father was an alcoholic. By age 12, Cadle was emulating his father, drinking and out of control. Soon he was in the grip of sex, gambling, and the Midwest crime syndicate.

"Always remember, Son," his worried mother often said, "that at eight o'clock every night I'll be kneeling beside your bed, asking God to protect my precious boy." But her prayers didn't seem to slow him until one evening on a rampage he pulled a gun on a man and squeezed the trigger. The weapon never fired and someone quickly knocked it away. Cadle noticed that it was exactly eight o'clock.

Presently his health broke, and the doctor told him he had only six months to live. Dragging himself home, penniless and pitiful, he collapsed in his mother's arms, saying, "Mother, I've broken your heart. I'd like to be saved, but I've sinned too much."

The old woman opened her Bible and read Isaiah 1:18—"Though your sins are like scarlet, They shall be as white as snow." That windswept morning, March 14, 1914, E. Howard Cadle started life anew. With Christ now in his heart, he turned his con skills into honest pursuits and started making money hand over fist, giving 75 percent of it to the Lord's work. He helped finance Gipsy Smith's crusades in which thousands were converted. Then he began preaching on Cincinnati's powerful WLW, becoming one of America's most popular radio evangelists, saying:

Until He calls me, I shall preach the same gospel that caused my sainted mother to pray for me. And when I have gone to the last city and preached my last sermon, I want to sit at His feet and say, "Thank You, Jesus, for saving me that dark and stormy day from a drunkard's and a gambler's hell."

Today's Suggested Reading

Isaiah 1:1–18

"Come now, and let us reason together," says the Lord. "Though your sins are like scarlet, they shall be as white as snow; though they are red like crimson, they shall be as wool." Isaiah 1:18

L'Abri

Christianity alone offers hope to the human soul. "There is no other sufficient philosophical answer," taught Francis Schaeffer. "It is not that this is the best answer to existence; it is the only answer."

That message drew swarms of students to Francis and Edith Schaeffer's Swiss home in the mid-1950s, and thus their L'Abri Fellowship was born. But in the early days, Edith worried about things like funding and strength and privacy.

I was sitting at my typewriter, feeling the heaviness that went with the uncertainties ahead. I propped my Bible up on the typewriter, and asked God to give me help and comfort. My reading took me to the book of Isaiah. Now I believe the Bible is, to the spiritual life of a Christian, what warm, fresh wheat bread is to the physical life—both nourishing and appetizing! There are also times when God speaks to some of His children in the very words of the Bible, written hundreds of years ago, yet seemingly written as a message for the situation of the moment.

*Let me tell you what happened that day (as I read Isaiah 2:2–3). I reached for my pencil and wrote in the margin: "Jan '55 promise . . . Yes, L'Abri." For I had the tremendous surge of assurance that although this had another basic meaning, it was being used by God to tell me something. I did not feel that "all nations" were literally going to come to our home for help, but I did feel that it spoke of people from many different nations coming to a house that God would establish for the purpose of making His ways known to them. It seemed to me that God was putting His hand on my shoulder in a very real way and saying that there would be a work which would be His work, not ours. I felt that this work was going to be L'Abri.**

Today's Suggested Reading
Isaiah 2:1–5

Now it shall come to pass in the latter days that the mountain of the Lord's house shall be established on the top of the mountains, and shall be exalted above the hills; and all nations shall flow to it. Isaiah 2:2

---

*From *L'Abri,* by Edith Schaeffer, copyright © 1969, pp. 65–71. Used by permission of Good News Publishers/Crossway Books, Wheaton, Illinois 60187.

April **21**

Go Forth

Perhaps no missionary lived up to his name better than the one called Goforth. Jonathan Goforth, a Canadian by birth, has been called "China's most outstanding evangelist." Missionary historian Ruth Tucker writes, "Of all the missionaries who served in the Orient during the nineteenth and early twentieth centuries, none saw a greater immediate response to his personal ministry than did Jonathan Goforth."

Dr. Charles Trumbull said about him, "God's missionary program for the past half century would not have been complete without him." Goforth became a powerful evangelist throughout Asia, a rarity for a Westerner, and his crowds sometimes numbered 25,000. His Chinese home was open to inquirers—one day alone over 2,000 showed up. Multitudes throughout the Orient came to Christ through Jonathan and his wife Rosaline. During his missionary career, fifty Chinese converts went out as ministers or evangelists.

What led Jonathan Goforth overseas?

He came to Christ at age 18, and shortly afterward yielded himself to fulltime service after reading Robert Murray M'Cheyne's *Memoirs*. But it was Dr. George Mackay, veteran missionary to Formosa (Taiwan), who drew him to overseas work. Mackay had been traveling across North America for two years trying to recruit young men for Asian evangelism, but he grew bitterly discouraged. One night as Jonathan, a college student at the time, listened, Mackay pronounced himself a failure. All his travels had been in vain, for not one young man had said, "Yes." The missionary had no choice but to return to Formosa alone, without anyone to carry on the work.

Mackay didn't realize it, but his work wasn't in vain after all.

Jonathan later said about that evening: *I heard the voice of the Lord saying: "Whom shall I send, and who will go for us?" and I answered: "Here am I, send me." From that hour I became a foreign missionary.*

Today's Suggested Reading

Isaiah 6:1–8

Also I heard the voice of the Lord, saying: "Whom shall I send, and who will go for Us?" Then I said, "Here am I! Send me." Isaiah 6:8

Veitch's Victory

It was an upsetting night in 1680 when soldiers burst into the peaceful home of William and Marion Veitch and dragged him off to prison for his faith in Christ. The children were terrified, but Marion, finding strength in the Lord, read to them from Scripture. Then as soon as she could arrange it, she set off to visit her husband. It appeared he would be removed far away and executed, so there was no time to lose.

Marion's journey took place on a bitterly cold January day. The snow was blinding, and she had to fight the weather on horseback. Night fell, and she trudged on, finally arriving at the prison, half-frozen, about midnight.

The guards wouldn't disturb her husband until morning, so Marion sat by the fire and waited. The next day, she was given only a moment with him in the presence of guards before being torn away. Marion went to a friend's house, wept her fill, and opened her Bible. The words of Isaiah 8:12–13 spoke powerfully to her: ". . . Nor be afraid of their threats, nor be troubled. The Lord of hosts, Him you shall hallow; Let Him be your fear, and let Him be your dread." She rested herself in the Lord and cast her burden on Him.

A day or two later, their archenemy, Vicar Thomas Bell, who was responsible for William's arrest, called on a friend. He lingered until 10 P.M., when he said he must be going home. It was another frigid night, and his host urged him to wait for morning. But Bell had work to do and victims to prosecute. He rode away warmed by alcohol, and his body was found two days later, standing up to his arms in a block of ice in the river.

William was soon freed, and the restored couple worked side-by-side until William's death forty years later.

Today's Suggested Reading

Isaiah 8:11–18

. . . Nor be afraid of their threats, nor be troubled. The Lord of hosts, Him you shall hallow; let Him be your fear, and let Him be your dread.
Isaiah 8:12–13

With Joy

It was the biggest decision of her life. Virginia Miller was an efficient secretary for a team of doctors in Los Angeles, and she enjoyed her single, professional life, her plush office, her business associations. But something nagged at her. It was the early 1940s, and she had heard of the new evangelical organizations springing up—Wycliffe Bible Translators, Missionary Aviation Fellowship, Far East Broadcasting Company. Virginia sometimes wondered if she should devote her skills to one of these ministries.

But, no, there were professional and financial considerations. Salaries at faith ministries were neither secure nor substantial. Most of the organizations were fledgling, like the one started by her friend, Joy Ridderhof. Joy was running Gospel Recordings, Inc. out of her crowded bedroom attic. Yes, recordings of the gospel were finding their way to remote areas where missionaries were unavailable or could not go, but it was still a spartan, shoestring operation.

That day Virginia had bumped into Joy at a wedding reception, and the meeting had been surprising. Virginia had asked casually, "How's it going?" Joy had unexpectedly said, "Getting on fine, but we sure need you!" Now Virginia couldn't get those words off her mind. "We sure need you . . . we need you . . . need you . . . you. . . ."

To leave her plush office for a penniless group, to sacrifice the luxury hotels, the expensive luncheons, the generous income. . . . What should she do? Before going to bed that night, Virginia prayed, "Lord, do you want me to go and help Joy?" The next day her Bible reading was in Isaiah 12, and the words hit her like bricks: "Therefore with joy you will draw water from the wells of salvation."

With Joy! Draw water from the wells of salvation with Joy! The answer was so simple and direct that she could not doubt it. She promptly gave notice at work, joined Joy Ridderhof, and became the first fulltime employee of Gospel Recordings, Inc.

Today's Suggested Reading

Isaiah 12:1–6

Therefore with joy you will draw water from the wells of salvation. Isaiah 12:3

My Consuming Thought

Today's verse is good for those who are pregnant and sick, in strange hospitals, and alone in distant cities, as Shirley Lauthern learned in October, 1960. She was seven months along when her husband Jim asked her to accompany him to a convention in St. Louis. The doctor agreed, and the two made a holiday of it, visiting the sights and rambling all over town with friends. That evening Shirley grew ill and was hospitalized with toxemia. The doctors insisted she stay absolutely flat on her back for a full week. In those days, hospitals had no in-room phones, radios, or televisions, and Shirley had nothing to do but stare at the ceiling and worry. Jim returned home to care for their infant son, and Shirley felt "forgotten by everyone—even God."

But a dear Christian pastor and his wife who lived in St. Louis heard I was in the hospital, and they came every day to visit. On their first visit, he left his card with Isaiah 26:3 written on the back. That verse became my consuming thought as I read and re-read the words: "Thou wilt keep him in perfect peace, whose mind is stayed on thee: because he trusteth in thee."

It was like balm to her soul; and soon Shirley felt well enough to travel home where she gave birth to a healthy daughter.

But her testimony doesn't stop there. *Twenty-eight years later, I was hospitalized again, this time in Nashville for a biopsy. Cancer was suspected, and I was apprehensive. A friend who came to see me found me asleep from the anesthetic, but she left a small piece of paper for me. On it she had scribbled the words of Isaiah 26:3. As I read that verse, I was again flooded with the same sweet peace I had experienced in that other stark room years before. The Lord bestowed the same precious promise, the same perfect peace.***

Today's Suggested Reading

Isaiah 26:1–3

*Thou wilt keep him in perfect peace, whose mind is stayed on thee: because he trusteth in thee. Isaiah 26:3**

---

*King James Version

**Lauthern, Shirley—As told to the Author.

April **25**

Give Me One Soul

Peter Cartwright was a colorful, eccentric preacher, a backwoods, trailblazing Methodist who helped transform the frontier. He once wrote, *We went from fort to fort, camp to camp, cabin to cabin, with or without road or path. We slept on buffalo skins before a fire, our saddlebags for pillows. We crossed creeks and rivers without bridges, often swam them on horseback or crossed on trees that had fallen over the streams, often waded waist deep.*

What propelled Cartwright into such a rigorous ministry? He had grown up in Kentucky, devoting his early teens to drinking, card playing, horse racing, and dancing. All that changed in 1801 when Peter was converted. The next year he was licensed to preach. He was 17.

At last I gave up the world, bidding farewell to father and mother, brothers and sisters, and met brother Lotspeich at an appointment in Logan County. He told me I must preach that night. This I had never done. I tried to beg off, but he urged me to make the effort. I went out and prayed fervently for aid from heaven. All at once it seemed to me as if I could never preach at all, but I struggled in prayer. At length I asked God, if He had called me to preach, to give me aid that night, and give me one soul as evidence I was called to this work.

I went into the house, rose, gave them for a text Isaiah 26:4: "Trust ye in the Lord forever; for in the Lord Jehovah there is everlasting strength." The Lord gave light, liberty, and power; the congregation melted into tears. There was present a professed infidel. The word reached his heart by the eternal Spirit. He was powerfully convicted, and joined the church, and afterward became a useful member of the same.

Cartwright traveled for 53 years through Kentucky, Tennessee, and Illinois, preaching over 14,000 sermons and winning tens of thousands to Jesus Christ.

Today's Suggested Reading
Isaiah 26:4–6

*Trust ye in the Lord for ever: for in the Lord Jehovah is everlasting strength. Isaiah 26:4**

---

*King James Version

That Soul-Refreshing Text April **26**

About the time the Pilgrims sailed to America in search of religious liberty from the intolerance of established religion, one man decided to remain in the United Kingdom and preach with intrepidity. His name was Donald Cargill, and the nature of his life is reflected in the effusive title of his biography: "Some Remarkable Passages in the Life and Death of that Singular, Exemplary, Holy-in-Life, Zealous, and Faithful-unto-the-Death, Mr. Donald Cargill."

Cargill always preached on the run. On one occasion, soldiers pursued him to a raging river. To their astonishment, he dashed up a rocky ledge and took a flying leap over the torrent, safely landing on the other side. None of the troops dared follow him, and he escaped. The spot has ever since been known as "Cargill's Leap."

At length, however, the net tightened around him. His last sermon was from Isaiah 26. Patrick Walker, author of the prior-mentioned biography, wrote: *I had the happiness to hear blest Cargill preach his last public sermon in Dunsyre Common, where he preached upon that soul-refreshing text, Isaiah 26, the last two verses, "Come, My people, enter into your chambers. . . ."*

He insisted what kind of chambers these were, of protection and safety, and exhorted us all earnestly to dwell in the clefts of the rock, to bind ourselves in the wounds of Christ, and to wrap ourselves in the believing application of the promises flowing therefrom, and to make our refuge under the shadow of His wings, until these sad calamities pass over, and the dove come back with the olive leaf in her mouth. These were the last words of his sermon.

Cargill was thereafter captured, imprisoned, and condemned. As he climbed the steps to the scaffold, he turned back and shouted, "The Lord knows I go up this ladder with less fear than ever I entered a pulpit to preach." Minutes later he was with the Lord.

Today's Suggested Reading
Isaiah 26:19–21

Come, My people, enter your chambers, and shut your doors behind you; hide yourself, as it were, for a little moment, until the indignation is past. Isaiah 26:20

High Matters

If only there had been voice recorders in the days of Thomas Chalmers. He was one of Scotland's most beloved and spellbinding preachers, pastor to 2,000 poor families in Glasgow. One of his most vivid sermons, last preached the year before his death in 1846, was from Isaiah 27:4–5. Chalmers said:

My brethren, think how certainly death will come upon you all. The very youngest among you know very well that manhood will come, and old age will come, and the dying bed will come, and the very last look you shall ever cast on your acquaintances will come, and the agony of the parting breath will come, and the time when you are stretched a lifeless corpse before the eyes of weeping relatives will come, and the coffin that is to enclose you will come, and the throwing in of the loose earth into the narrow house where you are laid, and the spreading of the green sod over it—all, all will come on every living creature who now hears me. And in a few little years the minister who now speaks, and the people who now listen, will be carried to their last homes and make room for another generation. Lay it seriously to heart, and no longer trifle and delay, when the high matters of death and judgment and eternity are thus set before you. Yes, the day of final reckoning will come, and the appearance of the Son of God in heaven will come, and the opening of the books will come, and the standing of all generations before the judgment-seat will come. Yes, and if you refuse to be reconciled in the name of Christ, I must tell you what that sentence is to be—"Depart from me, ye cursed, into everlasting fire, prepared for the devil and his angels."

There is a way of escape from the fury of this tremendous storm. There is a pathway. A way of redemption has been found in Jesus Christ our Lord.

Today's Suggested Reading

Isaiah 27:1–5

Fury is not in Me. Who would set briers and thorns against Me in battle? I would go through them, I would burn them together. Or let him take hold of My strength, that he may make peace with Me; and he shall make peace with Me. Isaiah 27:4–5

Bread and Water

Sophia's husband John, an ardent soul-winner, spent his short life preaching on the streets, in the parks, in halls and theaters, wherever he could. But at age 27, he contracted typhoid and quickly died, leaving Sophia Ironside with two small boys and no income.

One of the boys, Harry (later the world-famous pastor of Moody Memorial Church), watched his mother closely. On one occasion, he recalled company coming for supper. Sophia's cupboard was nearly bare, but she scraped together a meal with the little that remained. After the visitors left, she found under one of their plates a ten-dollar bill—a vast sum in those days. With eyes full of tears, she offered thanks to God.

Some time later, the cupboard was again empty. Sophia gathered her two sons to the table for breakfast, but their plates were empty, and there was only water to drink. "We will give thanks, boys," she said. Closing her eyes, she prayed, "Father, Thou hast promised in Thy Word, 'Your bread shall be given you, and your water shall be sure.' We have the water, and we thank Thee for it. And now, we trust Thee for the bread, or for that which will take its place."

Just as she finished praying, the doorbell rang, and the boys ran to the door to find a man there. "Mrs. Ironside," he said, "I feel very bad. We have been owing you for months for that dress you made for my wife. We've had no money to pay you. But just now we're harvesting our potatoes, and we wondered if you would take a bushel or two on account of the old bill."

"Indeed, I'll be glad to," replied Sophia.

In a few minutes, the potatoes were sizzling in the frying pan, and the boys had answered prayer for breakfast.

Today's Suggested Reading
Isaiah 33:14–16

He will dwell on high; his place of defense will be the fortress of rocks; bread will be given him, his water will be sure. Isaiah 33:16

April **29** Listening in the Doorway

While working in a dentist's office in the 1920s, Mabel Bailey felt God calling her into missionary service. Her heart accepted, but her fiancé wasn't so enthusiastic. He broke the engagement and quickly fell in love with another girl.

Mabel, undeterred, went to Toccoa Falls Bible Institute, then enrolled in Nyack Bible College on the Hudson, where one day she was asked to speak before the faculty and student body regarding the needs of India. She was nervous about addressing so many people, especially after hearing the dean of women say, "Well, I know she would be good, if only we can understand her"—referring to Mabel's Georgia drawl.

I worked diligently on that speech. I even took a week off from work to rest and read about India. Finally my message was ready, but emotionally I was not prepared. I would be speaking before 3,000 people. I was afraid. The day before I was to speak, I was sick. Yet I felt that for the land of India and my beloved Lord I must do my best the next day. The morning of February 22, alone in my room, I knelt.

I opened my Bible to Isaiah. "Oh, God," I prayed, "give me strength from your word." My eyes fell on 33:17. I recorded it in my diary for that day. "Thine eyes shall see the king in his beauty: they shall behold the land that is very far off." Fear left my heart and I had perfect peace.

Mabel spoke that afternoon without missing a word. Unknown to her, a young man, having slipped into the back of the auditorium, stood listening in the doorway, unable to find a seat. He was instantly attracted to Mabel and afterward asked to be introduced.

His name was Tom Willey. In years to come, Tom and Mabel Willey were renowned for their missionary work in Cuba before and during the Communist Revolution, and they helped launch the missions movement for their denomination, the National Association of Free Will Baptists.**

Today's Suggested Reading
Isaiah 33:17–24

*Thine eyes shall see the king in his beauty: they shall behold the land that is very far off. Isaiah 33:17**

---

*King James Version

**Adapted from *Beyond the Gate: The Autobiography of Mabel Bailey Willey* (Nashville, TN: Randal House Publications, 1998).

Isaiah's Ornithology

One day last year I sat down to study a verse, wanting to preach from it. I discovered it almost too lofty to contemplate. My insights, and those of the commentaries I consulted, seemed inadequate to convey the grandeur of the passage. "What did Isaiah mean?" I wondered. "To mount up with wings like eagles? To soar on eagles' wings?" I laid aside my pen, drove to the local library, and spent the afternoon reading up on ornithology, the study of birds.

I learned that most birds fly by flapping their wings. But not eagles. They are built for soaring, not flapping; that allows them to travel much farther on less energy. It seems that God built into our planet invisible columns of hot air called thermals which rise up here and there from the earth's surface. Eagles know where to find thermals. They fly into these invisible updrafts, stretch out their wings, and are lifted higher and higher into the sky as though ascending on an elevator. They may rise as high as 14,000 feet, so high they cannot be seen from earth with the naked eye. When they reach those heights, they emerge from the updraft, their wings still spread, and they soar this way and that way, downward and sideward, traveling for miles with very little exertion of strength.

It is a perfect picture. God Himself is an invisible, uplifting thermal current. When we claim His promises and trust His Word, we are spreading out the wings of faith and are caught up to a higher plane. We mount up with wings like eagles. We run without growing weary. We walk and do not faint.

The strength we need for holy, effective, victorious living comes not from frantically flapping through the air like sparrows in distress, but from gliding in the currents of God's grace.

How Isaiah knew all this is a mystery, but his theology was as good as his ornithology.

Today's Suggested Reading
Isaiah 40:25–31

But those who wait on the Lord shall renew their strength; they shall mount up with wings like eagles, they shall run and not be weary, they shall walk and not faint. Isaiah 40:31

May

Worthless Wood

Look to Me

Without Distraction

Carroll's Countenance

Our Concernments

A Good Run

In 1980, Lake Speed made his Winston Cup debut, and two years later won the Transouth 500 at Darlington. In 1985, a first-class NASCAR racing team asked Lake to be their new driver, but they didn't have a sponsor. Lake prayed earnestly, packed his bags, and moved. *As the team prepared for the racing season, I prayed every day for a sponsor. I often read from Isaiah 41, "For I, the Lord your God, will hold your right hand, Saying to you, 'Fear not, I will help you.'" For several months, I helped the team owners, calling people, having meetings, and doing everything I could to get money. It was discouraging, but several times I heard that voice say, "Lake, why don't you trust Me?" The Daytona 500 is the Super Bowl of stock car racing and is the first race of the season. The team was running out of money and no sponsor had appeared. We decided to race anyway. If the team had to shut down after Daytona, so be it.*

But on Saturday as Lake watched a preliminary race, a man approached him, curious about racing. The two hit it off, and Lake answered the man's questions and patiently explained the race to him. Afterward, the gentleman said, "This is the most exciting thing I've ever seen. I'm with Nationwide Auto Parts. I came here to work out a sponsorship with a team, but I've never been able to connect with them."

The next day, Lake Speed started the Daytona 500 with the painted-on sponsor's name still wet on his car. He had a terrific race, finishing second only to Bill Elliott. Afterward, with TV cameras rolling, *I burst into tears and started bawling like a baby. I don't remember what I said, but I thanked the Lord for giving me a good run and answering my prayers.**

Today's Suggested Reading

Isaiah 41:8–13

For I, the Lord your God, will hold your right hand, saying to you, "Fear not, I will help you." Isaiah 41:13

---

*Adapted from P. J. Richardson & Robert Darden, *Wheels of Thunder* (Nashville: Thomas Nelson Publishers, 1997), pp. 17–22.

That Old Depression

Many Americans are disgusted with our increasingly debased entertainment industry and are rediscovering the old programs from a simpler time, like *The Donna Reed Show,* which originally aired 1958 through 1966.

Donna Reed was born in Denison, Iowa, in 1921, one of four children who grew up on a farm. Her family suffered during the Depression, and her neighbors struggled with drought, withered crops, and dust storms. Family after family loaded their goods into rickety automobiles and left. Her parents worked hard to survive, up early and late to bed, day after day, laboring to exhaustion with little to show for it. How did they bear up?

On Sundays I'd get a glimpse of the answer. Dad would pile Mom and the four kids into the old car and we'd rattle to the Methodist Church in Denison. You could get strength just from sitting next to Dad. When the minister read from the Bible, Dad would lean forward. We children could see that the ancient words were food to his spirit, strength to get him through one more week.

Our minister used to read from those books of the Bible that rang with hope. Only recently, I searched through the Bible to see if I couldn't find some of the familiar passages and there, in Isaiah, I came across some verses which brought back the whole experience as though I were there again, sitting in the pew next to Dad: "The poor and needy seek water, but there is none. Their tongues fail for thirst. I, the Lord, will hear them. . . . I will make the wilderness a pool of water, and the dry land springs of water."

Dad was a family man, a real family man. "If there is family strength," he used to say, "that old Depression's not going to get us." And the Depression did pass and it did not get us.

Today's Suggested Reading
Isaiah 41:17–20

The poor and needy seek water, but there is none. Their tongues fail for thirst. I, the Lord, will hear them; I, the God of Israel, will not forsake them. I will open rivers in desolate heights, and fountains in the midst of the valleys; I will make the wilderness a pool of water, and the dry land springs of water. Isaiah 41:17–18

Passing Through the Waters

Robert Morrison was the first Protestant missionary to China, sent out by the London Missionary Society in 1807. Arriving in Canton, he moved into a cellar and was rarely seen in public, pouring himself into a study of the language. He made such good progress that he was hired by the East India Company as an interpreter and spent the next 25 years thus employed. This arrangement allowed him the opportunity of translating the Bible, tracts, hymnbooks, and prayer books from English into Chinese. He prepared an Anglo-Chinese dictionary and a Chinese grammar book.

During his lifetime, Morrison saw but three or four conversions, but his work paved the way for all the missionaries who followed.

He found Isaiah 43:2 as a young man on a voyage from Newcastle to London. He was on his way to school, and the seas were rough. Morrison suffered a bout of seasickness, but he nonetheless managed his daily intake of Scripture. He wrote his father:

I was happily surprised, when lying sick in the state room, by hearing a number of persons sing psalms in the cabin; and every night when the weather would permit, we had prayers and reading of Scriptures. The passage was very rough, in some parts of it; one night they let the ship drive, and another night pitched away her bowsprit, which last occurrence was very serious, as it endangered the loss of our masts.

I mention these circumstances to excite thankfulness to God, who brought us safely through. I pleaded the promise, in its literal sense, "When thou passest through the waters, I will be with thee," and blessed by God, it was fulfilled.

It was a promise he was to claim many times to come.

Today's Suggested Reading
Isaiah 43:1–7

*When thou passest through the waters, I will be with thee; and through the rivers, they shall not overflow thee: when thou walkest through the fire, thou shalt not be burned; neither shall the flame kindle upon thee. Isaiah 43:2**

---

*King James Version

Worthless Wood

Before he was murdered in Polynesia, John Williams had a full and fruitful ministry. He had been a wild youth back in England, but all that had changed on a Sunday night when he ducked into a church to hide from the wild gang that chased him. There in the back row he heard the gospel. And there, on another Sunday, he heard the call of God to missions. He was sent to Polynesia from the London Missionary Society in 1816 and immediately began going from island to island sharing Christ.

Several of the islands were ruled by an evil chief named Romatane, to whom Williams preached from Isaiah 44:15–17 on the folly of idolatry. A man cuts down a tree and uses some of it for firewood, "And the rest of it he makes into a god, his carved image. He falls down before it and worships it, prays to it and says, 'Deliver me, for you are my god!'" How foolish!

That day the chief began to glimpse the truth of the gospel, and he stayed up all night talking to John. In the morning, he called together his people and ordered them to destroy all their idols.

"Will not the gods punish us?" cried the people.

"No," said Romatane. "Each god is a worthless piece of wood that we have decorated. Pile them up and make a bonfire."

They did, and it was indicative of John's success everywhere. During his ministry, fifty different South Sea islands received the gospel.

He was only forty-three when he set off for a new group of islands, the New Hebrides. After a difficult passage, he disembarked with seven others on the cannibalistic island of Erromanga and began following a small creek inland. He heard a noise behind him, turned, ran, tripped, and fell. His skull was smashed in two blows, then his backbone was broken.

His soul went to heaven. His body was eaten.

Today's Suggested Reading
Isaiah 44:14–22

And the rest of it he makes into a god, his carved image. He falls down before it and worships it, prays to it and says, "Deliver me, for you are my god!"
Isaiah 44:17

Look to Me

Charles Haddon Spurgeon's mind was phenomenal. His library contained 12,000 volumes, he read six books a week, he preached as many as ten times a week, and he once said he counted eight sets of thought passing through his mind at the same time while he was preaching.

But only one thing was on his mind on Sunday, January 6, 1850. That was the day he came to Christ. A blizzard had struck, and Charles, 15, ducked into a small church for shelter. *The minister did not come that morning; snowed up, I suppose. At last, a thin-looking man, a shoemaker or tailor or something of that sort, went up into the pulpit. Now, preachers should be instructed, but this man was really stupid. He was obliged to stick to his text, for the simple reason that he had little else to say. The text was: "Look unto Me, and be saved, all the ends of the earth."*

The preacher began: "My friends, this is a very simple text. It says, 'Look.' Well, a man needn't go to college to learn to look. You may be the biggest fool, and yet you can look. Anyone can look. Even a child can look. The text says, 'Look to Me.'"

When he had managed to spin out ten minutes or so, he was at the end of his tether. Then fixing his eye on me as if he knew all my heart, he said, "Young man, you look miserable." Well, I did; but I had not been accustomed to have remarks made from the pulpit on my appearance before. However, it was a good blow, struck right at home. He continued, "and you will always be miserable—in life and in death—if you don't obey my text. But if you obey now, this moment, you will be saved." Then lifting up his hands, he shouted, "Young man, look to Jesus Christ! Look! Look! Look! You have nothing to do but to look and live!"

Spurgeon did look, and that day he was saved.

Today's Suggested Reading
Isaiah 45:20–25

Look to Me, and be saved, all you ends of the earth! For I am God, and there is no other. Isaiah 45:22

Deliverance

When the Communists overran mainland China in the 1940s, a thousand workers of the China Inland Mission were trapped behind the bamboo curtain. CIM ordered the greatest evacuation of missionaries in history, but no one knew who would be allowed to leave.

Missionaries Arthur and Wilda Mathews applied for exit visas and waited. Days turned to months, and their emotions became like "stretched rubber." At length, Arthur was summoned to police headquarters where a Chinese official tried to recruit him as a spy for the Communists. This continued several days, and every evening on his way home, Arthur noticed large posters on walls throughout the city, giving the names of all to be executed the next day. From his kitchen, he heard the shots. What if he were executed? What would happen to Wilda and to their toddler?

Finally the pressure put on Arthur reached its peak, and he shot back, "I am not a Judas. To do as you ask would be treason to the cause of Christ!" He was summarily sent home, expecting his name to be on the next day's execution list. That evening Arthur and Wilda, overwhelmed with fear, knelt in their little kitchen and cried, "Lord, speak to us!" Their Bible opened to Isaiah 49:25: ". . . the prey of the terrible be delivered; for I will contend with him who contends with you, and I will save your children." As they rose to their feet, their hearts overflowed with joy. "We have His promise," said Arthur, "we are not the prey of the terrible. We are the prisoners of the Lord Jesus Christ—just lent to evil men to show forth the abundance of His power!"

The next Sunday as the Christians nervously gathered, Arthur told of his terrible experience and of God's answer in Isaiah 49:25. That was to be his final message to Chinese Christians. Arthur Mathews and his family did finally escape from Communist China, Arthur being the last CIM missionary to exit the country.

Today's Suggested Reading

Isaiah 49:25–26

But thus says the Lord: "Even the captives of the mighty shall be taken away, and the prey of the terrible be delivered; for I will contend with him who contends with you, and I will save your children. Isaiah 49:25

With Such a God

Few men have encountered more dangers, delays, and difficulties than Alexander Mackay, an engineer sent to Africa in 1876 by Scotland's Church Missionary Society. He labored through it all, never returning to Scotland, but leaving behind him a legacy of solid missionary work.

When he arrived at Entebbe, capital of Uganda, King M'tesa welcomed him and gave him wide freedom to preach the gospel. Mackay was always surrounded by children, and everyone, young and old, longed to hear his message. Soon a church was established, and Mackay was busy translating the Scriptures.

But all that changed when King M'tesa died and was replaced by his cruel, 18-year-old son M'wanga. Thirty boys, Mackay's young disciples, were roasted alive for resisting M'wanga's homosexual passions. Three other boys were tortured before death, having their arms cut off in front of a jeering mob. Others among his converts were strangled or clubbed to death. And now M'wanga was rumored to have Mackay in his sights.

Almost beside himself with grief, the missionary fell to his knees, his Bible open before him. The passage he read was Isaiah 51:

Listen to Me, you who know righteousness,
You people in whose heart is My law:
Do not fear the reproach of men,
Nor be afraid of their insults. . . .
I, even I, am He who comforts you.
Who are you that you should be afraid
Of a man who will die,
And of the son of a man who will be made like grass?
I am the Lord your God. . . .
I have put My words in your mouth;
I have covered you with the shadow of My hand.

Alexander Mackay rose from his knees to continue his work. "With such a promise," he said, "and such a God, who shall be afraid?"

Today's Suggested Reading

Isaiah 51:12–16

I am the Lord your God. . . . And I have put My words in your mouth; I have covered you with the shadow of My hand. Isaiah 51:15–16

Prayer Meeting Hill

Lyman Jewett had seen little fruit at his missions post in remotest India despite seventeen years of laborious effort, yet when the American Baptist Mission Board wanted to close it down, Jewett pleaded with them for a little more time. The Board agreed, but the outpost was dubbed "Forlorn Hope."

Early on New Year's Day, 1854, Jewett and his native helpers climbed to the top of the hill behind Forlorn Hope to begin the year in prayer. They arrived before daybreak, at four in the morning, and read these words from Isaiah 52: "How beautiful upon the mountains are the feet of him who brings good news, who proclaims peace, who brings glad tidings of good things, who proclaims salvation, who says to Zion, 'Your God reigns!' "

Having so read, they joined in prayer, pleading with God to send just the man who could break through the barrenness of their field. They finished praying just as the sun rose above the horizon. The mountain came to be called Prayer Meeting Hill.

Ten years later, farmer John Clough was working atop a reaper in his wheat field in Iowa when he received news that his application had been accepted by the American Baptist Foreign Mission Society. They were going to send him to a place called Forlorn Hope.

Arriving in India, John went right to work, preaching, praying, leading, and working tirelessly to feed the hungry and organize famine relief during the great drought of 1876–1878. The Indians came to love him because of his works of mercy, and increasing numbers responded to his message. A powerful revival swept the area, and on one day alone Clough and his workers baptized 2,222 converts. The conversions continued, and in 39 days, they baptized 8,691 new Christians. Twenty-four national ministers were ordained to oversee the young, exploding church; and during the course of the revival, over 20,000 came to the Lord.

Forlorn Hope had proved no match for Prayer Meeting Hill.

Today's Suggested Reading
Isaiah 52:4–10

How beautiful upon the mountains are the feet of him who brings good news, who proclaims peace, who brings glad tidings of good things, who proclaims salvation, who says to Zion, "Your God reigns!" Isaiah 52:7

A Better Explanation

Solomon Ginsburg was one of the most colorful and effective of missionaries. His adventures are the stuff of movies. Solomon was born in Poland in 1867 to a Jewish rabbi who named him after the most glorious of all the kings of Israel. Rabbi Ginsburg wanted his boy growing up in his footsteps, a spiritual leader for the Jews of Eastern Europe.

One day Solomon and his father were celebrating the Feast of Tabernacles by staying overnight in a small tent near their home. The boy picked up a copy of the Prophets and turned haphazardly to Isaiah 53. As he read the opening verses, his curiosity was stirred. "To whom does the prophet refer in this chapter?" he asked. When his father answered with "profound silence," Solomon repeated the question. This time his father snatched the book from his hand and slapped him across the face.

Years later Solomon traveled to London. Passing down Whitechapel Street, he met a Jewish friend who invited him to Mildmay Mission. "I am going to speak on the 53rd chapter of Isaiah," said the friend. "Won't you come?" Solomon attended, curious "to see if he had a better explanation than the one my father had given."

As he listened, he grew troubled. Christ seemed to have perfectly fulfilled Isaiah's prophecies in chapter 53. Solomon purchased a copy of the New Testament and was soon convinced that Christ was the Messiah, and for three months a terrible war raged within him. What would his father think? His uncles? His family?

At last, he heard Rev. John Wilkinson preach a powerful sermon on the text, "He that loveth father or mother more than me is not worthy of me." Returning home, Solomon paced the floor till midnight, finally surrendering his life to Christ in the wee hours.

He was abandoned by his family, beaten and nearly killed by angry friends. But *I knew I was forgiven and accepted. I felt my load was lifted. I knew that my sins were washed away by the precious blood of Jesus.*

Today's Suggested Reading

Isaiah 53:1–5

But he was wounded for our transgressions, He was bruised for our iniquities; The chastisement for our peace was upon Him, and by His stripes we are healed. Isaiah 53:5

He Is Here Present

John Marrant, a 14-year-old black in colonial Charleston, was converted through the preaching of George Whitefield, but his family disapproved of his new faith. John, dispirited, left home with only a small Bible and a little hymnbook in his pocket. He wandered through the wilderness several days, eating little and sleeping in trees for fear of beasts.

At length, he was seized by a Cherokee hunter. *He asked me how I did live. I said I was supported by the Lord. He asked me how I slept. I answered the Lord provided. He inquired what preserved me from being devoured by wild beasts? I replied, the Lord Jesus kept me from them. He stood astonished, and said, "You say the Lord Jesus Christ does this, and does that, and does everything for you; He must be a fine man; where is He?" I replied, "He is here present." To this he made no answer.*

Back in the hunter's village, John was promptly condemned to death. *The executioner showed me a basket of turpentine wood stuck full of small skewers. He told me I was to be stripped naked and laid down in the basket, and these sharp pegs were to be stuck into me, then set on fire, and when they burnt to my body, I was to be thrown into the flame, which was to finish my execution.*

John immediately burst into prayer, and his pitiful words so moved the executioners they took him to the chief. Opening his little Bible to Isaiah 53, John read: "All we like sheep have gone astray; we have turned, every one to his own way; and the Lord has laid on Him the iniquity of us all." Turning here and there in the Bible, John preached the gospel, converting among others the chief himself. For the next two years, the teenager remained among the Cherokees, preaching and teaching and making disciples.

Today's Suggested Reading
Isaiah 53:6–12

All we like sheep have gone astray; we have turned, every one to his own way; and the Lord has laid on Him the iniquity of us all. Isaiah 53:6

The Cobbler of Paulerspury May **11**

There appeared nothing special about William Carey. He was born in the village of Paulerspury, England, in 1761. His father was a poor shoemaker, and William was a sickly child who grew up failing in most of the occupations he tried. But he had vision. He avidly read both the Bible and *Captain Cook's Voyages,* and, putting the two together, he began to envision reaching the globe for Christ. This was a novel idea, for in Carey's day there were no organized Protestant missions. He hung a homemade map of the world behind his cobbler's workbench and began to talk openly of world evangelism.

He was pooh-poohed by the hyper-Calvinists among his fellow Baptists, who told him that God would convert the heathen when he was good and ready, "without any help from us." Undaunted, Carey wrote a book entitled *An Enquiry Into the Obligations of Christians,* which he followed with a powerful sermon at an annual conference. His text was from Isaiah 54:2–3: "Enlarge the place of thy tent," and concluded with an unforgettable cry: "Attempt great things for God! Expect great things from God!"

The men were moved, one of them later writing, "If all the people had lifted up their voices and wept, I should not have wondered. It would only have seemed proportionate to the cause; so clearly did Mr. Carey prove the criminality of our supineness in the cause of God."

Still, the ministers seemed willing to adjourn without acting on Carey's pleas. As the group filed out, Carey gripped the arm of his friend Andrew Fuller, crying, "Is nothing again going to be done?"

Something was done. A Baptist society was soon formed "for the propagation of the gospel among the heathen, according to the recommendations of Carey's *Enquiry,*" and Carey went out as their first missionary.

Thus was born Protestant foreign missions, and to this day the obscure cobbler of Paulerspury is called "The Father of Modern Missions."

Today's Suggested Reading
Isaiah 54:1–3

Enlarge the place of your tent, and let them stretch out the curtains of your dwellings; do not spare; lengthen your cords, and strengthen your stakes. For you shall expand to the right and to the left, and your descendants will inherit the nations, and make the desolate cities inhabited. Isaiah 54:2–3

Her Husband

Mrs. Agnes is asking for you," the caller said, "but come quickly. She doesn't have long." I was saddened, for Mrs. Agnes Frazier was one of a kind. She had devoted her life to educating young people; and her wit, warmth, and Christian witness had left a mark on many a life. She had tirelessly corresponded with and prayed for missionaries around the globe. She had spearheaded her denomination's efforts to launch a women's ministry. She had walked with God, and now He seemed to be dispatching His angels for her.

"You sent for me?" I asked, bending over Mrs. Frazier's bed.

"Yes, Brother Morgan. I want you to tell me who those men are."

"What men?"

"Those men at the foot of my bed."

"There haven't been any men here," I said. "Just Sally, who is taking care of you."

"Brother Morgan, there are men at the foot of my bed," she insisted, "and they are dressed in white. I don't know who they are. What do I tell them?"

I pondered her question and decided there *were* perhaps men in white near her bed. "Tell them," I said, "that you belong to Jesus."

Agnes died a few days later, and she left her Bible to me, a well-worn, heavily-marked red one. Thumbing through it, I saw underlined Isaiah 54:5, and recalled another story about Mrs. Frazier. She and her husband Emmett were married over fifty years, and every morning they had sat at the breakfast table and shared morning devotions. On the morning after his death, Agnes sat alone at the breakfast table, face in her hands, praying, "Lord, I don't think I can sit here any more and have my devotions. My husband is dead."

She nonetheless bravely opened her Bible, and her day's reading brought her to this verse: "For your Maker is your husband, the Lord of hosts is His name."

She smiled, wiped away a tear, and said, "Thank you, Lord."

Today's Suggested Reading

Isaiah 54:4–8

For your Maker is your husband, the Lord of hosts is His name. Isaiah 54:5

Sermon from a Tombstone

In a letter to Lady Huntingdon in 1768, Henry Venn, close friend of evangelist George Whitefield, described a typical Whitefield meeting. The evangelist had preached from this text while standing on a tombstone in the churchyard of Cheltenham Parish Church, permission being denied him to preach in the church. Venn wrote:

To give your ladyship any just description of what our eyes witnessed and our hearts felt within the last few days at Cheltenham, exceeds my feeble powers. My inmost soul is penetrated with an overwhelming sense of the power and presence of Jehovah who has visited us with an effusion of His Spirit in a very eminent manner. There was a visible appearance of much soul-concern among the crowd that filled every part of the burial ground. Many were overcome with fainting; others sobbed deeply; some wept silently; and a solemn concern appeared on the countenance of almost the whole assembly. But when he pressed the injunction of his text, Isaiah 55:1, on the unconverted and ungodly, his words seemed to act like a sword, and many burst out into piercing cries. At this juncture, Mr. Whitefield made an awful pause of a few seconds, and he wept himself. During the interval, Mr. Madan and myself stood up and requested the people, as much as possible, to restrain themselves from making a noise. Oh, with what eloquence, what energy, what melting tenderness, did Mr. Whitefield beseech sinners to be reconciled to God, to come to Him for life everlasting, and to rest their weary souls on Christ the Savior! When the sermon was ended the people seemed chained to the ground. Mr. Madan and myself found ample employment trying to comfort those who seemed broken down under a sense of guilt. We separated in different directions among the crowd, and each was quickly surrounded by an attentive audience still eager to hear all the words of life.

Today's Suggested Reading
Isaiah 55:1–7

"Ho! Everyone who thirsts, come to the waters; and you who have no money, come, buy and eat. Yes, come, buy wine and milk without money and without price. Isaiah 55:1

Carroll's Countenance

Both wounded and embittered, B. H. Carroll returned from the Civil War. His side had lost, and he could walk only with the aid of crutches. Being angry with God, he swore to never again set foot in a church. But his mother begged him to attend a Methodist camp meeting for her sake. He attended, though *I had not an atom of interest. The meeting closed without any change upon my part. The last sermon had been preached, the benediction pronounced, and the congregation was dispersing. A few ladies remained near the pulpit, engaged in singing. Suddenly there flashed upon my mind, like a light from heaven: "Come unto Me all ye that labor and I will give you rest." I seemed to see Him standing before me, inviting me come to Him. In a moment I went, once and forever, casting myself at Christ's feet.*

I gave no public expression of the change which had passed over me, but spent the night in the enjoyment of it. I understood the scripture I had so often heard my mother repeat: "For ye shall go out with joy, and be led forth with peace: the mountains and the hills shall break forth before you into singing, and all the trees of the field shall clap their hands."

When I reached home, I said nothing to my mother about the experience, but went at once to my room, lay down on the bed, and covered my face with my hands. I heard her coming. She pulled my hands away from my face and gazed long and steadfastly upon me without a word. A light came over her face, then, with trembling lips, she said, "My son, you have found the Lord."

B. H. Carroll went on to become a potent preacher of the gospel, and influential in founding Southwestern Baptist Theological Seminary, today the largest seminary on earth.

Today's Suggested Reading
Isaiah 55:8–13

For ye shall go out with joy, and be led forth with peace: the mountains and the hills shall break forth before you into singing, and all the trees of the field shall clap their hands. Isaiah 55:12*

---

*King James Version

A Mile in Every Message

When Jesus Christ entered the ministry at age 30, He returned to His hometown of Nazareth to preach before His family and friends, and He chose text from Isaiah, announcing Himself as its ultimate fulfillment.

Many preachers since Christ have sensed a certain application of these words to themselves as well, for no one can minister effectively without the anointing and empowering of the Holy Spirit. Consider, for example, the unconventional Billy Sunday, who won thousands to Christ though his voice was husky and strained and his words ordinary and crude.

Sunday preached in a sensational style—shouting, jumping, swinging fists, running from one end of the stage to the other. One editor estimated he traveled a mile in every message. As a former baseball player, Sunday had the physique of an athlete, and he used every muscle. He sometimes slid across the platform as if stealing a base, or leaped atop his pulpit or onto the pews. Some of his acrobatics made audiences gasp.

Yet his content was hardly spontaneous. Sunday painstakingly composed elaborate notes, bound in large, black leather notebooks. Arriving at the pulpit, he habitually placed his notes atop a Bible opened to Isaiah 61:1—"The Spirit of the Lord God is upon Me, because the Lord has anointed Me to preach good tidings."

Sunday considered most preaching devoid of spiritual power. *While at Pentecost one sermon saved 3,000 people, now it takes 3,000 sermons to get one old buttermilk-eyed, whiskey-soaked blasphemer. Ever since God saved my soul and sent me out to preach, I have prayed Him to enable me to pronounce two words, and put into those words all they mean. One word is "Lost" and the other is "Eternity." Ten thousand years from now we will all be somewhere. I never preach a sermon but that I think it may be the last one some fellow will hear or the last I shall ever be privileged to preach.*

Today's Suggested Reading

Isaiah 61:1

The Spirit of the Lord God is upon Me, because the Lord has anointed Me to preach good tidings to the poor; He has sent Me to heal the brokenhearted, to proclaim liberty to the captives, and the opening of the prison to those who are bound. Isaiah 61:1

Give the Lord No Rest

In Isaiah, Jerusalem's soldiers and sentries are told to pray so persistently that the Lord will have no rest till He answers their cry. One translation says, "They must remind the Lord of His promises. . . . They must give Him no rest until He restores Jerusalem."*

Remind God of His promises? Give Him no rest till He answers? How many of us pray like that?

One man did, and as a result he was nicknamed "Praying."

John "Praying" Hyde grew up in Carthage, Illinois, in a minister's home. At McCormick Theological Seminary, he committed himself to overseas evangelism, and following graduation, he went to India. His itinerant ministry took him from village to village, but his preaching produced few converts until he discovered the truth of Isaiah 62:6–7 and took these words literally.

At the beginning of 1908, he prayed to win at least one soul to Christ every day. By December 31, he had recorded over 400 converts. The following year, the Lord laid two souls per day on his heart, and his prayer was again answered. The next year he prayed for four souls daily with similar results.

Once, stopping at a cottage for water, Praying Hyde pleaded with God for ten souls. He presented the gospel to the family, and by the end of his visit all nine members of the family had been saved. But what of number ten? Suddenly a nephew who had been playing outside ran into the room and was promptly converted.

Hyde's great missionary work flowed from his prayer life like water from a fountain, and he finally wore himself out in prayer, staying on his knees, night after night, year after year, reminding God of his promises and giving the Lord no rest. The great prayer warrior died on February 17, 1912, his last words being: *Bol, Visu Masih, Ki Jah*—"Shout the victory of Jesus Christ!"

Today's Suggested Reading
Isaiah 62:1–7

I have set watchmen on your walls, O Jerusalem; they shall never hold their peace day or night; you who make mention of the Lord, do not keep silent, and give Him no rest till He establishes and till He makes Jerusalem a praise in the earth. Isaiah 62:6–7

---

*Today's English Version

Playing with Fire

Gilead, a mountainous region east of the Jordan River, was far-famed for its medicinal salve. Jeremiah asserted that not even Gilead's balm can heal the soul, but only the Great Physician.

This was the truth that led 15-year-old Lorenzo Dow to Christ. He was attending a Methodist meeting, and the evangelist preached from Jeremiah 8:22. Later that evening, Lorenzo slept little. His mind tossed and turned and struggled until finally he shouted, "Lord, I give up! I submit! I yield."

Lorenzo began preaching all across New England, trudging through the snow with only a blanket for warmth. His clothes grew tattered, his hair long. He looked like a wild man, and sometimes acted like one, preaching with fury, then running out the back door to the next village. He was called "The man who raises the devil."

Once while preaching through the South, Dow stayed in the home of a woman whose husband was away. From his room, he heard the wife entertaining a man in the couple's bed. Suddenly the woman's husband returned home unexpectedly, and the frightened woman hid her lover under the bedcovers. When her boisterous husband entered the bedroom, she tried to calm him, saying, "Be quiet! Lorenzo Dow is staying here; you'll awaken him."

"The man who raises the devil?" cried her husband. "Fetch him. I'd like to see the devil raised." Into the room came Dow, who finally agreed to raise the devil. Taking the candle, he touched the cotton and shouted, "Come forth, old boy!" As flames engulfed the bedclothes, the hidden man shot out and raced from the room like a demon.

The story provided Dow with a good sermon illustration—living proof of Proverbs 6:27ff: "Can a man take fire to his bosom, and his clothes not be burned? So is everyone who goes in to his neighbor's wife. . . ."

Today's Suggested Reading
Jeremiah 8:18–22

Is there no balm in Gilead, is there no physician there? Why then is there no recovery for the health of the daughter of my people? Jeremiah 8:22

All My Children

Here is Karlanne's story:

I became a Christian at age 29, unmarried, seven months pregnant. When Kevin was born, I had to go to work, but the Lord raised up women in the church who helped with child care.

When Kevin was three, I married Bill, whom I had met at church. He adopted Kevin, and about two years later we had a daughter, Kaitlin. I was hoping to stay at home with Kaitlin and prayed that God would provide a miracle in Bill's job situation with his salary. But the miracle never happened. I grew angry concerning my perception of God's unfairness toward me, and I remember complaining one day to Him about having to go back to work. A little while later, I went to my Bible to look up a passage, and the Lord had another verse to show me, Jeremiah 10:23—"O Lord, I know the way of man is not in himself; it is not in man who walks to direct his own steps." I knew God was speaking to me concerning my desire to stay home.

Shortly afterward, my mother-in-law offered to come to our house every day and watch our children. I pay her for child care, so this helps my in-laws financially since they are retired. As you can see, God has been faithful to provide for us.

My testimony would be incomplete if I didn't tell you I have two other children that God Himself is taking care of. Before becoming a Christian, I had two abortions. I lived in anguish over them until one day when God spoke to my heart, saying, "Why do you keep feeling guilty about this? I'm taking care of your children now." If God had not shown me that truth, I would never have had peace in my life.

*I know now the Lord is watching over my children, all of them.**

Today's Suggested Reading

Jeremiah 10:19–25

O Lord, I know the way of man is not in himself; it is not in man who walks to direct his own steps. Jeremiah 10:23

---

*Coates, Karlanne—Letter to the Author.

Without Distraction

According to 1 Corinthians 7, there are many advantages to remaining single, for "He who is unmarried cares about the things of the Lord—how he may please the Lord . . . without distraction." Evangelist John Berridge offers living proof.

Had John lived in London or Edinburgh, he would have been famous for his powerful preaching, but the Lord placed him in out-of-the-way villages where he became the "Whitefield of the countryside." John was quaint and eccentric, but his strange ways merely added to the appeal and power of his ministry. He preached to great crowds in rural England, in one year alone leading over 4,000 people to Christ—and he evangelized nonstop for 30 years.

He insisted he could best minister unmarried, and he worried that the Wesley brothers and George Whitefield didn't do likewise. George Whitefield had married a woman with whom he had spent less than a week; she died in 1768. And poor John Wesley had marital woes. Writing to Lady Huntingdon, patron of the English evangelists, Berridge observed: *No trap* [*is*] *so mischievous to the field-preacher as wedlock; and it is laid for him at every hedge corner. Matrimony has quite maimed poor Charles* [*Wesley*], *and might have spoiled John* [*Wesley*] *and George* [*Whitefield*], *if a wise Master had not graciously sent them a brace* [*pair*] *of ferrets. Dear George has his liberty again; and he will escape well if he is not caught by another tenterhook. Eight or nine years ago, having been grievously tormented with housekeeping, I thought of looking out for a Jezebel myself. But it seemed highly needful to ask advice of the Lord. So, kneeling down before the table, with a Bible between my hands, I besought the Lord to give me direction.*

The Lord gave John Berridge Jeremiah 16:2—"You shall not take a wife, nor shall you have sons and daughters in this place. . . ." Thus he relinquished all thoughts of marriage and gave himself to pleasing the Lord "without distraction."

Today's Suggested Reading
Jeremiah 16:1–13

You shall not take a wife, nor shall you have sons or daughters in this place. Jeremiah 16:2

Green Leaf

About a thousand workers with the China Inland Mission were trapped by the Communist Revolution in China, and every missionary was in deadly peril. One of them, Isobel Kuhn, "slipped over China's back fence" in 1950. From her new perch in Thailand, she anxiously awaited word on the others.

One morning in a prayer meeting, a coworker prayed for those left behind, saying "O Lord, keep their leaf green in times of drought!" Isobel's mind flew to Jeremiah 17:8, and she felt God was using that verse to reassure her about her colleagues. *That was it! There was an unseen Source of secret nourishment, which the Communists could not find and from which they could not cut them off.*

One by one, all the missionaries except two slipped from the mainland; and then . . .

It was July 23, 1953, when we got the news. We were in Base Camp, Chiengmai, North Thailand, and in those hot countries, houses are built more for airiness than privacy, so John's shout rang through every room. "Dr. Clarke and Arthur Mathews are OUT! Safe in Hong Kong!" He had just received the telegram.

I was on my way to the kitchen, but I just stood where I was and shouted, "Praise God!" and from each room in the house I heard echoes of the same. Spontaneously we all lifted our voices and sang, "Praise God from whom all blessings flow."

It was not just that these much-tried brethren, held by the Communists in the farthest corner of northern China, were now at liberty. It was that they were the last of our CIM family to be delivered. Now we could say, "We, the largest Protestant Mission group in China, have all been brought through this Red Sea trial, and no one martyred."

Isobel Kuhn later wrote the thrilling story of the escape of the last CIM missionaries from China, titling her book *Green Leaf in Drought-Time.**

Today's Suggested Reading
Jeremiah 17:5–8

For he shall be like a tree planted by the waters, which spreads out its roots by the river, and will not fear when heat comes; but its leaf will be green. Jeremiah 17:8

---

*Adapted from *Green Leaf in Drought-Time,* by Isobel Kuhn. Copyright © 1957, Moody Bible Institute of Chicago. Moody Press.

A Verse for Billy Frank

Before her death, Morrow Coffey Graham wrote a little book about her experiences as the mother of the man who would preach the gospel to more people than any other in history.

My husband and I established a family altar the day we were married and we carried that through. In the breakfast room I always kept a Scripture calendar with a verse for the day. Each morning we read that, too, and prayed to the Lord. As we gathered at the breakfast table, everyone would bow his head and fold his hands as my husband asked the blessing. Often as I packed the children's school lunches, I could hear my husband talking to the children. He helped them memorize literally hundreds of Bible verses.

I looked forward to our evenings together as a family. Everyone gathered in the family room. We did this right after the dinner dishes were put away. It was the most important thing in our life, this time of Bible reading and prayer. I know that today Billy recalls those instructional periods as among the most important in his life, helping him to become saturated with the Bible.

Since my children have married and gone their separate ways, and since my husband's death, I have found myself with more time to devote to prayer. I pray without ceasing for Billy Frank.

In the early days of Billy's ministry, his mother accompanied him on a trip. Seeing his busy schedule, the throngs of people, and the stresses he encountered, she grew alarmed. But the Lord gave her Jeremiah 23:23, and it became her theme verse in praying for him: "Am I a God near at hand," says the Lord, "And not a God afar off?"

*I knew God had a long arm; He was wholly trustworthy. I have always had great confidence in the Lord's watchcare over Billy, and I have not feared, therefore, for his life.**

Today's Suggested Reading
Jeremiah 23:21–24

"Am I a God near at hand," says the Lord, "And not a God afar off?" Jeremiah 23:23

*Adapted from Morrow Coffey Graham, *They Call Me Mother Graham* (Grand Rapids, MI: Fleming H. Revell, a division of Baker Book House Co., 1977), passim.

May **22** One Last Season

Which professional baseball player entered the 1997 season . . .

- *the oldest starting outfielder and lead-off man?*
- *ranked first in triples among active players?*
- *fourth in stolen bases? seventh in runs?*
- *twenty-fifth in on-base percentage?*
- *having the smallest feet in the major leagues?*

The answer: Los Angeles Dodger Brett Butler. But his mind was elsewhere that year, for a tickle in his throat had led to the discovery of squamous cell carcinoma—cancer. The news jolted Brett and his family like an earthquake, but he told the press, "Even more than baseball, my faith in Christ is my strength."

I read and reread a verse Vince Nauss, head of Baseball Chapel, sent me. "For I know the plans I have for you . . . plans to prosper you and not to harm you, plans to give you hope and a future." Finally I came to a point of peace. "All right, Lord, just give me the strength to get through it, whatever it is, whether by death or in life." I wanted God to be glorified in all of this. After all, he had given me so much.*

Shortly, Brett needed surgery to remove lymph nodes where the cancer might have spread, then radiation treatments started. Yet the Lord allowed Brett to go back to the Dodgers for several games in 1997, including a career game in which he went 5-for-5, raising his batting average to .311 and his on-base percentage to .446, tops in the National League for lead-off hitters.

*I am thankful for one last season. God allowed that to happen. My future is in God's hands. He knows best. Everything that happens to us happens for a reason. Our job is to determine that reason and make sure God gets the glory.***

Today's Suggested Reading
Jeremiah 29:1–11

For I know the thoughts that I think toward you, says the Lord, thoughts of peace and not of evil, to give you a future and a hope. Jeremiah 29:11

---

*New International Version

**Adapted from "Cancer Won't Strike Me Out," by Brett Butler with Jerry B. Jenkins, excerpted from "Field of Hope," in *Christian Reader,* September/October, 1997, pp. 91–101.

. . . Whom I Abhorred

Sundar Singh was born into a devout Hindu family in North India in September, 1889, the youngest son of a wealthy Sikh. As a teenager, he enrolled in a mission school sponsored by American Presbyterians, but upon learning he would have to study the Bible, he was furious. He tore the pages from his Bible and led other students in open revolt. But even while attacking the Scripture, Sundar found it piquing his curiosity. He began reading it and was immediately attracted to the Savior. Still, he bitterly resisted its message. He withdrew from the mission school and publicly burned a New Testament. Once he spent a solid hour scrubbing himself after the shadow of a missionary fell across his body.

Yet he remained entranced by the Bible, and, almost against his will, he would open it to secretly read its message. One day he turned to Jeremiah 29:13 and was pricked by the words: "And you will seek Me and find Me, when you search for Me with all your heart." The battle within him became intense.

I arose at three in the morning, determined to find peace or to end my life by casting myself before the train that passed near the house at five o'clock. After taking a bath, I spent an hour and a half in prayer. I kept praying, "O God, if there be a God, reveal Thyself to me. . . ." I hoped to see Krishna or Buddha. Presently I saw a globe of light in the room and in the light there appeared, not the form I had hoped to see, but the Living Christ whom I abhorred. He showed me His hands and said, "Why do you persecute me?"

That day Sundar Singh embraced Christianity. He went on to become a powerful evangelist who experienced one breathtaking adventure after another for Christ.

Today's Suggested Reading

Jeremiah 29:12–14

And you will seek Me and find Me, when you search for Me with all your heart. Jeremiah 29:13

God's "I Wills"

The Japanese occupation of China during World War II was brutal, not only for the Chinese but for missionaries. John and Edith Bell of Canada served the Lord in China's western regions. Their three children, far away in Chefoo, were seized and imprisoned at Weihsien Concentration Camp.

One day a man arrived on the Bell's doorstep with news that the children were well cared for with food and clothing. Some time later, he came again. This time he said, "Mrs. Bell, I have some very sad news. All the students in the Weihsien Camp have been murdered."

Edith's mind reeled, and she fought to stave off total panic. Suddenly she remembered Jeremiah 31:16–17, verses the Lord had given her just after her children were interred: "Refrain your voice from weeping, and your eyes from tears . . . they shall come back from the land of the enemy. There is hope in your future, says the Lord, That your children shall come back to their own border."

She quickly found the verses in her Chinese Bible and said to the man, "Doctor, you read this." He read it, then angrily threw down the Bible and stomped from the house. He was an infiltrator, trying to destroy the Christians' morale with lies.

Sometime later, John and Edith had to flee through India. They eventually booked passage to America without knowing the condition of their children. As they disembarked in New York, a Red Cross worker greeted them with news their children had been liberated and had arrived back in Canada ahead of them.

"I was completely overcome," Edith said. "My children not only came from the land of the enemy, they came to their own border as the verse in Jeremiah had promised."

The Bells caught the next train to Ontario where "we stepped down and were almost knocked over by our three children. It was joy unspeakable and full of glory. God's 'I wills' had not failed, and we knew they never would."

Today's Suggested Reading
Jeremiah 31:13–17

Thus says the Lord: "Refrain your voice from weeping, and your eyes from tears; for your work shall be rewarded, says the Lord, and they shall come back from the land of the enemy. There is hope in your future, says the Lord, that your children shall come back to their own border." Jeremiah 31:16–17

A 70-Year-Old Sermon

Charles E. Fuller became one of America's first nationwide radio evangelists, preaching from Long Beach Municipal Auditorium every week during his "Old Fashioned Revival Hour." He also helped establish Fuller Seminary in 1947. Jeremiah 33:3 became his favorite verse through its impact on his life—and on his wife.

In 1932, Charles and Grace Fuller were overwhelmed with pressure. Their young son was near death, suffering pneumonia. The Great Depression had wiped out their financial support, and Charles desperately sought ways to remain solvent. He was forced to sell off his valuable orange groves and to exhaust his wife's inheritance in order to meet their bills. Grace faced major surgery, and Charles was forced from his pastorate. A severe earthquake struck their home in Southern California, and their financial woes multiplied.

Grace felt she could stand the strain no longer, and she cried out to God for help. Entering her husband's study, she opened a book of Spurgeon's sermons, and found a message he had preached seventy years before from Jeremiah 33:3.

When I called upon God in desperation in August, 1933, He answered me by directing me unmistakably to the library shelf on which this book stood and to this sermon. It brought great comfort and enabled me to trust God and to await the unfolding of His plans for us.

She later said that God lifted her burden so remarkably that when Charles returned from another hard day with the lawyers, trying to find a way to ward off bankruptcy, she was able to tell him, "Never mind how black things look now. God has assured me that He has great and mighty things in store for us in the future—things which we can't even imagine now."

As time passed, Charles and Grace Fuller traced in that moment the faint beginnings of their incredible ministry of radio, evangelism, and education. Ever after, Charles would pen this verse under his signature.

Today's Suggested Reading
Jeremiah 33:1–9

Call to Me, and I will answer you, and show you great and mighty things, which you do not know. Jeremiah 33:3

"I Thundered Greatly"

Howell Harris became a Welsh schoolteacher with a love for dice-playing, love-making, beer-drinking, and his own appearance. He was the center of his social circle. But at age 21, Harris heard a Palm Sunday sermon in which the minister declared that those without Christ are not fit to live or to die. The words hit him like a blow to the solar plexus and soon led to his conversion. Immediately Harris began sharing his faith. *I could not meet or travel with anyone, rich or poor, young or old, without speaking to them concerning their souls.*

He soon started preaching, and his sermons were fearless, furious and long, sometimes lasting four or five hours. "He used to speak of hell," said one listener, "as though he had been there himself."

Harris once claimed that God had filled his mouth with "terrors and threatenings. I was given a commission to rend and break sinners in the most dreadful manner. I thundered greatly."

As he preached across the land, he made frequent use of Jeremiah 49:10: "I have made Esau bare; I have uncovered his secret place, and he shall not be able to hide himself." Harris warned people there was no hiding from the searching eyes of God.

This was the message Wales needed, for the whole land was seeped in sin and ignorance. Under Harris's preaching, hundreds were converted, including notorious sinners.

Harris shocked Great Britain by moving his sermons out-of-doors and preaching in the open air. The established clergy denounced this innovation; but one man, watching from afar, was stirred to the depths—George Whitefield.

It was Harris who gave Whitefield the vision for field preaching, and it was Harris who taught him how to do it. It was Harris who set Wales afire, but it was Whitefield who became the greatest open-air evangelist in the English-speaking world.

Today's Suggested Reading
Jeremiah 49:7–10

But I have made Esau bare; I have uncovered his secret places, and he shall not be able to hide himself. His descendants are plundered, his brethren and his neighbors, and he is no more. Jeremiah 49:10

Our Concernments

What a joy to read and re-read *Pilgrim's Progress*. It was written by John Bunyan, the Puritan tinker (mender of pots and pans) in Bedford, England. After his conversion, Bunyan joined the nearby Baptist church; but after Charles II was restored to the British throne in 1660, John was arrested for preaching without receiving permission from the Established Church. He remained in Bedford jail for over twelve years, suffering, preaching as he could, and writing books. His family meanwhile encountered great burdens.

In his autobiography, Bunyan wrote: *I found myself compassed with infirmities; the parting with my wife and poor children hath oft been to me in this place as the pulling the flesh from my bones, and that not only because I am somewhat too fond of those great mercies, but also because I have often brought to mind the many hardships, miseries, and wants that my poor family was to meet with, especially my poor blind child, who lay nearer my heart than all I had besides; O the thoughts of the hardship I thought my blind one might go under would break my heart to pieces. Poor child, thought I, what sorrow art thou like to have for thy portion in this world? Thou must beg, suffer hunger, cold, nakedness, and a thousand calamities, though I cannot now endure the wind should blow upon thee.*

But that which helped me in this temptation was the consideration of [*this*] *Scripture, "Leave thy fatherless children, I will preserve them alive, and let thy widows trust in Me." I had this consideration, that if I should now venture all for God, I engaged God to take care of my concernments.*

Bunyan realized that his "concernments" would be well-tended *if left at God's feet, while I stood for His name, as they would be if they were under my own tuition. This was a smarting consideration, and was as spurs unto my flesh.*

Today's Suggested Reading
Jeremiah 49:11–19

Leave your fatherless children, I will preserve them alive; and let your widows trust in Me. Jeremiah 49:11

"Great Is Thy Faithfulness"

When I was in college, I was often fairly unmoved during chapel services; but for some reason I would always tear up when we sang "Great Is Thy Faithfulness," the great hymn based on Lamentations 3. Now I consider it a barometer of my spiritual life, whether or not my eyes still moisten during this song.

It was written by Thomas Chisholm, who was born Lincoln-like in a log cabin in Kentucky. As a young adult, he was converted by evangelist H. C. Morrison. Chisholm's health was unstable, and he alternated between bouts of illness and gainful employment, in which he did everything from journalism to insurance to evangelistic work. Through all the ups and downs, he discovered new blessings from God every morning. Lamentations 3 became precious to him, and he wrote this hymn after 30 years of serving Christ.

It was relatively unknown until popularized around the world by George Beverly Shea and the choirs at the Billy Graham Crusades.

At Graham's 1954 Harringay Crusade, Wilber Konkel first heard "Great Is Thy Faithfulness," and a flood of memories coursed through his mind. He recalled the dark nights of World War II, when London was nearly bombed to oblivion. "Each night as the enemy planes came over," Konkel wrote, "we cast our care upon Him. I quoted [this Scripture] to myself. I used it in my prayers. Those were dark days. At times they seemed hopeless. It was in those darkest hours that God proved His faithfulness to me. We were so near death. Yet it is the Lord's mercies that we are not consumed, because His compassions fail not. They are new every morning."

Perhaps we should all shed an occasional tear of thanksgiving whenever we sing:

Great is Thy Faithfulness! Great is Thy Faithfulness!
Morning by morning new mercies I see.
All I have needed Thy hand hath provided.
Great is Thy Faithfulness, Lord, unto me.

Today's Suggested Reading
Lamentations 3:22–26

Through the Lord's mercies we are not consumed, because His compassions fail not. They are new every morning; great is Your faithfulness.
Lamentations 3:22–23

A Poor Man's One Eye

Misery loves company; we can often better face our trials when we discover biblical characters who encountered similar troubles. Thus Jeremiah, the author of Lamentations, comforted Samuel Rutherford.

Rutherford was a Scottish pastor in the town of Anwoth, who was attacked by the government for not conforming to the Established Church. Found guilty, he was stripped of his pastorate and banished to Aberdeen. His letters back to his flock have become classics. One of them is dated 13 July 1637:

Dearly beloved and longed-for in the Lord, Grace be to you and peace. God knoweth the sad and heavy Sabbaths I have had since I laid down my shepherd's staves. I have been often saying, as it is written, "My enemies chased me sore like a bird, without cause: they have cut off my life in the dungeon, and cast a stone upon me." For next to Christ, I have but one joy, to preach Christ my Lord; and they have violently plucked that away from me. It was to me like the poor man's one eye; and they have put out that eye, and quenched my light. But my eye is toward the Lord. I know I shall see the salvation of God and that my hope shall not always be forgotten.

O if I had paper as broad as heaven and earth, and ink as the sea and all the rivers and fountains of the earth, and were able to write the love, the worth, the excellency, the sweetness and due praises of our dearest and fairest Well-beloved! And then if you could read and understand it!

Let heaven and earth be consolidated into pure gold, it will not weigh the thousandth part of Christ's love to a soul, even to me a poor prisoner. . . . Keep in mind what I taught you. . . . Remember me to God in your prayers; I cannot forget you.

The grace of the Lord Jesus Christ be with you all.

Today's Suggested Reading

Lamentations 3:52–53

*My enemies chased me sore, like a bird, without cause. They have cut off my life in the dungeon, and cast a stone upon me. Lamentations 3:52–53**

---

*King James Version

Big 'Un

Alvin York, a poorly-educated, red-headed, strapping Tennessean whom his friends called "Big 'Un," became the greatest hero of World War I. On September 26, 1918, he and his men were ambushed by Germans in the Argonne Forest. His bunkmate was peppered with so many rounds his uniform was torn off. Others dropped to York's left and right, and the surviving Americans were pinned down. Rising to his feet, York stepped into the hail of bullets and started firing. When his rifle ammunition ran out, he drew his pistol. Bullets and bayonets rained down on him, but in the end York didn't suffer a scratch. He killed the nest of 24 machine gunners, captured 132 prisoners, and singlehandedly saved his men. It was "the greatest single exploit" of World War I.

Ironically, York was a dedicated Christian who had originally requested exemption as a pacifist. The Sixth Commandment seemed clear to him, and he had no desire to fire at anything more than rabbits and squirrels. When his request was denied, York reported for duty deeply troubled.

But in the army, he met Major George Edward Buxton. One evening the two engaged in a gentle debate of Scriptures. When York quoted the Sixth Commandment, Buxton turned to Luke 22:36: ". . . he who has no sword, let him sell his garment and buy one." York quoted the passage about turning the other cheek, and Buxton countered with Christ's driving out the moneychangers. York said, "Blessed are the peacemakers," and Buxton said, "Render unto Caesar the things that are Caesar's."

Finally, Buxton turned to Ezekiel 33 and read how Israel's watchmen were to blow their trumpets and defend their city. Buxton's eyes met York's, and it was then, York later wrote, that *I knowed I would go to war. I knowed I would be protected from all harm, and that so long as I believed in Him He would not allow even a hair on my head to be harmed.*

Today's Suggested Reading
Ezekiel 33:1–9

So you, son of man: I have made you a watchman for the house of Israel. . . . Ezekiel 33:7

His Greatest Sermon

Among the Scottish Presbyterians—the "Covenanters"—was John Livingstone, born at Kilsyth, Scotland, in 1603, the son of a minister. John attended college intending to become a doctor, but he grew troubled about his life's calling and resolved to set aside a day for prayer. *Accordingly, on the day appointed, he retired to Cleghorn wood, where, after much confusion in the state of his soul, he at last thought it was made out to him that he must preach Jesus Christ.*

On January 2, 1625, he preached his first sermon in his father's pulpit. He was soon preaching regularly. For a while, Livingstone wrote out all his sermons, reading to the people from a manuscript. But one day when he rose to preach, he spotted some friends who had already heard the sermon he planned to give. He quickly chose a new text and scribbled some notes. He discovered *more assistance and more emotion in his own heart than ever he had found before; which made him never afterwards write any more of his sermons, except such short notes for the help of his memory.*

His greatest sermon was delivered on Monday, June 21, 1630. The night before, he and his companions had devoted the entire evening to prayer. Now Livingstone felt weak and frightened as he stepped into the pulpit, but, mustering his strength, he read his text, Ezekiel 36:25–26.

Here he was led out in such a melting strain, that, by the downpouring of the Spirit from on high, a most discernible change was wrought upon above 500 of the hearers, who either dated their conversion, or some remarkable confirmation, from that day forward.

It was the highlight of his ministry, but it wasn't the end of it. He continued preaching in Scotland until driven to Holland where he served the Lord in exile until his death at age 78.

Today's Suggested Reading

Ezekiel 36:22–26

Then I will sprinkle clean water on you, and you shall be clean; I will cleanse you from all your filthiness and from all your idols. I will give you a new heart and put a new spirit within you. Ezekiel 36:25–26

June

The Lord's Maidservant

Luther's Verse

Apostle to the Indians

Tune My Heart

The Trumpeter and the Little Horn

The Great Deliverance Came

William Carvosso had slight talent, no education, and little money. He couldn't read or write. He appeared the most ordinary of men, and few expected him to make much of himself. He didn't.

He made much of Christ.

Carvosso was converted at age 21 from a "life of sin" and, growing in the Lord, wanted more and more of God's power in his life.

What I now wanted was "inward holiness," and for this I prayed and searched the Scriptures. Among the number of promises which I found in the Bible, my mind was particularly directed to Ezekiel 36:25–27—". . . I will put My Spirit within you and cause you to walk in My statutes, and you will keep My judgments and do them." This is the great and precious promise of the eternal Jehovah and I laid hold of it, determined not to stop short of my privilege; for I saw clearly the will of God was my sanctification.

At length one evening, while engaged in prayer meeting, the great deliverance came. I began to exercise faith by believing, "I shall have the blessing now." Just at that moment, a heavenly influence filled the room; and no sooner had I uttered or spoken the words from my heart, "I shall have the blessing now," than refining fire went "through my heart—illuminated my soul"—scattered its life through every part, and sanctified the whole. I then received the full witness of the Spirit that the blood of Jesus Christ has cleansed me from all sin. I cried out, "This is what I wanted! I have now got a new heart." O what boundless, boundless happiness there is in Christ, and all for such a poor sinner as I am!

The date was March 13, 1772, and Carvosso spent the next 60 years as a powerful soul-winner for the Methodist church of England.

Today's Suggested Reading

Ezekiel 36:27–38

I will put My Spirit within you and cause you to walk in My statutes, and you will keep My judgments and do them. Ezekiel 36:27

June **2**

Apostle to the Indians

John Eliot was born in England and educated at Cambridge, where he distinguished himself in languages. He came to Massachusetts Bay Colony in search of religious liberty, and soon began a 52-year pastorate at Roxbury, a frontier settlement two miles outside Boston. His first years were occupied with his flock, but in the 1640s, Eliot, 40, felt a gradual burden for reaching the nearby Algonquian Indians with the gospel.

Helped by an Indian named Cockenoe, he began working on the language. Algonquian speech patterns compressed complex ideas into extended single words, and were full of guttural sounds. But Eliot was brilliant with languages, and within two years he could speak broken Algonquian.

In October 1646, he ventured to a nearby village and entered the wigwam of a peaceful Indian named Waban. There at the council fire Eliot preached the first Protestant sermon in the Indian tongue in North America. His text was Ezekiel 37:9, and the Indians immediately began asking questions about God, such as:

- *How could God hear the Indian prayers when He is used to hearing English prayers?*
- *Am I not too old to come to Christ?*
- *Why has no white man ever told us these things before?*

As Eliot left the village, he passed out treats, sweetmeats and apples for the children, and tobacco for the men. He returned every two weeks, preaching and answering questions. Soon numbers of Native Americans were discovering Christ. The New Testament, then the entire Bible appeared in the Algonquian tongue. In 1651, a settlement was established and named Natick, a Christian Indian town. Homes were built on both sides of the Charles River, with a bridge to connect them. Streets were laid out, and a two-story building was erected as school, church, and warehouse.

Today Natick is a residential, industrial, and commercial center, and on the site of the original meeting house stands Eliot Church, named for the man who is known to history as "Apostle to the Indians."

Today's Suggested Reading
Ezekiel 37:1–10

Also He said to me, "Prophesy to the breath, prophesy, son of man, and say to the breath, 'Thus says the Lord God: "Come from the four winds, O breath, and breathe on these slain, that they may live."'" Ezekiel 37:9

But If Not . . .

While serving in Korea in the 1920s, missionary Stanley Soltau met Chinsoo Kim, a student whom he embraced as a son. Chinsoo went on to seminary, and was ordained a minister. The two men became the closest of friends.

In 1936, the occupying Japanese government ordered all Korean schools to bow before the goddess Amaterasu-Omi-Kami, patron saint of the Japanese army. Mission schools were not exempt, and Christians faced the same challenge encountered by Shadrach, Meshach, and Abed-Nego. Stanley, refusing to compromise, recommended closing the mission schools if necessary. "Not so much as a nod of the head should be offered," he said. Intense persecution raged against the Christians, with over 60,000 arrests.

As Stanley left Korea, Chinsoo met him at the station. "Father," Chinsoo said as the train prepared to depart, "I fear hard times ahead for us. . . . The stand we are taking against shrine worship—tell me again that we are doing the right thing."

"There is no question about it," said Stanley. As he boarded the train, Chinsoo pressed a paper into his hand. Stanley read: "Of one thing I am certain, you will never feel ashamed of your son. Whatever comes, I am looking to the Lord for his enabling power. . . ."

Stanley did not return to Korea until 1952 and learned of Chinsoo's fate. Soon after their parting, Chinsoo had been arrested by the Japanese police because of his refusal to bow before the Shinto shrine. He was imprisoned and brutally tortured. One winter day, a friend passing the jail saw a pile of corpses, frozen, stacked like firewood. Among them was Chinsoo.

From the day Stanley heard it until he died quietly in 1972, he carried Chinsoo's death around with him just as he carried the death of Christ in his heart. He understood that Chinsoo, his son and fellow-servant, was one of God's "But if nots. . . ."*

Today's Suggested Reading

Daniel 3:13–18

Shadrach, Meshach, and Abed-Nego answered and said to the king, . . . "our God whom we serve is able to deliver us from the burning fiery furnace . . . we do not serve your gods, nor will we worship the gold image which you have set up." Daniel 3:16–18

---

*Adapted from "T. Stanley Soltau" by Charles Turner in *Chosen Vessels: Portraits of Ten Outstanding Christian Men,* ed. by Charles Turner (Ann Arbor, Mich: Vine Books, 1985), ch. 9.

"I Can't Stand This"

Henry Venn was an Anglican clergyman, born near London and ordained in 1749, whose sermons fascinated the industrial and manufacturing classes of eighteenth-century England. The records of his ministry are sparse, but among them is this story:

One day at his church in Huddersfield, Venn preached from Daniel 5:27, describing the stubborn, pleasure-soaked reign of King Belshazzar. He described Belshazzar's feast for a thousand lords, God's handwriting on the wall, and Daniel's thundering words to the vile monarch: "You have been weighed in the balances, and found wanting."

In the congregation sat Mr. William Brook with his 19-year-old uncle, W. Mellor, who had been drawn into the church by noticing the great crowds. People on every side were weeping quietly as Venn pealed forth. As they left the church, neither man spoke. They silently walked to the nearby fields, then Mellor stopped, leaned against the wall of a farm building, and burst into tears, saying, "I can't stand this."

William later wrote: *His conviction of sin was from that time most powerful, and he became quite a changed character. I was not so much affected at that time; but I could not after that sermon be easy in sin. I began to pray regularly; and so, by degrees, I was brought to seek salvation in earnest.*

The people used to go in droves to Huddersfield Church. Some of them came out of church together; and they used to stop and talk over, for some time, what they had heard, before they separated to go to their homes. That place has been to me like a little heaven below.

I never heard a minister like him. He was most powerful in unfolding the terrors of the law. When doing so, he had a stern look that would make you tremble. Then he would turn off to the offers of grace, and begin to smile, and go on entreating till his eyes filled with tears.

Today's Suggested Reading
Daniel 5:25–31

Tekel: You have been weighed in the balances, and found wanting. Daniel 5:27

Grit and Backbone

Daniel preferred to spend a night with the lions than miss a day in prayer. He slept better under angelic guard in the lions' den than the king in the palace bedroom. After all, said Spurgeon, "How could the lions eat him when most of him was grit and backbone!"

I first became acquainted with Daniel's story in the big Scofield Bible my parents gave me as a child. C. I. Scofield, its editor, had fought in the Civil War. President Grant later appointed him United States Attorney for Kansas, and Scofield was considered a brilliant lawyer. But his career was marred by alcoholism—until his conversion to Christ at age 36. Scofield then became a great Bible student, a pastor and evangelist, founder of the Central American Mission, and editor of his famous reference Bible. He once said:

Shortly after I was saved, I passed the window of a store in St. Louis where I saw a painting of Daniel in the lions' den. That great man of faith, with his hands behind his back and those beasts circling him, was looking up and answering the king, who was anxious to know if God had protected him.

As I stood there, great hope flooded my heart. Only a few days had passed since I, a drunken lawyer, had been converted; and no one had yet told me anything about the keeping power of Jesus Christ. I thought to myself, there are lions all about me too, such as my old habits and sins. But the One who shut the lions' mouths for Daniel can also shut them for me! I knew that I could not win the battle in my own strength. The painting made me realize that while I was weak and helpless, my God was strong and able. He had saved me, and now He would also be able to deliver me from the wild beasts in my life. O what a rest of spirit that truth brought me.

Today's Suggested Reading
Daniel 6:16–23

My God sent His angel and shut the lions' mouths, so that they have not hurt me. Daniel 6:22

June **6**

The Trumpeter and the Little Horn

In Daniel, there is a description of the coming antichrist, the man of lawlessness who will rage against both God and Israel during the Great Tribulation. But 1 John 2:18 says there is a sense in which many antichrists have already come. In sixteenth-century Scotland, John Knox was quite sure he spotted some.

Knox was born about 1514 in a village south of Edinburgh. He finished his education just as the winds of Reformation were blowing in from the Continent. Patrick Hamilton and, after him, George Wishart took up the Protestant cause. Both were burned at the stake. Advocates of the Scottish Reformation then turned to young Knox, asking him to assume spiritual leadership of the movement. Knox burst into tears and declined, but the group endorsed his call with acclamation, and Knox reluctantly agreed.

His first sermon was to Protestant soldiers who had seized St. Andrew's Castle where the Protestants were holed up. He chose for his text Daniel 7:24–25, concerning the little horn that would arise to terrorize the earth. Knox preached that the Roman Church had arisen from the wrecked Roman Empire and was the Antichrist. He described the debauched lives of various popes. He attacked the corrupted doctrines and practices of the priests. His message was so vivid, moving, fiery, and grounded in the theology of justification by grace through faith that Knox was afterward called the "Trumpeter of God."

But it was a sermon for which he paid dearly. St. Andrew's fell, and its occupants, including Knox, were condemned to perpetual captivity aboard a galley ship. There in the ship's bowels, he was chained to an oar, his scant clothing offering little protection from the drummaster's whips. He suffered there for nineteen months before being released, upon which he promptly returned to the British Isles to continue the struggle for Reformation.

Today's Suggested Reading

Daniel 7:21–28

The ten horns are ten kings who shall arise from this kingdom. And another shall rise after them; He shall be different from the first ones, and shall subdue three kings. He shall speak pompous words against the Most High, shall persecute the saints of the Most High, and shall intend to change times and law. . . . Daniel 7:24–25

Treachery, Tyranny, and Trickery

Here's another story about Donald Cargill, who followed Knox by a hundred years as a leader in Scotland's Reformation. Cargill was born about 1619, and, like Knox, benefited from a quality education. At his father's request, Donald entered the ministry; but he was unhappy at the division he found in the church between advocates of the Reformation and supporters of the Royal or State Church. His disillusionment grew, and he finally decided to abandon his church and leave the ministry.

But as he mounted his horse, an old woman pushed her way to him, demanding, "Sir, you have promised to preach on Thursday, and you have appointed a meal for poor, starving people, and will you go away and not give it? If you do, the curse of God will certainly go with you."

Her words pierced Donald to the bone, and he dismounted, determined to press on with his ministry. He became increasingly caught up in the Reformation, and on a Sunday shortly afterward he preached a blistering sermon from Hosea 9:1: "Do not rejoice, O Israel, with joy like other peoples, for you have played the harlot against your God. You have made love for hire on every threshing floor."

In his sermon, he attacked the king of Scotland for forcing his influence upon Scotland's church: "The king will be the woefullest sight that ever the poor Church of Scotland saw: woe, woe, woe unto him. His name shall stink while the world stands, for treachery, tyranny, and trickery."

This didn't go over well with his majesty, and the next day a company of dragoons burst into his study, asking for "that vile traitor, Donald Cargill." Cargill fled to a friend's house, and spent the rest of his life preaching on the run until at length he was captured. He went to the scaffold and to his death, cheerfully singing Psalm 118: "O, give thanks to the Lord, for He is good! For His mercy endures forever."

Today's Suggested Reading

Hosea 9:1–4

Do not rejoice, O Israel, with joy like other peoples, for you have played the harlot against your God. You have made love for hire on every threshing floor. Hosea 9:1

With Fasting

The biblical practice of fasting is neglected by most Christians today, for it runs counter to the modern spirit of consumerism. But Sandy Sheppard decided to try it when her husband, Rick, came down with a chronic illness. *I wondered how—with two school-age children and a toddler at home—I could fast without complicating life for the rest of my family. I resolved to fast one day a week, skipping breakfast and lunch and eating dinner as usual.*

The next Tuesday night she joined her family for dinner, but avoided evening snacks and skipped breakfast and lunch the next day. *In mid-afternoon my thoughts turned to fixing the family's dinner. The hours between 2 and 6 proved the most difficult. Ordinary meatloaf had never smelled so tempting.*

As the weeks passed, Sandy embarked on a more thorough study of the Bible's teaching about fasting. She found in the book of Joel a verse that deeply impressed her. *I knew God heard my prayers even before I began fasting. But practicing self-denial added a new dimension to my spiritual life, and I gained a deeper understanding of God's instruction in Joel 2:12, "Return to me with all your heart, with fasting and weeping and mourning."* The discomfort of hunger reminded me to fix my eyes on God.*

Andrew Murray wrote in With Christ in the School of Prayer, *"Prayer needs fasting for its full growth. . . . Prayer is the one hand with which we grasp the invisible; fasting, the other, with which we let loose and cast away the visible." Giving up eating—which I truly enjoyed—made me more aware of my weakness in contrast to God's strength.*

Rick's condition worsened for several months, then began to improve. In the meantime, Sandy learned that fasting and praying for the physical healing of another is a sure method of growing stronger in one's own heart.**

Today's Suggested Reading

Joel 2:12–14

"Now, therefore," says the Lord, "Turn to Me with all your heart, with fasting, with weeping, and with mourning." Joel 2:12

---

*New International Version

**Adapted from "Fasting 101" by Sandy Sheppard in *Moody Magazine*, July/August 1996, pp. 50–52.

Where Is Your God?

June **9**

Vance Havner's inimitable preaching had audiences laughing one minute, crying the next, nodding agreement, then shuddering with conviction. His sermon from Joel 2:17 is a prime example:

There ought to be enough divine electricity in every church to give everybody in the congregation either a charge or a shock! It is time God's ministers grew tired of hearing the pagans sneer, "Where is your God?" We claim to have the answer to every need of humanity. If we really believed this, no auditorium would hold the people. There is something wrong with our Christianity when we have to beg most of our crowd to come to church to hear about it. Like Joel, we ought to be ashamed when the world goes by looking at a corporal's guard huddled in a lumberyard of empty seats singing, "Revive us again." If I were a non-Christian who dropped into an average church during a so-called revival and saw a handful trying to enlist more recruits in the army of the Lord when most of the outfit already was AWOL, I would either conclude that Christianity is not what it is supposed to be or that Christians had been inoculated with a mild form of the faith and immunized against the real thing. I would feel like rising from a back pew to ask, "Where is your God?"

What do you mean by singing "Onward Christian Soldiers" when most of your army has deserted?

I agree with Joel. I'm embarrassed when pagans walk by our empty churches, look in on our feeble ceremonies, see us swapping members from church to church, moving corpses from one mortician to another, preaching a dynamite gospel and living firecracker lives.

*We need to repent, confess, and forsake sin, renounce the world, make Jesus Lord, and be filled with the Spirit. When we do, no longer will the pagans sneer, "Where is your God?"**

Today's Suggested Reading

Joel 2:15–19

Why should they say among the peoples, "Where is their God?" Joel 2:17

---

*Vance Havner, *In Times Like These* (Grand Rapids, MI: Fleming H. Revell, a division of Baker Book House Co., 1969), pp. 71–76.

June **10** The Lord's Maidservant

The word "maidservants" in this verse encouraged the Quakers to involve women fully in their ministry from the beginning. George Fox, founder of the Quakers, quoted from Joel when answering critics who insisted on a more conservative role for women in the church. Mary Fisher, Fox's convert and recruit, also got a lot of mileage from Joel 2.

Mary was a Yorkshire maid who joined the Quakers after hearing Fox preach in 1651. She soon began witnessing and preaching, acts for which she was jailed for 16 months. She used the time to study Quaker doctrine, including Joel 2:29, and left prison more outspoken than ever. She was arrested again for preaching at Sidney Sussex College, and this time she was stripped to the waist, tied to a post, and whipped "till the blood ran down her body." As the lashes fell, she sang, "The Lord be blessed, the Lord be praised, who hath thus honored us and strengthened us to suffer for His name." At the end of the ordeal, she said to the examiner, "If you think you have not done enough, we are ready to suffer more for our Savior."

In 1655, Mary sailed to America, where the authorities in Boston burned her library, imprisoned her, and boarded up her jailhouse window, denying her light so that no one could see or talk with her. She was strip-searched, ridiculed, roughly handled, and eventually deported to Barbados.

Returning to England, Mary, now 34, journeyed to Turkey as a Quaker missionary, still convinced she was God's maidservant in the tradition of Joel 2:29. There she preached to the Sultan himself.

At length, Mary returned to England where she met and married William Bayly, a seaman and Quaker preacher. For the next 40 years, she ministered as a mother and homemaker, raising three children and devoting her spare time to the women's work among the Quakers.

Today's Suggested Reading
Joel 2:28–32

And also on My menservants and on My maidservants I will pour out My Spirit in those days. Joel 2:29

Worse and Worse

His mother didn't like it, but John Marrant, a young, free black man in colonial America, became a musician. His violin and French horn were a hit at balls and parties in Old Charleston, South Carolina, and John was the toast of the town. All that changed one evening as he sauntered down the street on his way to play his horn somewhere. He saw a crowd outside a church and was told "a crazy man was hallooing" inside. Marrant pushed in, intending to break up the meeting by blasting his instrument.

The "crazy man," evangelist George Whitefield, was preaching from Amos 4:12. As Marrant entered, Whitefield pointed his finger directly at him and shouted, "Prepare to meet your God." The words hit the young man with such force he collapsed to the floor unconscious. When he came to, Whitefield was still preaching. "Every word," said Marrant, "was like a parcel of swords thrust into me." He was carried to a side room, and after the service, Whitefield called on him, saying, "Jesus Christ has got thee at last."

Marrant was carried home and his sister sent for doctors. For three days, he barely ate or drank. One of Whitefield's associates visited him, and the two men knelt together by Marrant's bed. After their prayer, the minister asked Marrant how he felt.

"Much worse," came the reply. They prayed again, and the minister again asked how he felt.

"Worse and worse."

They prayed a third time. *Near the close of his prayer, the Lord was pleased to set my soul at liberty, and being filled with joy, I began to praise the Lord immediately. My sorrows were turned into peace and love.*

This time when the minister asked how he felt, Marrant replied, "All is well, all is happy." John Marrant was just fourteen at the time, but he went on to become a dramatic preacher throughout North America.

Today's Suggested Reading
Amos 4:11–13

"Therefore thus will I do to you, O Israel; because I will do this to you, prepare to meet your God, O Israel." *Amos 4:12*

June **12**

Oswald in His Presence

Few readers of *My Utmost for His Highest* realize its author was a gifted painter who might have enjoyed a long and distinguished career. But a sermon by Charles Spurgeon changed that, and Oswald Chambers lay down his brushes, sensing God's call to ministry. From 1906 to 1910, he preached around the world, and from 1911 until 1915, he directed a Bible college.

At the outbreak of World War I, Chambers offered to minister among soldiers in Egypt. Under his leadership there, mission huts sprang up for British troops near Cairo and at the Suez. Men turned out in droves to hear his sermons and lectures.

During these days, Chambers typically rose at 5:30 A.M. for his hour alone with God. Watching the sunrise over the ancient desert always filled him with wonder, and he sometimes described it in his journal, using an artist's tongue: "It is a lovely morning, the sun rose in a real marvel of glorious light. Each sunrise here looks as if it were a new thought from God. . . ."

Chambers spent his last mornings in the minor prophets. He noted that the blasts and plagues described in Amos seemed to come from "the powerful hand of God, and not the blind cause and effect." He sensed God's overruling providence, even in disasters, even in the midst of war.

One day Chambers described in his diary the brilliant sunrise "like a celestial scheme of shot silk." He meditated on the power of a God who could make even the desert spectacular, then he read Amos 5, claiming verse 8: "He made the Pleiades and Orion; He turns the shadow of death into morning; . . . the Lord is His name." Having thus reassured himself of the sovereignty and supremacy of God, Chambers plunged into another day.

He had only a handful left. A couple of weeks later he underwent an emergency appendectomy in the Red Cross hospital. Two weeks later, his wife cabled four words to his family and friends: "Oswald in His Presence."

Today's Suggested Reading

Amos 5:8–15

He made the Pleiades and Orion; He turns the shadow of death into morning and makes the day dark as night; He calls for the waters of the sea and pours them out on the face of the earth; the Lord is His name. Amos 5:8

Brother Jonah

We remember Jonah mainly as whale bait, forgetting he became one of the greatest itinerant preachers in history, converting a huge city with an eight-word sermon.

Today his example inspires another Jonah, a man in China, who risks life and liberty traveling around with a knapsack of Bibles. As Jonah preaches, he often takes his text from Jonah 3:4, telling audiences they are like the Ninevites: "You live in defiance of the true God who will judge you if you don't repent."

On a recent weekend, Jonah found himself wedged in a crowded third-class railway carriage. By and by, a soldier leaned over and said, "Old man, tell us why you seem so happy."

Jonah replied, "What do you think? What would be the happiest thing that could ever happen to you?"

The man next to Jonah replied, "I want to be loved by a beautiful woman." A lady said, "A big house would make me the happiest person in the world." Another said, "A passport to America." The soldier said, "If I had the power to command the People's Liberation Army, I'd be happy."

"Let me see, now," said Jonah. "I have a mansion so large an emperor would envy; I am loved by the most beautiful person in the world; I have freedom to go wherever I wish; and I happen to be a close friend of the most powerful man on earth. In fact, I have received all this from one person; His name is Jesus Christ."

As the train jostled across Communist China, Jonah pulled out an old Bible and spent the next 20 hours giving his listeners an all-night seminar about the Christian faith.

Disembarking the train, he bicycled another five hours, dodging authorities who had been tipped off by an informant on the train. All in all that weekend, Jonah traveled 40 hours on trains, 9 hours on buses, 9 hours peddling a bicycle; he led 50 people to Christ—all at age 73.*

Today's Suggested Reading

Jonah 3:1–10

And Jonah began to enter the city on the first day's walk. Then he cried out and said, "Yet forty days, and Nineveh shall be overthrown!" Jonah 3:4

*Adapted from "On the Road With Brother Jonah" by Ron MacMillan in *World Vision*, February/March, 1992, pp. 7–10.

June **14** Flickering in Its Socket

On November 18, 1845, David Marks, forty years old and dying, addressed the students of Oberlin College. He was introduced by his dear friend Charles Finney, who announced that it was uncertain Brother Marks would survive his sermon. He said Dr. Dascomb could find no pulse in one wrist, and only "a little tremulous motion" in the other. If he should die while preaching, the students were to remain calm and not leave their seats.

Thus introduced, Marks began his last sermon. His text was Micah 2:10.

My dear friends, I feel to thank God that I have the prospect of addressing you once more, and for the last time. This has been the desire of my heart. The lamp of life has for some time been flickering in its socket, and in the opinion of friends I have but a few hours to live. I suppose my coffin is being made.

My extreme weakness, and the distress of suffocation in consequence of the dropsical difficulty in my chest, and which is probably drowning my heart, has not allowed me to spend a moment in preparation for this meeting. Hence my remarks must be made off hand. The first and leading thought of which I wish to dwell, is that God has not designed this place as our final home. As the prophet said, "Arise and depart, for this is not your rest. . . ." The light of a blessed immortality dawns beyond the tomb. Christ is so near and so precious that I cannot fear death. O, my brethren, no reality is so sure, none so sweet, none so glorious, as the Christian's hope. . . .

He spoke of the brevity of life, the certainty of heaven, then he ended by urging the students, *O live for God and your generation! You enter life at a glorious time to live—there is so much to do for God. Farewell. Brother Finney, I want to give you my hand. All of you who love God, Farewell.*

None of the students ever forgot that dramatic sermon. Two weeks later, Marks "arose and departed" to his rest.

Today's Suggested Reading
Micah 2:1–13

Arise ye, and depart; for this is not your rest: because it is polluted, it shall destroy you, even with a sore destruction Micah 2:10*

---

*King James Version

Unchanging Principles

Jimmy had learned a lot of Bible verses during his Sunday school years, and he put them to good use. They came to mind during times of crisis, times of opportunity, times of disappointment, and times of great challenge. Now, as he faced the biggest challenge of his life, two dear old verses forced their way to the forefront of his thoughts—2 Chronicles 7:14 and Micah 6:8. He and his wife discussed them, prayed over them, and he decided to use the latter one as his theme in an upcoming speech.

Well, it wasn't just a speech. It was his inaugural address as the incoming 39th president of the United States. Standing on the bunting-draped, ornate platform on the east front of the Capitol, Jimmy Carter scanned the multitudes and wanted to draw his nation back to its spiritual roots.

In this outward and physical ceremony, we attest once again to the inner and spiritual strength of our Nation. As my high school teacher, Miss Julia Coleman, used to say, "We must adjust to changing times and still hold to unchanging principles." Here before me is the Bible used in the inauguration of our first president, in 1789, and I have just taken the oath of office on the Bible my mother gave me a few years ago, opened to a timeless admonition from the ancient prophet Micah: "He hath shewed thee, O man, what is good; and what doth the Lord require of thee, but to do justly, and to love mercy, and to walk humbly with thy God?"

Carter went on to articulate his goals and dreams for the nation, that Americans would learn to live together, work together, and pray together; then he ended his address as he had begun it: *I hope that when my time as your president has ended, people might say this about our nation: that we remember the words of Micah.*

Today's Suggested Reading
Micah 6:1–8

*He hath shewed thee, O man, what is good; and what doth the Lord require of thee, but to do justly, and to love mercy, and to walk humbly with thy God? Micah 6:8**

*King James Version

Slapped with a Bible

George Fox was a large man, young, muscular, with piercing eyes, long hair, and a foghorn voice. He felt called by God to battle ungodliness; and occasionally he would run through the villages in stocking feet, shouting, "Woe to the bloody city! Woe to Lichfield! Woe to Nottingham! It is full of lies and robbery!"

Most thought him crazy, but no one ever forgot those words.

Fox was born in 1624, and grew up noticing how few professing Christians displayed the joy and reality of the indwelling Christ. At age 23, he dramatically encountered the Lord. *One day when I had been walking, I was taken up in the love of God, so that I could not but admire the greatness of his love. While in that condition, it was opened unto me by the eternal light and power, and I saw clearly that all was done, and to be done, in and by Christ. I saw the harvest white, and the seed of God lying thick on the ground, and none to gather it; for this I mourned with tears.*

He began preaching with power that made his audiences quake and tremble, thus giving rise to the name by which they were called—Quakers. Using Nahum 3:1, Fox went from one "bloody" city to another, preaching repentance. In Tickhill, a clerk hit him so hard in the face with a Bible that the blood flowed, then he was dragged out, stoned, beaten, and thrown over the hedge.

Fox spent a total of six years in filthy prisons, dark and caked with repulsive build-ups of excrement. His cells had no benches or mattresses, and they teemed with lice and vermin.

But George Fox pressed on, and by his death in 1691, there were 50,000 Quakers in England and Ireland. Around the globe today, there are a quarter of a million.

Today's Suggested Reading
Nahum 3:1–8

Woe to the bloody city! It is all full of lies and robbery. Its victim never departs. Nahum 3:1

Luther's Verse

One famous verse in the Bible is repeated three times in the New Testament—Romans 1:17, Galatians 3:11, and Hebrews 10:38.

That was too many times for Martin Luther to miss.

Luther had intended to become a lawyer, but while caught in a violent lightning storm, he cried, "Help me, St. Anne! I will become a monk!" So off he went to the monastery, and within two years he was a priest. But Luther had no inward peace, and he grew increasingly terrified by the wrath of God.

These words, *The just shall live by faith,* kept coming to Luther. While it is difficult to pinpoint the moment this phrase first impacted him toward personal conversion, there is an interesting handwritten letter displayed in a glass case in the Library of Rudolstadt in Germany. It is written by the reformer's youngest son, Dr. Paul Luther.

In the year 1544, my late dearest father, in the presence of us all, narrated the whole story of his journey to Rome. He acknowledged with great joy that, in that city, through the Spirit of Jesus Christ, he had come to the knowledge of the truth of the everlasting gospel. It happened in this way. As he repeated his prayers on the Lateran staircase, the words of the prophet Habakkuk came suddenly to his mind: "The just shall live by faith." Thereupon he ceased his prayers, returned to Wittenburg, and took this as the chief foundation of all his doctrine.

In the preface to his collected Latin works, Martin Luther described an event that occurred sometime after returning to Wittenburg, while he was in the "toilet"—monastic slang for "in the pits." As he meditated on Habakkuk's words as quoted in Romans 1:17, *I began to understand. This immediately made me feel as though I had been born again, and as though I had entered through open gates into paradise itself. From that moment, I saw the whole face of Scripture in a new light.*

The Christian world was never again the same.

Today's Suggested Reading
Habakkuk 2:1–4

Behold the proud, his soul is not upright in him; but the just shall live by his faith. Habakkuk 2:4

Yet Will I Rejoice

John's childhood was unbearably lonely. His mother died when he was seven, and his father, a severe sea captain, was seldom home. At eight, John was sent to boarding school, where his education consisted primarily of floggings. At eleven, he took to the sea with his dad, and there, at the onset of adolescence, he learned the ways of sailors.

One day, waiting for his ship to sail, John visited the Catlett family, who had tended his mother during her illness. There he met 14-year-old Mary, who was helping her mother with supper. John, finding in her the love he had always needed, tarried and missed his ship.

His dad arranged another voyage, but he again missed it because of Mary. This time he was seized and pressed into service aboard the warship *Harwich*. He again slipped off to visit Mary, but by now her exasperated parents told him the relationship was over. John returned to the *Harwich* so distraught that he jumped ship and returned to plead. He was captured, flogged, demoted, and placed aboard a slave ship.

The story gets worse before getting better, but in the end John Newton found Jesus Christ, and he wrote the hymn *Amazing Grace* as his testimony. He married Mary, and the two devoted themselves to joint ministry.

Their love deepened as the years passed. But one day Mary was diagnosed with cancer. As she declined, John wrote love letters, calling her, *My dear, sweet, precious, beautiful, own dearest dear.* His emotional pain was almost unbearable, but he found strength in Habakkuk 3:17–18.

And on the day of Mary's funeral, John slowly mounted the pulpit of his little London church and preached from that text, which he viewed as a model of how Christians should handle grief: "Though the fig tree may not blossom, nor fruit be on the vines; though the labor of the olive may fail, and the fields yield no food. . . . Yet I will rejoice in the Lord, I will joy in the God of my salvation."

Today's Suggested Reading

Habakkuk 3:14–19

Yet I will rejoice in the Lord, I will joy in the God of my salvation. Habakkuk 3:18

The Victorious Christian Life

For some odd reason, his parents assigned him the unlikely name of Handley Carr Glyn Moule. His friends, however, called him "Bishop," for he came to be one of England's most respected churchmen.

His conversion to Christ occurred at age 25, during the Christmas season of 1866. Writing to his father, he said: *This very Christmas vacation, after much mental wretchedness, I was able to find and to accept pardon and peace through the satisfaction of the Redeemer, as I had never done before.*

Yet some years later when he entered the ministry, he felt spiritually unfit. Writing again to his father, he said: *I sadly feel the need of tenfold grace before I can hope to be either a very happy Christian or—as a minister of Jesus Christ—a very useful one.*

He pressed on in ministry, but the feeling of powerlessness increased. His mother wrote to him of being filled with the Spirit, and he replied: *Oh, to be made to feel a little more my hold on the Lord Jesus Christ.*

In 1882, D. L. Moody and Ira Sankey came to Cambridge and their flaming power and victorious message stirred his heart. A year later, some Keswick speakers came along preaching of rest and victory in Christ. Handley attended the meeting, held in a great barn. A Christian businessman, William Sloan, spoke from Haggai 1:6: "You eat, but do not have enough." Sloan said that when "Self" rules our hearts instead of Christ, our souls are lean. Only the life fully committed to Christ is Spirit-filled and victorious.

That evening Moule yielded himself without reservation to be the Lord's bondservant, and he trusted Christ to fill him with power for joyful living and effective service. A peace filled him like the ocean, and from that day until his death in 1920, Handley Carr Glyn Moule demonstrated Christ to all who met him.

Today's Suggested Reading

Haggai 1:1–11

You have sown much, and bring in little; you eat, but do not have enough; you drink, but you are not filled with drink; your clothe yourselves, but no one is warm; and he who earns wages, earns wages to put into a bag with holes. Haggai 1:6

Apple of My Eye

John Hyde (1865–1912) was a missionary to India who became so famous for his effective and powerful praying that he is known to history as "Praying Hyde." He once told of the "most salutary" lesson the Lord ever taught him about prayer. It occurred while he was praying for a national pastor in India, a man who was both having—and causing—problems.

Hyde began his prayer, "O God, Thou knowest this brother, how. . . ." He was going to say "cold," when suddenly he was smitten in his spirit. A voice seemed to whisper sharply to him, "He that touches him touches the apple of My eye." A great horror swept over Hyde, and he felt he had been guilty before God of "accusing the brethren."

Falling to his knees, Hyde confessed his own sin, and he remembered the words of Paul, that we should think on things that are lovely and good. "Father," cried Hyde, "show me what things are lovely and of good report in my brother's life."

Like a flash, Hyde remembered the many sacrifices this pastor had made for the Lord, how he had given up all for Christ, how he had suffered deeply for Christ. He thought of the many years of difficult labor this man had invested in the kingdom, and the wisdom with which he had resolved congregational conflict. Hyde remembered the man's devotion to his wife and family, and how he had provided a model to the church of godly husbanding.

John Hyde spent his prayer time that day praising the Lord for this brother's faithfulness.

Shortly afterward, Hyde journeyed into the plains to see this pastor, and he learned that the man had just received a great spiritual uplift, as if a personal revival had refreshed his heart like a springtime breeze.

While Hyde had been praising, God had been blessing.

Today's Suggested Reading
Zechariah 2:1–12

. . . for he who touches you touches the apple of His eye. Zechariah 2:8

Plucked from the Fire

John Wesley grew up in dingy little Epworth, England, where his father, Samuel, was a penniless and unpopular pastor whose sermons were blunt and without tact. As a result Samuel occasionally became the victim of ruffians. His crops were burned, his livestock maimed, and twice someone tried to torch his house.

The third attempt succeeded. About midnight on February 9, 1709, Susanna Wesley was awakened by sparks falling from the roof onto the bed of little Hetty. Samuel woke with a start and cried, "Fire! Fire!" Opening the door, he found the house full of smoke and flames. It was a three-storied timbered house liberally daubed with plaster. The thatched roof exploded in a mass of flames, and the fire spread like a sheet of lightning. The parents, flying to rescue their bevy of children, were almost trapped in the burning building, but finally managed to escape through windows and the garden door.

But a head count showed one child missing. Peering back, they saw John's terrified face pressed against an upstairs window. He was only five. Instantly a human ladder formed; and just as the house caved in, John was snatched to safety. He never forgot the rescue: *I remember the circumstances as distinctly as though it were but yesterday. Seeing the room was very light, I put my head out and saw streaks of fire on top of the room. I got up and ran to the door, but could get no further, the floor beyond it being in a blaze. I climbed up a chest that stood near a window. One in the yard saw me. . . .*

Samuel gathered his family around him and offered thanksgiving to God that none had perished. Susanna then made an exclamation that stayed with John all his life: "Is this not a brand plucked out of the burning?" In later years, he had this phrase engraved under his portraits.

After the fire, Susanna gave herself to prepare John for the ministry, believing that God surely had some special work for him to do.

Today's Suggested Reading
Zechariah 3:1–10

And the Lord said to Satan, "The Lord rebuke you, Satan! The Lord who has chosen Jerusalem rebuke you! Is this not a brand plucked from the fire?" Zechariah 3:2

June **22** Rebuking the Devourer

In his book *Proving God,* Al Taylor tells the story of Arlie Rogers of Selma, California, who came to be known as the "Sweet Potato King" because of his vast farming operations in the San Joaquin Valley. Arlie and his brother first arrived to California with little money. By scraping and saving, they finally managed to purchase a farm. At that time, the money crop was cotton, so the two brothers invested every penny they could get in sowing cotton.

When the cotton plants were just out of the ground, a great sandstorm blew through the valley, destroying everyone's crops. The Rogers brothers were disconsolate.

Arlie called the church and asked their pastor to visit. As Pastor Burnham walked across the devastated fields, the brothers poured out their troubles. "Everything we had was in that crop. We don't have any money or credit left to replant. We are completely ruined. Now we will lose everything."

Pastor Burnham knew these brothers as dedicated Christians, active in their church, and faithful in giving their tithes to the Lord. Squinting at them, he replied, "No, fellows, it's really not that bad. The God we serve raised His own Son from the dead after three days. I know He can raise cotton."

With that, the pastor sank to his knees in the dirt and prayed a simple little prayer. "Father," he said, "these men are tithers. You said You would rebuke the devourer for a tither. I am asking You to manifest the power of Your Word and fulfill that promise right here in this cotton field. Bring this cotton back and give these men a good crop in Jesus' name. Amen."

He rose, brushed the dust from his knees, and said, "That ought to take care of it."

It did. A few days later the Rogers brothers called him back. There before their eyes a good crop was rising from the ground. God had rebuked the devourer.*

Today's Suggested Reading

Malachi 3:8–12

Bring all the tithes into the storehouse. . . . And I will rebuke the devourer for your sakes, so that he will not destroy the fruit of your ground. Malachi 3:10–11

---

*Adapted from Al Taylor, *Proving God* (Cleveland, Tennessee: Pathway Press, 1991), pp. 102–103.

I Only Got Fourteen

Missionary Christine Tinling once visited a leper colony in Foochow, China, where she heard of an old man who had showed up one day asking for a room in which to die. He wore only a bit of burlap tied by a few strings. He had no relatives, but the Christians took him in and loved him like their own.

One day the Chinese pastor visited the old man and began sharing the gospel, but when the pastor asked him if he wanted to become a Christian, he said, "No. Jesus gave Himself to me, but I have nothing to give Him in return for a gift like that."

"But He wants no gift except yourself," said the pastor. It took awhile for the old man to comprehend this. He kept asking, "How could He possibly want an ill-smelling, rotten old leper like me?" But finally one day, he believed and received Jesus as Savior.

The man quickly learned to love the Word of God and he began sharing Christ with fellow lepers, going from room to room, until the disease caused his feet to drop off and his eyes to fall out.

As he lay dying, his one regret was that he had done so little for the Lord. He had learned the gospel too late, when he was hardly able to move about. Looking up at his pastor, he asked this question: "When I reach Father's house, will Jesus blame me for not getting any more, or will He remember I was just a rotten old leper?" Then he added: "I only got fourteen."

Fourteen souls he had won to Jesus Christ.

On the resurrection day, said Christine Tinling in recounting the story, *from a grave outside Foochow, will rise this child of God, who, in the days of his flesh, was a leper and an outcast. He will have his own place in the blessed company of whom it is written: "They will be Mine in that day when I make them My jewels."*

Today's Suggested Reading

Malachi 3:16–18

"They shall be Mine," says the Lord of hosts, "On the day that I make them My jewels." Malachi 3:17

Tune My Heart

The 17-year-old grinned mischievously as he poured another drink for the fortune-teller. He and his buddies, relaxed by their alcohol, laughed as the gypsy tried to tell their futures through her drunken haze. But he stopped laughing when she pointed a quivering finger at him and said, "And you, young man, you will live to see your children and grandchildren."

Something about those words bothered young Robert Robinson, and his mood changed. "Let's go," he told his friends, "She's too drunk to know what she's saying. Leave her alone."

But her words bothered Robert, for he thought, "If I'm going to live to see my children and grandchildren, I'll have to change my ways. I can't keep on like I'm going now."

That evening, Robert suddenly suggested to his buddies they attend the evangelistic meeting being held by world-famous George Whitefield. "Sure," they said, "maybe we can break up the meeting."

But that evening Whitefield, preaching from Matthew 3:7, thundered out the words, "Flee from the wrath to come!" The effects of Robert's day-long drinking disappeared, and he sobered up immediately. He felt Whitefield was preaching directly to him, and the words haunted him for two years and seven months. Then, on December 10, 1755, he gave his heart to Christ.

Robert Robinson joined the Methodists and was appointed by John Wesley to minister in Norfolk, England. Three years later, he wrote a poem for one of his sermons, and it was soon published as a hymn. It has been a favorite of the church ever since:

Come, Thou Fount of every blessing,
Tune my heart to sing Thy grace;
Streams of mercy, never ceasing,
Call for songs of loudest praise:
Teach me some melodious sonnet,
Sung by flaming tongues above;
Praise the mount—I'm fixed upon it—
Mount of Thy redeeming love.

Today's Suggested Reading
Matthew 3:1–12

But when he saw many of the Pharisees and Sadducees coming to his baptism, he said to them, "Brood of vipers! Who warned you to flee from the wrath to come?" Matthew 3:7

God and the Gulag

When Georgi Vins died January 11, 1998, he left behind the legacy of a hero. Years before, in 1966, Vins had made a bold stand for the Lord in downtown Moscow. Five hundred delegates of the church of Evangelical Baptist Christians had traveled there to protest the treatment of believers by Communist authorities. All day long they stood before the headquarters of the Central Committee for the Communist Party of the USSR, holding in their hands a petition addressed to General Secretary Leonid Brezhnev. And all night the 500 stood in the rain as cars drove by, throwing dirt and mud on them. Authorities proposed a meeting with minor officials, but the leaders refused, holding out for a meeting with Brezhnev himself.

At 1:45 P.M., 28 military buses roared in. The believers formed a ring, joined hands, and sang hymns. The police began beating them, young and old. Some were singled out, dragged away by the hair, and beaten till unconscious. Many were then loaded on the buses and shipped to prisons, labor camps, and torture chambers.

Georgi Vins was not among those arrested, but he recalled that the preaching ministry of Jesus had begun upon the arrest of John the Baptist. Going to the Communist headquarters in Moscow, he stood on the street and proclaimed the very words Jesus had said on that occasion: "Repent, for the kingdom of heaven is at hand."

He was promptly arrested. His whereabouts were withheld from friends and family, but it was later learned he had been sent to Leftorovskaia Prison. All in all, Georgi Vins spent nine brutal years in the Soviet Gulag for his faith. He was finally released in 1979 in a swap arranged by President Jimmy Carter.

Vins devoted the rest of his days to advancing the cause of the church behind the Iron Curtain, and God allowed him to see the collapse of the Communist system under which he had so nobly suffered.

Today's Suggested Reading
Matthew 4:17–25

From that time Jesus began to preach and to say, "Repent, for the kingdom of heaven is at hand." Matthew 4:17

A Radical Solution

When young George Whitefield began attracting large crowds in England, the British clergy barred him from their churches. He was brash and evangelical, and they considered him a threat. In Bristol, England, as George wrestled with his dilemma, a radical solution came to him—presenting the gospel without chancel, pulpit, pew, or pipe organ! To stand on a makeshift platform and preach in the open air! It was unheard of, and even Wesley called it a "mad notion."

But on February 17, 1739, Whitefield and three friends ventured to the coal fields outside Bristol to experiment. The coal miners were among the most despised of people—illiterate, dirty, poverty-stricken, living in blackened huts. They were thought of as "gin-devils, wife-beaters, and sodomites." They knew little of God, and no pastors served them.

Whitefield arrived just as the miners were leaving the pits. Standing on a little rise of ground, he laughed nervously and muttered that the Lord Jesus, too, had used "a mount for his pulpit and the heavens for his sounding board." Then, lifting up his magnificent voice, he cried out to the miners who were about a hundred yards away: *Matthew, Chapter 5, verses 1 to 3!*

Some of the men stopped and stared. They had no idea who Matthew was or what "Chapter 5" meant, but about 200 of them came nearer. Whitefield continued: *And seeing the multitudes, He went up on a mountain, and when He was seated His disciples came to Him. Then He opened His mouth and taught them, saying: "Blessed are the poor in spirit, for theirs is the kingdom of heaven."*

George then told a story that made the miners laugh; and as his three nervous friends prayed earnestly, he launched into his sermon, his words pouring out in a torrent. By and by he noticed white streaks forming on the miner's sooted faces, as tears began cutting through the grime. Within days the crowds had increased to 10,000.

It was a good beginning for the 24-year-old evangelist.

Today's Suggested Reading
Matthew 5:1–5

Blessed are the poor in spirit, for theirs is the kingdom of heaven. Matthew 5:3

Conceited? June **27**

Some verses from Matthew have strengthened many a persecuted Christian, such as the Bohemian reformer, John Hus. Just before he was martyred in Constance, he wrote his friends, "I am greatly comforted by that saying of our Lord, 'Blessed shall you be when men shall hate you. . . .'"

Though Charles Spurgeon was never burned at the stake like Hus, he did suffer a firestorm of criticism when beginning his ministry in London. A steady stream of articles trashed his sermons, and pamphlets appeared denouncing his methods, motives, mannerisms, and messages. He was vilified in cartoons and caricatures. Several writers questioned whether he was converted.

At first, this storm of cynicism and censure deeply hurt Spurgeon, who described himself as "broken in agony." But his wife prepared a plaque of Matthew 5:11–12 for the wall of their room where Charles would see it first thing every day: "Blessed are you when they revile and persecute you, and say all kinds of evil against you falsely for My sake. Rejoice and be exceedingly glad, for great is your reward in heaven."

The verse did its work, and in time Spurgeon learned to take criticism in stride. Not long before his death years later, a friend, visiting him in his study, said, "Do you know, Mr. Spurgeon, some people think you conceited?"

The great preacher paused a moment, then he smiled and said with a twinkle in his eye, "Do you see those bookshelves? They contain hundreds, nay, thousands of my sermons translated into every language under heaven. Well, now, add to this that ever since I was twenty years old there never has been built a place large enough to hold the numbers of people who wished to hear me preach, and, upon my honor, when I think of it, I wonder I am not more conceited than I am!"

Today's Suggested Reading
Matthew 5:6–11

Blessed are you when they revile and persecute you, and say all kinds of evil against you falsely for My sake. Rejoice and be exceedingly glad, for great is your reward in heaven. Matthew 5:11–12

Bat Out of Hell

Mitsuo Fuchida, commander of the Japanese Air Force, led the squadron of 860 planes that attacked Pearl Harbor on December 7, 1941.

American bomber Jacob DeShazer was eager to strike back, and the following April 18th, he flew his B-25 bomber, the "Bat Out of Hell," on a dangerous raid over Japan. After dropping his bombs on Nagoya, DeShazer lost his way in heavy fog and bailed out as his plane ran out of fuel. He was taken prisoner, tortured by the Japanese, and threatened with imminent death. For almost two years, DeShazer suffered hunger, cold, and dysentery.

In May of 1944, he was given a Bible. "You can keep it for three weeks," said the guard. DeShazer grabbed it, clutched it to his chest, and started reading in Genesis. Scarcely sleeping, he read the Bible through several times, memorizing key passages. On June 8, coming to Romans 10:9, Jacob prayed to receive Jesus Christ as his Savior.

Immediately Matthew 5:44 became a critical text for DeShazer as he determined to treat his Japanese guards differently. His hostility toward them evaporated, and every morning he greeted them warmly. He prayed for them and sought to witness to them. He noticed their attitude toward him also changed, and they would often slip him food or supplies.

After the war, DeShazer returned to Japan as a missionary. Copies of his testimony, "I Was a Prisoner of the Japanese," flooded the country, and thousands wanted to see the man who could love and forgive his enemies. DeShazer settled down to establish a church in Nagoya, the city he had bombed.

One man in particular, deeply affected by DeShazer's testimony, was led to Christ by Glenn Wagner of the Pocket Testament League. Shortly afterward, the man paid a visit to Jacob DeShazer at his home, and the two became dear friends and brothers. It was Mitsuo Fuchida, who had led the Pearl Harbor attack. As DeShazer served as a missionary in Japan, Fuchida became a powerful evangelist, preaching throughout Japan and around the world.

Today's Suggested Reading
Matthew 5:43–48

But I say to you, love your enemies, bless those who curse you, do good to those who hate you, and pray for those who despitefully use you and persecute you, that you may be sons of your Father in heaven. . . . Matthew 5:44–45

Hallowed Be Thy Name

During the reign of England's Mary I—Bloody Mary—Rev. John Hooper was imprisoned for his faith and sentenced to die. About 9 o'clock on the morning of February 9, 1555, he was taken to the center of Gloucester. About 7,000 were present, it being market day. Hooper nodded cheerfully to friends; then arriving at the stake, he removed his outer clothes while sacks of gunpowder were tied to his armpits and between his legs.

As the silent crowd gazed in terror, Hooper raised his voice and asked them to join him in the Lord's Prayer. The winter sky echoed with 7,000 voices: "Our Father which art in heaven, Hallowed be Thy name. Thy kingdom come. Thy will be done in earth, as it is in heaven. . . ."

The final "Amen" was spoken, and the multitudes watched through tear-clouded eyes as a metal hoop was placed around Hooper's chest to hold him to the stake. The fire was set, but too much green wood had been used, and the wind was strong. It created a slow torture, with Hooper's hair burning a little and his skin swelling from the heat, but without any lethal flames.

Finally the lower part of his body began to smoke as the executioners got a blaze going. Even when his face and mouth blackened, he could be seen praying until his lips finally burned away. John Foxe wrote in his *Book of Martyrs: Hooper struck at his chest until one of his arms fell off, and then continued striking his chest with the other hand while fat, water, and blood spurted out his fingertips. Hooper was about 45 minutes to an hour in the fire. Even so he was like a lamb. Now he reigns as a blessed martyr in the joys of heaven prepared for the faithful in Christ before the foundations of the world.**

Today's Suggested Reading
Matthew 6:8–15

In this manner, therefore, pray: Our Father in heaven, hallowed be Your name. . . . Matthew 6:9

---

*John Foxe, *The New Foxe's Book of Martyrs,* written and updated by Harold J. Chadwick (New Brunswick, NJ: Bridge-Logos Publishers, 1997), p. 177.

June **30**

Treasures in Heaven

Venerable W. A. Criswell used to preach from Joel, ending his sermon with these words: *John Rascus put $300 in the collection plate when it passed, and he said softly, "I'll see you in heaven." Those around him said, "Old John is getting senile. He says he is going to see that $300 in heaven. He may meet his Maker over there, but he certainly won't meet his money."*

Now, the church treasurer used some of that $300 to pay the electric bill. He gave some of it to the preacher to buy gasoline. Some went to ministerial students, and some to the mission field.

Early one morning, John Rascus died in his sleep. On that first Lord's Day in glory, he walked down the golden streets and a young fellow came up and said, "Thank you, brother John. I was cold and lonely and it was a dark night. I saw the lights of the church. Just to get out of the dark, I went in. While there, the darkness left my soul and I found Jesus."

Another came to him saying, "The preacher came to the filling station. As I filled his tank, he told me about Jesus and I gave my heart to the Lord."

Next John met a throng of people who said, "I want to thank you for those students you helped. They preached the gospel to my family, and we found the Lord."

He next met those of strange tongues who said, "Thank you, brother, for sending us the gospel across the seas." Finally old John came to Hallelujah Square and, turning to an angel, he said, "I feel sorry for you angels. You have never known what it is to be saved by the blood of Jesus, My Lord."

John Rascus mused a moment, then added, "And you do not know what it is to transform the possessions of earth into the treasures of heaven."

*"Sir," replied the angel, "all we do is just watch it from the streets of glory."**

Today's Suggested Reading

Matthew 6:16–23

Do not lay up for yourselves treasures on earth, where moth and rust destroy and where thieves break in and steal; but lay up for yourselves treasures in heaven. . . . Matthew 6:19–20

---

*Adapted from *Great Doctrines of the Bible* by W. A. Criswell. Copyright © 1986 by The Zondervan Corporation. Used by permission of Zondervan Publishing House.

July

The Unsinkable Ship

Making Light of Christ

The Sabbath That Never Came

Tolstoy's Tale

From Riches
to Righteousness

Where Your Treasure Is

Jerome is remembered as one of history's great Bible translators. He was a brilliant, brooding fourth-century Christian who rendered the Bible into the Latin version—the Vulgate—which was used for over a thousand years in the Western world.

Jerome had been born in northeast Italy to well-to-do Christian parents who found him so precocious they sent him to study in Rome at the age of twelve. There he remained through his teen years, enjoying the city's sins as well as its schools. And there he was baptized at age nineteen after having visited the catacombs.

Jerome spent his early twenties in retirement, studying pagan literature. Then, wanting a deeper experience with God, he started off toward the Holy Land. The deaths of two friends and a series of other misfortunes drove him again to the Greek and Latin classics; he had learned to escape his problems by burying himself in study.

During a severe illness, Jerome had a life-changing dream, which he later related to his pupil Eustochium: *Such a dazzling light radiated from those who stood by, that, prostrate on the ground, I dared not raise my eyes. When I was asked what my profession was, I said, "I am a Christian." "You lie," said He who presided. "You are . . . not a Christian: where your treasure is, there shall your heart be also."*

Jerome suddenly knew he must forsake the pagan classics and devote himself exclusively to God's Word. He eventually settled in Bethlehem near the Church of the Nativity, plunging into his life's work of studying the Bible and making it available in the common language. He never completely lost his bad temper, but he nonetheless became a hero for generations to come. No one was more frequently portrayed in Medieval or Renaissance art, sometimes being pictured in the desert, sometimes in ecstasy, sometimes in study, sometimes as a church official, and often alongside a lion.

Today's Suggested Reading
Matthew 6:21–24

For where your treasure is, there your heart will be also. Matthew 6:21

Escape from Saigon

In 1975, the Far East Broadcasting Company in Vietnam was caught in the nightmare of the fall of Saigon. South Vietnamese intelligence had intercepted a North Vietnam Communist hit list, and the FEBC personnel were near the top due to their evangelistic efforts.

Robert Bowman, FEBC's president, flew briefly into Vietnam to consult with his staff, and he was asked to address them as they huddled in fear in their broadcast studios. Feeling utterly inadequate, Bob chose to read from Matthew 6:25–27: "Therefore I say to you, do not worry about your life. . . ."

Bob returned to Hong Kong as he and his stateside staff frantically contacted every American official who would talk with them. The fall of Saigon seemed imminent, and normal emigration channels were useless. Finally, the refugees tried a desperate scheme—booking passage on a refugee boat from Saigon Harbor, hoping to evade gunboats in the Mekong Delta and to be rescued on the open seas. But their van developed engine problems, and they missed the launch.

"That wasn't a very dignified way to go anyhow," one of the refugees said laconically. "God is going to fly us out." (As it turned out, the boat was captured on the Mekong and its human cargo seized.)

Returning to their hiding place, the group hoped against hope for word from the American Embassy which was evacuating refugees by helicopters from its roof. Finally the group decided to split up for the night. Just after they had scattered hither and yon through the panicked city, an urgent message arrived from the Embassy: "Come at once! Immediate departure!"

Nothing short of a miracle plucked the various staff members from the frenzied streets of Saigon. They jumped into embassy sedans and were shuttled past checkpoints to the American military terminal to be evacuated to the Philippines. Today some of these faithful workers are still beaming the gospel back to their homeland day and night.

When the Lord "worries" about us, we have no cause to worry.

Today's Suggested Reading
Matthew 6:25–30

Therefore I say to you, do not worry about your life, what you will eat or what you will drink; nor about your body, what you will put on. Matthew 6:25

Adrift

Captain Eddie Rickenbacker and seven crew members ditched their plane into the Pacific on October 21, 1942, and found themselves stranded on three rafts with no water and only four oranges. Tying their boats together, they drifted day after day without food or water, sometimes delirious, tortured by the relentless sun, and constantly encircled by the triangular dorsal fins of sharks.

What followed is one of the most incredible stories of our times. "If it weren't for the fact that I had seven witnesses," Rickenbacker later said, "I wouldn't dare tell this story because it seems so fantastic."

The men credited their amazing survival to something in the pocket of Private Johnny Bartek—a New Testament: pocket-sized, khaki-bound, with a zipper arrangement that made it waterproof. From the beginning, Bartek, a devoted Bible student, maintained his morning and evening devotions. All the men began joining him. Starting in Matthew's Gospel, they soon came to 6:31–34. It immediately became their hope, inspiration, and prayer: *What shall we eat? What shall we drink?—Your heavenly Father knows that you need all these things.*

As the men read those verses day after day, provisions arrived in the nick of time and in bizarre ways. Just when they were near starvation, for example, a bird would inexplicably land on Rickenbacker's head and they would grab it, carve it up for food, and use its innards for fishing bait. Just when they were near death by thirst, a cloud would drift over and fill their raft with water.

Later one of the men, Lieutenant James Whittaker, wrote a best-selling account of the ordeal entitled *We Thought We Heard the Angels Sing,* in which he described finding the Lord during those 21 never-to-be-forgotten days. "I don't think there was a man of us who didn't thank God for that little khaki-covered book," he said. "It led us to prayer and prayer led us to safety."

Today's Suggested Reading

Matthew 6:31–32

. . . your heavenly Father knows that you need all these things. Matthew 6:32

Calculating God's Promises July 4

Some people seem to read this verse from Matthew backward, as though spiritually dyslexic: "Add all these things to your life, and if you have any leftover time, seek the kingdom of God and His righteousness."

But blessed are those who read it as Jesus intended.

Wanamaker Department Stores in the Northeast was started by nineteenth-century businessman John Wanamaker, who was active in Christian causes. He served as the president of the world's largest Sunday school, spoke widely, and advised such evangelical leaders as D. L. Moody. To top it off, he was named Postmaster General of the United States. When someone asked him how he could hold all those positions at once, he replied, "Early in life I read, 'Seek ye first the kingdom of God, and His righteousness, and all these things shall be added unto you.' The Sunday school is my business, and the rest are the things."

As one missionary put it, "If you take care of the things that are important to God, He will take care of the things that are important to you."

Richard Greene of Cary, North Carolina, learned this lesson while in college. He was fretting over bills one day, trying to balance his checkbook. He grew agitated and afraid. "Where will the extra money come from?" he asked aloud. "Please, Lord, help me pay these bills."

As he finished balancing his checkbook, he noticed the final digits on his pocket calculator—6.33. He had six dollars, thirty-three cents left. Suddenly he remembered a verse he had just discovered: Matthew 6:33. He laughed, and took it as a message from the Lord.

Shortly afterward, he received an unexpected scholarship. A little later a friend handed him a check for his month's rent. God provided his needs throughout college, and today Richard is director of public relations for Trans World Radio, beaming the message of Scripture (including Matthew 6:33) around the world.*

Today's Suggested Reading

Matthew 6:33–34

But seek first the kingdom of God and His righteousness, and all these things shall be added to you. Matthew 6:33

---

*Adapted from Richard S. Greene, "Where Will the Money Come From?" in *Decision Magazine*, May, 1997, pp. 32–33.

July 5 A Dead Undertaker Lives

In his little book *The Romance of a Doctor's Visit,* Dr. Walter Wilson told of being asked to assist in the burial of a certain lady. A cold, driving rain was falling on the day of the funeral, and the cemetery road was unpaved. Rather than taking his own car, Wilson asked if he could ride with the young undertaker. As they drove through the mire, Wilson asked, "What do you suppose the Bible means by saying, 'Let the dead bury their dead'?"

"There isn't any Scripture like that in the Bible," replied the undertaker.

"Yes, there is."

"Well, it must be a wrong translation, because it doesn't make any sense. How could a dead person bury a dead person?"

"No, it's not a wrong translation," said Wilson. "These words were spoken by the Lord Jesus Himself."

The undertaker flipped his cigarette out the window and said, "Do you know anything about me, doctor? Has anyone told you about my life? I have been burying many people lately, and it has caused me to think about my own case. Last night after supper, I got out the Bible and read until two o'clock this morning, trying to find out how to become a Christian. Tell me, what did Jesus mean by those words?"

Wilson replied, "You are a dead undertaker driving to the cemetery to bury the dead friend in the back of this hearse. The friend is dead to her family, and you are dead to God. She does not respond to their caresses, their calls, their commands; neither do you respond to the call and love of God."

Wilson went on to explain that Christ had come to give us life in abundance. "We arrived at the cemetery with a live undertaker," he wrote, "though we had started on the journey with a dead one. He who was dead in trespasses and sins was now alive in Christ, having trusted Him who gave His life for his salvation."*

Today's Suggested Reading

Matthew 8:16–22

But Jesus said to him, "Follow Me, and let the dead bury their own dead." Matthew 8:22

---

*Adapted from *The Romance of a Doctor's Visit* by Dr. Walter Wilson (Chicago: Moody Press).

From Riches to Righteousness

So many legends have invaded the story of St. Francis that it is difficult to cull the false from the true. This much, however, is certain: He was a devout man whose love and generosity in Christ's name have inspired Christians for nearly a thousand years.

Francis grew up in a wealthy family in Assisi, Italy, where his father was a textile merchant. As a young man, Francis was spoiled and frivolous; but when a nearby war broke out, he enlisted in the army, was captured, and suffered as a POW until ransomed by his father. His incarceration seems to have changed him; and after his release, he visited Rome, where he was moved by the city's poor. He even exchanged clothes with a beggar to feel what poverty was like.

The young man's growing concern with outcasts angered his father, and the two had a violent argument in which Francis stripped off every scrap of his fine clothing and returned it to his father. The local priest loaned him a robe, and Francis spent the following years caring for lepers and repairing church buildings.

On February 24, 1208, as Francis was worshiping in the church of Portiuncula, the priest read Matthew 10:7–19, in which Christ commissioned the disciples. In particular, Francis was moved by verses 9–10: "Provide neither gold nor silver nor copper in your money belts, nor bag for your journey, nor two tunics, nor sandals, nor staffs; for a worker is worthy of his food."

Francis decided then and there to become an itinerant social worker and evangelistic preacher. He embraced poverty and spent the rest of his life wandering through towns and villages, preaching the gospel and helping the needy. Scores of followers joined him, thus beginning the Franciscan Order (today the largest religious order in the Roman Catholic church).

His ministry and lifestyle took a toll, and Francis grew blind, diseased, and emaciated. He probably died from tuberculoid leprosy in his mid-forties; but his example has lived on mightily.

Today's Suggested Reading
Matthew 10:1–10

Provide neither gold nor silver nor copper in your money belts, nor bag for your journey, nor two tunics, nor sandals, nor staffs; for a worker is worthy of his food. Matthew 10:9–10

The Nestlings

One day a storm knocked a bird's nest onto a friend's roof and four little hatchlings fell through the drainpipe. Doug's young daughters found them, made them a home in a shoe box, and fed them endless amounts of worms. But a couple of mornings later, Audrey came in from the deck saying, "I don't think the birds are alive this morning. It got kind of cold last night."

She disappeared into her bedroom, and presently Doug went to check on her. There she was, a tiny bird in her hand, trying to warm it by the bulb of her desklamp. A tear escaped her eye. "It's my fault, Dad," she said. "I left them out in the cold last night."

That morning Doug drove to the library to study the nesting habits of birds. He learned that many mother birds don't just feed their chicks, they swallow the worms and bugs, partially digest them, then regurgitate them into the babies' mouths. Others hold the food in their mouths while flying to the nest in order to coat it with their own digestive juices. Some mother birds don't just drop the food into the mouths of their young. They actually stick their long beaks almost into the stomachs of the little ones. The feeding is nonstop, with parents making as many as a thousand trips a day. And the mother's own feathers and warmth are necessary at night, for chicks are unable to regulate their own body heat.

Armed with all that and more, Doug sat down to reassure his little girl. In the process, Matthew 10:31 came to his mind. Jesus evidently loved us so much that He Himself fell to earth through the drainpipe of history. He was laid like a nestling in the straw of a barnyard feedbox, and He died like the doves being offered on the altar of the temple in Jerusalem. Now He gathers us tenderly under the security of His wings, saying, "Do not fear therefore; you are of more value than many sparrows."

It was a never-to-be-forgotten bird's-eye view of grace.

Today's Suggested Reading
Matthew 10:27–31

Do not fear therefore; you are of more value than many sparrows. Matthew 10:31

The Cause Demands It

Otis Robinson Bacheler was a Harvard-trained physician who sailed to India as a medical missionary in 1840 for the Free Baptists. He bore heavy family obligations—fathering a total of ten children—and his wife fell ill just as his work in India was beginning to bear fruit. Reluctantly, he gathered his brood and returned to America. En route, four-year-old daughter Katie died and was buried in London. The Bachelers arrived in America exhausted and penniless.

Ten years passed, but all the while Bacheler's heart was in India. His wife's health finally improved, and the family made plans to return to the mission field. But mission funds were too low to finance the relocation of a large family. As he studied Matthew 10:37–39, Bacheler sensed the Lord telling him to return to India alone if necessary. It was a brutal sacrifice, but on July 12, 1862, Dr. Bacheler boarded ship by himself. As the shores of America disappeared, he wrote in a letter: *It may be asked, "Why this departure?" The cause demands it. I am going alone because the state of our treasury is such that my family, even a small portion of it, cannot accompany me. We have been under appointment to return for nearly three years, and waiting for the means to be supplied, but they have not been available. I accept the opportunity with the understanding that, should the means be supplied, my family may follow hereafter.*

The propriety of this arrangement may be questioned by some, but my authority may be found in Matthew 10:37–39.

And now let me say that, though sad thoughts come over me when I think of the dear ones I have left, yet I go forth to the work with a joyful heart, counting it an exalted privilege to labor again in the dark lands of heathenism.

The result was a great ingathering with hundreds coming to Christ during his 53 years as a missionary. A son and a daughter both followed in his footsteps, becoming doctors serving the poor of India in Christ's name.

Today's Suggested Reading
Matthew 10:34–39

He who loves father or mother more than Me is not worthy of Me. And he who loves son or daughter more than Me is not worthy of Me. And he who does not take his cross and follow after Me is not worthy of Me.
Matthew 10:37–38

July **9**

Land of Opportunity

"Everyone in America is rich! I've heard there is gold in the streets for the taking." Those words convinced Weir Seir, living in the slums of Liberia, to stow away aboard a steamer and jump ship in America. But all he found in America's streets was trouble; he was arrested after a string of robberies and sent to the Kansas State Penitentiary.

His first three years of incarceration took a heavy toll. He was caged like an animal, abused by prisoners and guards, and overwhelmed with remorse and shame.

One rainy Sunday he took his place in the "Negro Section" in the prison chapel. Dr. Walter Wilson rose to speak, turning in his Bible to Matthew 11:28. Wilson said that life is hard without Christ, and we become weary and burdened. But Jesus gives inward rest and peace to all who come to Him. Wilson stressed the word "all"—"Come to Me, *all* you who labor. . . ."

Few of the prisoners seemed to listen, and Dr. Wilson left discouraged. But a few days later, he received a letter from Weir Seir. Returning to his cell, the Liberian had read Matthew 11:27–28 repeatedly. Then he said aloud to Christ, "You told me to come, and I am coming right now."

The change in Seir's attitude was immediate, and soon the other prisoners were calling him, "The Parson."

Shortly afterward, Seir was eligible for parole, but he turned it down, saying he wanted to win his prison friends to Christ—which he did.

When finally released, he was given a new suit of clothes and a one-way ticket to Liberia. Weir Seir returned to his native land and became a preacher of the gospel.

He didn't find gold in the streets of America, but he found God in its prisons.

Today's Suggested Reading

Matthew 11:25–30

Come to Me, all you who labor and are heavy laden, and I will give you rest. Matthew 11:28

A Wild Little Company

Robert Raikes is considered the founder of the Sunday school, but Hannah Ball actually beat him to it. She was born on March 13, 1733, one of twelve children in a modest home. Her early years were spent in labor and toil, and it wasn't until 1762, during a violent thunderstorm, that she began thinking of spiritual things. For the next three years, she read her Bible and studied the sermons of various preachers. Then on January 8, 1765, she heard 63-year-old John Wesley preaching from Matthew 15:28: "O woman, great is your faith!" She was so moved by his sermon that she lived "under conviction of sin" for five months before finding "peace and deliverance" on June 3, 1765.

In 1769 (fourteen years before Raikes's school), Hannah began teaching the Bible to children on Sundays and Mondays: *They are a wild little company, but seem willing to be instructed. I labor among them, earnestly desiring to promote the interest of Christ.*

Hannah began corresponding with John Wesley about her work, and he reassured her during discouragement. In 1771, he wrote: "It pleases Him sometimes to let us sow much seed before there is any fruit. But frequently much grows up upon a sudden, at a time and in a manner we least expected."

Wesley sought to duplicate her Sunday schools among his Methodists. "I love Sunday schools much," he wrote. "I verily think these Sunday schools are one of the noblest specimens of charity which have been set on foot in England since the time of William the Conqueror."

In the meantime, the Sunday schools started by newspaper publisher Raikes were taking off, and he had the advantage of media promotion. The Ball and Raikes movements combined to create one of the most powerful forces in modern Christian history. He has gotten the credit, but Hannah Ball paved the way.

And all because the Lord had spoken to her on January 8, 1765, saying: "O woman, great is your faith!"

Today's Suggested Reading
Matthew 15:21–28

Then Jesus answered and said to her, "O woman, great is your faith! Let it be to you as you desire." Matthew 15:28

The Bibleless Peoples

The world's largest missionary force, Wycliffe Bible Translators, was started by a question posed in 1918 to missionary Cameron Townsend. Townsend had come to Guatemala to sell Spanish Bibles, which many of the nation's tribal groups could not read. As Townsend tried to distribute his wares among the quarter-million Cakchiquel-speaking people, one man asked him an unforgettable question: "If your God is so great, why can't He speak my language?"

Townsend was so challenged that he settled among the Cakchiquel, studied their language, and began translating the Bible. A local religious leader called it "the work of the devil," but having little else to read, this man devoured the Cakchiquel Bible and was converted. He burned his false gods, saying, "I served them all my life. I thought it was time they served me, so I made kindling wood out of them and cooked my beans." Thus the Cakchiquel Church was born.

Townsend soon began asking, "If God is so great, why couldn't He speak all the languages of Brazil and Mexico and Africa and Asia?" Traveling to Chicago, he shared his vision with missionary leaders, but they advised him to devote his life to the Cakchiquels.

Townsend returned deeply troubled, uncertain of himself, unsure of the future. In desperation, he asked God to guide him, then opened his Bible and put his finger on a verse at random. It was Matthew 18:12: "What do you think? If a man has a hundred sheep, and one goes astray, does he not leave the ninety-nine and go to the mountains to seek the one that is straying?"

That was Townsend's answer. "Yes, Lord," he prayed, "I'll leave the 250,000 Cakchiquel and go in quest of the Bibleless peoples."

The worldwide work of Wycliffe began in the heart of "Uncle Cam" Townsend then and there. Over 2,000 language groups have now at least part of the Bible in their language, and nearly 6,000 translators are currently working in over 50 countries.

Today's Suggested Reading

Matthew 18:1–14

What do you think? If a man has a hundred sheep, and one of them goes astray, does he not leave the ninety-nine and go to the mountains to seek the one that is straying? Matthew 18:12

My Dear Ann

Over 100 years ago in his book *The Ministry of Healing,* A. J. Gordon told of Ann Mather, a young woman "afflicted with lameness in the feet, for some years having no use of her limbs." Gordon quoted the following from the journal of Ann's father, Methodist leader Joseph Benson:

My dear Ann remained without use of her limbs and indeed without the least feeling of them, or ability to walk a step. We prayed however, incessantly, that it would please the Lord, for the sake of her three little children, to restore her.

This day my family and some of my pious friends went to take tea at her house; Mr. Mather bringing her down in his arms into the dining room. After tea I spoke of the certainty of God's hearing his faithful people, and repeated many of his promises. I also enlarged on Christ's being the same yesterday, today, and forever.

We then kneeled down, and Ann took her infant child and gave it the breast, that it might not disturb us with crying while we were engaged in prayer. I prayed first, then Mr. McDonald; all the company joining fervently. We pleaded the Lord's promises, and especially that whatever two or three of his people should agree to ask, it should be done for them (Matt 18:19). Immediately on rising from our knees, Ann beckoned the nurse to take the child, and then instantly rose up and said, "I can walk, I feel I can!" and proceeded over the room: when her husband, afraid she should fall, stepped to her, saying, "My dear Ann, what are you about?"

She put him off, saying, "I don't need you: I can walk alone," and then walked three times over the floor; after which, going to a corner, she knelt down and said, "O let us give God thanks!"

It was indeed the most affecting scene I ever witnessed in my life. She afterward, without any help, walked up the stairs into her lodging room, and with her husband kneeling down, joined in prayer and praise.

Today's Suggested Reading

Matthew 18:15–20

Again I say to you that if two of you agree on earth concerning anything that they ask, it will be done for them by My Father in heaven. Matthew 18:19

. . . And Harlots

Eva J. Alexander was born to believing parents in Chennai, India, and born again at age 12 during a Billy Graham meeting. In 1963, she married R. D. Alexander, and the two took positions with the Indian government. Eva's job exposed her to the plight of women in her country, and she began speaking out about their status and suffering. For awhile, she became so socially active that her spiritual life suffered. Politics became more important than religion.

But the Lord sent a serious illness that brought her to her knees. "God, if you're real," she prayed, hovering near death in the hospital, "do not allow me to die. I will serve you." Returning home, Eva began reading her Bible again and two words in Matthew 21:31 tore through her mind like torpedoes—*and harlots*. Jesus wanted to bring harlots into His kingdom.

A week later, a nearby pastor told her of a prostitute who had run away from the brothels, and he asked Eva to provide a room for her. "I can't," said Eva. "You keep her." Eva had a husband and four children at home, including two teenage sons. But the Lord again brought Matthew 21:31 to mind, and Eva relented.

Her family was aghast: "What is this? You're turning our house into a brothel!" But their attitudes soon changed, and they accepted this ministry as coming from God. Other girls began showing up, and the Alexander home became a rehabilitation center. Police officers and prisons referred troubled women to Eva, and today up to 15 women live in the Alexander home at any one time. The Alexanders provide medical treatment, job training, and a strong gospel witness. Eva has started a home for the children of prostitutes where 60 children, age 12 months to 13 years, find refuge.

Her husband and children joined her work, and, spurred on by Matthew 21:31, they are bringing many harlots into the Kingdom.*

Today's Suggested Reading
Matthew 21:28–32

Jesus said unto them, "Assuredly, I say to you that tax collectors and harlots enter the kingdom of God before you." Matthew 21:31

---

*Adapted from "Rescuing Women," by Eva J. Alexander in *Decision,* October, 1997, pp. 4–5.

Making Light of Christ

Despite his poor health, Richard Baxter was among the most prolific men of the seventeenth century. By his death in 1691, he had written 160 books, some of them popular to this day. He spent 18 months in the Tower of London for his Puritan views, yet he preached more sermons than perhaps any other vicar of his era. One of his most potent messages was based on Matthew 22:5, on making light of Christ.

It is one of the wonders of the world, that when God hath so loved the world as to send His Son, that most of the world should make light of it. God takes no pleasure in the death of sinners, but rather that they return and live. But men take such pleasure in sin that they will die before they will return. The Lord Jesus was content to be their Physician, and hath provided a sufficient plaster of His own blood: but if men make light of it, and will not apply it, what wonder if they perish after all?

As a sinner, thou art viler than a toad: yet Christ was so far from making light of thee that He came down into the flesh and lived a life of suffering. How can you have any quietness in your minds! How can you eat, or drink, or rest till you have some ground of everlasting consolation!

The time is near when Christ and salvation will not be made light of as they are now. When God hath shaken those careless souls out of their bodies, and you must answer for all your sins, then what would you give for a savior!

You that can not make light of a little sickness or want, or of natural death, no, not of a tooth-ache, but groan as if you were undone; how will you then make light of the fury of the Lord, which will burn against the despisers of his grace! Doth it not behoove you beforehand to think of these things?

Today's Suggested Reading
Matthew 22:1–14

But they made light of it. Matthew 22:5

July 15 Saved by His Own Sermon

Quaint, bizarre, eccentric, peculiar—those words describe a little, wiry coal miner named Billy Bray, of Cornwell, England. Before his conversion in November, 1832, Billy lived a vile life. After finding Christ, he became a flaming evangelist and lay preacher.

On a mountain near his home lived a cluster of non-Christian families. Billy, after working underground all day, would emerge from the mines and set out for the mountain, where he visited door-to-door, evangelizing the families. Soon every inhabitant was converted, and a church house was built.

The Church of England sent Rev. W. Haslam to shepherd the families, but when Billy heard the new parson preach, he was upset. Haslam didn't seem to know the gospel. Billy felt the pastor wasn't truly a Christian himself, and he told him so.

Haslam was shaken. The next Sunday as he stood to preach, he announced his text, Matthew 22:42: "What think ye of Christ?" As he began delivering his message, he felt himself trusting Christ as Savior. He was converted while preaching his own sermon.

Billy heard of it and came for a visit. When Haslam came to the door, Billy asked, "Converted, kind sir?" The man said, "Yes, thank God, I am." Billy was so happy, he threw his arms around him, lifted him up, and carried him around the room shouting, "Glory, glory, the parson's converted! Glory be to God."

Mrs. Haslam, hearing the commotion, entered the room, and Billy cried, "Be the missis converted?" She replied, "Yes, thank God." Billy started toward her, but instead of picking her up, he just grinned ear to ear and said, "Oh, I be so happy I can hardly live. Glory! Glory be to God!"

Today's Suggested Reading
Matthew 22:41–46

*What think ye of Christ? Matthew 22:42**

*King James Version

Fuel

Only the computers of heaven will be able to tabulate the number of Christians who will populate eternity because of the ministry of A. B. Simpson. Born in Canada's maritime provinces in 1843, Simpson became a powerful soul-winner and missionary statesman. He was a pastor, the editor of *Alliance Weekly,* and the author of more than 70 books and many poems and hymns. But Simpson is primarily remembered as the founder of two missionary societies which combined in 1897 as the Christian and Missionary Alliance; and for establishing a Bible and missionary training school in Nyack, New York, which is active to this day.

Matthew 24:14 fueled Simpson's energy.

In the early days of the Christian and Missionary Alliance, a reporter from the *New York Journal* called on Simpson for an interview. They discussed the hundreds of CMA missionaries who were spanning the globe, and the hundreds of thousands of dollars going for their support. Then the reporter abruptly asked, "Do you know when the Lord is coming back?"

"Yes," said Simpson. "And I will tell you if you will promise to print just what I say, references and all."

The reporter nodded and readied his pencil.

"Put this down," said Simpson. "'And this gospel of the kingdom shall be preached in all the world as a witness unto all nations; and then shall the end come'—Matthew 24:14. Have you written down the reference?"

"Yes, what more?"

"Nothing more."

"Do you mean to say you believe that when the gospel has been preached to all nations, Jesus will return?"

"Just that," said Simpson.

"Then," said the reporter, "I think I begin to see daylight."

"What do you think you see?"

"Why I see the motive in this movement."

"Then," said Dr. Simpson, "you see more than some of the doctors of divinity."

Today's Suggested Reading

Matthew 24:1–14

*And this gospel of the kingdom shall be preached in all the world for a witness unto all nations; and then shall the end come. Matthew 24:14**

---

*King James Version

The Darkened Moon

When Bible translator Jim Walton first entered the primeval jungles of La Sabana in Colombia, South America, he thought no one there had previously heard the gospel.

Then he met Andres.

Andres was the oldest son of Chief Fernando of the Muinane tribe, and by occupation a tapper of latex from rubber trees. He lived three days from La Sabana, and he tended about 200 rubber trees over a 100-acre section of jungle. Andres had been asking himself questions about life—where we came from, what happens after death—but had found no satisfying answers.

One night in boredom, Andres had begun fiddling with a transistor radio given him by a rubber baron. Suddenly he picked up a sharp, clear signal from Trans World Radio in Bonaire. A man was reading these words: "The sun (shall) be darkened, and the moon shall not give her light, and the stars shall fall from heaven, and the powers of the heavens shall be shaken: And then shall appear the sign of the Son of man coming in the clouds of heaven. . . ."

By strange coincidence, that very evening the moon did not give its light. Though Andres didn't understand it at the time, a total lunar eclipse had covered the entire jungle with blackness. The young Colombian was deeply stirred.

Andres soon returned home, and the next day Jim Walton arrived unexpectedly and, opening his New Testament in front of Chief Fernando's guest house, began to read. Andres was spellbound.

When I saw you reading that book, I knew it was the book from the radio, the book that had the truth. And when you said it was God's Word, and you wanted to put it in my language, I determined to help you.

He did help. For the next 18 years, Andres served Jim as co-translator, helping complete the first draft of the New Testament and portions of the Old Testament.

Today's Suggested Reading

Matthew 24:29–35

*Immediately after the tribulation of those days shall the sun be darkened, and the moon shall not give her light, and the stars shall fall from heaven, and the powers of the heavens shall be shaken. Matthew 24:29**

---

*King James Version

Well Done

July **18**

During a bitterly cold January in 1875, Rev. Richard S. Storrs of Brooklyn warmed the minds of the ministerial students of Union Theological Seminary as guest lecturer on the subject *Preaching Without Notes.* Storrs had originally prepared for the bar. He had seen America's greatest lawyers sway stubborn juries and judges by looking them in the eye and speaking persuasively without notes.

I could not see, therefore, why a minister should not do before his congregation [*that*] *which lawyers do all the time in the courts; and when my plans of life changed under the impulse of God's Spirit and I devoted myself to the ministry, I determined to preach without manuscript.*

For three weeks, Storrs stirred the students, telling them why and how to preach without notes; then on January 27, 1875, he ended his lectures, saying:

Your success may not come at the precise time when you expect it, or in the way which you anticipate. It may not come so that you yourselves shall see it on earth. The Master seemed to have but small success: twelve apostles, and one of them a traitor. Paul, the greatest preacher, did not appear to achieve large success: a few scattered congregations, error and dissension among them. But success is certain in the end. Out of the work come consequences of good—immense if unseen. In all your life remember this! Expect the time when the Son of Man, no more invisible, shall be revealed; and when by Him shall be opened to you that grand and bright expanse of heaven in which he may say to all of us: "On earth ye have been the rulers over a few things; a few facilities, a few knowledges, a few opportunities: Lo, I will make you rulers over many things, in this kingdom of my Father."

Today's Suggested Reading

Matthew 25:14–30

Well done, good and faithful servant; you were faithful over a few things, I will make you ruler over many things. Enter into the joy of your lord. Matthew 25:21

Tolstoy's Tale

At about age 50, Russian novelist Leo Tolstoy developed a profound interest in spiritual things and began studying the Gospels in earnest. Unfortunately, he rejected more than he accepted, repudiating belief in miracles, the deity of Christ, the personality of God, and the plan of salvation. Tolstoy reduced Christianity to little more than charity and good works.

He nonetheless wrote about it beautifully, and nothing sums up his philosophy better than this story which Tolstoy based on one of his favorite passages, Matthew 25:31–40:

One night Martin Avdeitch, a humble shoemaker, dozing over his open Bible, suddenly seemed to hear a voice saying, "Martin! Look thou into the street tomorrow, for I am coming to visit thee." Convinced the Lord Jesus was going to visit him, Martin awoke the next morning with nervous excitement. But no one showed up that day except a succession of penniless and pitiful souls: an aged veteran, a shivering mother and newborn, an old peddler woman and a frightened boy who had filched one of her apples.

With a kind heart, Martin cared for each person; but as evening fell, he was disappointed that Jesus had not visited that day. Putting on his spectacles, he took up his Bible with a sigh, and it opened to Matthew 25. Martin read: "For I was hungry and you gave Me food; I was thirsty and you gave Me drink; I was a stranger and you took Me in."

Lord, when did we do these things?

Looking on down the page, Martin read: "Assuredly, I say to you, inasmuch as you did it to one of the least of these My brethren, you did it to Me."

Then Avdeitch understood that the vision had come true, and that his Savior had in very truth visited him that day, and that he had received Him.

Today's Suggested Reading
Matthew 25:31–46

And the King will answer and say to them, "Assuredly, I say to you, inasmuch as you did it to one of the least of these My brethren, you did it to Me."
Matthew 25:40

The Sabbath That Never Came

On October 8, 1871, D. L. Moody preached in Chicago's Farwell Hall. Our eternal destiny, he said, depends on our answer to Pilate's question: "What shall I do with Jesus?" At the conclusion of his sermon, Moody said: *I wish you would take this text home with you and turn it over in your minds during the week, and next Sabbath we will decide what to do with Jesus of Nazareth.*

But there was no next Sabbath. As soloist Ira Sankey closed the meeting singing, "Today the Savior Calls," his voice was suddenly drowned out by cries of alarm. The Great Chicago Fire had started and was sweeping toward the Hall. That night, the city and many of its citizens perished.

Twenty-two years later on the anniversary of the fire, Moody again spoke in Chicago from Matthew 27:22, saying: *What a mistake! I remember Mr. Sankey's singing, and how his voice rang: "Today the Savior calls, for refuge fly! The storm of justice falls, and death is nigh!"*

I have never seen that congregation since. I have hard work to keep back the tears today. Twenty-two years have passed away, and I have not seen that congregation since, and I never will meet those people again until I meet them in another world. But I want to tell you of one lesson I learned that night, which I have never forgotten, and that is, when I preach, to press Christ upon the people then and there, and try to bring them to a decision on the spot.

You will notice that Pilate was just in the condition of my audience that night, just the condition that you are in today—he had to decide then and there what to do with Jesus. The thing was sprung on him suddenly.

I have asked God many times to forgive me for telling people that night to take a week to think it over. I have never dared to give an audience a week to think of their salvation since.

Today's Suggested Reading
Matthew 27:15–26

Pilate said to them, "What then shall I do with Jesus who is called Christ?" Matthew 27:22

July **21**

How to Thaw the Heart

I once read of a man in Dundee, Scotland, who was confined to bed for forty years, having broken his neck in a fall at age fifteen. But his spirit remained unbroken, and his cheer and courage so inspired people that he enjoyed a constant stream of guests. One day a visitor asked him, "Doesn't Satan ever tempt you to doubt God?"

"Oh, yes," replied the man. "He does try to tempt me. I lie here and see my old schoolmates driving along in their carriages and Satan whispers, 'If God is so good, why does He keep you here all these years? Why did he permit your neck to be broken?' "

"What do you do when Satan whispers those things?" asked the guest.

"Ah," replied the invalid, "I take him to Calvary, show him Christ, and point to those deep wounds, and say, 'You see, he *does* love me.' And Satan has no answer to that. He flees every time."

That story reminds me of another, this one having to do with Dr. Eric Frykenberg, veteran missionary to India. Frykenberg was a great storyteller, and he could vividly describe scenes and events from his fifty-plus years in Asia. One day someone asked him, "Dr. Frykenberg, what is the most difficult problem you ever faced?"

Without hesitation, he answered, "It was when my heart would grow cold before God. When that happened, I knew I was too busy. I also knew it was time to get away. So I would take my Bible and go off to the hills alone. I'd open my Bible to Matthew 27, the story of the crucifixion, and I would wrap my arms around the cross."

"And then," Frykenberg said, "I'd be ready to go back to work."

Today's Suggested Reading

Matthew 27:27–35

Then they crucified Him. Matthew 27:35

"On Those Words I Staked Everything"

July **22**

As David Livingstone, the great missionary and explorer, journeyed down the Zambezi River, searching for the ultimate entrance into Central Africa from the Eastern Coast, he was wide-eyed. The country teemed with elephants, buffalo, and all kinds of wildlife. A thousand dangers encompassed him, from snakes to fevers to savages.

He gradually left friendlier areas and pressed on toward uncharted regions filled with hostile tribes. His guides were nervous, nerves taut, motions quick. Reports filtered in of warriors and headhunters massing against them, ready to massacre his whole party.

Livingstone pulled his Bible from his baggage, opened it, and ran his finger again across his favorite passage, Matthew 28:20, and his courage revived like the rising sun.

In his journal that evening, January 14, 1856, he wrote: *Felt much turmoil of spirit in prospect of having all my plans for the welfare of this great region and this teeming population knocked on the head. But I read that Jesus said, "Lo, I am with you alway, even unto the end of the world." It is the word of a gentleman of the most strict and sacred honor, so there's an end of it! I feel quite calm now, thank God!*

The next morning, he pressed on. *Nothing earthly shall make me give up my work in despair. I encourage myself in the Lord my God, and go forward.*

Later, having returned to Scotland and England on furlough, Livingstone was considered a national hero. When Glasgow University arranged a well-publicized ceremony honoring him, Livingstone spoke freely of his determination to soon return to Africa: *But I return without misgiving and with great gladness. For would you like me to tell you what supported me through all the years of exile among people whose language I could not understand, and whose attitude toward me was often hostile? It was this: "Lo, I am with you alway, even unto the end of the world." On those words I staked everything, and they never failed.*

Today's Suggested Reading

Matthew 28:16–20

*"Go ye therefore, and teach all nations . . . and, lo, I am with you alway, even unto the end of the world." Matthew 28:19–20**

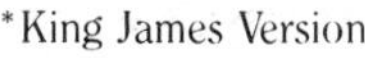

*King James Version

July **23**

One Sermon, 20,000 Converts

For fifty years A. B. Earle evangelized America, traveling 325,000 miles, preaching 19,780 times, and witnessing 150,000 conversions. He trekked from city to city, uniting local churches into powerful crusade services.

The surprising thing is that Earle was no great preacher. His skill was but average; his voice, plain; his facial expressions, unattractive; his sermons, dated. He wasn't highly emotional, and his grammar and rhetoric were faulty.

But his listeners were gripped by God's presence and power. The reality of the Holy Spirit seemed to descend, and people were often heard praying at midnight in the streets and houses following his services.

His secret? Earle started preaching in 1830 at age 18, but it was in 1860 that *I began to feel an inexpressible longing for the fullness of Christ. I loved the ministry, but felt inward unrest. Seasons of joy would be followed by doubt. In this state I was exposed to severe attacks of the enemy.*

In November 1863, Earle renewed his surrender to Christ during a period of intense prayer *and all at once a heavenly peace filled the vacuum, leaving no unrest. For the first time in my life, I had the rest which is more than peace. Jesus has been my all since then. And my success in leading souls to Jesus has been much greater.*

About that success, Earle said, *I have found that the severest threatenings of the law of God have a prominent place in leading men to Christ. They must see themselves LOST before they will cry for mercy. They will not escape danger until they see it. I have reason to believe a single sermon I have often preached on "The Sin That Hath Never Forgiveness" (Mark 3:29), has been the means of more than 20,000 conversions. I have known scores to give themselves to Christ under this sermon again and again. The wicked will never flee from the wrath to come until they are fully satisfied there IS wrath.*

Today's Suggested Reading

Mark 3:23–34

. . . but he who blasphemes against the Holy Spirit never has forgiveness, but is subject to eternal condemnation. Mark 3:29

The Unsinkable Ship

One of Scripture's finest cameos is of a wearied Jesus asleep in the stern of a rowboat as his frantic followers battle the elements. It paints itself vividly in our minds and leaps easily from the page to the pulpit.

Though I can't confirm this story, I read once that this is the text used in Belfast on the Sunday following the sinking of the *Titanic*. The great ship had been built in Belfast, and a tremendous amount of local pride went down with the ship—along with sixteen skilled mechanics, all members of the local church. Even strong men meeting on the city's streets, grasped hands, burst into tears, and parted without speaking a word.

That Sunday, the minister read this story and told his somber congregation that only one vessel in all history had been truly unsinkable: the frail boat occupied by the sleeping Savior. And, he added, the only hearts that can weather the storms are those in which the Lord likewise abides.

This was also the text used by Charles Fuller to launch his far-famed radio ministry. In February, 1929, Fuller spoke for ten days at the Cadle Tabernacle in Indianapolis. One day without warning, he was asked to fill in for the regular speaker on a local gospel radio program. Radio was a newfangled invention, and for Fuller, a new experience. He quickly selected Mark 4:35–41, using these four points: A Great Peril; A Great Plea; A Great Peace; A Great Personage.

The switchboard lit up, and large volumes of mail arrived; and as Fuller traveled by train back to southern California, he was seized by a burden for radio work. Somewhere in the night, tossing and turning in his railway berth, Fuller told the Lord he would go on the radio regularly should the door open.

It did open. Fuller was soon preaching to twenty million listeners each week on his Old-Fashioned Revival Hour from Long Beach Auditorium, and his ministry shaped the history of radio evangelism.

Today's Suggested Reading
Mark 4:22–41

Then He arose and rebuked the wind, and said to the sea, "Peace, be still!" And the wind ceased and there was a great calm. Mark 4:39

Coming Apart

Jesus spoke these words of today's reading, thinking not just of his disciples but of his vast army who would occupy subsequent Christian history. We all need little "Sabbaths" now and again to keep us healthy. "If we don't come apart," Vance Havner once quipped, "we *will* come apart."

Many learn this the hard way. Asahel Nettleton, for example, was an assiduous preacher in the early 1800s whose ministry was nearly cut short by an attack of exhaustion and typhus fever.

Nettleton had been converted during the Great Revival of 1800, and, after graduating from Yale, became a revivalist himself. From his first sermons, Nettleton began winning crowds of people to Christ; and he was in great demand throughout Connecticut, Massachusetts, and New York. But his exacting schedule brought him to the gates of death in 1822, and for two years he was laid aside from ministry. He never fully recovered his health. Though he resumed preaching in 1824, he never regained his strength.

Once while resting in the Catskills, he wrote to a theological student about the physical and spiritual benefits of rest: *Every itinerant preacher, especially if he has been engaged in a revival of religion, must feel the need of this direction, "Come ye yourselves apart into a desert place, and rest awhile," or suffer greatly if he long neglect it. I could not advise any one to be employed in a powerful revival more than three months, without retiring into solitude for a short time, to review the past, and to attend to his own heart. He will find much to lament, and much to correct; and it is by deep and solemn reflection upon the past, and by this only, that he can reap the advantages of past experience.*

As it turned out, Nettleton still had a number of years left, and before he died in his early 60s, he won vast numbers to the Lord. Much of his latter success came from pacing himself, by "doing more by doing less."

Today's Suggested Reading

Mark 6:30–34

And He said to them, "Come aside by yourselves to a deserted place and rest awhile." Mark 6:31

Finishing His Chapter

It sometimes takes a while for young people to find their way.

Consider Thomas. At 16, he wanted to be a teacher, but soon changed his mind. He next decided to seek his fortune in the West Indies, but aborted plans just before boarding ship. He then tried one thing after another, but couldn't find his niche. Traveling down to London, he drifted around town looking for work and finding none. Giving his last coin to a beggar, he was reduced to poverty himself.

But Thomas Nelson was a Christian, born to praying Scottish parents, and the Lord brought news to his ears about a job as a publisher's apprentice on Paternoster Row. Nelson checked it out, and there he found his calling. He had always loved Christian books, and now he discovered pleasure in printing them. He started weekly Bible clubs in London, thus sharing the gospel by both print and voice. He prospered and soon saved enough to return to Edinburgh to open a used bookshop. Soon he was publishing his own materials, aiming them toward the masses, seeking to provide affordable Christian literature for an eager and expanding market.

Eventually his teenage sons joined the business, and by 1853 Thomas Nelson and Sons had become the largest publishing house in Scotland. The next year, Thomas, Jr. sailed to New York to open an office there, making Nelson the first British publisher to establish a branch in America.

Today, over 200 years later, Thomas Nelson is the largest publisher of Bibles and Christian literature in the world. Not bad for a boy who had trouble finding his way.

It's no wonder that when he learned in 1861 that he was dying, Nelson was unruffled. "I thought so," he said. "My days are wholly in God's hands. He doeth all things well. His will be done!"

Then picking up the Bible by his bed, he said, "Now I must finish my chapter."

Today's Suggested Reading

Mark 7:31–37

And they were astonished beyond measure, saying, "He has done all things well. He makes both the deaf to hear and the mute to speak." Mark 7:37

July **27** Who Is General Jackson?

Charlemagne, it is said, gave instructions to be buried in the royal posture of a king upon his throne, with the Gospels opened on his knees, his sword beside him, and his crown upon his head.

When his tomb was later uncovered, there he was. The crown was still perched on his skull, and a bony finger rested on these words: "What will it profit a man if he gains the whole world, and loses his own soul?"

American evangelist Peter Cartwright was preaching from the same text in 1818 at a Presbyterian Church in Nashville. It was a beautiful October evening, and the church was packed. Just as Cartwright bellowed the words, "What will it profit a man if he gains the whole world, and loses his own soul?" in walked General Andrew Jackson who was staying nearby.

Jackson (who didn't come to Christ until late in life) was a fiery-tempered, hard-drinking, horse-racing, duel-fighting hero. Instantly a buzz swept over the congregation and heads turned. The host pastor, Rev. Mac, excitedly pulled Cartwright's coattail and whispered, "General Jackson has come in."

Cartwright roared back, "Who is General Jackson? Who is General Jackson?" He then declared that if the General didn't get his soul converted, God will damn him to hell as quickly as a pagan savage.

Rev. Mac was horrified, and the next morning rose at the crack of dawn to apologize to the General. But later in the day, Cartwright and Jackson met each other on the street. Reaching out his hand, Jackson said, "Cartwright, you are a man after my own heart. I am surprised at Mr. Mac, to think I would be offended at you. No, sir; I told him I highly approved of your independence; that a minister of Jesus Christ ought to love everybody and fear no mortal man. I told Mr. Mac that if I had a few thousand such independent, fearless officers as you are, and a well-drilled army, I could take old England."

Today's Suggested Reading
Mark 8:31–38

For what will it profit a man if he gains the whole world, and loses his own soul? Mark 8:36

Dropped from Heaven

David Marks, born in 1805, so craved education that, when 13 years old, he walked 368 miles to enroll in a school in Providence, Rhode Island, only to be sent back home for lack of finances. Marks found solace, however, among the Free Will Baptists of New England who accepted him as a "boy preacher" and sent him out as a young itinerant. Leaving home was a bittersweet experience.

My parents followed me to the corner of the house. My weeping father then took me by the hand, and in a faltering voice, said, "Whenever you wish to return, my house shall be your home. God bless you, my son. Farewell." My dear mother then giving me a dollar, grasped my hand, and pressed it affectionately. On casting a look at her features, I saw they were convulsed; the big swelling tears rolling fast from her eyes. Her chin quivered, her lips moved, and she faintly articulated, "Adieu! my child, adieu! The Lord go with thee." My spirit almost failed within me.

Coming to a rise of ground in sight of my father's house, I turned to view once more the beloved forms of those dear parents, and cast on them my last look.

But while grief was almost bursting my heart, the sweet promise of Christ, contained in Mark 10:29–30, dropped as if from heaven into my soul: "There is no man that hath left house, or brethren, or sisters, or father, or mother, or wife, or children, or lands, for my sake, and the gospel's, but he shall receive a hundredfold now in this time . . . and in the world to come eternal life." My mourning was now turned into rejoicing, and my tears into songs of praise.

Marks went on to evangelize vast portions of New England and the young American Midwest, dying in 1845, more or less from exhaustion, at age 40.

Today's Suggested Reading
Mark 10:27–31

*Verily I say unto you, There is no man that hath left house, or brethren, or sisters, or father, or mother, or wife, or children, or lands, for my sake, and the gospel's, but he shall receive a hundredfold now in this time, houses, and brethren, and sisters, and mothers, and children, and lands, with persecutions; and in the world to come eternal life. Mark 10:29–30**

*King James Version

The Wounded Healer

In his book *Healing for Damaged Emotions,* pastor David Seamands tells of counseling a woman named Betty and her husband. The couple was deeply committed to Christ. They were even preparing for Christian service. They loved each other, and their marriage was solid.

But they had recently sensed a growing distance between them, and Betty had become depressed and withdrawn. To her surprise, as they met with Seamands, she began crying uncontrollably.

In the next session, Betty began sharing her story. She was born to parents who didn't want her, to parents who married each other merely because she had been an "accident." Three years later, as another baby was on the way, Betty's father became involved in an adulterous affair. The resulting divorce was deeply and painfully scratched into Betty's memory. *She vividly remembered that final day when her father walked out the door and left home. She remembered being in her own little crib-bed in the room when it happened; hearing the vicious quarrel and the terrifying moment when he left. It had left an aching, malignant core of deep pain within her.*

As Seamands helped Betty to process her feelings, he asked, "If you could have said something to your father from your crib at that moment—what would you have said?"

With sobs, Betty cried, "Oh Daddy, please don't leave me!"

*Later, as we prayed together, it dawned on me that if we were to translate Christ's cry of dereliction from the cross ("My God, My God, why hast Thou forsaken Me?") into a paraphrase for a child, we couldn't improve on Betty's words. Suddenly I realized that because of what Jesus experienced on that cross, He understands the cries heard so often in our day, the cries of millions of little children, "Daddy," or "Mommy, please don't leave me!" But they do leave. And the Wounded Healer understands those cries and is touched with the feelings of those children.**

Today's Suggested Reading

Mark 15:33–39

And at the ninth hour Jesus cried out with a loud voice, saying, "Eloi, eloi, lama sabachthani?" which is translated, "My God, My God, why have You forsaken Me?" Mark 15:34

---

*Adapted from David Seamands, *Healing For Damaged Emotions* (Wheaton, IL: Victor Books, 1986), pp. 139–143.

Henry and Hiram

They found the 17-year-old crumpled up on the steps of Yale University in New Haven, weeping. He was from Hawaii, and three years before he had watched his parents slain before his eyes. Having fled the islands by working on ships, he gradually made his way to Yale, only to be rejected for admission.

But some theology students found Henry Obookiah on the steps, took an interest in him, and led him to Christ. One of the students was named Hiram Bingham, and Henry and Hiram became good friends. As they studied the Bible together, they were deeply impressed with the Great Commission as stated in Mark 16:15: "Go into all the world and preach the gospel to every creature." Henry Obookiah died shortly afterward, and a grieving Hiram felt he should sail to Henry's homeland as a missionary. "We can hardly fail the injunction, 'Go ye into all the world and preach the gospel to every creature,'" he wrote.

Once in Hawaii, Hiram and his fellow workers began translating the New Testament, establishing schools, and tending the sick and diseased. As he preached the gospel, he often used his favorite text, Mark 16:15. A typical journal entry reads: "I discoursed on the great commission given by Christ to his disciples to proclaim his gospel to all the world."

He baptized his first convert in the summer of 1823, Keopuolani, mother of the king. Within five years, over 12,000 people were regularly attending Sunday services at several stations, and 26,000 students were enrolled in mission schools. By 1838, the islands were in a state of full revival, with thousands coming to Christ. Over 1,705 people were baptized on a single day, July 1, 1838.

Hiram Bingham returned home, broken in health, in 1841; but he had been an active participant in one of the greatest evangelistic efforts in Christian history.

Today's Suggested Reading

Mark 16:1–15

And He said to them, "Go into all the world and preach the gospel to every creature." Mark 16:15

July **31**

That Old Serpent

The first massive missions effort among Protestants occurred when the Moravians of central Europe fanned around the globe with the message of Christ. One of them, Louis Daehne, settled along the northern coast of South America, among the Arawak Indians in Dutch Guiana (Surinam). There he found enough danger for a dozen lifetimes.

Often Daehne was awakened at night by the roar of jaguars prowling around his hut for food. He was once attacked by poisonous black ants, each one an inch long and packed with venom, which stung him until he dropped to the ground senseless. On another occasion, his hut was surrounded by fifty bloodthirsty Indians wanting to kill him. Coming out to meet them, he began telling them of the Lord Jesus, and the headhunters were completely disarmed by the gospel.

But perhaps his most harrowing experience involved a large snake that slithered into his hut and coiled on a shelf above his hammock. When Daehne unwittingly threw himself on his hammock to rest, the snake uncoiled and slithered over his head and face, biting him in the neck and injecting him with its venom.

Daehne gripped the writhing serpent, but in the scuffle it bit him several more times, fastening hard on his head and winding its cable-like body around his neck. The missionary struggled furiously, but the snake was a powerful one. Finally giving up, Daehne reached for a piece of chalk and wrote on the table by the hammock, "A serpent has killed me."

But just as he finished writing those words, Mark 16:18 flashed to his mind: "They will take up serpents . . . it will by no means hurt them." Summoning his last ounce of strength, Daehne gripped the snake again, wrenched it loose, and flung it from the hut.

After recovering from the shock, Louis Daehne suffered no ill effects.

Today's Suggested Reading
Mark 16:16–20

. . . they will take up serpents; and if they drink anything deadly, it will by no means hurt them; they will lay hands on the sick, and they will recover. Mark 16:18

August

The Lord's Handmaid

The Transformation

White for the Harvest

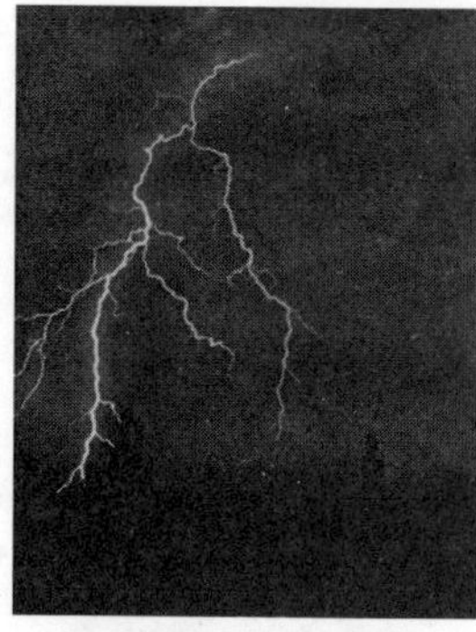

Neither Lucifer
nor Lightning

A Long Hard Row

August 1 The Lord's Handmaid

Ann Hasseltine, born in Massachusetts in 1789, grew up in a distinguished family. She was highly intelligent and much sought after. As a teenager, Ann gave herself to the Lord, praying: "Direct me in Thy service, and I ask no more. I would not choose my position of work, or place of labor. Only let me know Thy will, and I will readily comply."

She was a 21-year-old schoolteacher when she met young Adoniram Judson, who wanted to become a missionary; and when Adoniram later wrote to Ann's father asking for her hand, he said: *I have now to ask whether you can consent to part with your daughter early next spring to see her no more in this world. Whether you can consent to her departure for a heathen land, and her subjection to the hardships of a missionary life. Whether you can consent to her exposure to every kind of want and distress, insult, persecution, and perhaps a violent death. . . .*

Ann, meanwhile, was pondering the same questions. In her journal, she wrote: *God has an undoubted right to do with me as seemeth good in His sight. I rejoice that I am in His hand—that He is everywhere present and can protect me in one place as well as another. When I am called to face danger, to pass through scenes of terror and distress, He can inspire me with fortitude, and enable me to trust Him. Whether I spend my days in India or America, I desire to spend them in the service of God, and to spend eternity in His presence. I am quite willing to give up temporal comforts and live a life of hardship and trial, if it be the will of God. "Behold the handmaid of the Lord; be it unto me according to thy word" (Luke 1:38).*

So it was that Adoniram and Ann Judson became the first foreign missionaries ever sent from the shores of America.

Today's Suggested Reading
Luke 1:26–38

*And Mary said, Behold the handmaid of the Lord; be it unto me according to thy word. Luke 1:38**

*King James Version

Come and Worship

When the Moravian Christians of Europe launched Protestant missions, they did it at a cost. Many of them had to leave their children behind in boarding schools across England and the continent.

And so it was that the Montgomery family reluctantly placed six-year-old James in such an institution as they shipped off as foreign missionaries to the West Indies. When they later perished, James, left with nothing, spent his teenage years drifting from pillar to post, writing poetry and trying his hand at one thing then another.

In his early twenties, he began working for a British newspaper, the *Sheffield Iris,* and there he found his niche. When his editorials proved unpopular with the local officials, he was thrown into jail and fined twenty pounds. But he emerged from prison a celebrity, and he used his newly acquired fame to promote his favorite issues.

Chief among them was the gospel. Despite the loss of his parents and all his hardships, James Montgomery remained devoted to Christ and the Scriptures.

As the years passed, he became the most respected leader in Sheffield, and his writings were eagerly read by its citizens. Early on Christmas Eve, 1816, James, 45, opened his Bible to Luke 2, and was deeply impressed by verse 13. Pondering the story of the heralding angels, he took his pen and started writing. By the end of the day, his new Christmas poem was being delivered to England in the pages of his newspaper. It was later set to music and was first sung on Christmas Day, 1821, in a Moravian Church in England.

His parents would have been proud.

Angels from the realms of glory,
Wing your flight o'er all the earth;
Ye who sang creation's story,
Now proclaim Messiah's birth;
Come and worship, Come and worship,
Worship Christ the new-born King.

Today's Suggested Reading
Luke 2:1–14

And suddenly there was with the angel a multitude of the heavenly host praising God. Luke 2:13

August **3**

The Awful Separation

Jean-Baptiste Massillon was France's George Whitefield, a master in the pulpit, a prince of preachers, known for his brilliant thinking, powerful voice, and wide-ranging emotions. King Louis XIV once told him, "Father, I have heard many great orators in this chapel, and have been highly pleased with them, but whenever I hear you, I go away displeased with myself, for I see my own character."

One of Massillon's greatest sermons was based on Luke 4:27:

The number of lepers was great in the time of Elijah; and Naaman was only cured. In all times the number of the saved has been small. The family of Noah alone was saved from the general flood; Abraham was chosen from among men to be the sole depository of the covenant with God; Joshua and Caleb the only two of 600,000 Hebrews who saw the Land of Promise. Job the only upright man in the land of Uz. Lot in Sodom. [*There are*] *two roads—one narrow, rugged, and of small number; the other broad, open, strewed with flowers, and almost the general path of men.*

Now I ask you, I ask it with dread—were Jesus Christ to appear in this assembly to judge us, to make the awful separation between the sheep and the goats, do you believe that most of us would be placed at His right hand? Do you believe the number of us would be equal? Do you believe there would even be found ten upright servants of the Lord? I ask you!

My brethren, our ruin is almost certain! Yet we think not of it!

In the midst of the world, you are to live for God's glory, and not follow the multitude. It is Thou, O Lord! whom we ought to adore. If you wish to be of the small number, say in the secrecy of your heart, "It is Thou alone, O my God! whom we ought to adore. I will have no other law than Thy holy law. Thou wilt be my God in the midst of Babylon, as Thou wilt one day be in Jerusalem above!"

Today's Suggested Reading

Luke 4:23–30

And many lepers were in Israel in the time of Elisha the prophet, and none of them was cleansed except Naaman the Syrian. Luke 4:27

Down to His Underwear August 4

How literally to interpret this verse from Luke is a matter of opinion, but one man determined to obey it to the letter. He was Henry Richards, missionary to Africa with the Livingstone Inland Mission. He decided to begin his ministry in the village of Banza Mateke by translating the Gospel of Luke into the local tribal language. He would translate a handful of verses each day, and regularly preach to the tribe from the verses he had translated.

It all went well until he came to Luke 6:30. How could he read this verse to the people, he wondered, and how could he possibly explain it? The village was full of beggars; and, in fact, it was commonplace for the curious villagers to ask him for everything he possessed. He feared that if he actually gave his sparse missionary possessions to everyone who asked for them, he would be soon reduced to his underwear.

Richards went back to chapter one and started preaching through Luke again, to reinforce the Gospel message—and to give himself more time to ponder the problem posed by Luke 6:30. In time, he grew convinced that it meant exactly what it said, so when he came to it, he read it plainly.

Immediately the villagers in Banza Mateke began asking him for his belongings. He began distributing his goods as requested, and was soon reduced to near-underwear status. But to Richards' surprise, the people suddenly began returning his things, and before long every single item was back in its place. "What did it mean?" wondered the missionary.

As the villagers had talked among themselves, they concluded that such an unselfish man must indeed be God's man, and that his message must be God's message, for God "so loved that He gave. . . ." Now the people of Banza Mateke were ready to listen to Henry Richards, and a period of widespread revival and awakening transformed the village.

Today's Suggested Reading

Luke 6:27–31

Give to everyone who asks of you. And from him who takes away your goods do not ask them back. Luke 6:30

"It's Gone!"

It was very cold in Northern China in February, 1932, as missionaries and Chinese Christians worshiped around a stove in the seminary in Hwanghsien. Midway through the service, a woman interrupted the speaker. She was the wife of a national evangelist, and she confessed to nagging her husband mercilessly to make more money, thus forcing him to stay on the road for extended periods.

Soon others were confessing sins, and all day and night a spirit of revival poured forth. Attendance grew to 200. The preacher didn't deliver another sermon, for the Holy Spirit seemed in control of the meetings.

As the prayers continued, missionary Wiley Glass suddenly saw a man's face come to mind, and he thought, "How will I feel when I meet that man in heaven?" This man had once insulted Wiley's wife Eunice, and Wiley had been angry enough to kill him. *I had given him over to God; but I had presumed that God would, of course, send him to hell. Now I realized that bitterness had lingered in me all those years. I was shocked. While I had preached to others, "Love your enemies," I had let hate stay in my own heart. I had never prayed for that man to be saved. The force of conviction was terrific. When the Holy Spirit began pointing out my sin, I groaned and wept. The next day, still in great humiliation, after asking Charlie Culpepper to pray for me, I left the meeting and went home. When repentance washed the guilt away and the peace of forgiveness filled my soul, I knew an ecstasy of joy beyond description. Although I was nearly 58 years old, I ran the mile across the fields from Nanlo to Charlie's house and bounded over the fence like a schoolboy. Grabbing him in a bear hug, I shouted, "It's gone, it's gone."*

Wiley Glass continued ministering with renewed passion and amid great revival until forced home in 1942 by the Japanese Invasion of China.*

Today's Suggested Reading
Luke 6:32–36

But love your enemies, do good, and lend, hoping for nothing in return; and your reward will be great, and you will be sons of the Most High. For He is kind to the unthankful and evil. Luke 6:35

---

*Adapted from Eloise Glass Cauthen, *Higher Ground* (Nashville: Broadman Press, 1978), pp. 147–152.

A Hundred Pounds

Lorenzo Dow was an eccentric Methodist whose long hair, peculiar clothing, and sharp manner caused him to be called "Crazy Dow." But as he traveled thousands of miles on foot and horseback, he won multitudes to Christ.

As a teenager, Dow had been greatly troubled over the doctrine of predestination, and at one point became so convinced that he was among the condemned that he nearly took his own life with a pistol. But about that time, Methodist evangelist Hope Hull came through Connecticut, and his message pierced the youth. Lorenzo was so overcome with conviction that he had to hold to his cousin to keep from falling off his seat. People were being converted all around him, and Lorenzo was almost beside himself with a desire for peace with God. On his way home, he fell down on the road several times and hardly knew where he was. Reaching home at last, he prayed till exhausted, then fell into a slumber in which he experienced a nightmare of being in hell. He awoke in terror, *and, oh! how glad I was to find it was only a dream.*

He resumed his earnest prayers. *"Lord! I give up; I submit; I yield; if there be mercy in heaven for me, let me know it; and if not, let me go down to hell and know the worst of my case." As these words flowed from my heart, I saw the Mediator step in, as it were, between the Father's justice and my soul, and these words were applied to my mind with great power: "Son, thy sins which are many are forgiven thee; thy faith hath saved thee; go in peace."*

The burden of sin and guilt and the fear of hell vanished from my mind as perceptibly as a hundred pounds falling from a man's shoulder. My soul was so happy that I could scarcely settle to work; and I spent the greatest part of the day in going from house to house through the neighborhood, to tell the people what God had done for me.

Today's Suggested Reading
Luke 7:47

Therefore I say to you, her sins, which are many, are forgiven, for she loved much. But to whom little is forgiven, the same loves little. Luke 7:47

Death of a Dog

One day as Dick Hillis preached in a Chinese village, his sermon was suddenly interrupted by a piercing cry. Everyone rushed toward the scream, and Dick's coworker, Mr. Kong, whispered that an evil spirit had seized a man. "That is heathen superstition," said Dick, who had not previously encountered demon possession.

A woman pushed through the crowd toward them. "I beg you help me!" she cried. "An evil spirit has again possessed the father of my children and is trying to kill him."

Kong stepped over a filthy old dog lying in the doorway, and faced the madman. The room was charged with a sense of evil. "An evil spirit has possessed Farmer Ho," Kong told the onlookers. "Our God, the 'Nothing-He-Cannot-Do One' is more powerful than any spirit, and He can deliver this man. First, you must promise you will burn your idols and trust in Jesus, son of the Supreme Emperor."

The people nodded. Kong asked Dick to begin singing the hymn "There is Power in the Blood." With great hesitation, Dick began to sing, "Would you be free from your burden of sin. . . ."

"Now," continued Kong, "in the name of Jesus we will command the evil spirit to leave this man." Kong began praying fervently. Suddenly, the old dog in the doorway vaulted into the air, screeching, yelping, whirling in circles snapping wildly at his tail. Kong continued praying, and the dog abruptly dropped over dead.

Instantly Dick remembered Luke 8, the demons of the Gadarenes who invisibly flew into the herd of swine. As Kong finished praying, Farmer Ho seemed quiet and relaxed, and soon he was strong enough to burn his idols. At his baptism shortly afterward, he testified, "I was possessed by an evil spirit who boasted he had already killed five people and was going to kill me. But God sent Mr. Kong at just the right moment, and in Jesus I am free."

Today's Suggested Reading

Luke 8:26–37

Then the demons went out of the man and entered the swine, and the herd ran violently down the steep place into the lake and drowned. Luke 8:33

Three Friends

They were best friends, the three. Alanson Work was sandy haired, married, father of four. George Thompson was young and single, with thick black hair and a five-feet frame. The third man, James Burr, was six-feet-four. But they were united by a common devotion to Christ and a joint hatred of slavery.

In 1841, arrested for trying to smuggle slaves from Missouri, they were chained to each other and held without bail. Outside, a mob chanted for their deaths, while inside the three knelt in prayer. Thompson later wrote: *Our singing and happy contentment in our prisonhouse much annoyed the consciences of the* [*town's*] *inhabitants.* They preached to the crowds before and during their trial, then were sentenced to 12 years hard labor at the state penitentiary.

Arriving in prison, the men's heads were shaved, they were garbed in prison rags, and were repeatedly threatened with forty lashes. Their food consisted of hard cornbread, rotting bacon, cold potatoes, and "various animal intestines." During the cold winters, they nearly froze until they were allowed to sleep together. *We could take turns getting into the middle. If an outside one was becoming frostbitten, he only had to request the middle one to exchange places awhile.*

Night after night, the men read to one another from the Bible and joined together in singing and praying. Soon they were evangelizing and teaching the other prisoners. On Sunday, May 14, 1843, George Thompson's sermon from Luke 9:23 sparked a prison revival.

The most glorious day I have seen! The power of God wonderfully displayed. In prayer meeting, four new cases of conversion; cell crowded to overflowing; converts mounting higher and growing stronger; while the long-harded tremble like Belshazzar. Preached to 12 converts, in my cell, from Luke 9:23. In the afternoon, a powerful sermon—six new ones came forward. I talked and prayed with them, no man forbidding. Glory to God.

Work was finally released in 1845. Burr and Thompson were pardoned the next year, the latter becoming a missionary to Africa.

Today's Suggested Reading

Luke 9:23

Then He said to them all, "If anyone desires to come after Me, let him deny himself, and take up his cross daily, and follow Me. Luke 9:23

August **9**

Neither Lucifer nor Lightning

Wycliffe missionaries Doug and Beth Wright live among the Logo people in Zaire, where they are translating the Bible into Logoti. One Saturday, they arrived home after dark to find all their electrical circuits burned out. They soon learned that a powerful bolt of lightning had struck a large mango tree near their house. Attracted by underground water pipes, the charge had then plowed through five feet of porch cement and traveled to the other end of the house where it scorched the flowers and killed a goat. Two Zairian children at that end of the house were struck as they collected water from the overflow barrels.

The neighbors, hearing the blast, swarmed to the house and found the girl lying at the base of the mango tree, about 30 feet from the water barrels. She was conscious, but dazed and unable to get up. The boy had gotten up, but was delirious. Both later recovered.

As Doug and Beth surveyed the damage, they found that the surge had traveled through all the plugged-in electrical equipment in the house, destroying almost all the computers and equipment containing the Logoti Project. Part of Doug's desk and some of the equipment were charred. It was a huge loss to them. But they suddenly remembered that on the Friday before the blast they had been translating Luke 10:17—"The seventy-seven returned with joy and said, 'Lord, even the demons submit to us in your name.' He replied, 'I saw Satan fall like lightning from heaven.'"

The Wrights knew that in translating the Word of God into Logoti, they were putting themselves on the front line of spiritual warfare. But they would not be deterred. Gathering their notes and asking for prayer, they resumed their work, dissuaded by neither Lucifer nor lightning.*

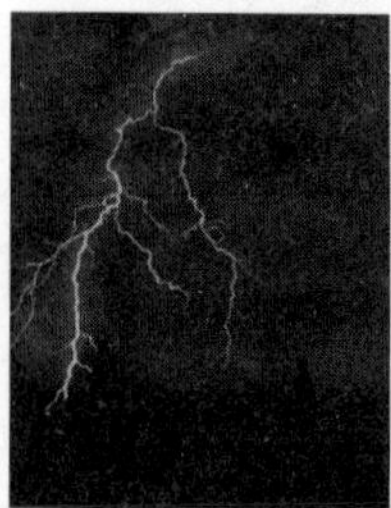

Today's Suggested Reading
Luke 10:1–20

And He said to them, "I saw Satan fall like lightning from heaven." Luke 10:18

*Adapted from "A Force So Powerful" by Doug and Beth Wright in *In Other Words*, September 1996, pp. 6–7.

How Much More

August **10**

As a young man, Oswald Chambers, of *My Utmost for His Highest* fame, battled a persistent sense of barrenness in his Christian life. He finally wrote: *I was getting desperate. I knew no one who had what I wanted; in fact I did not know what I did want. But I knew that if what I had was all the Christianity there was, the thing was a fraud.*

Then Luke 11:13 got hold of me.

At a little meeting in Dunoon, a well-known lady was asked to take the after meeting. She did not speak, but set us to prayer, and then sang, "Touch me again, Lord." I felt nothing, but I knew emphatically my time had come. I rose to my feet. Then and there I claimed the gift of the Holy Spirit in dogged committal on Luke 11:13.

I had no vision of heaven or of angels, I had nothing. I was as dry and empty as ever, no power or realization of God, no witness of the Holy Spirit. Then I was asked to speak at a meeting and forty souls came out to the front! I came to realize that God intended me, having asked, to simply take it by faith, and that power would be there. I might see it only by the backward look, but I was to reckon on the fact that God would be with me.

From that point on, Oswald Chambers ministered with unusual power. His words and writings touched people around the world, especially when he taught, as he frequently did, from his favorite verse, Luke 11:13. And when Oswald died at an early age in Egypt during World War I, an old Australian soldier whom he had led to Christ had a Bible carved in stone for his grave. Its pages were turned to Luke 11:13.

Today's Suggested Reading
Luke 11:1–13

If you, then, being evil, know how to give good gifts to your children, how much more will your heavenly Father give the Holy Spirit to those who ask Him! Luke 11:13

August **11**

Angel Near Her Shoulder

The island nation of Taiwan (formerly Formosa) became the home of missionary Lillian Dickson, who served there with her husband. She dreamed of establishing a work in the very middle of the island, in the mountain town of Po-li. She envisioned a medical clinic, a sewing room, a library, and a church conference center. But in the mid-1950s, uncertainty about the status of Taiwan hindered funds for such a project.

Lillian doggedly pressed on, trying to establish the work from her own limited resources. *So we went on building even though we hadn't enough to finish, even if it would always be a burden to buy medicines and to keep the clinic staffed. The need was there. . . .*

Bob Pierce of World Vision got behind the project, and the clinic was finally opened on January 16, 1956. It was a bright, beautiful day. In the distance, snow-capped mountains; in the valley, pink cherry blossoms. Immediately the clinic was swamped, and many of the cases were tuberculosis. The crowds were so great that 15 patients had to be housed in the tool shed the first night. By morning, the little shed was stuffed with 70 people, so crowded that most could not even sit.

Lillian was beside herself with concern. How could she do anything worthwhile against such staggering need? *Hurrying again to Po-li and reading my Bible for an answer to all this, I came upon a wonderful promise, pointed out to me by the angel near my shoulder. "Your Father will give the Holy Spirit to those who ask Him." Burdens seemed to drop off my shoulders in every direction as I asked the Father again for His Spirit and knew He would answer. So in Po-li, out of great confusion, clearly and unmistakably God showed us His plan. . . .*

And as God's Holy Spirit guided her, Lillian Dickson built a remarkable work in Po-li for God's glory.

Today's Suggested Reading
Luke 11:13–23

. . . your heavenly Father give the Holy Spirit to those who ask Him! Luke 11:13

A Fool No More

August **12**

The first time I visited Chicago, I searched out the Old Pacific Garden Mission and asked a worker to show me around. To my surprise, he grabbed my arm and pulled me out the door after him. "Here," he said, stuffing my hands full of New Testaments, "you can see the Mission later." It was during the height of the Vietnam War, and young soldiers were pouring into Chicago in waves. I spent the rest of the evening at the train station, giving out literature, evangelizing soldiers, and inviting them to the Old Pacific Garden Mission—the granddaddy of all urban rescue missions.

The Pacific Garden Mission boasts of thousands of stories of men and women who have been "unshackled" by its message. An older man, for example, nicknamed "Sunshine" Harris spent most of his life on Chicago's streets, living on stale wine and cigarette butts. He wandered in and out of the Mission, and one day someone there gave him a New Testament.

As he flipped through its pages, his eyes fell on Luke 12:20—"Fool! This night your soul will be required of you. . . ." Sunshine angrily snapped the book shut but later wanted to read the verse again. When he couldn't find it, he grew furious. Unwilling to be stymied, he started in Matthew 1:1, with the genealogies of Christ, and kept reading until he finally found Luke 12:20.

Rereading the parable, he noticed that it was spoken of a rich man, and Sunshine knew he was poor. But that didn't seem to matter. The story spoke to him, and that evening, when the invitation was given at the Mission, he raised his hand and a lady led him to Christ.

The year was 1899, and Sunshine was 71 years old. He spent the rest of his life, night after night, working at the Old Pacific Garden Mission and telling everyone who would listen how Christ had changed his life.

Today's Suggested Reading

Luke 12:16–21

But God said to him, "Fool! This night your soul will be required of you; then whose will those things be which you have provided?" Luke 12:20

John Pounds

It was a terrible fall, and it sickened those who saw it. John Pounds, a tall, muscular teen laborer at the docks of Portsmouth, England, slipped and plunged from the top of a ship's mast, pitching headfirst into the bowels of the vessel. When fellow workers reached him, he was nothing but a mass of broken bones. For two years he lay in bed as his bones healed crookedly. His pain never ceased. Out of boredom, he began to read the Bible.

At length, John crawled from bed, hoping to find something he could do with his life. A shoemaker hired him, and day after day, John sat at his cobbler's bench, a Bible open on his lap. Soon he was born again.

John ultimately gathered enough money to purchase his own little shoeshop, and one day he developed a pair of surgical boots for his crippled nephew Johnny, whom he had taken in. Soon John was making corrective shoes for other children, and his little cobbler's shop became a miniature children's hospital.

As John's burden for children grew, he began receiving homeless ones, feeding them, teaching them to read, and telling them about the Lord. His shop became known as "The Ragged School," and John would limp around the waterfront, food in his pockets, looking for more children to tend.

During his lifetime, John Pounds rescued 500 children from despair and led every one of them to Christ. Moreover, his work became so famous that a "Ragged School Movement" swept England, and a series of laws were passed to establish schools for poor children in John's honor. Boys' homes, girls' homes, day schools, and evening schools were started, along with Bible classes in which thousands heard the gospel.

When John collapsed and died on New Year's Day, 1839, while tending to a boy's ulcerated foot, he was buried in a churchyard on High Street. All England mourned, and a monument was erected over his grave, reading: "Thou shalt be blessed, for they could not recompense thee."

Today's Suggested Reading

Luke 14:1–14

And you will be blessed, because they cannot repay you; for you shall be repaid at the resurrection of the just. Luke 14:14

Moody's Last Sermon

Evangelist D. L. Moody was overworked and overweight, and he had trouble keeping the killer pace he set for himself. He wrote a friend that his many speaking engagements had "used me up."

On November 12, 1899, he began a crusade in Kansas City, suffering chest pains ("I did not let my family know, for they would not have let me come here"). On November 16, he preached on *Excuses,* from Luke 14:16–24. He was unable to walk to the meeting, but once up to preach, he showed no signs of exhaustion.

Suppose we should write out tonight this excuse, how would it sound? "To the King of Heaven: While sitting in Convention Hall, Kansas City, Mo., November 16, 1899, I received a pressing invitation to be present at the marriage supper of your only begotten son. I pray Thee have me excused."

Would you sign that, young man? Would you, mother? I doubt if there is one here who would sign it. Will you, then, pay no attention to God's invitation? I beg you, do not make light of it. Go play with forked lightning, go trifle with pestilence and disease, but trifle not with God.

Is there one here who will say, "By the grace of God I accept the invitation now." May God bring you to a decision. If you would ever see the kingdom of God, you must decide this question one way or the other. I bring it to you in the name of my Master.

Hundreds were converted that night, but it was Moody's final sermon. Staggering back to his room, he collapsed in bed as his friends attended him. The remaining services were canceled, and Moody wired his family, "Doctor thinks I need rest. Am on my way home." He arrived back in Massachusetts on Sunday and went upstairs to prepare for supper, but climbing the stairs overtaxed his heart and he never came down again.

Today's Suggested Reading

Luke 14:16–24

But they all with one accord began to make excuses . . . . Luke 14:18

August **15**

Visit to a Prostitute

The insistent pounding finally roused Dr. P. W. Philpott of Hamilton, Canada, from his sleep. It was 3 A.M. "Will you go with me to a house of prostitution?" the stranger at the door asked. "A dying girl there has asked for you." Philpott followed the stranger into a seamy part of town and in the flicker of an old lamp, saw the poor teenager.

She said, "I knew you would come and pray with me, for I'm going to die. The girls here don't believe I'm going to die, but I know I am."

I wondered how I could bring her to Christ when she solved the problem by asking if there wasn't a story in the Bible about a sheep that had strayed far from the fold and of the Shepherd who had gone after it. "Can you find the story?" she asked.

I read her the story, then turned to the verse which tells of the Shepherd giving his life for the sheep. As I knelt to pray by the dying girl, the other girls knelt too, sobbing by their companion's bed. What an audience! When I looked up, I shall never forget the expression on her face. "Oh!" she cried, "it's wonderful! The Good Shepherd has found me and He's holding me close to His heart." She kept repeating it.

When I returned at dawn, one of the girls came out to meet me. "We wish you had been here when Mary passed away. She was so happy. She kept saying, 'The Shepherd has found me, and He's holding me close to His heart.'"

Years later, in another city, a woman came to me after a service and asked, "Don't you recognize me? I'm that girl that told you of Mary's passing that morning. But there was something else I wanted to tell you. That morning when the Good Shepherd brought Mary in on one shoulder, I came in on the other."

Today's Suggested Reading
Luke 15:1–7

Rejoice with me, for I have found my sheep which was lost! Luke 15:6

A Long, Hard Row

When thirteen-year-old Samuel Huddleston ran away from home and joined a tough gang, his grieving father fell to his knees. "Sammy," he said, "I feel sorry for you. You've got a long, hard row to hoe unless you surrender to Jesus soon." But Samuel was too angry to listen, and his father could do nothing but pray.

Samuel became an unmarried father at age 16, and soon thereafter began selling drugs. One night in 1971, drunk and frenzied, he and his cousin robbed a liquor store and killed the owner.

His father visited him on his first day in jail. "Sammy," said the old man, "we're in trouble, and I don't know what we're gonna do. But we're gonna make it. We're just praying that Jesus will work it out for your best."

Shortly afterward, Samuel, 17, was sentenced to the penitentiary, five years to life. His adjustment to prison was a nightmare, but his father visited frequently, always speaking to him of Christ.

Two years later, Samuel began reading his Bible and praying, and one day he invited Christ into his heart. His father, hearing the news, wept. "Nineteen years," he said, "nineteen years since the day you were born, I've been praying for you."

Samuel took his new faith seriously and grew quickly in Christ. A year later he was invited to speak at a nearby church. To his surprise, the prison authorities allowed it. The church was packed. Samuel's father sat halfway back, a huge smile across his face. Samuel turned to Luke 15 and read the story of the prodigal son, saying that despite prison bars, he had found freedom in Christ because neither his heavenly Father nor his earthly one had given up on him.

Samuel was eventually paroled, but he keeps returning to prison as a preacher and reformer whose work has been honored by the president of the United States.

His beaming father can't get over it. "This my son was dead and is alive again; he was lost and is found."*

Today's Suggested Reading
Luke 15:11–24

". . . for this my son was dead and is alive again; he was lost and is found." Luke 15:24

---

*Adapted from "One Family's Forgiveness" by Samuel Huddleston, in *Focus on the Family Magazine*, November 1991, pp. 5–7

Faithful in Much

When Eric Liddell, Olympic hero turned missionary, sensed the need for a pastor in the rural Chinese area of Siaochang, he volunteered, knowing it meant prolonged separation from his wife and children. He began his work there in 1937, just as Japan invaded China.

Though Eric's district covered 10,000 square miles, he faithfully covered it by foot or bicycle, visiting churches, preaching, and evangelizing in all conditions. But the encroaching war made his work difficult, and bullet-dodging became routine. Weddings, baptisms, and sermons occurred against the cacophony of gunfire.

On one of his forays, he heard of a man wounded by the Japanese and left to die in a temple 20 miles away. No one would help him for fear of reprisals, so Eric detoured to the spot, found the man, and loaded him in a borrowed cart, determined to get him to a hospital. But that night, Eric slept little. He worried about the danger to which he had exposed himself. If the Japanese caught him, he would surely be killed on the spot. Finally Eric rose from bed, wrapped his old sheepskin coat around him, and reached for his Chinese Bible. As he opened it, his eyes fell on Luke 16:10: "He who is faithful in what is least is faithful also in much; and he who is unjust in what is least is unjust also in much."

The words seemed straight from the Lord, and Eric returned to bed and slept soundly.

The next morning Japanese troops were everywhere, but for some reason they didn't search Eric's cart, and he made his way out of the territory. Along the way, he rescued another victim whose neck had been slashed execution-style by the Japanese. They arrived at the hospital at last. The first man died, but the second one recovered to eventually become an outstanding Chinese Christian artist.

Today's Suggested Reading
Luke 16:1–13

He who is faithful in what is least is faithful also in much; and he who is unjust in what is least is unjust also in much. Luke 16:10

Poor Me!

The Christian and Missionary Alliance Church in Atlanta made a deep impression on student Mabel Willey. Its missionary ardor permeated her, but . . . *I became aware of a lack in myself. Deep in my heart, I knew what God wanted me to do. But I also knew that in my life there was no power. I did not have the freedom to witness as I wished. One Sunday I attended a service with a visiting evangelist. "Is there anyone in this audience who feels your life is empty? You want to do, but there isn't the power, the strength of the Holy Spirit?" As the choir sang, I slipped quietly to the altar. "Lord, here I am. I can offer nothing but myself. That's all I have, but I want this power to serve you."*

Mabel enrolled in Toccoa Falls Bible Institute for missionary training, but with many lessons still to learn.

"Poor me! I always have to do everything," I complained to the Lord one morning. I was president of the graduating class. As a parting gift, the class voted to dedicate a gate for one of the entrances to the Institute. I was responsible for many details, but in spite of my hard work, no one else seemed interested. All the students were busy with their own concerns.

That morning I got up early and went to the falls. Selecting a rock as a seat, I contemplated those falls, higher than Niagara, and complained to the Lord. "No one will help me, Lord. Please give me a verse just for me right now." I opened my Bible expecting to find a gracious verse, full of love and sustenance for His poor, discouraged servant. Instead these words stood out in bold letters: "After you have done all, say I am an unworthy servant."

I walked back to the door with a changed attitude. As a result things began to fall into place and the project moved forward to completion.

It was a lesson Mabel recalled many times as a missionary to Cuba.*

Today's Suggested Reading
Luke 17:1–10

So likewise you, when you have done all those things which you are commanded, say, "We are unprofitable servants. We have done what was our duty to do." Luke 17:10

*Adapted from *Beyond the Gate: The Autobiography of Mabel Bailey Willey* (Nashville, TN: Randall House Publications, 1998).

A Boy's Prayer

In the 1898 book *Yates the Missionary,* Matthew Yates described how the Lord used both light and lightning to bring him to Christ as a boy. The light was supplied by a kindly evangelist named John Purefoy, who often stayed in the Yates' home.

I remember well Father Purefoy's putting his hand on my head and saying, "May the Lord make a preacher of him!" This blessing made an impression on my young heart, for his manner was kind and his tone serious.

Later he asked me if I ever prayed. I replied I did not know how to pray. He looked kindly at me as I held his horse for him to mount, and said, "I will tell you, 'God be merciful to me, a sinner.'" This was the first intimation I ever had that I was a sinner.

At a subsequent interview, Purefoy asked me when no one else was present if I had ever prayed as he taught me. I replied I did not know where to pray. He said, "Go into the woods where none but God can hear you."

The house where I was attending school stood under a magnificent white oak. During recess while we played under its spreading limbs, it was struck by lightning twice in as many seconds. We were pressed to the ground as if by a great weight, and each boy had a deep red spot on some part of his body caused by the electricity. The heavens had been overcast that day, but there had been neither rain nor thunder.

This incident, so sudden and unexpected, made me feel that I was a sinner and must pray. I went into a dense forest and found a large oak that was much inclined toward the south. There I erected my altar of prayer, and there I prayed, "God be merciful to me a sinner."

Matthew Yates went on to became a prominent Christian and a missionary mightily used in China.

Today's Suggested Reading

Luke 18:9–14

And the tax collector, standing afar off, would not so much as raise his eyes to heaven, but beat his breast, saying, "God, be merciful to me a sinner!" Luke 18:13

Atop the Berlin Wall

In 1963, Rüdiger Knechtel, a 21-year-old border guard on the newly built Berlin Wall, was haunted by the coarse joking of his comrades. They were laughing about those killed trying to escape. Rüdiger made a silent vow to never shoot border jumpers, and he quietly convinced other guards to do the same. But when word reached the authorities, Rüdiger was arrested and sentenced to hard labor in a military prison. His wife meanwhile fell in love with another man, and Rüdiger returned home to a shattered life.

In time, he discovered Christ as Savior and started working with recovering alcoholics. As a livelihood, Rüdiger began collecting and selling antiques and fine art, eventually amassing a fine collection of his own. Still the Stasi kept him under surveillance, sending informants and spies to entrap him.

In the early hours of July 28, 1982, seven men appeared at his door, arrested him, and seized his most valuable paintings. Among numerous charges filed against him, he was accused of not paying a special tax on his paintings. That accusation was true, for Rüdiger had dodged a particular levy on his art works. "You haven't paid your taxes," prosecutors taunted, "yet you claim to be a Christian. What kind of Christian is that?"

The question hurt Rüdiger because he knew Luke 20:25. He should have rendered to Caesar the things that are Caesar's, even though the regime was corrupt. "It was a terrible feeling," he recalls. "It became clear to me how far from real faith I had lived."

Rüdiger Knechtel emerged from his second imprisonment determined to live in renewed moral obedience to God—and this made him all the more dangerous to the Stasi. In 1989, he helped lead the movement to defeat Communism in his country; and still today he is at work, caring for the sick and dying.*

Today's Suggested Reading
Luke 20:19–26

And He said to them, "Render therefore to Caesar the things that are Caesar's, and to God the things that are God's." Luke 20:25

---

*Adapted from *Candles Behind the Wall* by Barbara Von Der Heydt (Grand Rapids: Eerdmans Publishing Co., 1993), pp. 3–24.

August **21**

The Rooster's Crow

I've often thought of Peter when noticing how easily men cry in my office. In my experience, more men than women have broken down during counseling sessions, and often because of guilt. The husband who ruined his marriage. The father whose temper drove away his son. The alcoholic who relapsed.

When the eyes of Jesus scorch a man, when he hears the rooster's crow and weeps bitterly, determined to change, he is then at last beyond regret, beyond remorse, to a level of sorrow called repentance. Two biblical characters, I've found, offer the best advice to men at such junctions.

Peter teaches *God-forgiveness.* Though Peter denied Jesus three times, the Lord appeared to him privately following the resurrection (1 Corinthians 15:5), with a view of restoring him (Luke 22:32). We have no record of the details of that meeting, but Peter undoubtedly confessed his sin in utter self-contempt and contrition; and there he vividly learned the power of the "precious blood of Christ" (1 Peter 1:19). Later by the sea, Jesus drew a three-fold affirmation of love from his wounded disciple (John 21:15–19, and the spiritual restoration was deepened.

But another layer of healing is necessary, for it is often easier to be forgiven by God than to forgive oneself. Here, the Old Testament hero Joseph helps us. Just as Jesus was betrayed by Peter, Joseph was betrayed by his own brothers who sold him into slavery. But years later, he said to them: "Do not be grieved or angry with yourselves because you sold me here; for God sent me before you to preserve life" (Genesis 45:5). In other words, "I've forgiven you. Now stop beating yourselves up over this. Don't wallow in it any longer. Put it behind you, for God, who overrules all, has used even this sin for good."

Our faults and failures are damning matters; but when we kneel before the risen Christ, confessing our sins, His blood forgives us thoroughly; and we rise from our knees to forgive ourselves and to get on with the Master's business.

Today's Suggested Reading

Luke 22:54–62

And the Lord turned and looked at Peter. And Peter remembered the word of the Lord, how He had said to him, "Before the rooster crows, you will deny Me three times." Then Peter went out and wept bitterly.
Luke 22:61–62

The Transformation

Those words by the dying thief drew this response from our Lord: "Assuredly, I say to you, today you will be with Me in Paradise."

When astronomer Nicholas Copernicus was dying, he requested the following epitaph be written on his tombstone: *Lord, I do not ask the kindness Thou didst show to Peter. I do not dare to ask the grace Thou didst grant to Paul; but, Lord, the mercy Thou didst show to the dying robber, that mercy show to me. That I earnestly pray.*

In sixteenth century Cambridge, William Perkins, an alcoholic, was converted to Christ and eventually became a pastor. His compassion for criminals and vagabonds was boundless. Winning the respect of the jailers, Perkins took great latitude in ministering to prisoners.

One day he accompanied a young man to the gallows. As hangings were public events, a multitude assembled to see the execution, and it was the custom for the condemned to address the crowd. But the young man, having climbed the ladder, merely lowered his head, pale and terrified. "Are you afraid of death?" asked William, looking up at him.

"No," replied the man softly. "Of something worse."

"Come down again then, and see what God's grace will do."

The young man climbed down the ladder, and Perkins took his time explaining to him the forgiveness God offers through Jesus Christ. The man burst into tears and prayed earnestly. Then he wept again, this time out of joy as Perkins shared verses of eternal assurance.

Soon the young prisoner again mounted the ladder, this time with alacrity, and he went to his death as though seeing heaven opened. The onlookers went home amazed, saying they had not been to a hanging but to a transfiguration.

As William Cowper once wrote:

The dying thief rejoiced to see
That fountain in his day
And there may I though vile as he
Wash all my sins away.

Today's Suggested Reading
Luke 23:39–43

Then he said to Jesus, "Lord, remember me when You come into Your kingdom." Luke 23:42

River Song

Felix Manz (1498–1527) was a leader of the Swiss Anabaptists, a group of early Protestants who concluded that infant baptism was unscriptural. Though condemned by Reformer Ulrich Zwingli and the Zurich City Council, Manz persisted in his beliefs. On a cold night in the winter of 1525, a dozen people gathered in his home in Zurich to be baptized upon their personal confession of Jesus Christ as Savior. In response, the Zurich Council ordered that anyone found "rebaptizing" would be drowned.

At length, Felix was arrested and incarcerated. He escaped, was arrested again, and then freed. But on October 12, 1526, he was again seized, and, on the following January 5, sentenced to death ". . . because contrary to Christian order and custom he had become involved in Anabaptism." The decree ordered Manz "delivered to the executioner, who shall tie his hands, put him into a boat, strip his bound hands down over his knees, place a stick between his knees and arms, and thus push him into the water and let him perish in the water, thereby he shall have atoned to the law and justice."

Accordingly, Felix was taken bound from Wellenberg prison past the fish market and placed in a boat moored on the Limmat River that ran through Zurich. Above the splash of the oars came his mother's voice from shore, entreating him to remain true to Christ. The officers went to work on his arms and legs, during which time Felix sang out with a loud voice: *In manus tuas, Domine, commedno spiritum meum" (Into thy hands, O Lord, I commend my spirit).*

With that song on his lips, he was rolled out of the boat, and the cold waters of the Limmat River at the mouth of Lake Zurich closed over his head.

Today's Suggested Reading

Luke 23:44–56

And when Jesus had cried out with a loud voice, He said, "Father, 'into your hands I commit My spirit.'" Having said this, He breathed His last. Luke 23:46

Words by an Unmarked Grave

August **24**

Their hearts were heavy, these friends of Jesus. They needed time to grieve by his tomb, but arriving early in the morning, they found it emptied. It was too much to bear—their dear friend tortured to death before their eyes, his abrupt burial, and now his tomb looted. They were at the breaking point.

They did not yet know that this was the flash point of history, that Jesus Christ had risen from the dead. But the angels told them, relaying the tidings with these simple words: "Why do you seek the living among the dead?"

That same question came abruptly to Pastor Stephen Brown after his brother and best friend, Ron, died suddenly of a heart attack. Ron was young—in his forties—and a popular public servant, a superb district attorney, a good father. His death devastated Stephen, who didn't even have a chance to say good-bye.

Several weeks after Ron's death, Stephen decided to visit his brother's grave. It was a cold, overcast afternoon in late winter, and Stephen stepped from his car into the drizzle. Ron's grave was not yet marked, and Stephen couldn't find it. As he groped through the mud, his grief overwhelmed him. Standing in the rain, Stephen began sobbing. "God, this has been the worst month of my life, and now I can't even find my brother's grave."

Suddenly Stephen sensed a presence near him, as though Jesus Christ had drawn along side to help. These words came to mind like a burst of light, as though Jesus himself were speaking them: "Why are you seeking the living among the dead?"

"Those words comforted me," Stephen later wrote, "and I haven't been back to the cemetery since. I don't need to go back. The One who loved Ron and knew him came to me in my grief. He promised never to leave, and that has made all the difference in the world."*

Today's Suggested Reading

Luke 24:1–12

Then, as they were afraid and bowed their faces to the earth, they said to them, "Why do you seek the living among the dead?" Luke 24:5

---

*Adapted from Stephen Brown, *When Your Rope Breaks* (Nashville, TN: Thomas Nelson Publishers, 1998), pp. 48–49.

August **25**

John Bunyan's Last Sermon

John Bunyan, author of *Pilgrim's Progress,* was a mender of pots and pans who, following his conversion, became a mender of souls. In 1660 he was imprisoned in Bedford, England, for his Puritan views, and his cell became his study, his pulpit, his prayer chamber, his counseling center, and his writing studio. Following his release, Bunyan served the Baptist church in Bedford (which had elected him pastor while he was still in prison).

In August, 1688, Bunyan, 60, was drenched in a rainstorm while traveling to London; but, arriving in the city, he proceeded to bring the Sunday morning sermon at a church in Whitechapel. He choose for his text John 1:13, and he ended his message saying: *O do not flatter yourselves with a portion among the sons, unless you live like sons. When we see a king's son play with a beggar, this is unbecoming; so if you be the king's children, live like the king's children; if you be risen with Christ, set your affections on the things above, and not on things below; when you come together, talk of what your Father promised you; you should all love your Father's will, and be content and pleased with the exercises you meet with in the world. If you are the children of God, live together lovingly; if the world quarrel with you, it is no matter; but it is sad if you quarrel together; if this be amongst you, it is a sign of ill-breeding; it is not according to the rules you have in the Word of God. Dost thou see a soul that has the image of God in him? Love him, love him; say, This man and I must go to heaven one day; serve one another, do good for one another, if any wrong you, pray to God to right you, and love the brotherhood.*

Two days later, Bunyan was gripped by a high fever and put to bed in his hotel. He died twelve days after his last sermon.

Today's Suggested Reading
John 1:1–13

. . . who were born, not of blood, nor of the will of the flesh, nor of the will of man, but of God. John 1:13

Behold the Lamb

George Cutting, British author and soul-winner, was bicycling one day through a certain English village when he felt impressed to shout out the words, "Behold! the Lamb of God who takes away the sin of the world!" No sooner had he spoken those syllables when he suddenly felt he should repeat them.

A half-year passed, and Cutting returned to evangelize door-to-door in the area. When a woman came to the door of one cottage, Cutting asked if she was saved. "Oh yes!" she exclaimed. "Six months ago I was in great distress about the salvation of my soul. I pleaded for God's help. Then a voice cried, 'Behold! The Lamb of God who takes away the sin of the world!' I asked God to repeat what he had said, and the voice came again."

A similar, better-known incident happened in the ministry of Charles H. Spurgeon. He was invited to preach in London's Crystal Palace on the "Day of National Humiliation." The meeting was described as "the largest ever addressed by a preacher of the gospel in Europe or the world." Several days before the service, Spurgeon went to the Crystal Palace to walk around the platform, gaze over the empty seats, and test the acoustics. He stepped to the podium, raised his voice, and shouted the words, "Behold! The Lamb of God who takes away the sins of the world."

Unknown to him, his words wafted through the hall and up into the rafters where a workman, busy in the upper galleries, heard them as though spoken from heaven. He was immediately smitten with conviction of sin and put down his tools, went home, and sought for Christ until he found Him.

Today's Suggested Reading
John 1:15–29

The next day John saw Jesus coming toward him, and said, "Behold! The Lamb of God who takes away the sin of the world!"
John 1:29

Operation Alice

Crotchety old Alice was a terror to neighborhood children, stray dogs, and delivery boys. Her face was sour and surly. She waved her garden trowels and hedge-clippers like weapons in the faces of visitors.

When James and Jean Mader moved next door, they mustered their courage to speak to Alice about the Lord, but she cut them off. "I've been a member of the church all my life," she snorted. "I don't need the Bible to tell me what to do."

The Maders looked for ways of befriending Alice, and slowly the relationship thawed. Stili, Alice wanted nothing to do with the gospel.

During a community evangelistic campaign, the Maders became involved with a plan called "Operation Andrew," based on John 1:42, about Andrew's introducing his brother, Simon, to Christ. They listed ten people to pray for and to invite to the meetings. Alice's name was at the top of the list, but she spurned their appeals. Still they prayed and looked for chances to witness.

One summer, returning from vacation, the Maders found Alice's house empty. She was in a nursing home, having suffered a stroke. They visited her, bringing flowers and news from the neighborhood. Alice was unable to speak. They returned frequently with their family photos and tasty snacks. One day several months later, when Jim asked if he could read Psalm 23, she nodded.

Jim and Jean stopped by often, always sharing a Scripture passage. They noticed that Alice began fixing her gaze on him as he read instead of staring straight ahead as she had previously done. Finally Jim felt the time was right and asked, "Alice, do you want the Lord Jesus to forgive your sins and give you peace with God?" Alice indicated that she did, bowing her head and praying silently as Jim led her. When she raised her head, her eyes were wet with tears.

It had taken over twelve years.

Today's Suggested Reading

John 1:40–43

Andrew . . . first found his own brother Simon and said to him, "We have found the Messiah (which is translated the Christ). And he brought him to Jesus. John 1:40–42

It's Lemuel's Sermon

Lemuel Haynes was born in the summer of 1753, in Connecticut, the illegitimate child of a black man and a white woman. Abandoned at birth, he became the infant indentured servant of Mr. and Mrs. David Rose in Granville, Massachusetts, who took him in, sent him to school, provided his needs, taught him of Jesus, and made him one of their own.

I remember I often had fearful apprehensions of going to hell. I was one evening greatly alarmed by the Aurora Borealis, or Northern Lights. It was in that day esteemed a presage of the day of judgment. I cannot express the terrors of mind I felt. One evening under an apple tree mourning my wretched situation, I found the Savior. I always visit that place when I come to Granville, and, when I can, I pluck some fruit from the tree and carry it home; it is sweet to my taste.

Lemuel fought in the Revolutionary War as one of Washington's minutemen, then returned to the Rose household and became an advocate for the abolition of slavery.

One night at family devotions, Lemuel read a sermon based on John 3:3. Afterward, Mr. Rose, deeply impressed, said, "Lemuel, whose work is that which you have been reading? Is it Davies' sermon, or Watts' or Whitefield's?"

"It's Lemuel's sermon," came the sheepish reply. He had been pouring himself into John 3:3, and out of it had come his first sermon. Encouraged by the Roses, Lemuel began preparing for the ministry, and eventually accepted a church in Rutland, Vermont. During his 30 years there, he preached 5,000 sermons, conducted 400 funerals, experienced two great revivals, and saw hundreds born again.

In 1833, Haynes, now old, made a final visit to Granville, where he visited the old apple tree—still standing—one last time. He died shortly afterward. The epitaph on his tombstone reads: "Here lies the dust of a poor hell-deserving sinner, who ventured into eternity trusting wholly on the merits of Christ for salvation."

Today's Suggested Reading

John 3:1–5

Jesus answered and said to him, "Most assuredly, I say to you, unless one is born again, he cannot see the kingdom of God." John 3:3

A New Bodyguard

A friend of mine, evangelist Rick Amato, tells of his search for meaning as a rebellious teenager in the mid 1970s. He fully participated in the drug culture and asked a lot of questions about the purpose of life. His gang in the back alleys of Detroit led him deeper into vice, and Rick appeared to be on a dead-end street.

But a friend invited him to church, and against all odds, Rick accepted. As the congregation sang "Just As I Am," he made his way to the altar and asked Christ to become his Lord and Savior. His drug use, vice, and destructive habits began to change, and he started reading the Bible. He also started witnessing.

At football practice, every time the coach would begin to swear, saying "Jesus Christ," Rick would say, "is Lord!"

My first "sermon" was preached to the high school choir. All the kids were gathered together in the choir room, waiting for the presidential address. And I was the president. I got up and said, "This year's presidential address is found in John 3:7. Jesus said, 'You must be born again.' "

One guy yelled, "Hey, man. This is a public school. You can't preach the Bible in public school."

I said, "Shut up! I'm the choir president, and this is the presidential address. I can do whatever I want." And I did. I told them that when I received Jesus, all my sins were forgiven. I told them how wonderful it was. Then the bell rang, and I lost my congregation.

All except for Norman, the biggest, strongest athlete in the school. Tarrying behind, Norman asked, "Do you really believe that if a person asks Jesus Christ into his life that He'll forgive everything that person ever did? You mean He will save me?" Rick wasn't actually sure how to lead Norman to Christ, but the two boys sank to their knees and prayed as best they could.

That day another searcher found what he was looking for. The school had a new All-American athlete, and Rick Amato had a new bodyguard.*

Today's Suggested Reading

John 3:6–8

Do not marvel that I said to you, "You must be born again." John 3:7

---

*Adapted from Rick Amato, *A Pocket Full of Pennies* (Nashville, TN: Thomas Nelson Publishers).

The Gospel in Miniature August **30**

John 3:16 may be the world's best loved text, but no one has loved it more than the nineteenth-century British evangelist Henry Moorehouse. Henry began preaching shortly after his conversion from a life of vile wickedness, and every time he stood to preach he gave John 3:16 as his text.

His sermons varied, but his text was always the same.

Once when Moorehouse decided to travel and preach throughout America, he sent D. L. Moody a letter offering to preach for him. Moody put him off but soon got another letter. Then a third. "What to do with him, I did not know," recalled Moody. "I had made up my mind he couldn't preach."

Moody was leaving on a trip just as Henry arrived in Chicago. "I don't think he can preach," Moody told his church leaders, "but let him try." When Moody returned, the church was astir. "He has preached two sermons from John 3:16," Mrs. Moody said. "He preaches a little different from what you do. He tells sinners God loves them."

"Well," replied Moody, "he is wrong."

"I think you will agree with him when you hear him," said his wife, "because he backs everything he says with the Word of God."

Moody trudged reluctantly to church that night, and Moorehouse announced his text—John 3:16. Moody later said, *He preached a most extraordinary sermon from that verse. I never knew up to that time that God loved us so much. This heart of mine began to thaw out, and I could not keep back the tears.*

Moorehouse preached for seven nights, always from John 3:16, and his message stirred D. L. Moody to his depths. From that week, Moody's great ministry took on a deeper, softer tone.

Some years passed and Henry Moorehouse came to his deathbed at age 40. His last words were: "If it were God's will to raise me up, I should like to preach from the text John 3:16. Praise be to the Lord."

Today's Suggested Reading

John 3:9–17

For God so loved the world that He gave His only begotten Son, that whoever believes in Him should not perish but have everlasting life. John 3:16

August **31** White for the Harvest

Multiplied millions of dollars have poured into overseas missions under the banner of Lottie Moon, the Southern Baptist whose name is used to promote that denomination's annual missionary offering. But who was Lottie Moon and what did she do?

Lottie (short for Charlotte) was born in 1840 and grew up in an old Virginia family. Her father's plantation house, Viewmont, overlooked the Blue Ridge Mountains. Her mother, a staunch Christian, read to her from the Bible, and as a girl Lottie developed a love for Scripture and for missionary biography. Since there was no church nearby, Mrs. Moon conducted services herself every Sunday for family, neighbors, and servants.

Lottie excelled in school and became one of the first Southern women to earn a Master's Degree, all the while pondering what to do with her life. In the spring of 1873, Lottie, 33, heard a sermon on John 4:35. As the preacher spoke of fields "white unto harvest," Lottie made up her mind then and there that she would become a missionary to China, and that fall she was on her way. When her ship was caught in a terrific storm and appeared to be sinking, she wrote: *As I watched the mad waste of waters, howling as if eager to engulf us, I think I should scarcely have been surprised to see a Divine Form walking upon them, so sweetly I heard in my inmost soul the consoling words, "It is I, be not afraid."*

For forty years, Lottie Moon worked unafraid in North China, serving faithfully amid storms of war, disease, poverty and plague. When, in her early seventies, a terrible famine swept China, she gave her food and her last dollar for famine relief. She grew so frail and undernourished the doctor ordered her home. She died en route on Christmas Eve, 1912.

"I would that I had a thousand lives that I might give them to the women of China," she said.

She gave her one life, and it has been multiplied a thousandfold.

Today's Suggested Reading
John 4:28–35

Do you not say, "There are still four months and then comes the harvest"? Behold, I say to you, lift up your eyes and look at the fields, for they are already white for the harvest. John 4:35

September

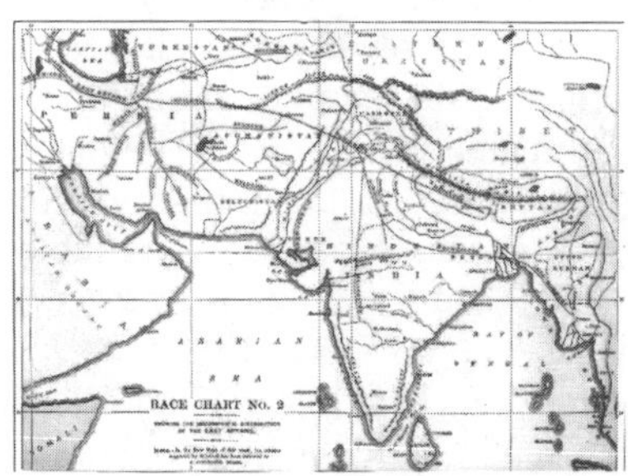

Crossing the Rubicon

The Exchanged Life

Sons of Satan

Dreading the Dentist

James Wilson's Verse

September **1**

I've Been Waiting for You

Minnesota pastor Tom Rakow's phone jingled. One of his parishioners was having emergency surgery for gallstones. Rakow sighed and resigned himself to making the hospital trip through snow and over icy roads. His feeling of weariness deepened.

On his way home after the visit, he saw a car stuck in a snowbank, and he pulled alongside to help. A man was sitting on the passenger side and the vehicle's engine was running. The man lowered his window as Tom approached. He spoke in wheezes. "My wife . . . was bringing me back from the hospital . . . and hit a slick spot. . . . Someone stopped . . . and she . . . went to get a wrecker."

"Do you mind if I wait till the wrecker comes?" Tom asked.

The man welcomed the company, and Tom slid behind the steering wheel. The man, whose name was John, explained he was suffering from cancer in the chest.

Immediately I knew that John and I were not sitting together in that car by mere coincidence. A question surfaced in my mind. At first I tried to suppress it. But then, sensing a great urgency, I asked, "John, have you accepted Jesus Christ as your Savior and Lord?"

John looked at me straight in the eyes. With great difficulty, he said, "I've been trying to find God—but I don't know how."

Tom explained the gospel simply and quietly, then read John 5:24: ". . . he who hears My word and believes in Him who sent Me has everlasting life, and shall not come into judgment, but has passed from death to life." The man prayed, trusting Jesus as his Savior, then he grabbed Tom's hand and said, "I've been waiting for you—for a long time."

John died a month later, and Pastor Rakow later wrote: *I can't help but marvel at how God used cancer, frigid weather, slick roads, breathing problems, and gallstones to accomplish His plan. But He did. God fused these factors together in order to bring John to Himself.**

Today's Suggested Reading

John 5:18–30

Most assuredly, I say to you, he who hears My word and believes in Him who sent Me has everlasting life, and shall not come into judgment, but has passed from death into life. John 5:24

---

*Adapted from Tom C. Rakow, "Meeting in a Snowbank," in *Decision*, January, 1997, p. 15, © 1997; published by the Billy Graham Evangelistic Association.

A Bible of Her Own

In 1792, a little peasant girl in Llanfilhangel, Wales, named Mary Jones, became intrigued with the Bible and longed to read from its pages. As her parents were too poor to afford one, she went to a neighbor's house and borrowed a New Testament. Her eyes fell on three words: *Search the Scriptures.*

Mary determined to purchase a Bible of her own, and for the next several years, she toiled with her hands sacrificing many other things in order to earn enough money to purchase her own copy of the Scriptures. Times were very difficult, pennies were hard to come by, and Bibles were rare. But in the spring of 1800, Mary walked 25 miles barefooted to a place called Bala, carrying her hard-earned money. She arrived there late in the day and found lodging with the local Methodist minister, but she could hardly sleep for the excitement of having a Bible of her own.

Early next morning, she proceeded to the house of Rev. Thomas Charles, who was reported to have Bibles for sale. Imagine her sorrow to learn that his stock of Bibles was exhausted. Her inconsolable grief so moved Thomas Charles that he said, "My dear child, I see that you *must* have a Bible. It is impossible to refuse you." Finding a copy that had been promised to another, he gave it to her.

But that's not the end of the story. Rev. Charles, deeply moved by that scene, developed a burning determination to do everything in his power to make the Bible available to any who desired it, to the millions in Christendom not having one.

He laid plans, garnered support, expended energy, and in 1894 the British and Foreign Bible Society was formed, the "granddaddy" of all the world's Bible societies.

Today's Suggested Reading
John 5:31–40

You search the Scriptures, for in them you think you have eternal life; and these are they which testify of Me. John 5:39

September **3** # Dreading the Dentist

When I was a child, my dentist had his office at the end of a long dark hallway on the sixth floor of an old downtown building. It was a terrifying trip filled with ominous dread that lingers to this day.

My dread, however, was nothing compared to the panic attacks that seized Elva Minette Martin before her dentist appointments. *I would worry and get an upset stomach, lie in bed with my mind racing and awaken in the clutches of terror. I was sure that I wouldn't be able to swallow or move when I sat in the dentist's chair.*

One week shortly before a routine visit, Elva was preparing to teach her Sunday school class from John 6, about the storm on the Sea of Galilee. Just as the disciples' panic reached its worst, Jesus came walking on the water and saying, "It is I; do not be afraid."

As she studied those words, Elva was suddenly convicted about her own fears.

That night I went to bed, but not to sleep. My mind knew that God was able to help me; yet I was still afraid. Acknowledging his Lordship in my life, I finally gave up my hold on fear. I prayed, "OK, Lord. Even when I go to the dentist, I will remember your promise."

As Elva headed toward her appointment, she was nervous yet excited, sensing the Lord would give her a breakthrough. *He calmed me, even relieved my grasp on the arms of the dentist's chair. Each time I began to worry, I remembered his promise: "It is I; do not be afraid."*

*What a joyous time! God suspended my fear. I had never thought that I could ever say that going to the dentist was a wonderful experience—but it was. Not because of what went on around me or what happened to me, but because of what was in my heart. With his help, I am learning to say, "God is in control; I will not be afraid."**

Today's Suggested Reading
John 6:16–21

But He said to them, "It is I; do not be afraid." John 6:20

*Adapted from Elva Minette Martin, "I Was Afraid," in *Decision*, November, 1997, p. 36, © 1997; published by the Billy Graham Evangelistic Association.

"Just as You Are" September **4**

She was an embittered woman, Charlotte Elliott of Brighton, England. Her health was broken, and her disability had hardened her. "If God loved me," she muttered, "He would not have treated me this way."

Hoping to help her, a Swiss minister named Dr. Cesar Malan visited the Elliotts on May 9, 1822. Over dinner, Charlotte lost her temper and railed against God and family in a violent outburst. Her embarrassed family left the room, and Dr. Malan, left alone with her, stared at her across the table.

"You are tired of yourself, aren't you?" he said at length. "You are holding to your hate and anger because you have nothing else in the world to cling to. Consequently, you have become sour, bitter, and resentful."

"What is your cure?" asked Charlotte.

"The faith you are trying to despise."

As they talked, Charlotte softened. "If I wanted to become a Christian and to share the peace and joy you possess," she finally asked, "what would I do?"

"You would give yourself to God just as you are now, with your fightings and fears, hates and loves, pride and shame."

"I would come to God just as I am? Is that right?"

Charlotte did come just as she was. Her heart was changed that day. As time passed, she found and claimed John 6:37 as a special verse for her: ". . . the one who comes to Me I will by no means cast out."

Several years later, her brother, Rev. Henry Elliott, was raising funds for a school for the children of poor clergymen. Charlotte wrote a poem, and it was printed and sold across England. The leaflet said: *Sold for the Benefit of St. Margaret's Hall, Brighton: Him that Cometh to Me I Will in No Wise Cast Out.* Underneath was Charlotte's poem—which has since become the most famous invitational hymn in history:

Just as I am, without one plea,
But that Thy blood was shed for me,
And that Thou bidd'st me come to Thee,
O Lamb of God, I come! I come!

Today's Suggested Reading
John 6:32–40

All that the Father gives Me will come to Me, and the one who comes to Me I will by no means cast out. John 6:37

September **5** Crossing the Rubicon

Trula Cronk, veteran missionary to India, tells of growing up homeless in the Appalachian mountains. She was eventually taken in by an orphanage (now the Trula Cronk Home for Children in Greeneville, Tennessee), and there she learned about the Lord Jesus—and about "foreign missions," an idea that initially bothered her.

One day the pastor's wife, a former missionary, spoke to my Sunday school class about India. She showed us artifacts and let us try on Indian costumes. Afterward she talked about the Great Commission. When she finished, my Sunday school teacher, Mrs. Dobson, turned to me and said, "Trula, wouldn't you like to be a missionary?"

"Never," was my quick reply. "You couldn't pay me to be a missionary."

The awful thing was that from that day I kept hearing that question in my mind.

As the years passed, that question haunted Trula relentlessly. She tried so hard to evade it she became physically ill. *Finally, sitting in my room feeling sorry for myself, I decided I would read the Bible for some light on this subject. I began reading in the New Testament. I got as far as St. John. When I reached the seventh chapter, I was struck by these words, "If anyone wills to do His will, he shall know concerning the doctrine, whether it is from God. . . ." I read the verse several times. I gathered from it that I would never understand about God until I became willing to do His will.*

Trula's struggle accelerated. One night, unable to sleep, she knelt by her bed and the tears began falling as she prayed. *Suddenly, I surprised myself by saying something like, "God, if you can make me willing to be a missionary, I will obey you." As soon as I had said amen, I knew I had crossed the Rubicon.*

Trula's attitude changed, and she soon found herself singing effortlessly, "I'll go where you want me to go, dear Lord, over mountain or plain or sea. . . ."

And she did go—all the way to India.*

Today's Suggested Reading
John 7:14–24

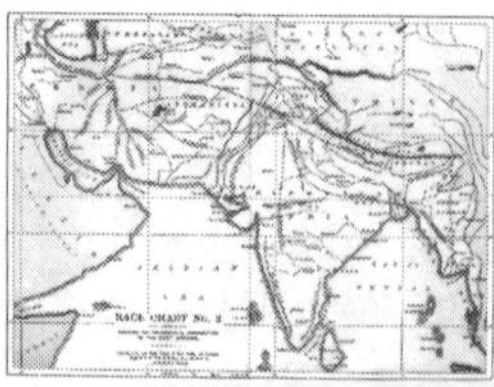

If anyone wills to do His will, he shall know concerning the doctrine, whether it is from God or whether I speak on My own authority. John 7:17

---

*Adapted from unpublished autobiography by Trula Cronk.

Rivers of Living Water September **6**

In his book, *The Life That Wins,* journalist Charles Trumbull tells how he discovered the "Victorious Christian Life." Though a Christian for many years, Trumbull was troubled by great fluctuations in his spiritual experience. One day he would be excited and triumphant; the next, discouraged and defeated by some temptation. He sought to win others to Christ, but saw little success. As the years passed, he became more vexed, especially after hearing a message at the World Missionary Conference in Edinburgh in 1910 on "The Resources of the Christian Life." The message had a clear and simple thrust: "The resources of the Christian life, my friends, are just—Jesus Christ."

Shortly afterward, Trumbull found himself the speaker at a summer missionary conference—*a week of daily work for which I was miserably, hopelessly unfit.* But on the first night of the conference, Trumbull's fellow-speaker rose to preach from John 7:37–39, saying that the Christian's life should flow continuously, not intermittently.

The next morning, Sunday, alone in my room, I prayed it out with God. And God, in His forgiveness and love, gave me what I asked for. It is hard to put into words, and yet it is, oh, so new, and real, and wonderful. At last I realized that Jesus Christ was actually and literally within me; and even more than that: that He had constituted Himself my very life, taking me into union with Himself—my body, mind, and spirit.

There has been an utterly new kind of victory, victory-by-freedom over certain besetting sins—the old ones that used to throttle and wreck me.

Jesus Christ does not want to be our helper; He wants to be our life. He does not want us to work for Him. He wants us to let Him do His work through us, using us as we use a pencil to write with—better still, using us as one of the fingers of His hand.

Today's Suggested Reading
John 7:35–46

If anyone thirsts, let him come to Me and drink. He who believes in Me, as the Scripture has said, out of his heart will flow rivers of living water. John 7:37–38

Eating Christianity

In her remarkable autobiography, *Queen of the Dark Chamber,* Christiana Tsai tells of growing up in imperial China where her father was an official of the Manchu dynasty. His twenty children lived in opulence and rarely ventured from their palatial compound. But as a teenager, Christiana begged to attend a Christian high school. Her father finally relented, saying, "Just be sure you don't eat [fall for] Christianity."

I made up my mind I was not going to "eat" Christianity, so I used to take a Chinese novel to chapel. I did not like the preaching. Another girl, a Miss Wu, hated this teaching, too, and we started to write a book denouncing all Christian teaching, insisting that Confucius and Buddha were our teachers.

But a famous American preacher was to speak in our church; for a little while I let down the bars on my heart and listened. His subject was "Jesus, the Light of the World," and he used an illustration that stuck in my mind. He said, "If a piece of wood is kept in a dark place, all kinds of ugly insects will hide under it. But if we expose it to the light, the insects will run away, for they love darkness and hate light. So with our hearts: if we do not have Jesus, the Light of the world, in our hearts, they will be dark too, and harbor evil thoughts. The moment we receive Him, the evil thoughts will be driven away." From childhood I had especially feared all kinds of insects, so this illustration made a deep impression on me. . . .

Later during a game of croquet, Christiana dislodged a stone and recoiled at the insects scurrying away. The minister's words came to mind and, dropping her mallet, she hurried home and knelt in prayer, asking Christ into her heart. *I got up quickly, my heart pounding, my face all red. At last I had found peace. The burden of sin and the pessimism of unbelief had gone from my soul! I had found Christ! From that time, I opened my heart to the study of the Bible and found comfort in it.**

Today's Suggested Reading
John 8:1–12

"I am the light of the world. He who follows Me shall not walk in darkness, but have the light of life." John 8:12

---

*Christiana Tsai, *Queen of the Dark Chamber* (Chicago: Moody Press, 1953), pp. 65–72.

Negative Circumstances, Positive God

September **8**

Debbie Stone had a lot of "Why's?" She had been conceived in the womb of a frightened unmarried girl who, fearful of her parents, had traveled to Los Angeles to "give birth to me in secret and place me for adoption."

Debbie had been adopted by a Jewish family, but at seven months she was paralyzed by polio. Her adopted parents placed her in a series of hospitals and institutions, and finally relinquished her to the courts, feeling unable to care for a quadriplegic child. Debbie's childhood was spent in hospitals. Ditto her teen years, with brief stays in foster homes. Growing bitter, she eventually moved into her own apartment, hired a live-in attendant, and enrolled in college. For the first time in her life, she began to make friends outside of a hospital. Among them was Alice Johnson.

Debbie recalls, *I spent a great deal of time asking her questions. Alice was a Christian, and as she talked about her relationship with Christ, I wanted to know Him as well. The two of us agreed to meet together to read the Gospel of John.*

My greatest unanswered question had always been the "why" of my disability and family loss. Alice read John 9:3, where Jesus said of a man born blind, "Neither this man nor his parents sinned, but that the works of God should be revealed in him." I was thrilled to learn that my circumstances were not punishment for anything that I or my parents had done, but that God had allowed these things to enter my life to bring glory to Himself.

I became excited about the possibility of Jesus Christ being exalted through my weakness. So when Alice invited me to her church, I was delighted to go. On December 6, 1970, I committed my life to Christ.

As I now look back on my life, I see how God has taken what appears to be a set of very negative circumstances and made something beautiful out of them.

He has a way of doing that.*

Today's Suggested Reading

John 9:1–11

Jesus answered, "Neither this man nor his parents sinned, but that the works of God should be revealed in him." John 9:3

---

*Adapted from Debbie Stone, "Adopted by Love," in *Moody Magazine,* April, 1986, p. 104.

I Once Was Blind

Recently I found an old book in a London shop—*Memories of the Mission Field* by Christine I. Tinling, undated, published in England. It tells of a Swedish missionary, a Mr. Tornvall, who arrived in Ping-Liang, China, uninvited and unwelcome. The missionary realized he would only be accepted by providing medical help, but he had no training—*only one small book and some homeopathic remedies.*

He began with an old woman, nearly blind, who was carried each day to ask alms. At night she was returned to her hut where a large stone was rolled across the door to keep out wolves, and there she had to stay until friends removed the stone the next morning. Tornvall stopped daily and treated her eyes with a salve. To the surprise of all, her eyesight was restored.

A soldier was then brought to Tornvall with a frostbitten leg requiring amputation. *I had no instruments except a Swedish penknife and an American saw, but I boiled them and did the best I could. I had a book on anatomy, and I kept it by me during the operation and looked at the diagrams to the leg as I cut. I did it on the verandah, and the neighbors gathered round to watch the performance. I had no ether or chloroform, but used a hot salt solution as a palliative.*

The operation was successful, and afterward the young soldier dried his dismembered leg in the sun so he could carry it home to his mother.

But the city fathers, unimpressed, called a public meeting to discuss driving Tornvall from their boundaries. The tide turned when the old beggar woman faced the crowd. "Do you want good people in this city or not?" she demanded. "You all know me, you know that I was almost blind, and now I see. This man has helped me."

Her words, strangely similar to those in John 9, moved the city, and Tornvall was allowed to stay in Ping-Liang where in time he established both a church and a medical center.

Today's Suggested Reading
John 9:17–25

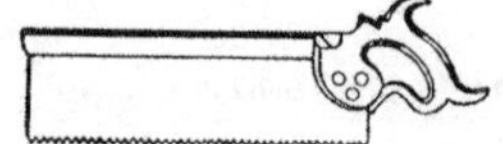

He answered and said, "Whether He is a sinner or not I do not know. One thing I know: that though I was blind, now I see." John 9:25

In Through the Window

In John 10, Jesus warned his followers of shepherds who do not enter the sheepfold by the door, but climb in some other way. Sixteen centuries later, his words stung the heart of a man named Alexander Henderson.

Henderson was born in Criech, Fifeshire, Scotland, in 1583, educated at St. Andrews, and sent to pastor the church at Leuchars. But he wasn't a kind and godly man. He was a churchman, but not a genuine Christian, and his appointment was unpopular with the people of Leuchars. Prior to his arrival, they shut and bolted the church door to keep him from their pulpit.

Arriving in town, Henderson was determined to claim his parish, and when he couldn't force open the door, he crawled through a window and thus began his ministry—such as it was—among them.

One day he heard of a group of Christians meeting for Bible study and worship. Their meeting was unauthorized by the state, and Henderson wanted to secretly discover what was being taught. He slipped through the shadows and took a back seat in a darkened corner.

The teacher rose and turned to the day's Bible lesson, John 10:1–2, and read: "Most assuredly, I say to you, he who does not enter the sheepfold by the door, but climbs up some other way, the same is a thief and a robber. But he who enters by the door is the shepherd of the sheep."

Henderson nearly fell from his chair, for those words brought to his mind his recent undignified scramble through the church window. His eyes were opened, and he recognized his own hypocrisy. In simple faith, he gave himself without reserve to Jesus Christ.

His village ministry immediately assumed a different tone, and for several years he tended his flock as a true shepherd. His reputation grew, and he became a leader in the Presbyterian movement to free Christianity in Scotland from the tyranny of state control.

Today's Suggested Reading

John 10:1–10

Most assuredly, I say to you, he who does not enter the sheepfold by the door, but climbs up some other way, the same is a thief and a robber.
John 10:1

Other Sheep

Peter Cameron Scott was born in Scotland in 1867 but emigrated to America with his parents when he was thirteen. In Philadelphia, young Peter was attracted to the stage. He had a powerful voice, and his training under a renowned Italian maestro convinced him he had a brilliant career with the opera. Overruling his parents' objections, he set out one day to respond to an advertisement for chorus singers.

On the steps of the opera house, he paused. It was a moment of life-changing decision. Should he pursue stage and fame, or should he respond to that nagging inner call of God to overseas church planting? His feet turned and walked away from the building, and shortly thereafter Peter and his brother John sailed for Africa.

It was a nightmare. John contracted a deadly tropical disease, and Peter was unable to save him. Constructing a crude coffin, Peter buried his brother with his own hands. Soon afterward, Peter himself fell ill to malaria and was forced to England, broken in both body and spirit.

While in London, badly needing hope and inner revival, Peter visited Westminster Abbey. As he walked through the vast cathedral, he came across the tomb of David Livingstone, the great African missionary and explorer. On Livingstone's tomb were engraved the words: "Other sheep I have which are not of this fold; them also I must bring."

Peter seemed to discover deep strength in that sentence, and he knelt there in prayer to rededicate himself to God's service in Africa, even if it meant his life. In 1895, along with A. T. Pierson and C. E. Hurlburt, Peter Cameron Scott founded the Africa Inland Mission with an initial missionary force of seven. Today 850 missionaries serve AIM International, advancing the gospel throughout Africa and around the globe.

Today's Suggested Reading

John 10:11–18

And other sheep I have which are not of this fold; them also I must bring, and they will hear My voice; and there will be one flock and one shepherd. John 10:16

Recalled from Death

Prayer," said Martin Luther, "is a climbing up of the heart into God. None can believe how powerful prayer is, and what it is able to effect, but those who have learned it by experience."

Luther spoke from his *own* experience, for he received many interesting answers to prayer. One of them occurred when his dearest friend and associate, Philip Melancthon, fell ill. According to an ancient biography, Luther arrived to find Philip about to "give up the ghost. His eyes were set; his consciousness was almost gone; his speech had failed, and also his hearing; his face had fallen; he knew no one, and had ceased to take either solids or liquids."

Luther, beside himself with grief, exclaimed, "Blessed Lord, how has the devil spoiled me of this instrument!" He turned toward the window and began praying aloud earnestly. Almost instantly Philip began to move, and he was soon completely restored. Melancthon later said, "I should have been a dead man had I not been recalled from death itself by the coming of Luther."

A similar event in 1541 involved Friedrich Myconius, another of Luther's friends, who was found in the last stages of tuberculosis and was almost speechless. Luther was unable to visit Myconius' bedside, so he wrote a prayer and sent it to him by courier, saying: *May God not let me hear so long as I live that you are dead, but cause you to survive me. I pray this earnestly, and will have it granted. Amen.*

Myconius later said, "I was so horrified when I read what the good man had written, that it seemed to me as though I had heard Christ say, 'Lazarus come forth!'"

And it so happened as Luther prayed. Myconius recovered and was kept from the grave until a short time after Luther's death in 1546.

Today's Suggested Reading
John 11:33–44

Now when He had said these things, He cried with a loud voice, "Lazarus, come forth!" John 11:43

September **13** Till We Meet Again

Anne Kotiadis grew up in New York City in the whirl of night clubs, dances, and gala parties. She was well schooled in etiquette and the social amenities, but her heart didn't seem satisfied. At Columbia University, she met a Christian named Ethel who invited her to an evangelistic rally. Jack Wyrtzen of Word of Life was the speaker, and that service led to Anne's conversion.

Some time later she met a young academic at Columbia University, Anthony Fortosis, and succeeded in eventually winning him to Christ. The two were married and settled down to a deeply satisfying marriage, blessed by four healthy boys and one beautiful daughter.

Then in the fall of 1967, Anne discovered a tumor. Despite the best medical attention, her situation grew serious. Dr. Fortosis recalled: *Through the long, pain-filled weeks that followed, I saw Anne hover between life and death. Those were dark days and yet some of the most blessed of our life together. Anne needed me as never before as her strength began to ebb. The disease spread to her spine and internal organs. The pains began to increase. Finally she entered the hospital for the last time. The doctor told me it was now only a matter of time.*

One afternoon we had our last "date." We talked about our beautiful 20 years together. After observing so many mediocre marriages, it occurred to us that God had crowned our union with abundant affection. She told me where she had hidden our love letters, and she said she wanted a very simple funeral. I kissed her and held her hand as she drifted into a coma. The next morning at 11 A.M. Anne's spirit departed to be with her glorious Lord.

*Why did the Lord send this most grievous of trials? Why did He take home a wife and mother so early in her ministry? Why? I am content that His will is always good and acceptable. "What I do thou knowest not now, but thou shalt know hereafter." John 13:7 is good enough for me.**

Today's Suggested Reading
John 13:1–11

Jesus answered and said to him, "What I am doing you do not understand now, but you will know after this." John 13:7

---

*Adapted from Anthony C. Fortosis, *Till We Meet Again* (Asheville, NC: Ben Lippen School, 1970), passim.

Let Not . . .

One weekend when President Jimmy Carter was at Camp David, a terrible scandal broke out concerning his brother Billy. Back at the White House, Rosalynn kept calling Jimmy, deeply distressed. Over the phone, Jimmy reminded her of John 14:1 which they had read the previous night during their devotions. They agreed to claim afresh the words of Jesus: "Let not your heart be troubled; you believe in God, believe also in Me." Thus they weathered the storm.

When Jabez Bunting was 19, he struggled with whether to enter the ministry. On a paper, he set forth the arguments for and against:

Pro:

1. *The want of labourers, especially such as are intelligent and well-informed.*
2. *The general duty of using every talent that God has imparted.*
3. *The deep-rooted and long-continued conviction that I am called to this work.*
4. *The opinion of those Christian friends whom I have consulted.*

Contra:

1. *My own deficiency in point of knowledge*
2. *My want of time for religious study.*
3. *My youth and inexperience.*
4. *My unfaithfulness to God's grace and my littleness of faith and love.*
5. *My rare opportunities of exercising.*

The "Pros" won, and on August 12, 1798, Jabez preached his first sermon in a cottage in a village called Sodom. His text was John 14:1. He grew to be a powerful leader of the early Methodist movement and the successor to John Wesley.

Howard Jones of the Billy Graham Evangelistic Association once preached from this verse to a remote tribe in the Sudan. He noticed his interpreter had difficulty with the text, and after the service he asked him about it. "Well," said the translator, "in the Sudanese language, the heart isn't the seat of the emotions; the liver is. So when I translated your words, it came out, 'Don't let your liver quiver!' "

Today's Suggested Reading

John 13:36—14:1

Let not your heart be troubled; you believe in God, believe also in Me.
John 14:1

Glimpsing Glory

Among America's greatest orators was John Jasper, a former slave, who once began a funeral sermon, saying, *Let me say a word about this William Ellyson. I say it the first and get it off my mind. Ellyson was no good man—didn't say he was; didn't try to be good, and they tell me he died as he lived, without God and without hope in the world. It's a bad tale to tell on him, but he fixed the story hisself.*

Jasper then shifted gears and took his audience on a breathtaking tour of heaven. *I loves to go down to the old muddy James, mighty red and muddy, but it goes along so grand and quite like it was tending to business. But that ain't nothing to the river which flows by the throne. I longs for its crystal waves, and the trees on the banks, and all manners of fruits. This old head of mine often gets hot with fever and rolls on the pillow, and I has many times desired to cool it in that blessed stream as it kisses the banks of that upper Canaan. The thought of seeing that river, drinking its water and resting under those trees. . . . Oh, to be there!*

After that, I'd stroll up them avenues where the children of God dwell, and view their mansions. Father Abraham, I'm sure he got a great palace. And David. And Paul, the mighty scholar who got struck down in the Damascus Road, I want to see his mansion. Then I cut round to the back streets and looks for the little home where my Savior set my mother up to housekeeping. I expect to know the house by the roses in the yard and the vine on the porch.

At that point, Jasper dramatically sprang back, clapped his hands, and shouted, *Look there! See that one! Hallelujah, it's John Jasper's. Said He was going to prepare a place for me. There it is! Too good for a poor sinner like me, but He built it for me, a turn-key job, and mine forever!*

Jasper waxed on like this for an hour and a half, but to the listeners it seemed like only a moment. That day, they glimpsed glory.

Today's Suggested Reading
John 14:2–3

In My Father's house are many mansions; if it were not so, I would have told you. I go to prepare a place for you. John 14:2

James Wilson's Verse September **16**

On board the missionary ship *Duff* one Sunday in December, 1796, Captain James Wilson shared his life's story with a group of missionaries he was transporting to the South Pacific.

I was the youngest of 19 children. While I was still a lad, my father, a ship captain, took me to sea. I grew up amid influences of the worst kind. When the war with the American colonies broke out, I enlisted in the king's service and fought in the bloody battle of Bunker Hill. Returning to England, I secured a berth on one of the vessels of the East India Company.

But while sailing toward India, Wilson's ship was captured by the French and he was thrown in jail. One night, learning he was going to be sold into Muslim slavery, he jumped from the prison ramparts into the river below, not knowing that it swarmed with alligators. Wilson barely made it out of the river, only to be captured by Muslim soldiers. He was stripped, bound, and driven on a forced march of 500 miles. *How I survived that terrible march or the tortures of prison, I cannot explain. It would be difficult to describe the horrors of those 22 months.*

Wilson suffered pitifully from the cold and starvation. At length, however, he was returned to England where, at age 34, he met Pastor John Griffin. *In three hours conversation, Griffin convinced me of the weakness of my belief in natural religion and planted in my mind certain truths which led to my conversion. The text he used with convincing effect was John 14:6.*

Wilson purchased a ship and became the first to transport missionaries to the South Pacific. Over and over in his preaching, he proclaimed John 14:6. It was also a verse he used to bolster his missionaries, saying: *Dwell much on John 14:6. Jesus is the only source of life abundant for discouraged Christians and the only source of eternal life and hope for a degraded race.*

Today's Suggested Reading
John 14:3–6

Jesus said to him, "I am the way, the truth, and the life. No one comes to the Father except through Me." John 14:6

September **17** The Exchanged Life

Hudson Taylor opened the interior of China to the gospel as no missionary had done before, but the effort brought him to the brink of collapse. A letter from fellow missionary John McCarthy turned the tide. The secret to inner victory, said McCarthy, is ". . . abiding, not striving nor struggling; looking off to Him, trusting Him for present power."

Taylor read those words in a little mission station at Chinkiang on an autumn Saturday in 1869, and . . . *as I read, I saw it all. I looked to Jesus; and when I saw, oh how the joy flowed.*

John 15 took center stage in his life as he realized the joy of abiding in Christ. He later wrote: *As to work, mine was never so plentiful or so difficult; but the weight and strain are now gone. The last month has been perhaps the happiest in my life; and I long to tell you a little of what the Lord has done for my soul.*

As I read [McCarthy's letter], I looked to Jesus and saw that He had said, "I will never leave you." Ah, there is rest. For has He not promised to abide with me? As I thought of the Vine and the branches, what light the blessed Spirit poured into my soul!

Later Hudson found a little booklet by Harriet Beecher Stowe that so articulated his experience that he sent it to all his missionaries. Mrs. Stowe wrote: *How does the branch bear fruit? Not by incessant effort for sunshine or air; not by vain struggles. It simply abides in the vine in undisturbed union, and blossoms and fruit appear as of spontaneous growth. How, then, shall a Christian bear fruit? By efforts and struggles? No. There must be a full concentration of the thoughts and affections on Christ; a complete surrender to Him; a constant looking to Him for grace.*

"Abide in Me," said Jesus, "and I in you. As the branch cannot bear fruit of itself . . . neither can you unless you abide in Me."

Today's Suggested Reading
John 15:1–8

Abide in Me, and I in you. As the branch cannot bear fruit of itself, unless it abides in the vine, neither can you, unless you abide in Me. John 15:4

Christ's Badge

Hugh Latimer, a founder of English Protestantism, was burned at the stake in 1555, but his voice still rings through his surviving sermons and influence. Here are excerpts from one of his sermons still popular today:

Seeing time is far spent, we will take no more in hand at this time than this one sentence, John 15:12—"This is My commandment, that you love one another . . . ," for it will be enough to consider well and to bear away with us. Our Savior Himself spake these words at His last supper. He makes love His badge and would have His servants known by their badge—love alone.

Moses, the great prophet of God, gave many laws, but he gave not the Spirit to fulfill the same laws; but Christ gave this law, and promised unto us, that when we call upon Him, He will give us His Holy Ghost, who shall make us able to fulfill His laws.

Then, using Paul's description of love in 1 Corinthians 13, Latimer went on to describe point by point the qualities of love produced by the Holy Ghost in God's people. Then ending his sermon, he said:

Now let us enter into ourselves, and examine our own hearts. And when we find ourselves to be out of His livery, let us repent and amend our lives, so that we may come again to the favor of God and spend our time in this world to His honor and glory, forgiving our neighbors all such things as they have done against us.

Now to make an end: Mark here who gave this precept of love—Christ our Savior Himself. When and at what time? At His departing, when He should suffer death. Therefore these words ought to be more regarded, seeing He himself spake them at His last departing from us. May God give us grace so to walk here in this world, charitably and friendly one with another, that we may attain the joy which God hath prepared for those that love Him. Amen.

Today's Suggested Reading
John 15:9–15

This is My commandment, that you love one another as I have loved you. John 15:12

"Mother, It Is Too Late"

Few missionaries have enjoyed such success as Jonathan and Rosalind Goforth of China. Their ministry swept multitudes into the kingdom and left an army of Christian workers in its wake. Rosalind, however, almost didn't make it to China because of her mother's protests.

I replied quietly, but firmly, "Mother, it is too late; I promised Jonathan Goforth last night to be his wife and go to China!"

Poor Mother! She almost fainted. For six weeks, I stayed with a brother, then came a letter from my sister pleading with me to return, as Mother was sobbing day and night and failing fast.

Reaching home, I was shocked at the change in Mother. She would not speak to me but seemed broken-hearted. My distress was very great. Could it be God's will for me to break my mother's heart? At last one day as I listened to her pacing her bedroom floor, weeping, I could bear the strain no longer and determined to find out God's will. Going down to the parlor where the large family Bible rested on a desk, I stood for a moment crying to the Lord for some word of light. Then I opened the Bible at random, and the first words my eyes lit on were: "Ye have not chosen me, but I have chosen you, and ordained you, that ye should go and bring forth fruit." I knew at once God was speaking His will to me through these words, and in an instant the crushing burden was gone. Running to Mother's room, I begged her to hear what I had to say. Unwillingly she unlocked the door and stood while I told her of my prayer and answer. For a moment she hesitated, then she threw her arms about me, saying, "O my child, I can fight against you, but I dare not fight against God." From that moment till her death, Mother's heart was entirely with me in the life I had chosen.

Today's Suggested Reading
John 15:16–27

You did not choose Me, but I chose you and appointed you that you should go and bear fruit, and that your fruit should remain. John 15:16

Fire

Blaise Pascal was without equal, a brilliant French philosopher, scientist, mathematician, and inventor. As a boy in Paris, his remarkable grasp of mathematics led to his involvement with the Academy of Science where he mingled with the greatest intellectuals of his day. At age 15, he was writing books and developing theorems that left his professors shaking their heads. As a teenager, he invented history's first calculating machine, and other discoveries led to the invention of the barometer, the vacuum pump, the air compressor, the syringe, and the hydraulic press.

But as a young man, Pascal had trouble with the spiritual equations of life, and he soon grew disillusioned with the pleasures of his fashionable society. One night he picked up a Bible and turned to John 17. As he began reading, verse 3 blazed out like a spark and seemed to set the room on fire—"And this is eternal life, that they may know You, the only true God, and Jesus Christ whom You have sent." His soul was instantly converted to Jesus Christ, and taking pen and parchment, he began quickly writing snatches of his thoughts:

In the year of Grace, 1654
On Monday, 23d of November
Fire
God of Abraham, God of Isaac, God of Jacob,
not of the philosophers and scholars.
Certitude. Certitude, Feeling. Joy. Peace.
Joy, joy, joy, tears of joy.
This is eternal life, that they may know You, the Only true God,
and Jesus Christ whom You have sent.
Jesus Christ. Let me never be separated from Him.

Pascal's life was changed forever, and he became a powerful Christian thinker and writer. The scrap of parchment was found after his death sewed into the lining of his coat, that it might ever be close to his heart.

Today's Suggested Reading
John 17:1–8

And this is eternal life, that they may know You, the only true God, and Jesus Christ whom You have sent. John 17:3

September **21**

The Power of Long Distance Prayer

On a day I shall never forget, recalled Hudson Taylor, the famous missionary to China, *when I was about 15 years of age, because my mother was absent from home, I had a holiday, and in the afternoon looked through my father's library to find some book with which to while away the hours. I turned over a basket of pamphlets, and selected from among them a gospel tract which looked interesting. I sat down to read the little book in an utterly unconcerned state of mind.*

Little did I know at the time what was going on in the heart of my mother, eighty miles away. She rose from dinner with an intense yearning for the conversion of her boy, and she went to her room and turned the key in the door, resolved not to leave until her prayer was answered. Hour after hour did she plead for me, until at length she was constrained to praise God for that which His Spirit taught her had been accomplished.

In the meantime I had taken up this little tract, and while reading was struck with the sentence, "The finished work of Christ." The thought passed through my mind, "Why does the author use this expression?" Immediately the words "It is finished" came to mind. What was finished? I replied, "A full and perfect atonement for sin: Christ died for our sins." A light flashed into my soul by the Spirit, that there was nothing to be done but to fall down on one's knees, and, accepting this Savior and His salvation, to praise him forever.

When mother came home a fortnight later, I was the first to meet her at the door to tell her I had glad news. I can almost feel her arms around my neck, as she said, "I know, my boy; I have been rejoicing for a fortnight."

You will agree with me that it would be strange indeed if I were not a believer in the power of prayer.

Today's Suggested Reading
John 19:25–30

So when Jesus had received the sour wine, He said, "It is finished!" And bowing His head, He gave up His spirit. John 19:30

Unconscious Influence

September **22**

Just as Horace Bushnell (1802–1876) began practicing law, he was converted, and, returning to Yale, he enrolled in divinity school and entered the ministry. Bushnell found sermons in texts where others saw none. His study of John 20:8, for example, led to this sermon entitled "Unconscious Influence."

We must answer not only for what we do with purpose, but for the influence we exert. Men are ever touching unconsciously the springs of motion in each other; thus it is that one man, without thought or intention, is ever leading some after him. Little does Peter think as he goes straight into the sepulcher that he is drawing his brother apostle after him. Little does John think, when he loses his misgivings and goes after Peter, that he is following his brother.

Just so, unawares to himself, is every man laying hold of his fellow man to lead him where otherwise he would not go. A Peter leads a John, a John goes after a Peter, both of them unconscious of any influence exerted or received.

Thus our life and conduct are ever propagating themselves through the circles in which we live. The Bible calls the good man's life a light, and it is the nature of light to flow out spontaneously in all directions and fill the world unconsciously with its beams. The Christian shines, not so much because he will, as because he is a luminous object. I verily believe that the insensible influences of good men are much more potent than their voluntary or active, as the great silent powers of nature are of greater consequence than her little disturbances and tumults.

The true philosophy of doing good is here explained. It is, first of all, to be good—to have a character. In order to act with effect on others, he must walk in the Spirit, he must be akin to God and so filled with His disposition that he shall seem to surround himself with a hallowed atmosphere.

And this, my brethren, is what God intends for you all.

Today's Suggested Reading
John 20:1–10

Then the other disciple, who came to the tomb first, went in also; and he saw and believed. John 20:8

"Lord, It's Not Happening"

Off the northwestern coast of Scotland are a group of 500 rugged islands called the Hebrides. In 1949, 50-year-old Duncan Campbell left the Scottish mainland to preach in the towns and villages of Lewis, the largest of the Hebrides. During his itinerant ministry there, a revival swept the island that is still talked about to this day. During those years, Duncan later said, you could stop any passerby and find that he was thinking about God and the state of his soul.

But one town, Arnol, remained indifferent to the gospel. Finding little response there to his preaching, Duncan invited a small group of men to join him for a prayer meeting. As they assembled, he asked the local blacksmith to lead them. "O God," said the man, "You made a promise to pour water upon him that is thirsty and floods upon the dry ground. Lord, it's not happening. I don't know how the others here stand, but Lord, if I know anything about my own heart I stand before Thee as an empty vessel. O Lord, Your honor is at stake, and I now challenge You to fulfill your covenant engagement and do what You have promised to do."

At that moment the house began to tremble and shake like a leaf in the wind. Someone whispered to Duncan, "An earth tremor. . . ." Duncan replied, "Yes," but his mind was thinking of Acts 4, when after "they had prayed, the place where they were assembled together was shaken; and they were all filled with the Holy Spirit. . . ."

Duncan walked from the church to find the whole village "alive with the awareness of God." From that moment, "a movement broke out that is spoken of in Scotland today as the Arnol revival, one of the mighty movements in the midst of this gracious visitation."

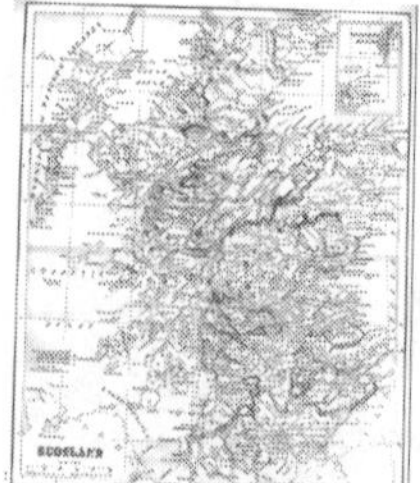

Today's Suggested Reading

Acts 4:23–31

And when they had prayed, the place where they were assembled together was shaken; and they were all filled with the Holy Spirit, and they spoke the word of God with boldness. Acts 4:31

A Swarm of Leeches September **24**

Peter's response to Jewish officials who ordered him to cease preaching the name of Jesus was bold and earned the apostles all a flogging. "They departed from the presence of the council, rejoicing that they were counted worthy to suffer shame for His name" (v. 41). Thus they set an example for generations yet to come.

The Indian Christian Sundar Singh once ventured into the forbidden land of Nepal on the borders of Tibet to preach Jesus. In a village there, as he distributed copies of Mark's Gospel, one of his listeners ripped the gospel apart and hurried to notify town officials. Sundar was promptly thrown into jail, but he used the time to witness to his fellow prisoners.

When the jailer forbade him from evangelizing, Sundar, sounding much like Peter, replied, "I must obey my Master and preach His gospel, regardless of threats and sufferings."

The jailer ordered the prisoners not to listen, but they replied, "This man tells us how we can become better, which is what we need."

Sundar was taken from the cell to a filthy cattle shed. The jailer stripped off his clothing, tied him down hand and foot, and threw upon him a swarm of leeches that had been collected from the jungle. These loathsome creatures latched onto his body and began sucking his blood. *But, I lifted up my heart to God in prayer, and He sent such heavenly peace into my soul that I soon began to sing His praises.*

After he had grown weak from loss of blood, the authorities released him and returned his clothes. Sundar was soon seen again in the center of town, preaching the gospel and telling the people, *It is a joy to suffer for my Savior. In bearing my cross, I hope to direct men to His cross with its offer of peace and pardon. In the cross of Christ alone, I will ever glory.*

Today's Suggested Reading

Acts 5:26–42

But Peter and the other apostles answered and said: "We ought to obey God rather than men." Acts 5:29

Blind Chang

The Boxer Rebellion in China was the largest massacre of Protestant missionaries in history, with 188 adults and children being killed. Thirty thousand Chinese Christians also perished during the summer of 1900 at the hands of the Boxers. Among them was Chang Shen, the best known evangelist in Manchuria.

Chang had been a notorious character prior to his conversion—a gambler, thief, and womanizer. At midlife he lost his eyesight, and neighbors considered it a judgment from God. Hearing of a missionary hospital in a distant area, Chang traveled hundreds of miles only to find all the beds full. The hospital chaplain kindly gave him his own bed, and over time, doctors partially restored Chang's vision. In the process they introduced him to Jesus Christ.

When Chang asked for baptism, missionary James Webster told him, "Go home and tell your neighbors you have changed. I'll visit you later, and if you are still following Jesus, I will baptize you." When Webster arrived in Chang's village five months later, he found hundreds of inquirers.

Chang's eyesight didn't last, but his evangelistic zeal did. He traveled from village to village, winning hundreds to Christ. Missionaries followed in his wake, baptizing and organizing churches of the converts he had won.

When he was finally arrested by the Boxers, he was put in an open cart and driven to a nearby graveyard while singing, "Jesus loves me, this I know. . . ." At the cemetery, he was shoved into a kneeling position. Three times he uttered the words of Stephen, "Lord Jesus, receive my spirit!" Then the sword sliced through his neck like a knife through butter.

The Boxers were so deeply shaken by Chang's quiet authority that they had his body drenched in oil and burned, so as to prevent, they thought, his resurrection. But still apprehensive, they retreated from the area altogether, thus saving other Christians from being butchered to death.

Today's Suggested Reading
Acts 7:51–60

And they stoned Stephen as he was calling on God and saying, "Lord Jesus, receive my spirit." Acts 7:59

Whole Every Whit

September **26**

Rev. Morgan Edwards, a respected New Jersey clergyman, told this well-documented story regarding a woman named Hannah Carman who died in Brunswick, New Jersey, in 1776. A. J. Gordon (1836–1895), in his book *The Ministry of Healing,* relayed it in Edwards' own words:

At the 25th year of her age, Hannah got a fall from a horse, which so hurt her back that she was bowed down and could in no wise lift herself up. Her limbs were so affected that she was a perfect cripple, not able to walk nor help herself in the smallest matters.

One day the young woman who cared for her went into the garden. She had not been long in the garden before she heard a rumbling noise in the house. She hastened in, thinking Hannah had tumbled out of her chair; but how was she surprised to see the cripple in the far end of the room praising God who had made her whole every whit.

Her neighbor came in haste and was equally astonished, for Hannah was in an ecstasy, running about the house, moving chairs and tables from place to place, going to her bedroom, walking, and every now and then falling on her knees to praise God.

Hannah soon explained, "While I was musing on the words, 'Aeneas, Jesus Christ maketh thee whole,' I could not help breathing out my heart in the following manner: 'O that I had been in Aeneas' place!' Upon that I heard an audible voice saying, 'Arise, take up thy bed and walk!' The suddenness of the voice made me start in my chair; but how was I astonished to find my back strengthening and my limbs recovering. I got up, and to convince myself that it was reality and not a vision, I lifted up my chair and whatever came in my way till I was convinced the cure was real and not a dream or delusion."

Today's Suggested Reading

Acts 9:31–35

*And Peter said unto him, Aeneas, Jesus Christ maketh thee whole: arise, and make thy bed. And he arose immediately. Acts 9:34**

---

*King James Version

Sons of Satan

From A. J. Gordon, whose nineteenth-century pen wrote the previous story, came another book entitled *The Holy Spirit in Missions,* in which he related an incident observed by Rev. Isaac D. Colburn, missionary to Burma. A group of Burmese Christians had gathered along the banks of a pool to witness the baptism of several new believers. Watching from a distance were many locals, some of them perched on rocky crags overlooking the water. Among these observers were two men, father and son, who detested the gospel and had done everything in their power to dissuade those about to be baptized.

As the Burmese pastor was opening the services by the pool, the father and son interrupted with blasphemous words, curses, and obscene gestures. The preacher rebuked them, but they continued all the more. Just as the pastor was about to plunge his first disciple into the water, the two antagonists stripped off their clothes and plunged naked into the water where they conducted their own malicious baptism, mocking the Christians by dipping each other in the water and uttering the name of the Trinity laced with profanities.

Standing on the bank was a native Karen evangelist named Sau Wah, who, before his conversion, had been a dreaded opponent of the gospel. Now he rose and, his voice stern with authority, demanded silence. Turning to the old man in the water, he said, "O full of all deceit and all fraud, you son of the devil, you enemy of all righteousness, will you not cease perverting the straight ways of the Lord?"

As he spoke, the Holy Spirit seemed to fall on the assembly. The two blasphemers, suddenly thunderstruck, raced from the pool and up the bank, but before going many yards, they fell to the earth. The Christians proceeded with their baptism. Afterward they found the father lying face down on the ground, dead. The son recovered consciousness and was carried to the village, but within a few months he followed his father to the grave.

Today's Suggested Reading
Acts 13:1–12

[Paul] said, "O full of all deceit and all fraud, you son of the devil, you enemy of all righteousness, will you not cease perverting the straight ways of the Lord?" Acts 13:10

The Devil's Old Regiment

Paul and Barnabas grew bold and said. . . ."

Benjamin Randall, founder of the Northern Free Will Baptists, discovered the same boldness while preaching in 1777. Preaching throughout New Hampshire, he faced bricks, bats, mobs, and threats of tar and feathers. *Persecution grew very hot, and such threatening language was used that I really felt my life in danger. But I gave myself to prayer, and the Lord wonderfully protected me.*

One day he decided to preach in a nearby town but was informed a mob had determined to stop him and the town was in an uproar. His friends appealed for cancellation of his plans, but Randall, undaunted, headed there anyway. Stopping at a friend's house, he learned that 40 men had gathered at a tavern, and someone had offered them a barrel of rum to kill him.

"That is the devil's old regiment," said Randall. "He raised 40 men to kill brother Paul. But he missed it then, and I believe he will now. I feel God has called me to preach in that town."

Arriving there at last, Randall gathered a few nervous souls and began preaching from Acts 13:46. Soon the dreaded mob drew near. The women in Randall's audience took fright and ran from the house, but the men remained put. Randall continued his sermon with one eye on the Master and the other on the mob. He later wrote: *I felt a most blessed degree of God's power drop into my soul. I felt assured that it would be impossible for them to touch my person. I felt completely shielded by the omnipotent hand.*

Suddenly a frightening thunderstorm broke over the village, with terrifying flashes of lightning and sonic booms of thunder. Randall preached over the storm, which dissipated most of the rabble, then left peacefully, shaking hands with a few troublemakers who lingered. Not one offered him an unpleasant word.

Today's Suggested Reading
Acts 13:42–48

Then Paul and Barnabas grew bold and said, "It was necessary that the word of God should be spoken to you first; but since you reject it, and judge yourselves unworthy of everlasting life, behold, we turn to the Gentiles." Acts 13:46

September **29** Come and Help Us

One incident helped change Western civilization—Paul's vision of a man from northern Greece led him to take the gospel westward into Europe instead of eastward into Asia—with far-reaching results.

Nearly 400 years later, a remarkably similar dream changed all of Irish history.

Patrick, a teenager in England, was kidnapped by pirates and scuttled away to Ireland where he was enslaved as a herdsman of swine. There he labored six years before escaping and returning to his relatives. Back in England, he resumed his education and prepared for his career.

But one evening—"in the depth of the night," he later said—he dreamed a man from Ireland appeared to him, saying, "Holy boy, we are asking you to come home and walk among us again." Patrick awoke "struck to the heart." To his family's dismay, he began making plans to return to Ireland, land of his captivity, this time as a slave of Christ. He felt God calling him there as a missionary.

Arriving in Ireland in A.D. 432, Patrick went to work on the west and northern sides of the island, seeking to evangelize the Celts. These were tribal peoples who lived in clans rather than towns, and who raised cattle and occasionally engaged in tribal warfare. Their religion consisted of Druid superstitions involving magic, and animal (even human) sacrifice.

Patrick traveled from village to village, preaching and evangelizing. In his *Confessions,* the first personal missionary accounts in history, he writes that he faced death twelve times; nevertheless, he continued for more than 30 years, planting some 200 churches and baptizing an estimated 100,000 people.

He gave credit to God, calling himself, "Patrick the sinner, an unlearned man to be sure, that none should ever say that it was my ignorance that accomplished any small thing; but judge ye and let it be most truly believed, that it was the gift of God."

Today's Suggested Reading
Acts 16:1–10

And a vision appeared to Paul in the night. A man of Macedonia stood and pleaded with him, saying, "Come over to Macedonia and help us." Acts 16:9

It Will Be Beautiful in the Morning

September **30**

John Harper jostled his luggage while helping Nina, age six, with her suitcase. Harper was a Baptist minister in Glasgow en route to a preaching engagement at Moody Memorial Church of Chicago. His wife had died at Nina's birth, so he was traveling with his young daughter, assisted by Nina's aunt, Miss Jessie Leitch. After settling themselves in the second-class passenger section, they took off to roam the ship. They felt especially fortunate to be on the maiden voyage of the greatest ocean liner ever built—the *Titanic.*

On the evening of April 14, 1912, Harper stood on deck admiring the sunset. "It will be beautiful in the morning," he said. Hours later when the collision occurred, he awakened his daughter, wrapped her in a blanket, and carried her to the deck.

When the ship sank, Nina was saved in lifeboat #11, sitting on her aunt's lap. For many years, she would not speak of that night, but before her death in 1986, she told of remembering the lights of the ship go out and of hearing the screams of the dying. But what of her father?

Months later, in a church in Hamilton, Canada, a man rose, saying, "I was on the *Titanic* the night she went down. I was thrown into the waters and managed to grab a spar and hang on for dear life. The waters were icy. Suddenly a wave brought a man near, John Harper of Glasgow. He too was holding to a piece of wreckage. He called out, 'Man, are you saved?' "

" 'No, I am not,' I replied."

"He shouted back through the darkness, 'Believe on the Lord Jesus Christ, and thou shalt be saved.' "*

"The waves bore him away, but a little later he was washed back alongside me. 'Are you saved now?' he called out."

" 'No,' I replied."

" 'Believe on the Lord Jesus Christ, and thou shalt be saved.' Then losing his hold on the wood, he sank. And there, alone in the night, with two miles of water under me, I trusted Christ as my Savior. I am John Harper's last convert."

Today's Suggested Reading
Acts 16:20–33

So they said, "Believe on the Lord Jesus Christ, and you will be saved, you and your household." Acts 16:31

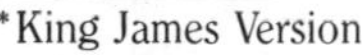

*King James Version

October

Ten Flights

A Blinding Flash

Dark Mines

To Her Brother's Killers

Jesus Is Victor

During World War II, many Germans, frightened about the future and unable to contact loved ones, turned to fortune-tellers. After the war, Corrie ten Boom, who had survived the Nazi concentration camp Ravensbruck, traveled throughout the country and found many people still entranced by sorcery and witchcraft. During her speaking engagements, she often dealt with the sins of witchcraft, fortune-telling, horoscopes, demonism, and the occult.

But whenever she spoke on such topics, she became unusually fatigued, so tired she could hardly reach her bed. A sickly feeling came over her, and her heart sometimes beat irregularly.

At length, she took it all to God in prayer, complaining that she could not continue in such shape. The exhaustion of fighting demonism was too great, and she doubted she could go on much longer. "Perhaps another month or two, and then my heart will give out," Corrie told the Lord.

But that day in her book of German Scripture readings, she came to Acts 18:9–10: "Do not be afraid, but speak and do not keep silent; for I am with you, and no one will attack you to hurt you; for I have many people in this city." There followed these words:

Though all the powers of hell attack,
Fear not, Jesus is Victor

Her heart filled with joy as she instantly took those words as a direct answer to her need. She began to pray again, this time in praise, claiming the promise of God's presence and protection and asking Him to shield her by His own blood from demonic attack

At that very moment, she sensed healing flow into her heart, and it began beating regularly. From that day whenever Corrie ten Boom spoke against witchcraft and sorcery, she felt as strong and as well as always. And ever after, her message when confronting the occult was: Jesus is Victor!

Today's Suggested Reading
Acts 18:1–11

Now the Lord spoke to Paul in the night by a vision, "Do not be afraid, but speak and do not keep silent; for I am with you, and no one will attack you to hurt you; for I have many people in this city."
Acts 18:9–10

Bonfire

I have a friend who came to me complaining of spiritual lethargy. He was a new Christian, but felt that no growth was occurring in his life. As we talked, he casually mentioned, "I have even stopped looking at the pile of pornographic material under my bed."

"Under your bed!" I said, alarmed. "Why haven't you burned it?"

"Well, I don't look at it any more, but I hate to destroy it because I spent so much money for it all—magazines, books, videos. . . . Maybe I could sell it or give it away."

"It's fit for nothing but the fire," I said, confident that his spiritual progress would be stymied until he cleaned under his bed.

"Does your life need a bonfire?" Vance Havner asked. "Are your heart and home filled with things that offend the Lord? His Word cannot grow and prevail until after the bonfire."

Clint Morgan, a friend in Africa, tells me that when villagers come to Christ, they commonly gather their neighbors to publicly burn their fetishes and false gods.

One of history's most famous bonfires was kindled in 1520, when the Roman pope sent a lengthy document excommunicating Professor Martin Luther of the University of Wittenberg. On the morning of December 10, the following notice was posted at the university: "Let whosoever adheres to the truth of the gospel be present at nine o'clock at the church of the Holy Cross—where the books of papal decree and scholastic theology will be burnt, according to ancient and apostolic usage. Come, pious and zealous youth, to this pious and religious crusade."

Students soon assembled and built a fire. Luther threw in his document of excommunication, saying, "Because you have corrupted God's truth, may God destroy you in this fire." As the flames leaped up, students threw in pile after pile of papal books from their own shelves and from the university library. The blaze continued until nightfall—and the Reformation was ignited.

Today's Suggested Reading
Acts 19:8–20

Also, many of those who had practiced magic brought their books together and burned them in the sight of all. And they counted up the value of them, and it totaled fifty thousand pieces of silver. Acts 19:19

So Great Treasure

In Acts 20:2–3, the apostle Paul arrived in southern Greece and settled himself for the winter of A.D. 56–57 in the villa of his friend Gaius. There he rested and prayed and plotted strategy, envisioning a new missionary journey to encompass western Europe as far as Spain. But he also made a contingency. In the event of his death, he wanted his core doctrines set forth in a systematic and methodical manner and deposited in the church at the very heart of the Roman Empire. And so, over a three-month period, he composed the book of Romans. In so doing, he changed the world. To this day, whenever, wherever the book of Romans is prayerfully preached and taught, souls are saved, revival occurs, and the people of God are encouraged.

It was the book of Romans that transformed St. Augustine from pagan to preacher.

It was the book of Romans that converted and consumed the great Reformer Martin Luther.

It was Luther's preface to the book of Romans that warmed John Wesley's heart and set it afire.

The book of Romans so affected English Bible translator William Tyndale that he wrote this about it: *Forsomuch as this epistle is the principal and most excellent part of the New Testament, and the most pure Euangelion, that is to say glad tidings and what we call gospel, and also a light and a way in unto the whole scripture, I think it meet that every Christian man not only know it by rote and without the book, but also exercise himself therein evermore continually, as with the daily bread of the soul. No man verily can read it too oft or study it too well: for the more it is studied the easier it is, the more it is chewed the pleasanter it is, and the more groundly it is searched the preciouser things are found in it, so great treasure of spiritual things lieth hid therein.*

"When the message of Romans gets into a man's heart," wrote J. I. Packer, "there is no telling what may happen."

Today's Suggested Reading

Romans 1:1–7

. . . concerning His Son Jesus Christ our Lord, who was born of the seed of David according to the flesh, and declared to be the Son of God with power . . . by the resurrection from the dead. Romans 1:3–4

Play the Man

One day in 1742, British evangelist George Whitefield was invited by a Quaker coal merchant to preach at the fair at Marylebone Field, west of London. "I'll build you a platform," promised the Quaker.

When Whitefield and his wife Elizabeth arrived at the fairgrounds, the sun was already down and the crowds seemed rowdy. Brawny prizefighters challenged all comers to bare-fisted fights in rings galore. Gambling booths were plentiful as fireflies, and the liquor flowed freely.

Whitefield seldom displayed fear, but that evening he was visibly nervous as he mounted the Quaker's rickety little platform. As he raised his magnificent voice, wisps of people began gathering. The crowds at nearby booths thinned, then emptied as Whitefield waxed louder. Shortly into his message, he saw a small army of battered, bare-chested fighters marching toward him, blood in their eyes. His voice faltered, but suddenly he felt a tug on his gown. "George," Elizabeth said, looking up at him. "Play the man for God!"

Boldness surged through Whitefield. "I am not ashamed of the gospel of Christ," he shouted, his voice ringing over babel and bedlam. "It is the power of God to salvation for everyone who believes." He threw out his arms in a dramatic gesture, and his platform nearly collapsed under him.

The fighters noticed Whitefield's wobbly platform, and they began crowding forward, hoping to topple it. But a group of Christians formed a circle around the evangelist, and Whitefield carried on, preaching as though on the deck of a tossing ship. A thrown rock struck him in the face, then a rotten egg, then a handful of manure. Still he preached on, his words flying like missiles into the crowd. Some people began to pray and others melted in tears. Still he preached on.

At last, his work done, the 27-year-old evangelist climbed from his perch and, escorted by friends, tried to get to his carriage. A young man lunged at him brandishing a sword, but it was deflected by a friend's cane.

Whitefield had played the man for God.

Today's Suggested Reading

Romans 1:8–17

For I am not ashamed of the gospel of Christ, for it is the power of God to salvation for everyone who believes, for the Jew first and also for the Greek. Romans 1:16

The Shantung Revival

One night in China, Southern Baptist missionary C. L. Culpepper stayed up late for devotions, but as he tried to pray he felt like stone. Finally he asked, "Lord, what is the matter?"

I had opened my Bible to Romans 2:17. It seemed the apostle Paul was speaking directly to me when he said, "But if you call yourself a Christian and rely upon the gospel, and boast of your relation to God, and know His will, and approve what is excellent; and if you are sure you are a guide to the blind, a light to those in darkness, a correction to the foolish, a teacher of children—you then who teach others, will you not teach yourself?"

The Holy Spirit used these verses like a sword to cut deeply into my heart. He said, "You are a hypocrite! You claim to be a Christian! What have you really done for Christ? The Lord said those who believed on Him would have rivers of living waters flowing from their inmost being! Do you have that kind of power?"

Culpepper awakened his wife, and they prayed into the night. The next morning at a prayer meeting with fellow workers, he confessed to pride and spiritual impotence, saying his heart was broken. The Holy Spirit began to so convict the others of sin that they could hardly bear it.

I watched their faces grow pale, then they began to cry and drop on their knees or fall prostrate on the floor. Missionaries went to missionaries confessing wrong feelings toward one another. Chinese preachers, guilty of envy, jealousy and hatred, confessed their sins to one another.

The revival spread through the seminary, the schools, the hospital, and the area churches.

The impression that the Shantung Revival wrote upon my soul lingers with me even today. Throughout the breadth and depth of Shantung Province, I discovered signs of revival. The churches were crowded as never before. Attendance multiplied. Countless people gave up their idols.

*Still today, my heart often returns to Shantung.**

Today's Suggested Reading

Romans 2:17–24

You, therefore, who teach another, do you not teach yourself? Romans 2:21

---

*Adapted from "The Shantung Revival" by C. L. Culpepper, in *Spirit of Revival,* October, 1991, pp. 10–15.

The Fountain

If Romans is the core of the gospel, Romans 3:21–26 is the spinning core of the book of Romans. Its powerful, succinctly stated truth has brought multitudes to Christ, and has given reassurance to more besides.

One of England's greatest poets was William Cowper (pronounced Cooper), but he lived a tormented life, wracked by depression, given to occasional attempts at suicide. The problems had started in boarding school, during which young William, a shy child, had been brutally hazed, his nerves shattered. He was afterward in and out of insane asylums, but he learned to ventilate his feelings through poetry.

One day he found a Bible on the bench in the garden, and he opened to the 11th chapter of John and read of Jesus' raising Lazarus from the dead. The thought fleetingly came to William that perhaps the power and goodness of Jesus could touch his own life. He opened the Bible again and this time read Romans 3:21–26. Verse 25 especially spoke to him, and instantly Cowper felt the burden roll from his shoulders. He was so enthusiastic about his encounter with Christ in these verses that he immediately dashed off a poem of 13 verses which began:

All at once my chains were broken
From my feet the fetters fell
And the word in pity spoken
Snatched me from the jaws of hell.

Though Cowper still suffered spells of depression, his faith in Christ (and his friendship with John Newton, author of "Amazing Grace") led to his writing some of our most loved Christian hymns. Among them: "God Moves in a Mysterious Way," "O For a Closer Walk with God," and . . .

There is a fountain filled with blood
Drawn from Immanuel's veins,
And sinners plunged beneath that flood
Lose all their guilty stains.

Today's Suggested Reading
Romans 3:21–26

. . . whom God set forth as a propitiation by His blood, through faith, to demonstrate His righteousness. Romans 3:25

"You Take Over"

Years ago while in college, I worked in several Billy Graham crusades as a "grunt." One of my more pleasant tasks was serving as chauffeur for the actress Jeannette Clift, who had just played the part of Corrie ten Boom in the film *The Hiding Place*. I found her to be so kind and pleasant that I was eager later to read her personal testimony of finding Christ as her Savior.

Jeannette was raised in a Christian home, but arrived on Broadway with little Christian influence. The exception was a small white Bible wrapped in cellophane that she always placed on her dressing room table whenever she opened a show. Though she seldom read it, she panicked if she couldn't find it. At length, however, she started reading it. She got bogged down in Leviticus, but asked the Lord to show her if he had any message for her other than what to do should her neighbor's ox fall into the ditch.

A few weeks later, she was waiting at a bus stop on her way to an audition when a burst of rain drenched the street. She ducked into a nearby bookstore, and as the rain worsened, Jeannette made her way into an adjacent auditorium. A man was speaking, and Jeannette, disinterested, stepped back onto the street under an awning. But then they rolled up the awning. Jeannette dashed back into the auditorium just as the speaker, Major Ian Thomas, was getting warmed up. She listened, and her heart creaked opened a little more.

One day shortly afterward, Jeannette discovered Romans 5:8, and suddenly she saw herself as a sinner whom God loved and for whom Christ died. Alone in her apartment, she cried out, "All right! Jesus Christ, whoever you are, you take over."

He did.

Today's Suggested Reading

Romans 5:1–9

But God demonstrates His own love toward us, in that while we were still sinners, Christ died for us. Romans 5:8

A Christmas Sermon

Christmas Evans was born on Christmas Day, 1766, and converted eighteen years later. He had been a wild, illiterate youth; and his old gang, angered by his newly embraced faith, attacked him on a mountain road, beat him and gouged out his right eye. But his grasp of the gospel and his power in presenting it made him among Wales' most celebrated preachers. One of his best sermons was from Romans 5:15. Describing the condition of a Christless person, Evans said:

Behold the wretched fallen creature! The pestilence pursues him. The leprosy cleaves to him. Consumption is wasting him. Inflammation is devouring his vitals. Burning fever has seized on the very springs of life. The destroying angel has overtaken the sinner in his sins. The hand of God is upon him. The fires of wrath are kindling about him, drying up every comfort and scorching all his hopes to ashes. Conscience is chastising him with scorpions. See how he writhes! Hear how he shrieks for help!

Is there no mercy? Is there no means of salvation? Hark! amidst all this prelude of wrath and ruin, comes a still small voice saying: "much more the grace of God, and the gift of grace, which is by one man, Jesus Christ, hath abounded unto many."

By grace ye are loved, redeemed, and justified. By grace ye are called, converted, reconciled, and sanctified. Salvation is wholly of grace. The plan, the process, the consummation are all of grace. Where sin abounded, grace much more abounds, manifested in the gift of Jesus Christ. Our sins were slain at His cross and buried in His tomb. His resurrection hath opened our graves and given us an assurance of immortality.

The work is finished. The ransom is effected. The kingdom of heaven is opened to all believers. Lift up your heads and rejoice! There is no debt unpaid, no devil unconquered, no enemy within your own hearts that has not received a mortal wound! Thanks be unto God who giveth us the victory through our Lord Jesus Christ.

Today's Suggested Reading
Romans 5:10–17

But the free gift is not like the offense. For if by the one man's offense many died, much more the grace of God and the gift by the grace of the one Man, Jesus Christ, abounded to many. Romans 5:15

Right Then

Successful NASCAR drivers owe as much to their pit crews as to their own skills behind the wheel. One of the finest crew chiefs on the NASCAR circuit is David Smith, who calls the shots in pit row for such drivers as Dale Earnhardt.

In the 1960s, David had plunged headlong into the hippie scene with its trademark consumption of alcohol and drugs. But his father, a new Christian, began witnessing to him.

"Dad," David said, "when I get old like you, I'll get religion."

"What if you were to die today? What if you go to one of these parties tonight and get shot? What if you wreck your car? Where do you think you'll be?"

"Well, I guess I'll be pushing up daisies!"

"No," his father replied, "you've got a soul. That soul is either going to spend eternity in heaven with the Lord, or in hell."

On his twenty-fifth birthday, his mother gave him a Bible, which he stowed away in a drawer and forgot about. But finally . . . *I realized things weren't fun anymore. I was drinking a lot, I was smoking a lot of dope, I was taking a lot of pills, but nothing seemed fun. Something impressed me to get that Bible out of my drawer. I sat down and just started reading. My mother had underlined a bunch of key Scriptures—John 3:16, Romans 3:23, and Romans 6:23: "For the wages of sin is death, but the gift of God is eternal life in Christ Jesus our Lord."*

That evening David read his Bible until far into the night, then found he couldn't sleep. The next morning at 6:30 he called his mom, only to discover she had been so burdened for him that she, too, had spent a sleepless night, on her knees.

David turned from his sins to Christ. *And I knew at that moment all the guilt was gone, the burden lifted off my shoulders. In its place a joy and warmness and a complete peace came into my life. Right then.**

Today's Suggested Reading

Romans 6:20–23

For the wages of sin is death, but the gift of God is eternal life in Christ Jesus our Lord. Romans 6:23

---

*Adapted from P. J. Richardson and Robert Darden, *Wheels of Thunder* (Nashville: Thomas Nelson, 1997), pp. 145–149.

October **10** A Prodigal Returns

Throughout his teen years, Franklin Graham, son of Billy and Ruth Graham, rebelled against God, charting his own course and venturing deeper and deeper into the "far country" as his parents worried and prayed. But by 1974, *the sinful life was not satisfying any longer. There was an emptiness—a big hole right. . . . The truth is, I felt miserable because my life wasn't right with God.*

One day in Switzerland, Franklin, 22, and his father took a walk. Billy turned somewhat nervously and said, "Franklin, your mother and I sense there's a struggle going on in your life. You're going to have to make a choice either to accept Christ or reject him. You can't continue to play the middle ground."

Shortly afterward in Rome, Franklin came upon his friend David Hill reading in Romans 7, where Paul vividly described struggling with sin. David read the chapter aloud, and Franklin, listening, *broke out in a sweat and lit a cigarette to ease the tension. David didn't say another word at that moment—he just stared at me. I made some excuse to leave, but I couldn't forget the words David had just read. I realized for the first time that sin had control over my life. I went back to my room and fished through my luggage for my New Testament and turned to Romans 8:1: "There is therefore now no condemnation to those who are in Christ Jesus."*

For several days Franklin struggled, haunted by his father's words and by those of Romans 7. He read Romans 8:1 repeatedly, until finally, while traveling in Israel, *I put my cigarette out and got down on my knees beside my bed. I'm not sure what I prayed, but I know that I poured out my heart to God and confessed my sin. I told Him I was sorry and that if He would take the pieces of my life and somehow put them back together, I was His.*

*My years of running and rebellion had ended.**

Today's Suggested Reading
Romans 8:1

There is therefore now no condemnation to those who are in Christ Jesus, who do not walk according to the flesh, but according to the Spirit. Romans 8:1

---

*Adapted from Franklin Graham, *Rebel with a Cause* (Nashville: Thomas Nelson, 1995), pp. 118–123.

For I Consider

October **11**

What comes to your mind when you think of God's faithfulness? How is he faithful? To what? To whom? Psalm 145:13 says, "The Lord is faithful to His promises."* Having filled His Word with promises, the Lord can be wholly expected to fulfill every one of them.

What comes to mind when you think of faith? According to Romans 4:21, faith is "being fully convinced that what He had promised He is able to perform." "Therefore take heart," said Paul, "for I believe God that it will be just as it was told me" (Acts 27:25).

How, then, should we meet and master the crises of life? By sinking our fingernails deep into God's promises and hanging on for dear life. Hudson Taylor once quipped during a trying time, "We have twenty-five cents—and all the promises of God."

Charles Spurgeon said that when troubled, he would find a promise of God, hammer it out into gold-leaf "and plate my whole existence with joy from it."

When my father was shut up in the hospital's intensive care ward, dying, I would try to sleep through the night in an adjacent waiting room. But the comings and goings of the doctor disturbed me. Hot irons of anxiety poked me from all sides, and I was worried sick. But this verse began coming to mind: "For I consider that the sufferings of this present time are not worthy to be compared with the glory which shall be revealed in us."

I knew that for my father, a devoted Christian, even the worst that could happen—death—couldn't compare to His everlasting glory in Christ. I knew that for those of us who remained, the pain of his passing would be temporary, and the reunion to follow, eternal.

I will never forget the tranquilizing power of that promise, how it helped me to rest at night and to recover my emotions by day.

"He who promised is faithful" (Heb. 10:23).

Today's Suggested Reading

Romans 8:18–25

For I consider that the sufferings of this present time are not worthy to be compared with the glory which shall be revealed in us. Romans 8:18

---

*Today's English Version

Dark Mines

I once grew concerned that I was leaning on a verse from Romans too much and claiming it too often. But the thought came to me that Romans 8:28 is indestructible. We can never wear it out.

My appreciation of Romans 8:28 then increased further as I studied its context. Verse 26 tells of the Holy Spirit's assistance in our weakness. Not knowing the future, we often don't know exactly what to pray. But the Holy Spirit, who *does* know both the future and the mind of God, prays for us "with groanings which cannot be uttered." The Heavenly Father both hears and answers the Spirit's intercessions, and as a result the unfolding events of our lives work out for our good.

This was the truth that sustained Barnard Gilpin when he was in deep political danger. Gilpin was called the "Apostle of the North" due to his powerful ministry in the north of England during the sixteenth century. He dearly loved Romans 8:28, and became famous for quoting it on all occasions. But when Bloody Queen Mary ascended the throne, his life was in danger. He was summoned to London to be tried and executed, but along the way he broke his leg. Some mockingly asked him if he imagined that his accident would work out for his good. "Yes," he said, "all things."

And it *did* work out for his good. His journey was delayed while he recovered at an inn, and before he reached London and its ominous prison and its cruel stake, word came that Queen Mary had died. He returned home to Houghton-le-Spring and labored for the Lord for another quarter of a century.

"From threatening clouds we get refreshing showers," said Charles Spurgeon. "In dark mines are found bright jewels; and so from our worst troubles come our best blessings."

Today's Suggested Reading
Romans 8:26–29

And we know that all things work together for good to those who love God, to those who are the called according to His purposes. Romans 8:28

Verses for Survival

The test was positive, she was pregnant, and it seemed like the end of the world. Jane Frank, 18, left the doctor's office in a daze and sought out her boyfriend, terrified he would abandon her. Instead he leaned near and held her. "I'm sorry," he said. "Don't worry, honey, things will work out."

Jane told him the doctor had advised checking into having an abortion. The couple sat silently, staring out the window, shell-shocked by the greatest dilemma of their young lives. "Our parents would kill us if they knew you were pregnant," Jerry said at last.

The next morning, Jane confided in a coworker who also advised having an abortion, even recommending a clinic that could "solve" her problem. Jane made an appointment and was ushered into a small, white examining room. "We get girls like you every day," said the counselor. "You're young, unmarried, and have no means to support a baby."

The abortion occurred the next Friday. But the pain lingered, and as the years passed Jane realized that her abortion "had not removed a blob of tissue, as I had been told; it had destroyed a baby."

At times, her anguish was almost unbearable, but finally through the help of a nearby crisis pregnancy center, Jane found relief through Jesus Christ. A wise counselor and a good support group helped. Jane allowed the natural grieving cycle to complete itself, knowing she could "either wallow in the past and let my failures engulf me, or allow God to use me for His work."

A passage of Scripture provided powerful spiritual medicine for her soul. It was Romans 8:33–39, describing the triumphant, overwhelming, soul-penetrating love of God: "For I am persuaded that neither death nor life, nor angels nor principalities nor powers, nor things present nor things to come, nor height nor depth, nor any other created thing shall be able to separate us from the love of God which is in Christ Jesus our Lord."

"Romans 8:33–39," said Jane, "became my verses for survival."*

Today's Suggested Reading

Romans 8:21–39

Yet in all these things we are more than conquerors through Him who loved us. Romans 8:37

---

*Adapted from "A Mark on My Heart" by Jane Frank in *Decision*, May, 1987, pp. 16–17, © 1987; published by Billy Graham Evangelistic Association.

20,000 Verses

Vast portions of the Bible were written to be memorized, evidenced by the number of psalms that are based on Hebrew acrostics, such as Psalm 119 or Psalm 145. Bible translator William Tyndale suggested the book of Romans as prime memory material: *I think it meet that every Christian man know it by rote and without the book.* Scripture memory stocks the mind with material for endless meditation, which, in turn, accelerates the transformation process. It keeps the heart from sin, and helps instill in us the mind of Christ.

In his book *Your Inner You,* pastor Leslie Flynn tells of his conversion to Christ during an evangelistic campaign led by Dr. Oscar Lowry, author of the book *Scripture Memorizing for Successful Soul-Winning.* Lowry admits that he entered Christian service as a young man with an undisciplined mind. Thinking he could not memorize Scripture, he filled the flyleaf of his Bible with references useful for counseling and evangelism, but it proved awkward to stop his conversations long enough to track down the right verse. Finally he determined to succeed at Scripture memory.

"If I can memorize one verse, I can memorize one more," he said, "and ten more, and even one hundred."

He rose early the next morning and chose what seemed to him a difficult passage, Romans 10:9–10. He paced the room, saying to himself, "I will do this thing." He struggled with this passage for half an hour, but finally succeeded in memorizing it completely. The next morning, he reviewed and reinforced those verses in his memory, then added a new one. He kept reviewing his chosen passages and adding new ones until it dawned on him one day that he could repeat one hundred verses without looking in his Bible.

By the end of his life, he had learned over 20,000 verses, and he could locate each by chapter and verse without his Bible. No wonder his Christian life was full of joy, his mind full of wisdom, and his evangelistic efforts full of success.*

Today's Suggested Reading

Romans 10:5–10

. . . if you confess with your mouth the Lord Jesus and believe in your heart that God has raised Him from the dead, you will be saved. Romans 10:9

---

*Adapted from Leslie B. Flynn, *Your Inner You* (Wheaton, IL: Victor Books, 1984), p. 60.

Magnifying the Ministry October **15**

Despite having no formal theological training, B. H. Carroll became a powerful Baptist leader who helped create Southwestern Baptist Theological Seminary—today the world's largest seminary—in 1910.

One of Carroll's most powerful sermons was preached from Romans 11:13 to Baptist pastors at Belton, Texas, in 1982. He spoke of the high calling of preaching the Word, whether in large, well-known pulpits or in small, obscure ones. "Just think of it seriously," he said. "When we stand to preach, we engage the attention of three worlds—men, angels, and devils. Eternal interests hinge on the sermon." He went on to say that every word of a sermon was either "a winged bullet of death or a message of reprieve from a death sentence."

Listening carefully that day was Dr. S. P. Brooks, who had been angry all his life about growing up in a rural parsonage, the son of a hardworking, downtrodden preacher. *I had resented all my life the hardships incident to the life of my own father who, as a country preacher, had labored on the farm and in the schoolroom for a living while he literally gave his life for others. I grew up in rebellion that my mother, a cultured woman, should endure the toils of the country pastor. Then came Dr. Carroll's sermon. He spoke in such terms that I began to see meaning in the pastoral ministry to which I had been a stranger.*

I left with a broken spirit. My heart was crushed. I went to bed that night with sleepless eyes. I cried the live long night. I could not get away from the picture Dr. Carroll had drawn. Morning came. With it, a joy that had not been mine before. I was glad my father was a preacher.

Brooks' heart was healed, and from that day he carried in his heart a pride for his parents—and a thanksgiving to God for his upbringing—that he had always longed to have.

Today's Suggested Reading
Romans 11:13–15

For I speak to you Gentiles; inasmuch as I am an apostle to the Gentiles, I magnify my ministry. Romans 11:13

Ten Flights

One Sunday in Copenhagen, Corrie ten Boom, 80, spoke from Romans, urging her audience to present their bodies to Christ as living sacrifices. After church two young nurses invited her to their apartment for lunch, and Corrie went with them—only to discover they lived on the tenth floor, and there was no elevator.

She didn't think she could mount the stairs, but as the nurses were so eager for her visit she decided to try. By the fifth floor, Corrie's heart was pounding, her breath coming in gulps, her legs buckling. She collapsed in a chair on the landing thinking she could go no further, and she complained bitterly to the Lord. Looking upward, the stairs seemed to ascend to infinity, and Corrie wondered if she might die en route. "Perhaps I am leaving earth to go to heaven," she thought.

But the Lord seemed to whisper that a special blessing awaited her on the tenth floor, so she bravely pressed on, one nurse in front of her and another following.

Finally reaching the apartment, Corrie found there the parents of one of the girls. She soon discovered that neither parent was a Christian, but both were eager to hear the gospel. Opening her Bible, Corrie carefully explained the plan of salvation. "I have traveled in more than sixty countries and have never found anyone who said they were sorry they had given their hearts to Jesus," she said. "You will not be sorry, either."

That day both prayed for Christ to enter their lives.

On her way down the steps, Corrie said, "Thank you, Lord, for making me walk up all these steps. And next time, Lord, help Corrie ten Boom listen to her own sermon about being willing to go anywhere you tell me to go—even up ten flights of stairs."*

Today's Suggested Reading
Romans 12:1–2

I beseech you therefore, brethren, by the mercies of God, that you present your bodies a living sacrifice, holy, acceptable to God, which is your reasonable service. Romans 12:1

---

*Adapted from Corrie ten Boom, *Clippings from My Notebook* (Nashville: Thomas Nelson Publishers, 1982), pp. 53–55.

Loud and Clear

As a terrified, wide-eyed boy in the Philippines during World War II, Fred Magbanua wondered if there was hope beyond death. After the war, he began listening to Far East Broadcasting Company and accepted Christ as his Savior. Later he became a civil engineer and, feeling he should use his talents only for the Lord, began working for FEBC.

One day he received a letter offering him a lucrative engineering job in New York. He was immediately attracted to the money, but his wife was bothered. Had he not committed himself to work only for Christ? But ignoring his wife's uneasiness, Fred began dreaming of America.

That night Fred's FEBC broadcast was from Romans 12:1–2. He recorded the program, then left the studios. Outside the building, he noticed a burned-out warning light atop the towering antenna and decided to change it at once. He threw the switch, not realizing the high voltage wasn't effectively grounded, and he climbed to the top of the 300-foot tower.

Suddenly a powerful electromagnetic field of 10,000 watts of radio frequency current seized him and began burning him alive. As he dangled by his neck, writhing in pain, unseen in the night, he was shocked to hear his own voice: "I beseech you therefore, brethren, by the mercies of God, that you present your bodies a living sacrifice. . . ." His own programming was going out over the antenna, and his head, locked by the radio frequency power, was acting as a conductor.

Fred lost consciousness and his body toppled toward the ground. Miraculously he fell only eight feet before catching on a brace. A fuse blew, saving him from burning to death. But a dozen deep burns seared through his head to his skull, and X-rays showed a black spot on his brain. During three months hospitalization, Fred suffered indescribable pain. But as Christians around the world prayed, he recovered. He left the hospital determined to be the Lord's living sacrifice, and served for many years with FEBC.

He had gotten the message loud and clear.*

Today's Suggested Reading
Romans 12:1–13

I beseech you therefore, brethren, by the mercies of God, that you present your bodies a living sacrifice, holy, acceptable to God, which is your reasonable service. Romans 12:1

---

*Adapted from Eleanor G. Bowman, *Eyes Beyond the Horizon* (Nashville: Thomas Nelson Publishers, 1991), pp. 115–118.

October **18** The Bible Thumper

Persecution comes in all sizes and shapes, and it strikes at people of all ages and conditions; even in America—and perhaps even on your street. Our response to attack and abuse can speak volumes to those considering Christianity for themselves.

Barbara Robidoux was intrigued with one of her neighbors, a Christian named Michelle, whom she dubbed her neighborhood "Bible Thumper." Michelle displayed a happy enthusiasm and cheer that brightened the street. Each summer during Vacation Bible School, she would stuff her van full of kids and plunge into church activities with them, providing blessed relief for parents and homemakers who were hard put to manage their summertime youngsters.

Barbara examined Michelle critically, looking for flaws, trying to discover what made her tick. What she found instead was compassion, kindness, humility, gentleness, and patience.

Then one afternoon, Michelle's son was attacked by a group of neighborhood bullies. He barged through the door, dripping with tears, having been pelted with stones, accompanied by jeers of "Jesus freak! Jesus freak!" Barbara watched as Michelle calmly comforted her son, and as she prayed for the souls of the bullies. When Barbara asked her how she could remain so composed, Michelle replied, "I'm so angry I can hardly talk, but Romans 12:14 tells us, 'Bless those who persecute you; bless and do not curse.'"

That incident haunted Barbara for days, and as time passed she questioned Michelle about her beliefs, and listened carefully to her answers.

"I don't know if any of the neighborhood children found Christ that summer because of Michelle's touch," said Barbara. "But I know that I did. I found Him because one family lived it in my neighborhood, and they lived it daily."*

Today's Suggested Reading

Romans 12:9–16

Bless those who persecute you; bless and do not curse. Romans 12:14

---

*Adapted from "Michelle's Touch" by Barbara Robidoux in *Discipleship Journal,* Issue 43, 1998, p. 12.

Take Up and Read

"Take up and read," said the voice. He did; he found a verse in Romans; and it changed both his life and all of subsequent Christian history.

He was St. Augustine of Hippo, born in A.D. 354 in North Africa to a pagan father and a devout mother. Patricius, the father, was described as a man of "fiery temper and dissolute habits," and Augustine followed robustly in his path. The young man was full of revelry and drunkenness, lewdness and lust. He enjoyed life with all its vices, and his mother Monica's warnings against fornication and false religions fell on deaf ears. By young adulthood, he had fathered a child, joined a cult, and become a professor of rhetoric and philosophy.

Years passed, but Augustine's mother Monica never stopped praying for her wayward son. Few men have been so assaulted by a mother's prayers. She followed him across the Mediterranean, praying for him and pleading with him to give his life to Christ. She nipped at his heels like the hound of heaven. In Milan she finally persuaded him to listen to the great Bishop Ambrose, and gradually the prodigal began contemplating Christianity. One day as Augustine sat in a friend's garden, he overheard a child chanting, "Take up and read!"

Restraining a rush of tears, I got up, concluding that I should open the Bible and read the first chapter I came to. I seized it, opened it and immediately read in silence the paragraph on which my eyes first fell: ". . . not in revelry and drunkenness, not in lewdness and lust, not in strife and envy. But put on the Lord Jesus Christ, and make no provision for the flesh, to fulfill its lusts." Instantly at the end of that sentence, as if a light had streamed into my heart, all the darkness of my doubt fled away.

Augustine went quickly to tell his overjoyed mother of his conversion. Monica died contentedly soon afterward, her prayers answered, her work done. But her illustrious son went on to become one of the greatest thinkers in church history.

Today's Suggested Reading
Romans 13:8–14

But put on the Lord Jesus Christ, and make no provision for the flesh, to fulfill its lusts. Romans 13:14

To Her Brother's Killers

Among the twentieth century's best known martyrs are five young missionaries who were speared to death in 1956 in the Ecuadorian jungle by the Aucas—Jim Elliot, Nate Saint, Pete Fleming, Ed McCulley, and Roger Youderian. The men had flown into Auca territory and established a camp on a sandbar in the Curaray river, hoping to make contact with this fierce tribe.

Nate Saint's older sister Rachel had already been serving with Wycliffe Bible Translators in Peru. When her brother had arrived in Ecuador, she, too, developed a burden for the Aucas and shortly thereafter, the doors opened for Wycliffe to work in Ecuador. In February, 1955, Rachel arrived at a base near Auca territory and began studying the language.

Rachel was away from Ecuador in 1956 when the dramatic news arrived that her brother had been killed. As she pored over Scripture, the Lord impressed her with the apostle Paul's words in Romans 15:21, and she felt as though they had been written just for her: "To whom He was not announced, they shall see; and those who have not heard shall understand." She felt God calling her to take up the work and bring the Aucas to Christ.

In the late 1950s, after months and years of prayer and preparation, Rachel Saint and Elisabeth Elliot ventured into Auca territory and lived among the villagers, learning their lifestyle and perfecting their grasp of the language. (It was later revealed that the Aucas allowed it because they were curious and bothered as to why the five young men had not fired their weapons or tried to defend themselves). Gospel Recordings sent in recordings of the gospel in Auca, and Wycliffe translators worked feverishly on the Gospel of Mark. The Aucas built an airstrip, and Missionary Aviation Fellowship pilots began touching down there.

Soon Auca tribesmen were coming to Christ—among them the very ones who had slain the missionaries. One of the killers, Kimo, became the pastor for the tribe, and it was he who baptized Steve and Kathy Saint, children of the man he and his companions had speared.

Today's Suggested Reading
Romans 15:14–21

. . . but as it is written, "To whom He was not announced, they shall see; and those who have not heard shall understand." Romans 15:21

Still My Determination October **21**

From the days of St. Luke, some of history's greatest preachers have originally trained as medical doctors. One of my favorites was Martyn Lloyd-Jones, born and reared in Wales, who moved to London in 1914 at age fourteen. He enrolled at St. Bartholomew's Hospital as a medical student, graduating in 1921. But as he treated people's physical needs, he became increasingly aware of their spiritual ones, and he felt a nagging call to the ministry of preaching. 1 Corinthians 2:2 burned in his heart: "I determined not to know anything among you except Jesus Christ and Him crucified."

In 1927, he began pastoring in his native Wales. His first sermon was from 1 Corinthians 2:2. Ten years later, he moved to London's great Westminster Chapel as assistant to G. Campbell Morgan. When Morgan retired in 1943, Lloyd-Jones stepped into the pulpit where, for 30 years, he preached "Jesus Christ and Him crucified," dissecting and dividing the Scripture with the precision of a surgeon's scalpel.

On February 6, 1977, he returned to his former church in Wales for the fiftieth anniversary of his ministry. After announcing his text, 1 Corinthians 2:2, he said: *I have a number of reasons for calling your attention tonight to this particular statement. One of them—and I think you will forgive me for it—is that it was actually the text I preached on, on the first Sunday night I ever visited this church. I call attention to it not merely for that reason, but rather because it is still my determination. . . .*

My dear friends, in the midst of life we are in death. This is not theory; this is personal; this is practical. How are you living? Are you satisfied? How do you face the future? Are you alarmed? Terrified? What will you have when the end comes? You will have nothing, unless you have Jesus Christ and Him crucified.

When Lloyd-Jones died four years later, these words were engraved on his tombstone: "For I determined not to know anything among you, save Jesus Christ, and him crucified."

Today's Suggested Reading

1 Corinthians 2:1–5

For I determined not to know anything among you except Jesus Christ and Him crucified. 1 Corinthians 2:2

Tone Deaf

The truth of 1 Corinthians 2:14 has sometimes been illustrated by a story about two British statesmen, William Wilberforce, leader in the movement for the abolition of slavery, and William Pitt, the Prime Minister. Both were brilliant men, both politicians, and they were very great friends. But Wilberforce was a Christian while Pitt, though a church-goer, was not truly converted.

This bothered Wilberforce, and at length he persuaded Pitt to go with him to hear popular evangelist Richard Cecil, who was preaching in London. Wilberforce was thrilled, and that evening Cecil was at his best. The great preacher flung out the gospel with eloquent power, his message crystal clear, his voice reaching every corner of the hall. Wilberforce, lifted to the heavens, could hardly contain himself; but he wondered how his friend Pitt was responding.

He soon found out. As they left the building, Pitt turned and said, "You know, Wilberforce, I have not the slightest idea what that man has been talking about."

William Wilberforce realized afresh that the natural man does not receive the things of the Spirit of God, for they are foolishness to him. The message that bore him to the skies, had only bored his unsaved friend. It was meaningless to him, for Pitt was tone deaf to the spiritual. Richard Cecil had might as well preached to a dead man.

Only the Spirit of God can open a person's heart to God's truth. Perhaps that's why Paul asked the Lord to give his readers "the spirit of wisdom and revelation in the knowledge of Him, the eyes of your understanding being enlightened; that you may know what is the hope of His calling, what are the riches of the glory of His inheritance in the saints, and what is the exceeding greatness of His power toward us who believe. . . ." (Ephesians 1:17–19).

Today's Suggested Reading
1 Corinthians 2:13–16

But the natural man does not receive the things of the Spirit of God, for they are foolishness to him; nor can he know them, because they are spiritually discerned. 1 Corinthians 2:14

The Solid Rock

A verse in 1 Corinthians provides the basis for a hymn that has been shaking the rafters of churches for over 150 years:

My hope is built on nothing less
Than Jesus' blood and righteousness;
I dare not trust the sweetest frame,
But wholly lean on Jesus' name.

On Christ the solid rock I stand,
All other ground is sinking sand.

The hymn first appeared anonymously in leaflet form in the mid-1830s, then it was printed in a hymnbook published by Edward Mote, who titled it, "The Immutable Basis of a Sinner's Hope." It proved instantly popular, and when speculation about its authorship grew feverish, Mote confessed it as his own. He said the song came to him on his way to work.

I began to meditate on the gracious experience of a Christian. Soon the chorus and then the first stanza came to my mind. On the following Sunday, as I came out of Lisle Street meeting, Brother King invited me to his home to try to encourage his critically ill wife. I had early tea that day; then I went to the Kings' home. Mr. King said, "I always sing a hymn, read Scripture, and pray. Will you join me?" He searched in vain for a hymnbook. I said, "I have some verses in my pocket, Brother King. If you like, we can sing them." Mrs. King's heart responded to the words, and Mr. King asked me to leave a copy with her.

Back at home I sat by the fireside musing on Mrs. King's reaction to the hymn; and soon the entire hymn was clear to my mind. I committed the words to paper, making a fresh copy for Mrs. King. Later the thought came to me that as these verses had met this dying woman's needs, perhaps they would help someone else. So I had a thousand leaflets printed for distribution.

Today's Suggested Reading
1 Corinthians 3:9–11

For no other foundation can anyone lay than that which is laid, which is Jesus Christ. 1 Corinthians 3:11

October **24** A Blinding Flash

When Amy Carmichael died in 1951, she left a legacy that still touches the world. Amy served as a missionary to India for the Church of England. Her distinctive work lay in rescuing girls who had been condemned to a life of slavery and shame in Hindu temples, and in establishing homes for children in South India, and as a writer of devotional books.

Her entire ministry flowed from an incident that had happened to her as a child growing up on the streets of Belfast. It was a damp Sunday morning, and she was returning with her family from church. They came upon a broken-down old woman who was quivering under a heavy bundle. With a surge of compassion, Amy and her siblings began helping this ragged woman. One took the bundle as the others grasped her hand and began helping her down the street.

This meant facing all the respectable people who were, like ourselves, on their way home. It was a horrid moment. We were only two boys and a girl, and not at all exalted Christians. We hated doing it. Crimson all over (at least we felt crimson), we plodded on, a wet wind blowing us about, and blowing, too, the rags of that poor old woman. But just as we passed a fountain, this mighty phrase suddenly flashed as it were through the gray drizzle: "Gold, silver, precious stones, wood, hay, stubble; every man's work shall be made manifest; for the day shall declare it, because it shall be revealed by fire; and the fire shall try every man's work of what sort it is. If anyone's work abide. . . ."

"If anyone's work abide—" I turned to see the voice that spoke with me. The fountain, the muddy street, the people with their politely surprised faces, all this I saw, but nothing else. The blinding flash had come and gone. I said nothing to anyone, but I knew that something had happened that had changed life's values. Nothing could ever matter again but the things that were eternal.

Today's Suggested Reading
1 Corinthians 3:12–15

. . . the fire will test each one's work. 1 Corinthians 3:13

The Blade and the Sword

Eli Fangidae, an Indonesian businessman, had a penchant for gambling. It was an insidious disease that left him increasingly depressed. Finally after a particularly devastating loss, he decided to take his own life. On December 12, 1971, he hanged himself in his room.

His brother-in-law found him dangling by the rope, cut him loose, and Eli fell to the floor with a thud and began breathing. Recovering, he railed at his family and forbade them from interfering further in his suicide plans. They sent for an officer, and Eli was taken into protective custody.

The police stripped Eli and the cell of anything that could be used for suicide, but they missed a small razor he had hidden near the toilet. That night when the officers had all gone, Eli retrieved the blade, sat at the table, and stretched out his left wrist. The veins were clearly visible, and with determined nerves, Eli grasped the blade in his right hand and took aim.

Suddenly his attention was drawn to a small book on the table, a Gideon New Testament. Out of curiosity, he opened it and his eyes fell on the words, "Do you not know that you are the temple of God and that the Spirit of God dwells in you? If anyone defiles the temple of God, God will destroy him."

How could the page be opened at that very moment when I was going to commit suicide? There were no earmarks, nor were the verses underlined. When I thought of those verses given me by God, I shook out of control. I knelt down and cried, "Oh God, forgive me. Have mercy on me." These words I repeated over and over until the policeman on duty sent for a minister who came and prayed for me. This was on December 15, 1971, and I have never been the same again.

The following year, Eli entered Batu Bible College in Malang, East Java, and later became the pastor of the Timor Evangelical Church in Kupang, Timor, Indonesia.*

Today's Suggested Reading

1 Corinthians 3:16–17

Do you not know that you are the temple of God and that the Spirit of God dwells in you? If anyone defiles the temple of God, God will destroy him. For the temple of God is holy, which temple you are. 1 Corinthians 3:16–17

---

*Adapted from *Converted and Called* (Nashville: The Gideons International, n.d.), pp. 37–38.

October **26** New Man in Her Life

She felt important only when she had men's attention. Brooke Ball cooked for them, hung to their every word, bought them presents, and followed them "like a well-trained puppy." But a series of affairs and broken relationships left her asking, "Why do the people I love leave me?"

One day she was sitting in the park, feeling depressed, making a gift for yet another marginally-interested man. A friend approached, one she hadn't seen in years. *As we talked, my troubles became obvious to her. She knew God could help me and suggested I attend a Bible conference in a nearby city with her.*

Brooke attended the conference, though with a defiant attitude. And yet one message sank in. *I don't recall the exact words; I only remember the teacher talked about immorality and God's disapproval of it. "Do not be deceived. Neither fornicators, nor idolaters, nor adulterers, or homosexuals, nor sodomites . . . will inherit the kingdom of God" (1 Cor. 6:9–10).*

Brooke gave her heart to Jesus Christ, and He gradually helped her change her unhealthy habits. *One day, after I had been wearing a tight T-shirt and short shorts, the thought came to me: "If you want to be treated like a lady (which I did), then you should dress like one." It was a gentle and sensible thought that I knew came from Jesus. Imagine the God of the universe caring about what I wore!*

Besides changing my attire, Christ began changing my desires about men. Instead of wanting to follow a man, I want to follow Christ. On a date with one handsome man, for instance, I was tempted to be immoral again. This time, however, I said no.

As I made more choices like that, an unexpected thing happened: I gained dignity and self-respect. Living life as God meant it to be protected me from being used and rejected.

*Because of the love Christ showed me, I learned to like myself.**

Today's Suggested Reading

1 Corinthians 6:7–14

Do not be deceived. Neither fornicators, nor idolaters, nor adulterers, nor homosexuals, nor sodomites, nor thieves, nor covetous, nor drunkards, nor revilers, nor extortioners will inherit the kingdom of God. 1 Corinthians 6:9–10

---

*Adapted from "Love That Won't Leave Me," by Brooke Ball in *Moody Magazine*, September, 1986, p. 104.

Into His Image

October **27**

Bill Borden began attending church in Chicago with his mother after she became a Christian. When he was eight years old, she gave him a verse of Scripture as a birthday present: "Do you not know that your body is the temple of the Holy Spirit . . . ? You were bought at a price; therefore glorify God in your body and in your spirit, which are God's" (1 Cor. 6:19–20). According to his biographer, those words became the keynote of his life.

While at Yale University, Bill, a handsome athlete worth $50 million, felt God calling him to evangelism. He gave his inheritance to Christian causes and joined China Inland Mission, hoping to reach the Muslims in China. But en route, in Egypt, Bill contracted spinal meningitis and died.

His mother arrived in Cairo just as he died and sent home this message: *I do not want you to think of us as overwhelmed, for we are not. God's loving care and mercy have been evident on every side; and it has been a real joy to be in the place where William, in those few short weeks, became so honored and loved.*

And yet, it is all more like a dream than reality. We had been in doubt as to whether to go to the hospital to see him, altered as he would inevitably be; but thank God, we did. We were told not to go near the bed, but that at a distance it would be safe. The door opened, and immediately we were in the presence of all that remained of our William.

I was shocked at the change, but Joyce said, "Mother, see how he looks like all the pictures of Christ?" I looked again, and then indeed I saw. It seemed as though William had been transformed into the very likeness of Christ, through suffering. It was as though we had been permitted a glimpse into the mystery of suffering, human and Divine, and seen that through it God had, so to speak, given the final touches to William's life.

Today's Suggested Reading

1 Corinthians 6:15–20

Or do you not know that your body is the temple of the Holy Spirit who is in you. 1 Corinthians 6:19

October **28** A Junkyard Dog

After Franklin Graham committed himself to Christ, he was surprised to find his taste for cigarettes was strong as ever. He determined to quit smoking, but three days later, he awoke with *an absolutely overwhelming—almost terrifying—desire for a cigarette. I wanted to smoke so bad that I couldn't think of anything else. It intensified with each passing minute. Throughout the day, the yearning for a cigarette grabbed me like the jaws of a junkyard dog.*

He finally shared his struggle with his friend Roy Gustafson. "Roy, I quit smoking, but I don't think I can hold out. I just don't think I have the power to say no any longer."

"Oh, you don't, huh?" replied Roy, looking up from a hamburger. "Why don't you just get down on your knees and tell God He's a liar?"

"What? I can't do that!"

Roy quoted 1 Corinthians 10:13 to him, then said, "You need to tell God He's a liar. You claimed that verse and it didn't work."

"I'm not going to call God a liar," said Franklin. "Besides, I haven't claimed that verse yet!"

"You haven't?" said Roy, sounding shocked. "Why don't you, then?"

Returning to his room, Franklin knelt beside his bed and prayed, "Lord, I've been wanting a cigarette all day. I don't want to smoke again, but I don't know if I can make it through this day. Will you take this overpowering desire from me?"

Though the desire didn't cease, Franklin's ability to resist it grew. Only once did he slip, on a flight the next day to Athens. *I lit up and took several puffs. Instead of the usual satisfied feeling I would get, the cigarette left a bad taste in my mouth. I snubbed it out, wadded up the pack, and threw it on an empty seat.*

It was his last smoke.*

Today's Suggested Reading
1 Corinthians 10:12–14

No temptation has overtaken you except such as is common to man; but God is faithful, who will not allow you to be tempted beyond what you are able, but with the temptation will also make the way of escape, that you may be able to bear it. 1 Corinthians 10:13

---

*Adapted from Franklin Graham, *Rebel with a Cause* (Nashville: Thomas Nelson, 1995), pp. 126–129.

The Boys and the Bee October **29**

Scripture pervaded the life of M. R. DeHaan, founder of the Radio Bible Class, and was seldom far from his thoughts. In his early years, Dr. DeHaan kept bees, and one day his young sons Marv and Richard went with him to raid the hives. One of the bees zeroed in on Richard and, attacking him like a dive bomber, stung him just above the eye. The boy swatted frantically at the bee, then fell to the ground in agony, kicking and screaming.

The same bee headed toward Marv and buzzed around his head. The terrified boy also hit the ground, rolling and screaming, hiding his head in the grass and crying for help.

Dr. DeHaan rushed over to Marv, picked him up, and told him to stop crying. "The bee is harmless," he said. "It can't hurt you. It has lost its sting." The two then went over to check on Richard. There stuck in the brow above his eye was a little black stinger. DeHaan removed the stinger and checked his son for damage.

"When the bee leaves its stinger in the victim," he told the boys, "from then on it is perfectly harmless. The bee can still buzz and scare you, but it is powerless to hurt you. Your brother took the sting away by being stung."

Unable to resist a sermon, DeHaan went on to quote 1 Corinthians 15:55: "O death, where is thy sting? O grave, where is thy victory?"

"The Lord Jesus, our older Brother," he said, "hung on the cross and took the sting out of death. And death, which has only one sting, can no longer hurt us. It can buzz around and scare us, but its sting is gone."

The boys never forgot the lesson—though Richard would have just as soon learned it some other way.

Today's Suggested Reading
1 Corinthians 15:50–58

*O death, where is thy sting? O grave, where is thy victory? 1 Corinthians 15:55**

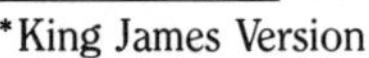

*King James Version

Anywhere

His contagious Christian influence as missionary, pastor, and college president touched thousands of lives, and his writings on the Victorious Christian Life moved millions more. V. Raymond Edman left a mark behind him—circled, underlined, and highlighted.

Early in his career, Edman nearly died of tropical disease while a missionary in Ecuador. Seeking to regain his strength, he took a Pacific voyage in 1928 aboard a Dutch freighter, the *Boskoop*. He missed his work terribly, and even though his weakness made it hard to leave his stateroom, he labored intently over the lectures he hoped to give at his Ecuadorian Bible institute.

As he outlined the book of 2 Corinthians, he reached chapter 2, and read the words, "Now thanks be to God who always leads us in triumph in Christ. . . ." He was staggered. He read the words several times, slowly, prayerfully, phrase-by-phrase.

He suddenly sensed a great contrast between that verse and his condition. Here he was, broken health, unsure future, anxious about his missionary service, not far from death's door. Yet to Paul, life was ongoing, unbroken triumph! Edman walked to the deck and began praying for a triumphant spirit. Quickly and quietly, the Lord seemed to whisper in his ear, "But are you willing to go anywhere for me?"

Slowly, with trembling heart, Edman replied, "Yes, Lord, anywhere in Ecuador Thou mayst send me."

"I did not say in Ecuador."

For a long time, Edman gazed across the Pacific, conscious that the Lord was standing beside him, awaiting an answer. Finally in deepest sincerity, Edman replied, "Yes, Lord, anywhere Thou sayest I will go, only that my life may be always a constant pageant of triumph in Thee." He stood there for a very long time, thinking of the testimony of George Mueller, who once told of the moment when he died to self, to ambition, to the praise or blame of men, only that he might live in Christ. Now he, too, had abandoned all—even his ministry goals—for the sake of Christ.

From that day, God began to use V. Raymond Edman in an unprecedented way.

Today's Suggested Reading
2 Corinthians 2:12–17

Now thanks be to God who always leads us in triumph in Christ, and through us diffuses the fragrance of His knowledge in every place.
2 Corinthians 2:14

If Our Earthly Tent . . . October **31**

Thomas Jonathan Jackson overcame many hardships in life. Orphaned at an early age, he worked hard and snatched up whatever schooling he could find. Through Herculean effort, he secured an appointment to the U.S. Military Academy and finished high in his class. While serving with U.S. forces in Central America, he began studying Christianity, gave himself to Christ, and was baptized at age 25.

In 1857, Major Jackson married Mary Anna Morrison, and immediately the young couple started tithing and having family devotions. Jackson used his lunch hour every day for intense Bible study. The couple joined a Presbyterian Church where Jackson started a Negro Sunday school class. "My Heavenly Father has condescended to use me as an instrument in getting up a large Sabbath school for the Negroes," he wrote. "He has greatly blessed it."

When Virginia seceded from the Union, Jackson sided with his fellow Southerners; and on Sunday, April 21, 1861, he and his cadets were ordered into the Confederate Army. Just past noon, Jackson knelt with his wife in their bedroom for prayer. They opened the Bible and Jackson read aloud these words of assurance: "For we know that if our earthly house, this tent, is destroyed, we have a building from God, a house not made with hands, eternal in the heavens. . . ."

Finishing the passage, he rose and left, never to return.

Jackson maintained his devotional life in the field, and his men soon learned that when they saw him stumbling over stumps and rocks, he wasn't drunk. He was just praying with his eyes closed as he walked. Jackson rode among the troops distributing tracts and often took part in the revivals that spread through the Rebel army.

In May 1863, General "Stonewall" Jackson went out at nightfall to scout and was shot by mistake by his own men.

"I always wanted to die on a Sunday," he said, and he did just that. His earthly tent had been dissolved.

Today's Suggested Reading

2 Corinthians 5:1–5

For we know that if our earthly house, this tent, is destroyed, we have a building from God, a house not made with hands, eternal in the heavens. 2 Corinthians 5:1

November

The Text on the Wall

Wesley's First Hymn

Two Great Monosyllables

Count Me Not as Dead

"I Will Be Patient"

A Transformed Man

November **1**

Pictures of Mel Trotter (1870–1940) show a distinguished gentleman with serious face, slight smile, silver hair, wire glasses around perceptive eyes. His favorite verse was 2 Corinthians 5:17, and for good reason.

Trotter's father, a bartender, taught Mel the trade at an early age. Despite the earnest prayers of his mother, Mel followed his dad headlong into runaway drinking, smoking, and gambling. When he married, his habits reduced his family to poverty. Mel sold the family possessions from under his wife's nose to replenish his drinking money, then he resorted to robbery to satisfy the craving for more booze.

One day Trotter staggered home to find his young son dead in his mother's arms. Over the boy's casket, Mel promised to never touch another drop of liquor as long as he lived, a resolve that barely lasted through the funeral.

Shortly afterward, Mel, age 27, hopped on a freight car for Chicago. It was a bitterly cold January night, but he sold his shoes for some drinking money. After being evicted from a bar on Clark Street, he headed toward Lake Michigan to commit suicide. Somehow he ended up at the Pacific Garden Mission so drunk the doorman had to prop him against a wall so he wouldn't fall off his chair.

Despite his inebriation, at the close of the service, Trotter raised his hand for prayer and trusted Christ as his Savior. The change was instant and remarkable. Mel Trotter became a new creation. 2 Corinthians 5:17 became his testimony verse, and he began sharing it everywhere. His wife came to Chicago to join him, and in time Mel Trotter became one of the most sought-after preachers, speakers, soul-winners, and rescue workers in America.

"The greatest day I ever lived was the 19th of January, 1897," he once said, "when the Lord Jesus came into my life and saved me from sin. That transaction revolutionized my entire life. Don't call me a reformed drunkard. I am a transformed man, a child of God."

Today's Suggested Reading

2 Corinthians 5:12–20

Therefore, if anyone is in Christ, he is a new creation; old things have passed away; behold, all things have become new. 2 Corinthians 5:17

November **2** # The Text on the Wall

Catherine Booth, the "Mother of the Salvation Army," worked side-by-side with her husband William in feeding, clothing, and saving impoverished souls in the name of Christ. Despite chronic illness, she pressed on, sustained by a verse she had memorized in childhood—2 Corinthians 12:9.

She kept the verse on the wall near her bed, making it the last thing she saw at night and the first thing she saw in the morning. When, at age 59, she was near death, her lips moved, desiring to speak, but no voice was heard. Instead, Catherine lifted a bony finger and pointed to the text on the wall. "It was," said the minister at her funeral, "*her* text."

"Gentlemen," said Charles Spurgeon one Friday to his ministerial students, "there are many passages of Scripture which you will never understand until some trying or singular experience shall interpret them to you. The other evening I was riding home after a heavy day's work; I was very wearied and sore depressed; and swiftly and suddenly as a lightning flash, that text laid hold on me: My grace is sufficient for thee! On reaching home, I looked it up in the original, and at last it came to me this way: MY grace is sufficient for THEE. 'Why,' I said to myself, 'I should think it is!' and I burst out laughing. It seemed to make unbelief so absurd. It was as though some little fish, being very thirsty, was troubled about drinking the river dry; and Father Thames said: 'Drink away, little fish, my stream is sufficient for thee!' Or as if a little mouse in the granaries of Egypt, after seven years of plenty, feared lest it should die of famine, and Joseph said, 'Cheer up, little mouse, my granaries are sufficient for thee!' Again, I imagined a man away up yonder on the mountain saying to himself, 'I fear I shall exhaust all the oxygen in the atmosphere.' But the earth cries: 'Breathe away, O man, and fill thy lungs; My atmosphere is sufficient for thee!' "

Today's Suggested Reading
2 Corinthians 12:1–10

And He said to me, "My grace is sufficient for you, for My strength is made perfect in weakness." Therefore most gladly I will rather boast in my infirmities, that the power of Christ may rest upon me. 2 Corinthians 12:9

Count Me Not as Dead

In his renowned *Book of Martyrs,* John Foxe devotes a chapter to Dr. Rowland Taylor, parish preacher for the English town of Hadley. Taylor was a beloved and honest man. Even the lowliest could approach him, and his sermons were like manna. But when Bloody Mary ascended the throne and reasserted Catholicism throughout England, Taylor was arrested.

One night when his young son came to visit, Taylor gave him an old Latin book with these words penned on the back flyleaf: *I believe they are blessed who die in the Lord. God cares for sparrows and for the hairs of our heads. Trust in Him by means of our dear Savior Christ's merits. Believe, love, fear, and obey Him. Pray to Him, for He has promised to help. Count me not as dead, for I shall certainly live, and never die. I go before, and you shall follow after, to our eternal home.*

I say to my dear friends of Hadley that I depart from here with a quiet conscience concerning my doctrine. I have, in keeping with my little talent, declared those lessons that I gathered out of God's Book. Therefore if I, or an angel from heaven, should preach to you any other gospel than that which you have received, God's great curse be upon that preacher!

Some days later, Taylor was led to the execution grounds, where he removed his outer garments and climbed into a pitch barrel placed around a stake. His body was secured with chains, and a soldier set fire to the kindling. Lifting his hands to heaven, the good pastor of Hadley cried, "Merciful Father of heaven, for Jesus Christ my Savior's sake, receive my soul into Thy hands."

"Then," writes Foxe, "he stood still in the fire without either crying or moving, with his hands folded together before him, until Soyce struck him on the head with a halberd and split his head open so that his brains fell out and his corpse collapsed into the fire."*

Today's Suggested Reading
Galatians 1:1–9

. . . if anyone preaches any other gospel to you than what you have received, let him be accursed. Galatians 1:9

*Adapted from John Foxe, *The New Foxe's Book of Martyrs,* written and updated by Harold J. Chadwick (New Brunswick, NJ: Bridge-Logos Publishers, 1997), pp. 179–194.

November **4** The Mouth of Gold

His name was John of Antioch, but history knows him as Chrysostom, a word which means "Mouth of Gold." His sermons in the fourth century are among the most eloquent in the history of the church. He was the Billy Graham of his day, combining careful exegesis of Scripture with incisive moral application to everyday life. His popular sermons were taken down in shorthand as he preached them and have been preserved through the centuries, making him the most quoted of the church's ancient preachers.

But Chrysostom often found himself in the crosshairs of Roman rulers who resented his powerful and unflinching message. In such times, he kept Galatians 1:10 close to his heart.

His archenemy was the Empress Eudoxia. Furious over Chrysostom's attacks on sin, she determined to rid Constantinople of him. He countered by preaching a blistering sermon about Elijah and Jezebel with obvious overtones. Eudoxia struck back and Chrysostom found himself deposed and shipped into exile. But the people of Constantinople rioted, angrily insisting on the preacher's return. At the same time an earthquake shook the city. Eudoxia, trembling, admitted defeat, and Chrysostom returned in triumph. He later expressed his feelings in these words:

When I was driven from the city, I felt no anxiety, but said to myself: If the empress wishes to banish me, let her do so. The earth is the Lord's. If she wants to have me sawn asunder, I have Isaiah for an example. If she wants me to be drowned in the ocean, I think of Jonah. If I am to be thrown into the fire, the three men in the furnace suffered the same. If cast before wild beasts, I remember Daniel in the lions' den. If she wants me to be stoned, I have before me Stephen, the first martyr. If she demands my head, let her do so; John the Baptist shines before me.

Paul reminds me, "If I still pleased men, I would not be the servant of Christ."

Today's Suggested Reading
Galatians 1:10–24

For do I now persuade men, or God? Or do I seek to please men? For if I still pleased men, I would not be a bondservant of Christ. Galatians 1:10

Wesley's First Hymn

He came from a large family, the eighteenth of nineteen children, and he barely survived his premature birth. He was wrapped in wool and lay silently for weeks as his anxious mother prayed. But he did live, and he did not stay silent. Charles Wesley become the greatest hymnist of the English church, composing 8,989 songs for Christ. Among them: "Hark! The Herald Angels Sing," "O for a Thousand Tongues," "Christ the Lord Is Risen Today," and "Rejoice the Lord Is King."

Here is his conversion story. In 1735, Charles and his brother John had sailed to Georgia as missionaries, but it proved a miserable experience. Charles—shot at, sick, shunned, and unsaved—bemoaned that he carried his hell around inside him. Back in England, he became friends with Peter Bohler, who one day asked him about going to heaven. Charles said he hoped to make it there because of his endeavors to serve God. When Bohler shook his head sadly, Charles was peeved; but shortly afterward while recovering from an illness, Charles began reading Luther's commentary on Galatians. The words of Galatians 2:20 stripped the blinders from his eyes as he realized that Christ "loved me and gave Himself for me." The following Sunday, Charles yielded his heart to Christ in simple faith, saying, "I now found myself at peace with God, and rejoiced in hope of loving Christ."

Three days later his brother John burst into his room, a troop of friends in tow, declaring, "I believe!" At about 10 P.M. Charles pulled out copies of a new hymn he had written celebrating his conversion. He had written hymns before, but this was his first as a genuine Christian. Around his sickbed by flickering candlelight they sang:

Where shall my wondering soul begin?
How shall I all to heaven aspire?
A slave redeemed from death and sin,
A brand plucked from eternal fire,
How shall I equal triumphs raise,
And sing my great Deliverer's praise!

Today's Suggested Reading
Galatians 2:17–21

I have been crucified with Christ; it is no longer I who live, but Christ lives in me; and the life which I now live in the flesh I live by faith in the Son of God, who loved me and gave Himself for me.
Galatians 2:20

November **6**

Redeemed from the Curse

Rabbi Ginsburg proudly named his newborn son Solomon and dreamed the boy might one day follow him as a leader of the Jews of Poland. But he was unprepared for the boy's teenage years. At age 14, Solomon rebelled against the pharisaical strictness of his home, particularly angered over the girl his father had arranged for him to marry. Leaving home, Solomon, 15, wandered around Europe, finally ending up in London where a friend spoke to him about Jesus from Isaiah 53. After months of anguished study and floor-pacing, Solomon embraced the Lord Jesus as both Messiah and Savior.

Family reaction was violent. The uncle with whom he stayed in London drove him away with curses, broomsticks, and hot water. He was disinherited. A group of Jews attacked him and beat him until he appeared dead. When he regained consciousness, he found himself in a garbage box, his bones broken and his clothes soaked with blood.

Then one day he was summoned before a family council. When he showed up, his relatives tried earnestly to dissuade him from following Christ, but starting at Isaiah 53, Solomon spoke to them of Jesus. One of the Jews began reading the bitter words of excommunication: "Cursed shall you be by day, cursed by night; cursed when standing and cursed when lying down . . ." and so on.

Solomon, cut to the core, quietly cried to the Lord. Suddenly it seemed he was gazing upon Christ, arms outstretched on the cross. Above his bleeding head, Solomon saw the words: "Christ has redeemed us from the curse of the law, having become a curse for us."

The youth's heart was suddenly filled with strange joy, and as he left the house he said, "I was so happy I did not know what I was doing. I walked right into the arms of a big policeman, who asked me if I was drunk. I replied, 'No, sir, but I am very happy.'"

Solomon Ginsburg never looked back, and he went on to become one of the most productive evangelists of his era.

Today's Suggested Reading

Galatians 3:10–14

Christ has redeemed us from the curse of the law, having become a curse for us (for it is written, "Cursed is everyone who hangs on a tree"), that the blessings of Abraham might come upon the Gentiles in Christ Jesus. . . . Galatians 3:13

The Freedom of the Heart

Reverend Walter H. Everett answered the phone, unprepared for the words he heard: "Scott was murdered last night." Walter's anger toward his son's killer raged through him like a violent riptide, growing even worse when a plea bargain resulted in a reduced sentence for the attacker.

My rage was affecting my entire life. "How am I going to let go of this anger?" I wondered. The answer came the first time I saw Mike, almost a year after Scott's death. Mike stood in court prior to his sentencing and said he was truly sorry for what he had done.

Three and a half weeks later, on the first anniversary of Scott's death, I wrote to Mike. I told him about my anger and asked some pointed questions. Then I wrote, "Having said all that, I want to thank you for what you said in court, and as hard as these words are for me to write, I forgive you." I wrote of God's love in Christ and invited Mike to write to me if he wished.

Three weeks later his letter arrived. He said that when he had read my letter, he couldn't believe it. No one had ever said to him, "I forgive you." That night he had knelt beside his bunk and prayed for, and received, the forgiveness of Jesus Christ.

Additional correspondence led to regular visits during which we spoke often of Mike's (and my) growing relationship with Christ. Later I spoke on Mike's behalf before a parole board, and he was given an early release. In November 1994, I was the officiating minister at his wedding.

When asked about his early release, Mike says, "It felt good, but I was already out of prison. God had set me free when I asked for His forgiveness."

*Can I truly forgive? I had wondered if it were possible. But I've discovered the meaning of the apostle Paul's words: "For freedom Christ has set us free."***

Today's Suggested Reading

Galatians 5:1–9

*It was for freedom that Christ set us free; therefore keep standing firm. . . . Galatians 5:1**

---

*NASV

**Adapted from "Forgiving the Man Who Killed My Son," by Walter H. Everett, in *Decision Magazine*, December, 1996, p. 32.

November **8**

The Boxer and the Businessman

Paul Rader, former wrestler and boxer, became one of the most powerful evangelists of the early 20th century. He was sometimes called the "New Elijah." In 1916, while pastoring Moody Memorial Church of Chicago, Rader, 30, was asked to preach at Los Angeles' Church of the Open Door.

On the Saturday before, California businessman Charles Fuller read about Rader's visit in the newspaper. Arriving at the church the next day, he found a seat behind a large pillar. Peering around, he studied Rader. The man was powerfully built, and Fuller visualized how he must have looked in the ring. But now Rader was fighting for souls, and as he stood to speak he proclaimed his text, Ephesians 1:18. Rader said that without Christ people are in a moral and spiritual cave, blinded, darkened, and unaware of the glories God has in store for them. Finding Christ is like emerging from the cave into the light.

As Fuller listened, he suddenly recognized his own spiritual blindness. Leaning his head on the seat in front of him, he trembled. After the service, he drove to nearby Hollywood and stopped his car in the shade of a eucalyptus tree in Franklin Park. Kneeling in the back seat, Fuller gave his life to Christ in prayer. He returned home and wrote his wife, who was away: *There has come a complete change into my life. Sunday I went up to Los Angeles and heard Paul Rader preach. I never heard such a sermon in all my life—Ephesians 1:18. Now my whole life's aims and ambitions are changed. I feel now that I want to serve God, if He can use me, instead of making the goal of my life the making of money. I may have a call to go to the mission field in Africa.*

In time, Fuller himself became a powerful evangelist, helping usher radio evangelism to the forefront with weekly broadcasts from Long Beach Municipal Auditorium, heard nationwide. He also helped found Fuller Seminary in 1947 and worked ceaselessly for Christ until his death in 1968.

Today's Suggested Reading
Ephesians 1:15–23

. . . the eyes of your understanding being enlightened; that you may know what is the hope of His calling, what are the riches of the glory of His inheritance in the saints. Ephesians 1:18

"Tell Them Again!"

November **9**

As the Reformation began spreading over Europe, authorities in Amsterdam sought to limit its effect. When a Protestant rally was announced on an estate outside the city, the city gates were shut to prevent people from attending. But many people swam out through the canals or escaped through small passages in the wall. Multitudes forced their way out when the gates were opened to let the milkmaids into the fields for the morning milking. By 11 o'clock, the city rulers gave in, and the gates were opened for all to attend the meeting. Over 5,000 people gathered to hear Pieter Gabriel preach a four-hour sermon from Ephesians 2:8–9: "For by grace you have been saved through faith. . . ." It helped establish the Reformation in Holland.

This Scripture also became the text of an unusual tag team sermon by Reverend James Spurgeon and his grandson Charles. The younger Spurgeon, who was just beginning to preach, had been invited to speak at a certain church, but due to the trains he was late. At length, James stood up and started the sermon in his place, choosing Ephesians 2:8–9 as his text. When Charles arrived, James interrupted himself, saying, "Here comes my grandson. He can preach the gospel better than I can, but you cannot preach a better gospel, can you?"

Charles mounted the pulpit and began right where his grandfather had left off. A few minutes later, when Charles was speaking about human sinfulness, James whispered, "I know most about that." Charles sat down, and James took over and finished that point; then he turned the pulpit back over to his grandson. As he resumed, Charles could hear his grandfather behind him, "Good! Good! Tell them that again, Charles."

For the rest of his life, whenever Charles read or preached from Ephesians, chapter 2, there came to him with recurring force his grandfather's words, "Tell them that again, Charles! Tell them that again."

Today's Suggested Reading

Ephesians 2:1–10

For by grace you have been saved through faith, and that not of yourselves; it is the gift of God, not of works, lest anyone should boast. Ephesians 2:8–9

Two Great Monosyllables

I wonder what entered the minds of Newton's parishioners as they watched their new pastor mount the pulpit for the first time. Vivid scenes from his earlier days? His being stripped and flogged by the Navy? His transporting chained African slaves? His immoral indulgences? His filthy mouth? His months of bondage to a sadistic woman?

Now this man, John Newton, was their pastor!

But apparently some were also troubled by his evangelical fervor. Newton had reportedly been so totally transformed by Jesus Christ that he preached the Bible with greater passion than other Anglican clergy. Were they getting a fanatic? An enthusiast?

So every eye watched Newton step into the pulpit of the little baroque church in the heart of London. He had chosen a text for his first sermon—Ephesians 4:15. The two great monosyllables in the phrase, "speaking the truth in love," he said, would mark his ministry. His voice rang out:

Every attempt to disguise or soften any part of the truth to accommodate the prevailing taste around us must be an affront to the Majesty of God. My conscience bears me witness that I mean to speak the truth among you. May the grace of God enable me always to do it.

But he also was prepared to care for his flock, *to feel the warmest emotions of friendship and tenderness toward them. This love which my heart bears, I offer as plea for the earnestness and importunity which I must use. Love will prompt me to be faithful and earnest.*

He admitted that he once was "a scorner and a despiser of the gospel," and he promised to hide nothing about his past life. But, he said, he stood before them "as a pattern of the long-suffering of God."

The little church, St. Mary's, was soon packed each Sunday. In time Newton's influence reached the highest members of the British government, and it was his ministry that fueled the movement for the abolition of the slave trade. Souls were saved, and all the world still sings his hymns, including one that begins, *Amazing grace, how sweet the sound. . . .*

Today's Suggested Reading
Ephesians 4:11–16

. . . but, speaking the truth in love, may grow up in all things into Him who is the head—Christ. Ephesians 4:15

My God, What a Task!

November **11**

Renouncing her lavish lifestyle, beautiful Mary Bosanquet opened an orphanage for London's street children; and for years she had little time to think of marriage. *I had no other thought but devoting myself to God in a single life; only I sometimes thought, were I to be married to Mr. Fletcher, would he not be a help to my soul.*

She was referring to John Fletcher, well-known Methodist leader and close friend of Wesley. And so it happened. On November 12, 1781, to the delight of their friends, the two married. Mary was over forty years old at the time; John was ten years her senior.

Returning from the wedding, the groom read Ephesians 5:25, telling their assembled friends, "Husbands, love your wives as Christ loved the church. My God, what a task! Help me, friends, by your prayers to fulfill it. As Christ loved the church! He laid aside His glory for her! O my God, none is able to fulfill this without Thine almighty aid."

He read the next words: "Wives, submit to your own husbands." Mary piped in, ". . . as unto the Lord," and Fletcher responded, "Well, my dear, only in the Lord. And if ever I wish you do any thing otherwise, resist me with all your might."

Some time later, this entry appears in Mary's journal: *I have such a husband as is in everything suited to me. He bears all my faults and failings, in a manner which continually reminds me of that word, "Love your wives as Christ loved the Church." He is in every sense the man my highest reason chooses to obey.*

At the same time, we find this in one of John's letters to a friend: *I was afraid at first to say much of the matter, for new-married people do not, at first, know each other; but having now lived fourteen months in my new state, I can tell you, Providence has reserved a prize for me, and that my wife is far better to me than the church to Christ.*

Today's Suggested Reading

Ephesians 5:17–33

Husbands, love your wives, just as Christ also loved the church and gave Himself for her. Ephesians 5:25

The Navigator

Years ago, a dorm buddy helped me grow in Christian maturity with Bible studies published by the Navigators, an organization started in 1943 by Dawson Trotman. Since then, Navigator material has been of endless enrichment to me.

The Navigators was started by Dawson Trotman who, as a high school student, had been class valedictorian and student body president. But his personal life was plagued by drinking, gambling, and questionable friends. One night he was arrested drunk at an amusement park. "Son, do you like this kind of life?" asked the officer. "Sir," Trotman replied, "I hate it." Two days later he attended a local church that encouraged Scripture memory. While memorizing verses, Dawson found himself praying, "Oh God, whatever it means to receive Jesus, I want to do it right now."

He was soon leading others to Christ, but doing little follow-through with his converts. One day he picked up a hitchhiker who swore a blue streak. Dawson recalled having picked up the same man a year before and having led him to Christ. Or so he thought.

Now there appeared no evidence of the man's conversion.

Dawson was deeply troubled, for it seemed Philippians 1:6 didn't work. Putting a cardboard under the verse, he actually started to cut the verse out of his Bible with a razor. But, hesitating, he decided to *study* the passage instead. As he did so, he realized he had been taking the verse out of context. He noticed Paul's ongoing concern for his Philippian converts, how he prayed for them in verses 3–4, how he held them in his heart in verse 7, how he longed for them with the affection of Christ in verse 8. With new insight, Dawson began focusing his efforts on follow-up and personal discipleship.

In 1933, he began teaching sailor Les Spencer the principles of Christian growth, spending hours with him in Bible study, memorization, and prayer. Soon Spencer was winning and teaching others on his ship until eventually 125 men of the U.S.S. *West Virginia* were growing in Christ and sharing their faith.

The Navigator ministry had begun.

Today's Suggested Reading
Philippians 1:1–11

. . . being confident of this very thing, that He who has begun a good work in you will complete it until the day of Jesus Christ. Philippians 1:6

The Stalwarts

November **13**

British pastor George Duncan was once invited to preach live from Keswick, England, on the BBC. He choose this text, saying it summed up the "full-orbed and balanced experience" of the Christian in "six unforgettable words, which in English at least are words of one syllable each, and should therefore not be beyond the understanding of the youngest or simplest of us." Victorious Christianity, Duncan said, is something personal—*to me*. . . . It is something practical—*to live*. . . . And it is something possible—*is Christ!*

It certainly proved that way for retired missionary/pastor Dan Merkh. Merkh recalls being part of a church youth group that called itself the "Stalwarts" and choose Philippians 1:20–21 as its theme. But Merkh wasn't very "stalwart" himself, for later while serving in the Marines, he drifted away from Christ and lived in a backslidden condition. He was assigned a desk job in the Marine Corps Depot of Supplies in Norfolk, and much paperwork passed over his desk. Someone gave him a glass paperweight in the shape of a half ball. The curve acted as a magnifying glass under which was to be placed a picture. Having nothing to put there, Dan remembered his old youth group theme and wrote the words, "To Live Is Christ and To Die Is Gain."

Every time he shuffled papers, his eyes fell on those words, and they eventually drilled into his heart. Later, rededicating his life to Christ and yielding himself to ministry, Philippians 1:20–21 became his life-verses.

Another missionary, Bill Wallace, a doctor in China, also loved these words. When he was arrested by the Communists and treated brutally, he would scribble verses like these on the walls of his cell to keep himself sane. After months of interrogation and abuse, he was found dead. The Communists claimed he had hanged himself, but his body showed signs of having been beaten to death. Defying the Communist authorities, his friends buried him with honor. Over his grave, they inscribed the words they felt described the motivation of his life: "For To Me To Live Is Christ."

Today's Suggested Reading

Philippians 1:12–26

For to me, to live is Christ, and to die is gain. *Philippians 1:21*

Never Better

Robert Baillie was a "Scottish Worthy," a sturdy seventeenth-century Presbyterian who defied persecution to advance the evangelical faith. Though viewed suspiciously by the Scottish crown, he was left relatively unmolested until August 1684. One night, old and feeble, he was scooped up by soldiers and tried in his nightshirt. His distraught sister accompanied him and gave him cordials to strengthen him, for he was too weak to stand. Nevertheless he was thrown into prison where he grew even weaker.

The State, unwilling for Baillie to suffer a natural death, condemned him on Christmas Eve, 1684, to be hanged at the Market Cross of Edinburgh between two and four that afternoon. His head was to be cut off and nailed in a public place. His body was to be stretched taut, carved into four pieces, and affixed to other sites.

Hearing his sentence, Baillie replied, "My lords, the time is short, the sentence is sharp, but I thank my God who hath made me as fit to die as you are to live."

While waiting in his cell for the appointed hour, Baillie thought of the promise in Philippians 3:21. At the resurrection God will transform our decayed, discarded bodies to be like the glorified body of the risen Christ. When someone asked him how he felt, Baillie answered, *Never better. And in a few hours I shall be well beyond all conception. They may hack and hew my body as they please, but I know assuredly nothing shall be lost; but that all these my members shall be wonderfully gathered, and made like Christ's glorious body.*

I have had sharp sufferings for a considerable time, he said in a final message to his friends, *and yet I must say to the commendation of the grace of God, my suffering time hath been my best time, and when my sufferings have been sharpest, my spiritual joys and consolations have been greatest. Let none be afraid of the cross of Christ, His cross is our greatest glory.*

Today's Suggested Reading
Philippians 3:17–21

. . . who will transform our lowly body that it may be conformed to His glorious body, according to the working by which He is able even to subdue all things to Himself. *Philippians 3:21*

All Things

It once dawned on me that the following well-worn verse is referring in its context to Christ's ability to give us contented hearts. "I have learned in whatever state I am, to be content . . . ," Paul wrote. "Everywhere and in all things I have learned both to be full and to be hungry, both to abound and to suffer need. I can do all things through Christ who strengthens me. . . ."

But the words have other applications as well.

I once heard Billy Graham speak of his exhaustion during crusades. "I sometimes feel I haven't strength for one more sermon. But often in such moments, this verse comes to me with assurance of God's strength for the task."

Robert Morrison became a Christian at age 15, and shortly after felt called to the ministry. Against his father's wishes, he traveled to London to enroll in theological and missionary training. It was very difficult, especially when his father wrote, complaining that the family business was suffering because of his absence and adding that he himself was not well. But by return post Robert tried to explain that having put his hand to the plow, he could not look back.

One day, the young man penned this prayer in his diary: *Jesus, I have given myself up to Thy service. The question with me is, where shall I serve Thee? I learn from Thy Word that it is Thy holy pleasure that the gospel shall be preached in all the world. My desire is, O Lord, to engage where laborers are most wanted. Perhaps one part of the field is more difficult than another. I am equally unfit for any, but through Thy strengthening me, I can do all things. O Lord, guide me in this. Enable me to count the cost, and having come to a resolution, to act consistently.*

His prayer was richly answered. Morrison became the first Protestant missionary to China. Though he saw only three or four converts during his 27 years of service, he paved the way for an army of workers to come.

Today's Suggested Reading

Philippians 4:4–14

I can do all things through Christ who strengthens me. Philippians 4:13

November **16** Question in the Night

No one who hears Stephen Olford's commanding voice can forget it. It seems to flash through the air as he preaches, with a British clip and a heavenly power that drives its message into listening ears. His expositional sermons ring with alliteration that makes each memorable.

Olford grew up in Africa where his parents were missionaries. On his seventh birthday, after the cakes and presents had been enjoyed, his mother, Bessie Santmire Olford, led family devotions. She read from John 14, emphasizing verse 3, the Lord's promise to return and receive His people to Himself. Pausing, she looked at Stephen and asked, "Stephen, when the Lord Jesus comes back, will you be ready to meet Him?"

The question was left unanswered. Stephen looked down, fidgeting with his hands and wishing he could be anywhere else at that moment. But that evening the question played on the boy's mind. His sleep was restless, and he tossed and turned in the African night. Suddenly the matter seemed to assume urgent proportions, and he called out in the darkness, "Mother!"

Bessie rushed in, expecting to find a hyena or other wild animal outside his window. She sat on the bed and held him, his little body trembling. No, it wasn't a wild animal. His fitful thoughts had imagined Jesus coming again, only to leave him behind. Bessie lit the lamp and opened her Bible to Colossians 1:27: "Christ in you, the hope of glory."

"If you want to be sure of going to heaven, Stephen, you must have Christ in you, in your heart. Do you want to invite Jesus into your heart?" Stephen nodded, and the two knelt by his bed to make the transaction.

"Before, my pillow seemed stuffed with bricks," Olford recalled, "but now a wonderful peace came into my heart. Mother was the undergirding of that conversion. In those early formative years, it was her training, her teaching, her example and counseling that drew me to the Lord."

Today's Suggested Reading
Colossians 1:24–29

To them God willed to make known what are the riches of the glory of this mystery among the Gentiles: which is Christ in you, the hope of glory.
Colossians 1:27

"I Was Only Fifteen" November **17**

In the former East Germany, fifteen-year-old Wilfried Gotter was summoned to appear in a closed room before the authorities—school leaders, local government officials, and Communist party functionaries. Would he or would he not join the Communist youth organizations? Would he or would he not join the Communist army?

The young man was in the tightest spot of his life, for he was a dedicated Christian who wanted nothing to do with the godlessness of Communism. He later recalled: *To sit there as a youngster and defend yourself against five men sitting opposite you who try to overwhelm you and intimidate you is not easy. My heart was pounding.*

At first Wilfried appeared frightened and unsure of what to say. But as he silently prayed, *I was given a word from God. It was Colossians 2:8—"See to it that no one takes you captive through hollow and deceptive philosophy, which depends on human tradition and the basic principles of the world, rather than on Christ."*

"When Wilfried quoted this verse in his defense," wrote journalist Barbara Von Der Heydt, "he was surprised to see how disarming the effect was. The men interrogating him had age, rank, and numbers on their side—yet this simple retort from the fifteen-year-old left them stymied. The interview halted, sputtered to an end, and they decided to let him go. They made no more attempts to change his mind."

"In that moment," Wilfried said, "I really experienced what it says in the Bible—that when you are led before the authorities, you shouldn't be concerned about what you will say. It was really a gift from God. To have such words in such a situation wasn't due to my quick-wittedness or anything—I was only fifteen. These are the practical experiences of faith in the everyday. They have a lasting effect when you experience them and realize that what's in the Bible is true."

Because of Wilfried's boldness, many of his friends also refused to submit to the Communist evils.*

Today's Suggested Reading

Colossians 2:1–10

Beware lest anyone cheat you through philosophy and empty deceit, according to the tradition of men, according to the basic principles of the world, and not according to Christ. Colossians 2:8

---

*Adapted from Barbara Von Der Heydt, *Candles Behind the Wall* (Grand Rapids: Eerdmans Publishing Co., 1993), pp. 112–114.

November **18**

The Barrenness of Busyness

All that God is . . . is available to the man who is available . . . to all that God is! No one has forgotten those words who heard them roll off the tongue of Major Ian Thomas, founder of Capenwray Missionary Fellowship and the international Torchbearer ministry.

As a university student in London, Thomas had exerted all his energy for Christ, becoming a windmill of activity, packing every day with preaching, talking, and counseling. But nobody was ever converted. *The more I did, the less happened; and I became deeply depressed because I really loved the Lord with all my heart. But I discovered that forever doubling and redoubling my efforts to win souls, rushing here and dashing there, taking part in this campaign, taking part in that campaign, preaching in the morning, preaching in the evening, witnessing to this one, counseling with another, did nothing, nothing to change the utter barrenness of my activity.*

"Oh God," Thomas prayed one night, near exhaustion, "I have tried to my uttermost and I am a hopeless failure." Suddenly a verse flashed through him that he didn't even know he knew. He couldn't remember hearing or reading it before, but now it rang in his mind like Big Ben: *Christ Who Is Our Life!*

Thomas realized he had been trying to do *for Christ* what only Christ could do *through him.* His own efforts were useless; he needed the power of Christ *in him* by the Holy Spirit. *Thou art the One Who is going to go out now, clothed with me to do all that I so hopelessly have been trying to do in the past.*

The following Sunday as he prepared to teach 90 boys, he prayed, "Well now, Lord, Thou art going to speak to that boys' class, isn't it wonderful? Yesterday I thought I was going to, but Thou art going to now."

That day 30 boys embraced Christ as Savior.

Ian Thomas had learned that . . . *All that God is is available to the man who is available to all that God is!*

Today's Suggested Reading
Colossians 3:1–4

When Christ who is our life appears, then you also will appear with Him in glory. Colossians 3:4

Richard Sherman recently wrote in *Moody Magazine* about trying to witness to his neighbor, a horoscope junkie. He briskly warned her one day that astrology was of the devil, but she snapped back, "You Christians! You talk about love, but you're filled with hate!" As she stomped off angrily, a sick and sluggish feeling settled over Richard.

That evening as he came to Colossians 3:12 in his reading he wondered if he could have been gentler. How could he have handled the conversation differently? Had he spoken with "kindness, humility, meekness, and longsuffering"? No, he admitted. Instead of being humble and gentle, he had sounded sharp and prickly. Returning to his study of Colossians 3, Richard noticed that verse 14 says, "But above all these things put on love, which is the bond of perfection."

Those verses took hold, and a few weeks later, Richard had another opportunity to witness. A hard-core evolutionist and hedonist dropped by to visit. This time Richard spoke gently, using his turns in the conversation to quietly share information about creationism. *My friend nodded. I sensed he appreciated my considerate approach. Rather than digging in his heels, he opened up. He shared how his views had been changing. He now believed in God—because he saw purpose in everything in the world. He admitted his fear of death and what would come after it. I gently stated that he didn't need to be uncertain. He knew that involved surrendering his life to Christ. His face dropped, "I'm not ready to do that yet," he said softly.*

Afterward, Richard reviewed the conversation, feeling good about the opportunity of planting the seed of the gospel and warming the soil, and praying that his friend will, in time, discover the One who can clothe us with tender mercies, kindness, humility, meekness, and longsuffering.*

Today's Suggested Reading

Colossians 3:12–17

Therefore, as the elect of God, holy and beloved, put on tender mercies, kindness, humility, meekness, longsuffering. Colossians 3:12

---

*Adapted from Richard E. Sherman, "What's Under My Armor?" in *Moody Magazine,* September/October, 1997, pp. 44–45.

November **20**

An Olympian's Motivation

Josh Davis, winner of three gold medals during the 1996 Olympics (the most gold medals won by any man in the entire U.S. delegation), is a Christian who, at evangelistic events for Athletes in Action and elsewhere, credits Christ with his success. One of the keys to his intensity as a Christian swimmer is Colossians 3:23: "And whatever you do, do it heartily, as to the Lord and not to men."

Recently in *Sports Spectrum,* Josh quoted this verse while sharing five ways in which young athletes can "make a splash with their coach."

1. *Be honest with yourself and with your coach. You will get upset at times, but you need to be truthful with yourself. Admit that you're feeling upset and analyze where those feelings are coming from. If they're legitimate, verbalize those feelings in a civilized manner to your coach.*
2. *Respect your coach as a person. There's never any reason to be rude or abrasive to another human being. I apply the biblical principle, "Do everything without complaining or arguing. . . ." (Philippians 2:14).*
3. *Realize that the things you do now will have an effect six months later.*
4. *We're in a society of instant gratification. You may have a tendency to want immediate satisfaction. You need to have a long-term perspective of perseverance.*
5. *Your intensity should not change, whether a coach is watching you or not. A biblical principle that helps me is, "Whatever you do, do it for the Lord and not for men" (Colossians 3:23).*

*I'm motivated to be a good steward of the talents God's given me. In my life, I've been given a gift of swimming fast, and I think God expects me to use that gift to the best of my ability. On top of that, He has given me the gift of eternal life. That and what Christ did on the cross supply me not only with the proper motivation but also with an everlasting motivation.**

Today's Suggested Reading
Colossians 3:17–25

And whatever you do, do it heartily, as to the Lord and not to men.
Colossians 3:23

---

*Adapted from "Flip Turn" by Roxanne Robbins in *Sports Spectrum,* March, 1995, pp. 24–26.

Pray Without Ceasing November **21**

Today's verse troubled me as a child, for I couldn't figure out how it could actually be done. Studying it again as an adult, I finally concluded that "praying without ceasing" meant that prayer should be, not necessarily *constantly occurring,* but *consistently recurring.*

Madame Jeanne Guyon, the French mystic, also pondered this verse at length. Her outspoken and aggressive Christianity led to her imprisonment in France's dreaded Bastille prison where, behind thick, cold, damp walls, in a tiny padlocked cell without light, ventilation, or heat, she wrote wonderful books.

Her works, numbering forty in all, include a volume titled *The Method of Prayer,* based on her study of 1 Thessalonians 5:17. Madame Guyon taught that inward holiness regulates outward life, and that inner strength comes from casting ourselves into the simple presence of God—from praying without ceasing. "Every Christian can elevate himself by meditation in the presence of God," she said, "in which the soul, without being inactive, acts no longer except by divine impulses."

A nameless old scrubwoman, knowing nothing of French mysticism, expressed the same truth in simpler language. According to an old story, some ministers were discussing 1 Thessalonians 5:17 one morning, but couldn't agree on its meaning. The woman, scrubbing on her knees, raised up and ventured an opinion.

"When I go to bed at night," she said, "I thank the Lord for the joy of resting in His everlasting arms. When I awaken, I ask Him to open my eyes to behold new things from His Word. When I build the fire, I ask Him to kindle love in my heart. When I bathe, I ask Him to cleanse me from secret faults. When I eat, I thank Him for my food. As I walk to work, I pray to be led in paths of righteousness. As I pass the church, I pray for my pastor. While scrubbing these floors, I ask Him to wash the hearts of those walking above me with His precious blood. . . ." And on she went.

She knew as much as Madame Guyon—and a good deal more than the preachers.

Today's Suggested Reading
1 Thessalonians 5:12–17

. . . pray without ceasing. 1 Thessalonians 5:17

November **22** # Father of a Hostage

A former college hallmate of mine, Chet Bitterman, Wycliffe missionary in Colombia, was kidnapped by guerrillas on January 19, 1981, in full view of his terrified wife and children. The news was quickly transmitted to Wycliffe headquarters by shortwave radio and by phone to the Bitterman home in Pennsylvania.

As Chet's father, Chester Allen Bitterman, listened in stunned silence, he scratched notes on the pad before him: *Radio message . . . guest house in Bogota broken into . . . radio equipment taken . . . Chet hostage?*

He was engulfed by a wave of depression and anger, and he stormed through the day in a rage—pacing, stalking, scheming, feeling like a bomb ready to explode. He visualized leading a commando force, tearing through the jungle to snatch his son from the hands of the thugs who held him. A portion of his rage was also directed toward God, and when Bitterman tried to pray, all that emerged were prayers of anger, hate, and vengeance.

But a verse, long ago memorized, appeared uninvited in his mind: . . . *in everything give thanks; for this is the will of God in Christ Jesus for you.*

The verse sounded like nonsense to Bitterman. "Paul never had a hostage son," he told himself. "It's absurd to give thanks in a time like this."

But the verse came again: *In everything give thanks. . . .* Then again. And again. Bitterman fought the verse with all his might, arguing and resisting. But he could not evade it: . . . *for this is the will of God in Christ Jesus for you.*

Finally, he fell to his knees in desperation and began sobbing, feeling in his heart he would never see Chet again. The hours passed. He prayed and pondered and wept; and slowly, very slowly, his heart changed. He began to sense blessings unrecognized, began to clasp a divine hand, began to grasp the power of prayer.

That night an anguished father felt the Father's heart.

In everything give thanks; for this is the will of God in Christ Jesus for you.

Today's Suggested Reading

1 Thessalonians 5:18–28

. . . in everything give thanks; for this is the will of God in Christ Jesus for you. 1 Thessalonians 5:18

Little Bilney

Hugh Latimer (c. 1485–1555), the "Preacher of the English Reformation," owed much to his mentor, Thomas Bilney.

Bilney, a quiet scholar at Cambridge University, acquired a Greek New Testament from the famous Erasmus. As he pored over it, one verse of Scripture seemed to be written in letters of light: *Christ Jesus came into the world to save sinners!*

"This one sentence," he later wrote, "through God's instruction and inward working, did so exhilarate my heart, which before was wounded with the guilt of my sins, that immediately I found wonderful comfort and quietness in my soul. My bruised bones leaped for joy."

Bilney wanted to share his conversion with others, but this was Reformation truth, and the Reformation had not yet reached England. Teachers such as Luther—and teachings like justification by grace through faith—were being fiercely attacked by English churchmen like Hugh Latimer.

But as Bilney listened to young Latimer rail against the Reformation, he prayed this unusual prayer: "O God, I am but 'little Bilney,' and shall never do any great thing for Thee. But give me the soul of that man, Hugh Latimer, and what wonders *he* shall do in Thy most holy name."

One day Bilney pulled Latimer aside, saying, "Oh, sir, for God's sake, hear my confession." Latimer sat and listened as Bilney spoke about Erasmus' Greek New Testament and shared what had happened to him through it. Reaching into his sleeve, he drew out the precious book, and it opened to a passage heavily underlined—1 Timothy 1:15.

As Latimer read those words, he himself saw the pure and simple truth of the gospel, that Jesus Christ came into the world to save sinners. The effect on Latimer was reminiscent of the conversion of Saul of Tarsus. Tears poured down his cheeks, and in that moment he, too, was born again.

Both men later perished at the stake, but their flames lit a candle in the English-speaking world that has never gone out.

Today's Suggested Reading
1 Timothy 1:1–15

This is a faithful saying and worthy of all acceptance, that Christ Jesus came into the world to save sinners, of whom I am chief. 1 Timothy 1:15

Edwards' Great Awakening

Despite his staunch Puritan background, Jonathan Edwards struggled spiritually during his years at Yale. *My convictions wore off; and I returned like a dog to his vomit, and went on in the ways of sin. Indeed, I was at times very uneasy, especially toward the latter part of my time at college; when it pleased God to seize me with pleurisy; in which He brought me nigh to the grave, and shook me over the pit of hell. And yet, it was not long after my recovery, before I fell again into my old ways of sin.*

The turning point came while . . . *reading 1 Timothy 1:17. As I read the words, there came into my soul a sense of the glory of the Divine Being, quite different from anything I ever experienced before. Never any words of Scripture seemed to me as these words did. I thought to myself, how excellent a Being that was, and how happy I should be, if I might enjoy that God, and be rapt up to Him in heaven, and be, as it were, swallowed up in Him forever! I kept saying and singing over these words of Scripture to myself; and went to pray to God that I might enjoy Him, and prayed in a manner quite different from what I used to do. From about that time, I began to have a new idea of Christ, and the work of redemption, and the glorious way of salvation by Him.*

Jonathan shared his experience with his father, and *was pretty much affected by the discourse we had together; and when the discourse was ended, I walked alone in a solitary place in my father's pasture, for contemplation. And as I was looking up on the sky and clouds, there came into my mind so sweet a sense of the glorious majesty and grace of God that I do not know how to express.*

Edwards spent the rest of his life trying to express it, and his sermons sparked the greatest revival in American church history.

Today's Suggested Reading
1 Timothy 1:16–20

Now to the King eternal, immortal, invisible, to God who alone is wise, be honor and glory forever and ever. Amen. 1 Timothy 1:17

Nightmare

On April 21, 1950, Rev. Wade Darby and his wife Mary returned from church visitation and retired for the evening. Near their bed, little Danny slept in his crib. At 2 A.M., Mary awoke to a nightmare. Someone was atop her, choking her. Her hand flew to Wade's pillow, but she felt a wet mass where his head should have been. As she struggled with her attacker, the bed heaved, slats falling out. Danny awakened and began crying.

Mary wrested free and flew into the closet, but the angry voice said, "If you don't come out, I'll kill you and this baby." As Mary prayed desperately, words sprang from her lips with no forethought: "Wade, get the gun from under the bed!" The couple had no gun, but the words did the trick, and the intruder fled.

Wade was rushed to the hospital with three skull fractures and a brain concussion, and both of them had knife wounds. But it soon became clear that physical healing would come easier than emotional healing. For weeks Mary lived with constant fear. Though the church relocated them in a new parsonage, the anxiety continued.

Such vicious, visceral fear yields to only one thing—the authoritative Word of God. The Lord gave Mary 2 Timothy 1:7: "For God has not given us a spirit of fear, but of power and of love and of a sound mind." She quoted those words in the darkness of the night. They came to mind when panic arose. They calmed her in moments of alarm. And they gradually dissolved the dread, allowing peace to return to her soul.

When Wade returned to the pulpit following his recovery, the church was packed. Hearts were touched, lives were changed; and the Lord used the adversity to enlarge their church numerically and to glorify Himself.

*Wade still carries the scars from that night, but those scars remind us of God's power and love. We have now been married for half a century, and we don't know to this day who the intruder was. But one thing I do know: God IS dependable.**

Today's Suggested Reading

2 Timothy 1:1–7

For God has not given us a spirit of fear, but of power and of love and of a sound mind. 2 Timothy 1:7

---

*Adapted from *Experiencing God Magazine* by Mary Darby.

November **26** Resting on Certainties

Several years before the *Titanic,* passengers on another ocean liner faced terror in the night. It was the *Empire State,* and a Methodist worker named Phoebe Palmer was aboard. The evening was very quiet, the waters placid. Suddenly a blast shuddered through the ship as a boiler burst, jolting the passengers from their beds in alarm. They might have panicked but for Phoebe Palmer who began singing hymns on deck. Others joined, and soon calm was restored. After the danger passed and all the passengers were safe, someone asked Phoebe, "Weren't you afraid?"

She replied, "No, thank God," explaining that from the very moment of the explosion, 2 Timothy 1:12 had come to her with such force that she could only sing of the One who was able to keep what was committed to Him.

The devotional writer Samuel D. Gordon knew a woman who had memorized much of the Bible, but age took from her memory all the verses but this one: . . . *I am not ashamed, for I know whom I have believed and am persuaded that He is able to keep what I have committed to Him until that Day.*

In time, she could only remember: . . . *what I have committed to Him.* When she came to her deathbed, her loved ones noticed her lips moving. Bending low, they heard her repeating one solitary word over and over: *Him, Him, Him.*

Dr. Gordon noted that she had lost the whole Bible but one word. But in that one word, she had the whole Bible.

This was also Michael Faraday's verse, the English scientist who pioneered research into electrolysis and the magnetic field. He was a dedicated Christian who lost no opportunity of testifying of the One in whom he believed.

People were so impressed with his knowledge and theories, that on his deathbed, he was asked, "What are your speculations?"

"Speculations?" he replied. "Speculation! I have none! I am resting on certainties. I know whom I have believed and am persuaded that He is able to keep that which I have committed unto Him against that Day!"

MICHAEL FARADAY

Today's Suggested Reading

2 Timothy 1:8–12

For this reason I also suffer these things; nevertheless I am not ashamed, for I know whom I have believed and am persuaded that He is able to keep what I have committed to Him until that Day. 2 Timothy 1:12

The Prince of Gospel Singers

Charles M. Alexander (1867–1920), "Prince of Gospel Singers," exhibited incredible ability to make people sing. He teamed up with evangelist Reuben A. Torrey, and the two became the first men to completely circle the globe in a quest for souls. He and his wife Helen Cadbury (of chocolate fame) helped organize the Pocket Testament League, and everywhere they went they pointed people to this verse.

2 Timothy 2:15 became Alexander's text in this way. He once had a friend, French Oliver, who had drifted away from Christ. Alexander, who led him back to the Lord and into Christian service, later wrote: *Oliver and I agreed to spend our next Christmas together. Those were two of the most profitable weeks I have ever spent. We sang and composed music, read the Bible, and talked over Christian work. On New Year's Eve we decided we would take a year-text, and the year-text was 2 Timothy 2:15. Instead of saying "Good night" to each other, one would call out "2 Timothy 2:15," and the other would answer, "2 Timothy 2:15."*

Finally the time came to part. I went to the depot to see him off. Many people were on the platform. My friend was standing at the back of the train, and instead of saying "Good-bye," I called out "2 Timothy 2:15!"

"2 Timothy 2:15!" he replied.

A year later, Alexander, teaching a class of young men, referred to this verse. One of them spoke up. "Twelve months ago," he said, "I was down at the depot when I heard a fellow shouting for all he was worth, '2 Timothy 2:15!' to a man on the end of the outgoing train, who was shouting back, '2 Timothy 2:15!' I thought, what is this? I made a beeline home and looked it up in my Bible. I wasn't a Christian then, but the words of that text hit me fairly between the eyes. I asked God to forgive my sins and help me to show myself approved, and thank God He has done it."*

Today's Suggested Reading

2 Timothy 2:14–19

Be diligent to present yourself approved to God, a worker who does not need to be ashamed, rightly dividing the word of truth. 2 Timothy 2:15

---

*Adapted from Helen C. Alexander and J. Kennedy Maclean, *Charles M. Alexander: A Romance of Song and Soul-Winning* (Murfreesboro, TN: Sword of the Lord Publishers, 1995), pp. 44–45.

Divine Calligraphy

The call to preach comes to different people in different ways. Under a lamppost, for example. On a Chicago street perhaps. Such was the case with Daniel Whittle of Chicopee Falls, Massachusetts. As a young man, Whittle relocated to Chicago where he entered the banking business, becoming a cashier for Wells Fargo. He was converted to Christ one day at work when he *went into the vault and in the dead silence of the quietest of places, I gave my life to my heavenly Father to use as He would.*

When the Civil War erupted, Whittle, 21, enlisted with the Union, marched with Sherman, and was wounded at Vicksburg. He rose to the rank of major, a title that stayed with him after the war. Returning to Chicago, Major Whittle became the treasurer of the Elgin Watch Company and struck up a friendship with evangelist D. L. Moody.

One night as he and Moody were walking through Chicago after a meeting, they paused under a lamppost where their ways parted. Whittle was somewhat discouraged, and he asked Moody what could be done to rouse the people. Opening his Bible, Moody read 2 Timothy 4:2: "Preach the word! Be ready in season and out of season. Convince, rebuke, exhort, with all longsuffering and teaching."

No more was said, but those words remained etched on Whittle's mind like divine calligraphy. After much thought and prayer, he resigned from the security of his position with Elgin and entered full-time evangelistic work. He soon become one of the leading evangelists of his day, working side by side with Moody and leading campaigns of his own throughout America and England.

All the while, Whittle also composed gospel songs like "Moment by Moment," "I Know Whom I Have Believed," and "There Shall Be Showers of Blessings."

Whittle's last work was done among soldiers fighting in the Spanish-American War where he literally wore himself out. He returned exhausted to Northfield, Massachusetts, where he died in 1901 at age 61.

Today's Suggested Reading
2 Timothy 3:16–4:2

Preach the word! Be ready in season and out of season. Convince, rebuke, exhort, with all longsuffering and teaching. 2 Timothy 4:2

"I Will Be Patient" November **29**

In his last known letter, the apostle Paul wrote Timothy from prison, asking him to *come before winter,* and to *bring the cloak that I left with Carpus . . . and the books, especially the parchments.*

Fifteen centuries later, this verse found its twin—a remarkable parallel in church history. It was from the hand of William Tyndale, who risked his life to translate the Bible into English. He was eventually arrested in Antwerp, imprisoned, and sentenced to death. Sometime during the winter of 1535, he wrote this letter to the governor of the castle where he was held. It is the only known writing in his hand still in existence.

I beg your Lordship, and that by the Lord Jesus, that if I am to remain here through the winter, you will request the Procurer to be kind enough to send me from my goods which he has in his possession, a warmer cap; for I suffer greatly from cold in the head, and am afflicted by a perpetual catarrh (mucous flow), which is much increased in this cell.

A warmer coat also, for this which I have is very thin; also a piece of cloth to patch my leggings. My overcoat is worn out; my shirts are also worn out. He has a woolen shirt of mine, if he will be kind enough to send it. He also has warmer caps for wearing at night. And I ask to be allowed to have a lamp in the evening; it is indeed wearisome sitting alone in the dark. But most of all, I beg and beseech your clemency to have the Hebrew Bible, Hebrew grammar, and the Hebrew dictionary, that I may spend my time with that study. And in return, may you obtain your dearest wish, provided always it be consistent with the salvation of your soul.

I will be patient, abiding the will of God to the glory of the grace of my Lord Jesus Christ, whose spirit, I pray, may ever direct your heart. Amen.

Today's Suggested Reading
2 Timothy 4:6–22

Bring the cloak that I left with Carpus at Troas when you come—and the books, especially the parchments. 2 Timothy 4:13

November **30**

Island of Tears

When visiting my wife's family in Maine, I often browse through used bookshops, looking for old volumes. One of my prizes is the autobiography of Lemuel Norton, who left a seafaring life to become a gospel preacher.

One day in the 1820s, Norton sailed over to Gott's Island, home of about a dozen families. As he stepped from the boat, a feeling of loneliness hit him, making him want to weep. As he visited house-to-house, he came to a man working in the field.

I told him Christ had come onto the island to visit the people, and that there was to be a meeting at four o'clock. The man seemed astonished and rather absently unyoked his oxen, sending them back to the barn. Norton followed him home, finding there a young lady in great despair, weeping over her sins.

Norton invited her to the afternoon meeting and left *weeping as I passed from house to house. I perceived Christ was there before me and loved to be where there was a good deal of weeping among the people.*

The meeting commenced at four, and Norton announced his text, Titus 3:4. *After showing how and when this kindness appeared, and speaking of the greatness of His love, I tried to persuade my hearers to love God in return. Just as I attempted to do this, the Holy Spirit descended with such power upon me that the only relief I could find was to speak with all my might. My hearers were bathed in tears; and what astonished me more was that seven young persons had already got on their knees, crying for mercy.*

Norton stopped preaching and sat crying, as were others. As the room filled with tears, a revival commenced that swept over the little community and on to other islands. Lives were healed, souls were saved, and churches were born. The kindness and love of God the Savior appeared that day amid the tears on Gott's Island.

Today's Suggested Reading

Titus 3:1–7

But when the kindness and the love of God our Savior toward man appeared. . . . Titus 3:4

December

When Coyotes Wail

"Mr. Whitefield Is Dead!"

The 66¢ Solution

Swarmed

The Pearly Gate

December **1**

Put Them on My Account

I remember sitting in church as a child, listening as our pastor waxed vividly from this text. He described the slave Onesimus, how he transgressed, how he confessed, and how he was reconciled to his master through Paul's entreaty.

Is not this a picture of the gospel? I think I see Him as He brings the needy sinner into God's presence, saying, "Father, he has wronged Thee; he owes Thee much, but all has been charged to My account. Let him go free."

Only years later did I discover that my pastor had preached one of Harry Ironside's most memorable sermons virtually word for word: *Charge that to My Account.*

Well, nothing is original. Ironside himself may have gotten the idea from the Methodist circuit rider, Daniel Curry. One night on the Nebraska prairie, Curry made himself a little campfire and fell asleep, using his saddle for a pillow. That night he dreamed of dying and going to heaven, where he was met by an angel who asked his reason for being there.

"My name is Daniel Curry," answered the preacher, "and I have come to claim the mansion Jesus promised me long ago." But the angel wouldn't let him in, and they got into a quarrel. Finally Curry was taken to argue his case before Almighty God Himself. But arriving at the throne, he was dumbstruck. It was ablaze with blinding light equal to a thousand suns, and Curry fell prostrate before the Lord, his eyes tightly shut. A stern voice cried, "Who art thou? What seekest thou?" Curry tried to rise, but he was too terrified to utter a sound.

Suddenly he heard sandaled feet drawing near. A hand touched him and pulled him to his feet. Daniel recognized the scars on the man's palms, and he heard Him speak these words: "Father, this is Daniel Curry. He confessed Me before men, and I am now confessing him before Thee. Whatever sins he has committed, whatever transgressions may blot his record, whatever iniquities may stain his past—charge them all to Me. Put them on My account."

Today's Suggested Reading

Philemon 1:1–25

*But if he has wronged you in any way, or owes you anything, charge that to my account. Philemon 1:18**

---

*New American Standard Version

"Mr. Whitefield Is Dead!"

December **2**

Benjamin Randall, great New England preacher and denominational leader, was born in 1749 to a sea captain and his wife on a rocky island off the coast of New Hampshire. In time, he became a tailor and sail-maker.

In September 1770, evangelist George Whitefield arrived in Portsmouth, New Hampshire. Randall attended the meetings unimpressed. Whitefield moved on. But a few days later, a horseman flew through town with dramatic news: "Mr. Whitefield is dead! Died this morning at Newburyport, about six o'clock!"

As I heard this an arrow pierced my heart. Mr. Whitefield was a man of God, and I had spoken reproachfully of him. That voice is not silent in death. On reaching home, I took to my room to mourn in solitude over my condition. My former religion seemed altogether worthless.

On October fifteenth, while musing on my condition, I fell into the following train of thought: "Once I was company for almost everyone, but now for none. I took pleasure in the world, but now there remains nothing of that. All things appear insipid." While thus musing, Hebrews 9:26 came to my mind: "But now, once in the end of the world hath He appeared to put away sin by the sacrifice of Himself." I was in such deep meditation that the words passed without particular notice. They came up the second time, however; then I began to think, "What can the passage mean?" While meditating upon the text my burden rolled off, leaving me calm and peaceful.

As my faith grasped the meaning of the text, I gave glory to God. And what a joy filled my soul! I could now see in Jesus Christ a blessed sacrifice for sin. How the character of Jesus shone in my soul! For a time I could do nothing but repeat the name of Jesus. Jesus! Jesus!! It seemed to me that if I had a thousand souls, I could trust them all in His hands.

Today's Suggested Reading
Hebrews 9:23–28

. . . but now, once at the end of the ages, He has appeared to put away sin by the sacrifice of Himself. Hebrews 9:26

December **3**

A Cold Night's Sermon

Sunday night, February 13, 1889, was bitterly cold. The thermometer registered twenty-two below zero, and most people huddled by their fires trying to stay alive. But Eugene Sallee, a brilliant student at Georgetown College in Kentucky, suggested to his roommate that they attend evening worship. "Let's go to church tonight," he said. "The pastor will not have many present."

He was right. The congregation consisted of Sallee, his roommate, and a small handful that braved the elements. Despite the small number, Pastor Z. T. Cody did his best, preaching on the subject, "Moses' Wise Choice," from Hebrews 11:24. For some reason, every sentence hit young Eugene like the blow of a hammer. Cody described how Moses, the darling of Pharaoh's household, had been trained in all the wisdom of Egypt. Wealth and position were his. But when God called him he obeyed, choosing "rather to suffer affliction with the people of God than to enjoy the passing pleasures of sin."

Until that night Sallee had planned for a career in law, but Dr. Cody's sermon perturbed him as he trudged through the dangerous cold back to his room. He wondered if the Lord was calling him to ministry. To missions? He pushed the thoughts aside and, graduating from Georgetown, he applied to Columbia Law School in New York.

Sallee spent the summer following his graduation in Missouri riding horseback across the countryside selling aluminum ware. But Cody's sermon from Hebrews 11 wouldn't release its grip on his soul. Finally one day as he rode along, Eugene came to a quiet stream. Tethering his horse to a tree, he wandered into the dense woods, found a place to pray, and there surrendered his life to fulltime Christian service.

In time, the Lord led him to China where he devoted 27 remarkable years in evangelization and church-planting. "For this cause came I into the world," he once said, "and to this end I was born, to preach the gospel in China."

Today's Suggested Reading
Hebrews 11:23–28

By faith Moses, when he became of age, refused to be called the son of Pharaoh's daughter, choosing rather to suffer affliction with the people of God than to enjoy the passing pleasures of sin. Hebrews 11:24–25

When Coyotes Wail

December **4**

Today's passage tells us how to win marathons, how to run with endurance. To be victorious in the Christian race, we must (1) strip away every sin like a runner discarding needless clothing; and (2) focus on Jesus, like a sprinter looking to the tape.

As to stripping away sin . . .

On August 24, 1662, 2,000 of England's finest ministers were ejected from their pulpits for resisting the Act of Uniformity. Among them was Thomas Manton who, in his final sermon, preached from this passage, giving five ways of stripping away sin. He told his people to:

- *Seriously purpose not to sin and promise God to yield Him unfeigned obedience. Take up a solemn purpose not to grieve the Spirit.*
- *Watch over thyself with a holy suspicion. Guard thy senses.*
- *Resist and strongly oppose the first risings of the flesh and the tickling and pleasing motions of sin.*
- *Bewail thy involuntary lapses and falls with penitential tears. Godly sorrow is of great use for laying aside sin as salt potions kill worms.*
- *Recover from thy falls, renew thy combat.*

As to looking to Christ . . .

When businessman Allan Emery was in the wool business, he once spent an evening with a shepherd on the Texas prairie. During the night, the long wail of coyotes pierced the air. The shepherd's dogs growled and peered into the darkness. The sheep, which had been sleeping, lumbered to their feet, alarmed, bleating pitifully. The shepherd tossed more logs onto the fire, and the flames shot up. In the glow, Allen looked out and saw thousands of little lights. He realized those were reflections of the fire in the eyes of the sheep.

"In the midst of danger," he observed, "the sheep were not looking out into the darkness but were keeping their eyes set in the direction of their safety, looking toward the shepherd. I couldn't help but think of Hebrews 12: 'looking unto Jesus, the author and finisher of our faith. . . .'"

Today's Suggested Reading

Hebrews 12:1–5

Therefore we also, since we are surrounded by so great a cloud of witnesses, let us lay aside every weight, and the sin which so easily ensnares us, and let us run with endurance the race that is set before us, looking unto Jesus. . . . Hebrews 12:1–2

Tuan Change

Ernie Presswood is one of thousands of missionaries whose ministries were broken up by World War II, but who nonetheless established a work for Christ that continues to this day.

Born to English immigrants on the Canadian prairie, Ernie gave his heart to Christ in Sunday school and later yielded to Christian service at a Gypsy Smith rally. In 1930, he was sent to the Sunda Islands of Southeast Asia by the Christian and Missionary Alliance. There Ernie's vivacious way of presenting the gospel earned him a special name among the Murut tribe—Tuan Change, for it was said, "he changed wicked natives and said they could have a new life."

In the mid-1930s Presswood married Laura Harmon, and in the remote wilderness Laura became pregnant. But complications following a miscarriage took her life, and Ernie buried her in a coffin made from boards he had been using to build them a home. A flood swept away the rest of Ernie's timber, ruining his unfinished house; and in his brokenness Ernie questioned whether God loved him at all.

At that difficult moment, Hebrews 12:6 took charge of his thoughts: ". . . whom the Lord loves He chastens." Those words, Ernie later said, brought comfort, courage, and the strength to face the future. In days to come, he witnessed a revival among the Muruts of Borneo. Into the mountains he pressed ever deeper, establishing churches, changing lives.

He was on the island of Celebes when the Japanese invasion engulfed him. He was seized and beaten, kept in a pig house, starved, and forced to labor in a prison camp where he watched fellow missionaries die while World War II raged across the Pacific.

In 1945, able to return at last to Borneo, Ernie seemed as effectual as ever. New revival fires spread among the Muruts. But while traveling by river, his boat capsized and he was dragged downstream 300 yards, much of it beneath raging waters. He managed to pull himself ashore, but the drenching ravaged his shattered constitution, and on February 1, 1946, he died.

He was 38.

Today's Suggested Reading
Hebrews 12:6–11

For whom the Lord loves He chastens, and scourges every son whom He receives. Hebrews 12:6

God's Kind of Comfort December **6**

Early on January 25, 1949, the chaplain of the United States Senate, Peter Marshall, awoke with severe chest pains. "Catherine," he said, "I'm in great pain. Will you call the doctor for me?" By the time the doctor arrived, Peter was feeling well enough to be transported to the hospital. At his insistence Catherine reluctantly remained home to get little Peter off to school.

At 8:28 A.M., the phone rang. Peter was dead. Catherine's head whirled and her legs wobbled. Little Peter, standing nearby, burst into sobs as Catherine turned to him in a daze and said, "Peter, the doctor told me that Daddy just died."

In her book, *To Live Again,* Catherine Marshall describes the anguished days and weeks that followed, during which she experienced the depths of anger, depression, fear, and self-pity. She blamed herself for not doing more to save Peter, and she blamed God: "Why did it have to end this way?"

Then one day, she realized that God often comforts us, not by coddling our self-pity, but by rebuking it. *God's comfort doesn't walk on tiptoe as in a sickroom; it marches. There is steel in its backbone. It makes us remember that the word "comfort" is derived from the word* fortis*—which means strong. I opened my New Testament and found there exactly that concept of comfort: "Discipline always seems for a time to be a thing of pain, not of joy; but those who are trained by it reap the fruit of it afterwards. . . . So up with your listless hands! Strengthen your weak knees! And make straight paths for your feet to walk in. . . . (Moffatt; Hebrews 12:11–12).*

God was asking me to grow up, to take a new step toward maturity.

Catherine began pulling herself together, claiming Scriptural promises, and in the process she learned a fathomless lesson for dealing with pain: *God is not interested in coddling us, but in liberating us for further creativity, for the new life that we are forced to make.**

Today's Suggested Reading
Hebrews 12:11–13

Now no chastening seems to be joyful for the present, but painful; nevertheless, afterward it yields the peaceable fruit of righteousness to those who have been trained by it. Hebrews 12:11

---

*Adapted from Catherine Marshall, *To Live Again* (New York: McGraw-Hill, 1957), pp. 1–37.

December 7 A Thousand Thousand Thoughts

Lifelong, serious Bible study pays its greatest dividends on the deathbed, for only the authority of the Word of God can brace the soul for its upward flight. For Richard Baxter, the comforting passage was Hebrews 12:22–24.

Baxter was a seventeenth-century Puritan whose sermons and writings established him as one of the most powerful men of his era. His book, *The Saint's Everlasting Rest,* is beloved to this day. But Baxter tended to be sickly, and in 1662 he was imprisoned in the Tower of London for his Puritan views. The imprisonment further damaged his health, and Baxter returned home weakened.

He was able to temporarily continue public ministry, then infirmity confined him to his rented house where, according to an old, undated biography, *he opened his doors, morning and evening, to all that would join in family worship with him; to whom he read the Holy Scriptures and taught those things which concern the Lord Jesus Christ. But, alas, his growing diseases and infirmities soon forbade this also, confining him first to his chamber, and after to his bed. There, through pain and sickness, his body wasted; but his soul abode strong.*

The description in Hebrews 12:22–24 was most animating to him, that he was going to the innumerable company of angels, and to the general assembly and church of the First-Born whose names are written in heaven; to God, the Judge of all, and to the spirits of just men made perfect, and to Jesus the Mediator of the new covenant. "That scripture," he said, "deserves a thousand thousand thoughts."

On Monday, December 7, 1691, Baxter was seized by trembling and chill and began crying to God for pity; *which cries and agony continued for some time, till at length he ceased those cries, and so lay in patient expectation of his change.*

About four the next morning, Richard Baxter was promoted to Mount Zion, the city of the living God, to that heavenly Jerusalem, and to the Saint's Everlasting Rest.

Today's Suggested Reading

Hebrews 12:22–29

But you have come to Mount Zion and to the city of the living God, the heavenly Jerusalem, to an innumerable company of angels. . . . Hebrews 12:22

Hand-Held Time Bombs

December **8**

I once heard Warren Wiersbe say he loved reading because of the joy of meeting people he has always wanted to know. "If it were announced that Hudson Taylor or Charles Spurgeon was speaking at a particular church," he quipped, "Christians from all over the world would show up. But when I open my book, Hudson Taylor opens his mouth. We have a great time together, and these people are my friends."

"Through a book," added Haddon Robinson, "we can wrestle with the thoughts of Augustine, rub shoulders with Calvin, make progress with Bunyan's pilgrim, enjoy the wit of C. S. Lewis, and hear the sermons of John Chrysostom."

Christian biographies have often proved hand-held time bombs which, when detonated through reading, can divert the course of a person's life. For example, God has used Elizabeth Elliot's biography of her husband Jim, martyr of the Ecuadorian Aucas, to direct many young people into missionary service.

Interestingly, Jim's own interest in missions was whetted while reading a biography. In *Shadow of the Almighty,* Elizabeth quotes from his journal, dated October 24, 1949: *I see the value of Christian biography tonight, as I have been reading Brainerd's* Diary *much today. It stirs me up much to pray and wonder at my nonchalance while I have not power from God. I have considered Hebrews 13:7 just now, regarding the remembrance of certain ones who spake the word of God, "consider the outcome of their life, and imitate their faith." I recall now the challenge of Goforth's* Life, *read in the summer of 1947, the encouragement of Hudson Taylor's* Spiritual Secret. *There are incidents which instruct me from the reading of J. G. Paton's biography last winter. And now this fresh Spirit-quickened history of Brainerd. O Lord, let me be granted grace to "imitate their faith."**

I wonder if Jim Elliot ever dreamed that his own biography would one day inspire multitudes.

Today's Suggested Reading

Hebrews 13:1–9

Remember those who rule over you, who have spoken the word of God to you, whose faith follow, considering the outcome of their conduct.
Hebrews 13:7

---

*Adapted from Elizabeth Elliot, *Shadow of the Almighty* (Grand Rapids: Zondervan, 1958), p. 108.

December **9**

Carey's Conversion Verse

If England hadn't been losing its war with the American colonies, William Carey might have never heard Hebrews 13:13, the verse that led to his conversion.

Carey had been born in 1761 into an impoverished home in an obscure English village. He was a sickly child, sensitive to the sun and afflicted by numerous allergies. By age 14, he was frequently in trouble, "addicted to swearing, lying, and unchaste conversation," skipping church, and running with a motley gang.

But he was apprenticed to a cobbler, John Warr, a zealous Christian who determined to win him to the Lord. Carey wanted none of it, but Warr, a Dissenter, was persistent in planting gospel truth in the young man's heart. Meanwhile, the Revolutionary War had broken out, and England found itself on the losing side. King George III, hoping for divine reversal, proclaimed a day of national prayer and fasting for Sunday, February 10, 1779, and Warr persuaded Carey to join him at a service of intercession.

Thomas Chater preached that day from Hebrews 13:13, urging his listeners to give their lives to Christ. As he quoted his text—"Let us go forth to Him, outside the camp, bearing His reproach"—the words spoke directly to 17-year-old William. He sensed God's telling him to take a stand for Christ by leaving the formality of the established church and becoming a dissenter and an evangelical Christian.

His heart slowly made its decision, and this has been called Carey's conversion experience. From that day, the direction of his life changed. Four years later he became a Baptist. Fourteen years later, a missionary. In time, William not only opened the floodgates of organized missions, he himself translated the complete Bible into six languages, and portions of the Bible into 29 others. (We assume he always gave special attention to the translation of Hebrews 13:13.)

Carey never returned to England, but labored for the Lord for nearly 41 years, until his death in India at age 73. He is called the "Father of Modern Missions."

Today's Suggested Reading

Hebrews 13:10–25

Therefore let us go forth to Him, outside the camp, bearing His reproach. Hebrews 13:13

Oil on Troubled Waters

Larry Miley grew up in the northeast corner of the Ivory Coast, where his father was a missionary physician. When he was 14, he was laid low by a bout of malaria, and his father gave him an injection. All seemed well at first, and Dr. Miley returned to his hospital, not knowing the injection would produce a severe reaction that would take Larry to the edge of the grave.

Mrs. Miley was preparing for her sewing and Bible class on the verandah when a blood-curdling scream filled the house. Rushing through the door, she saw her daughter Lynette standing in near hysteria before Larry, who seemed disoriented, confused, his twitching eyes recessing deeply into their sockets.

"There's something wrong with my eyes," Larry gasped. "Help me!"

As Lynette ran for her father, Mrs. Miley ushered Larry to the bed and covered his grotesque eyes with a washcloth. Just as the doctor arrived, Larry's body arched in a violent spasm. Like a woman in the throes of birth pains, regular contractions wracked him, sending him convulsing this way and that, threatening to cut off his respiration. Larry's heart grew fainter. Hours passed. The spasms grew stronger, and Larry became weaker. Dr. Miley knew well that Larry's survival in that remote outpost was unlikely.

Suddenly he remembered that James 5:14 says, "Call for the elders of the church." The only "elders" were fellow missionaries living nearby, and they were summoned at once. Eddie and Sandra Payne, Howard and Willie Gage, Lynette and her brother Lynn. As they knelt by the bed and prayed, Dr. Miley anointed Larry with the prescribed oil.

Mrs. Miley recalls: *Slowly, like oil being poured over troubled waters, a deep calm replaced the suffocating fear. We sensed before we even raised our eyes that the crisis had passed. Larry was asleep and slept peacefully through the night.*

*Next day as I prepared the noon meal, Larry came bouncing into the kitchen. "I'm all well now," he announced brightly, "so I think I'll go hunting."**

Today's Suggested Reading

James 5:14

Is anyone among you sick? Let him call for the elders of the church, and let them pray over him, anointing him with oil in the name of the Lord. James 5:14

---

*Adapted from Lorene Miley, *I Looked for a Man* (Nashville: Randall House Publications, 1983), pp. 152–154.

December **11** # Coming Home to Go Home

I wonder why Larry Miley survived, and Eunice Glass didn't.

Wiley and Eunice Glass were Southern Baptist missionaries in Hwanghsien, China, in the early years of the twentieth century. They lived in a two-story house in Hwanghsien, with bedrooms on the second floor, and a living room, dining room, and study below. There was no plumbing. Light was by kerosene lamp, water by well, transportation by pony.

Eunice gave birth to a beautiful little boy, but he grew ill and died. When another son died, she grew overanxious about Bently, their surviving son, and about their two young daughters. But it was Eunice herself who next fell ill. She had been soaked while crossing a bay, and Wiley took her to the mountains to recover. Local women brought eggs and milk, and the weather was beautiful. The children played happily on the mountainside. But Eunice grew weaker.

Her condition was finally diagnosed as tuberculosis, and when winter forced them back to their old house, Eunice told them that she had "come home to go home." She instructed her husband how to care for the children and she occasionally mustered her strength to sort through keepsakes. She grew painfully thin, surviving only on raw eggs. And then she was buried beside her two sons in the International Cemetery in Chefoo.

How did Wiley press on? By appropriating 1 Peter 1:13. It became his survival verse and gave him strength sufficient for his days. He leaned on it, and it never wavered under his weight.

Why did one missionary survive while another didn't? Only the Sovereign God—who orders all for our good—holds the answers to those kinds of questions. Christians, it seems, don't live by explanations but by promises. "Therefore," Peter said, "gird up the loins of your mind, be sober, and rest your hope fully upon the grace that is to be brought to you at the revelation of Jesus Christ."

A faith that can't be tested can't be trusted.

Today's Suggested Reading

1 Peter 1:1–13

Therefore gird up the loins of your mind, be sober, and rest your hope fully upon the grace that is to be brought to you at the revelation of Jesus Christ. 1 Peter 1:13

Never Mind My Age

December **12**

When Charlie made up his mind to enter the ministry, he trembled with excitement. Writing to his dad, he said, "How I long for the time when it may please God to make me, like you, my father, a successful preacher of the gospel. Oh that I might see one sinner constrained to come to Jesus! I almost envy you your exalted privilege."

Not long afterward, he and a companion were invited to participate in a Sunday night cottage service in the village of Taversham. While traveling to the house, Charlie turned to his friend and wished him God's blessings on the sermon. The friend turned in alarm, saying something to this effect, "But I'm not preaching! I thought you were. I have never preached before, can not do it, and will not. If you don't preach, there will be no sermon."

Charlie's heart skipped a beat, and his mind raced to find a solution. He had never before preached a sermon and was unprepared to do so now. All the while, they were drawing closer to the cottage, and the hour of the service was at hand. The boys ducked into the low, thatched cottage where a few farming families had gathered. The proceedings began. All too soon, it came time for the sermon. Charlie stood up and "got the text on his feet"—1 Peter 2:7: "Therefore, to you who believe, He is precious."

To everyone's surprise—most of all, his own—it was a marvelous sermon. The words came unabated. He didn't break down, did not stop in the middle, did not flounder for words. The thoughts flowed like water over a dam. His listeners were amazed and afterward crowded around him, asking his age.

"Never mind my age," Charlie said (he was 16), "think of the Lord Jesus Christ and His preciousness."

Those simple farming families had just enjoyed the privilege of hearing the first sermon—of Charles Haddon Spurgeon.

Today's Suggested Reading

1 Peter 2:1–10

Therefore, to you who believe, He is precious.
1 Peter 2:7

"I Am Willing"

The thing that impressed me about Chet was his cocky self-possession, exhibited chiefly in a smile that dangerously bordered on a smirk. He would stick his head through the door of my room at Columbia Bible College, flash his devil-may-care grin, ask how things were going, then disappear as quickly as he had come.

He always left too soon, and he seldom looked back.

When he knew God was calling him to be a missionary with Wycliffe Bible Translators in Latin American, Chet Bitterman penned this in his journal: *Maybe this is just some kind of self-inflicted martyr complex, but I find this recurring thought that perhaps God will call me to be martyred for Him in His service in Colombia. I am willing.*

Eight months later, Chet and Brenda entered Colombia to translate the Bible into the Carijona language. He was kidnapped by terrorists on January 19, 1981, and seven weeks later shot dead, a single bullet to the chest.

Prior to his kidnapping, Chet had memorized most of 1 Peter, a book that describes how Christians can live victoriously amidst persecution and suffering. During his captivity, Brenda prayed that he would remember those verses.

He did remember them. In a letter to Brenda two weeks after his abduction, Chet wrote: *The hardest thing for me so far has been thinking about how you are handling all this. It would help me more than anything to know that you are holding strong. The girls will cue their reactions off you. . . .*

He went on to fill the letter with passages of encouragement, then he ended by quoting this passage, 1 Peter 4:1–2: "Therefore, since Christ suffered for us in the flesh, arm yourselves also with the same mind, for he who has suffered in the flesh has ceased from sin, that he no longer should live the rest of his time in the flesh for the lusts of men, but for the will of God."

And that is exactly what Chet Bitterman did.

Today's Suggested Reading

I Peter 4:1–7

Therefore, since Christ suffered for us in the flesh, arm yourselves also with the same mind, for he who has suffered in the flesh has ceased from sin, that he no longer should live the rest of his time in the flesh for the lusts of men, but for the will of God. 1 Peter 4:1–2

When the News Comes

December **14**

Chet Bitterman is one of many. Through the centuries, thousands of Christians and missionaries have suffered and perished for Christ and His kingdom.

For example, Alexander Mackay and seven others were commissioned for missionary service in Africa on April 25, 1876, by the Church Missionary Society, an arm of the Anglican Church. The men dreamed of fulfilling Henry Stanley's vision of reaching Uganda.

In the poignant service that evening, Mackay, a well-educated Scottish engineer, told the crowd: *I want to remind the committee that within six months they will probably hear that some one of us is dead. Yes, is it at all likely that eight Englishmen should start for Central Africa and be alive six months after? One of us at least—it may be I—will surely fall before that. When the news comes, do not be cast down, but send someone else immediately to take the vacant place.*

And so it happened. Five of the men died the first year, and by the end of the second, Mackay alone was left, translating and broadcasting the gospel. In time he was able to set up a little printing press where he prepared a message for his oppressed disciples. On one side Mackay said: *In days of old, Christians were hated, hunted, driven out, and persecuted for Jesus' sake, and thus it is today. Beloved brethren, do not deny our Lord Jesus and He will not deny you on the last great day. Do not cease to pray exceedingly for our brothers who are in affliction and for those who do not know God.*

Mackay finished printing his message, then, turning the pages over, he selected a verse of Scripture to print on the back. It was 1 Peter 4:12–13, which summarized everything he wanted to say, and which summed up his life: *Beloved, do not think it strange concerning the fiery trial which is to try you, as though some strange thing happened to you; but rejoice to the extent that you partake of Christ's sufferings.*

Today's Suggested Reading
1 Peter 4:8–16

Beloved, do not think it strange concerning the fiery trial which is to try you, as though some strange thing happened to you; but rejoice to the extent that you partake of Christ's sufferings. 1 Peter 4:12–13

December **15** Boxed Up Hopes

Keith and Sarah Fletcher were married, dreaming of settling into a lifelong work for Christ, but they got off to a rough start. Sarah recalls: *A small church in North Carolina unanimously voted Keith in as their pastor—and nine months later voted him out. We were jobless, homeless, expecting our firstborn, and confused.*

Keith was next hired by a church in Oklahoma. We dug in, gave birth to our firstborn, and got to work. Nine months later, the church ran out of money and could no longer pay us. We were again on the street.

Keith found a staff position in an Indianapolis church, and this time we made it past nine months, but just barely. One day he went to work and the pastor said, "I don't think you're happy here. Maybe you'd better find another job." Actually, Keith had been happy, but we were nonetheless dismissed.

I was pregnant again, and very discouraged. All my wonderful hopes of a settled marriage and ministry had been boxed up and crushed in Ryders and U-Hauls; we were ready to get out of full-time ministry and go home, except we weren't exactly sure where home was.

Then one day in my Bible reading I discovered 1 Peter 5:10: ". . . may the God of all grace . . . after you have suffered a while . . . settle you." Before the Lord settles us, I thought, He sometimes allows us to pass through periods of suffering. That made sense. The Lord refines us, teaches us perseverance. Even more, He wants us to realize that no earthly location is our permanent address. We must instead be established and settled IN CHRIST.

Through the months and moves that followed, I clung to that promise, and the fog began to clear. Four months after moving from our house in Indianapolis, it burned down, killing its new occupants. With a shudder, I began to understand God's mysterious ways. New, better doors opened, leading us eventually to our current ministry. Keith now readily admits that part of his effectiveness in developing Christian resources for nationwide use comes from our having lived in a variety of places . . . like North Carolina, Oklahoma, and Indiana.

Today's Suggested Reading

1 Peter 5:6–11

But may the God of all grace, who called us to His eternal glory by Christ Jesus, after you have suffered a while, perfect, establish, strengthen, and settle you. 1 Peter 5:10

See How I've Ruined the Bible

December **16**

Some people seem to have Samsonian energy for the kingdom. R. A. Torrey, for example. After passing through a period of skepticism, he yielded to Christ and studied in Germany. He was tapped in 1889 by D. L. Moody to oversee the fledgling Moody Bible Institute, and he also served as pastor of Moody Memorial Church. Between 1902 and 1906, he traveled around the world conducting evangelistic crusades with Charles M. Alexander, and from 1912 until 1924 he served as dean of the Bible Institute of Los Angeles (Biola). All of this while speaking widely at Bible conferences and writing forty books.

His energy came from pouring himself into the Scripture.

Once a man approached him, a Dr. Congdon, complaining that he could get nothing out of his Bible study. The Scripture seemed to be dry as dust. "Please tell me how to study it so that it will mean something to me."

"Read it," replied Dr. Torrey.

"I *do* read it."

"Read it some more."

"How?"

"Take some book and read it twelve times a day for a month."

"What book could I read that many times a day, working as many hours as I do?"

"Try Second Peter," replied Torrey.

My wife and I read Second Peter three or four times in the morning, two or three times at noon, and two or three times at dinner. Soon I was talking Second Peter to everyone I met. It seemed as though the stars in the heavens were singing the story of Second Peter. I read Second Peter on my knees, marking passages. Teardrops mingled with the crayon colors, and I said to my wife, "See how I have ruined this part of my Bible."

"Yes," she said, "but as the pages have been getting black, your life has been getting white."

Today's Suggested Reading
2 Peter 1:1–11

Simon Peter, a bondservant and apostle of Jesus Christ, to those who have obtained like precious faith with us by the righteousness of our God and Savior Jesus Christ. 2 Peter 1:1

December **17** A Straw of Hope

The Bible is a machine gun with 31,173 bullets, for that's how many verses it contains. One of those bullets had Mark Sloan's name on it.

Mark combined alcohol and cocaine in lethal amounts, desperately trying all the while to stop. After one stay in a rehabilitation center, we invited him to live with us, thinking we could encourage his sobriety. For months all went well, then one morning he disappeared. We were unprepared for his relapse, and it seemed almost like losing a son. I would find him in despicable places, drunk, high, hurting, spiraling downward. Then several months passed with no word from him at all.

One day I heard he was in a basement across town. I found the place and banged on the door until he grudgingly let me in. He was badly depressed. I tried to persuade him to enter a treatment program, but he refused. It was time to die, he said. He had tried so hard to overcome his habits, and could not. His eyes were glazed over, his words slurred, and nothing I said fazed him.

"There's enough cocaine in this apartment to kill an elephant," he said, "and my body can't stand much more. A day or two, then it'll be over. You'll forget about me in a few weeks; we'll all be better off. It's meant to be . . . just let it be. It's meant to be."

I was turning to leave, choking back tears, when a verse suddenly popped from my mouth without forethought. "Mark," I said, "it *isn't* meant to be. The Bible says that God is not willing for any to perish, but for all to come to repentance." A flicker of hope registered in Mark's eyes. It was very faint, but unmistakable. I repeated the verse, and he listened as if trying to grasp a straw blowing past him.

In the years since, I've told Mark of that moment several times. He doesn't remember it, but I'll never forget it. I'm convinced that verse saved his life and eventually led to his becoming the sober, dedicated Christian he is today.

Today's Suggested Reading

2 Peter 3:8–13

The Lord is not slack concerning His promise, as some count slackness, but is longsuffering toward us, not willing that any should perish but that all should come to repentance. 2 Peter 3:9

Paralyzed

He heard his neck snap just as he made the tackle. When the players unstacked, he was unable to move; and Van Johnson, 15, found himself permanently paralyzed. Van embraced Christ as Savior while flat on his back, and he began growing as a Christian. His spiritual progress was marked by several critical junctures. One of them occurred one day while Van, lying in bed, was struck by a hell-launched missile of depression and self-pity.

Anger raged within me in mighty waves. I felt I was drowning. I wanted to kick, to flail my arms, to scream. Tears of anger and pity began to pour from my eyes. "You can't even wipe your tears away," I told myself. I beat my head against the mattress. "Maybe this will cause me to fall out of bed," I reasoned. "Then I'll be on the floor where I want to be."

Mom heard the commotion and came into my room to comfort me. "Van, what's wrong?" I refused to look at her, listen or answer her. Completely exhausted, I just lay there.

Van's rage faded into anguished guilt as he realized his pent-up anger and violent tantrum had been unwise, unhealthy, and dishonoring to God. *The words of 1 John 1:9 came to my mind: "If we confess our sins, He is faithful and just to forgive us our sins. . . ." My prayer was this: "God, please forgive me for my stupidity. I have sinned against You through my anger and self-pity. I confess my sins to You."*

His sweet presence came to me, and I felt a renewed sense of peace. I felt clean, because I knew as far as Jesus was concerned, it was all over—He would remember the episode no more.

*That experience taught me so much about life. I realized that the Christian never needs to stay discouraged or depressed, no matter the circumstances. From that day on, I determined within my heart that I would look away from my problems to see Jesus. This would be my choice.**

Today's Suggested Reading

1 John 1:1–9

If we confess our sins, He is faithful and just to forgive us our sins and to cleanse us from all unrighteousness. 1 John 1:9

---

*Adapted from Van Johnson, *Tackle the Impossible* (Melbourne, FL: Dove Christian Books, 1989), passim., particular quotes from pp. 121–125.

December **19**

Shalom, at Last

It was Max Federmann's misfortune to be a Jewish child in Hitler's Germany. He recalls the terror of the November night in 1938 when Nazi storm troopers marched through his village, destroying everything Jewish. He remembers his father and older brother being carried off to a concentration camp. His mother, too, was taken away to Auschwitz, where she perished. Max himself, 16, escaped to Yugoslavia, then to Italy.

After the war, Max married an Italian girl named Leda, and they had a daughter. After immigrating to California, two sons were added to the family. But tragedy struck again. The older son died in a car wreck, and this time Max lashed out at God: "How could you be a good God and bring such pain to me!"

Shortly afterward, Bernard, 14, was invited to church camp, and to Max's shock, he returned home believing in Jesus. Leda visited the church, and she, too, became a Christian.

At first, Max felt angry and rejected; but he decided to investigate their new faith in the light of his Hebrew Bible, studying what the Scriptures said about the Messiah. He also began reading the New Testament. He was stunned by how the prophecies in his Hebrew Bible seemed perfectly fulfilled by Jesus of Nazareth. He continued reading the New Testament, and *I fell to my knees when I came to 1 John 2:23 and understood the truth: "Whoever denies the Son does not have the Father either; he who acknowledges the Son has the Father also."*

I cried to God for forgiveness, and suddenly my heart was flooded with love for the Father and His Son, Jesus, the Messiah.

*My search had taken me almost a year. But from the moment I fell to my knees, I was able to love Jesus, my Messiah, with all my heart and mind and soul. I was even able to love those who had so cruelly persecuted my people. At last I understood the meaning of "Shalom!"**

Today's Suggested Reading

1 John 2:15–23

Whoever denies the Son does not have the Father either; he who acknowledges the Son has the Father also. 1 John 2:23

---

*Adapted from "True Shalom at Last," by Max Federmann as told to Chip Ricks in *Moody Magazine*, November/December, 1997, p. 96.

Five 'til Eight

December **20**

He cast a long shadow—a preacher for 67 years, a theological professor for 60 years, a seminary president for 13 years. John R. Sampey's influence touched multiple generations.

John was born in Alabama on his mother's birthday, September 27, 1863. One of his earliest memories occurred short years later when, as a young child, he watched his mother being baptized. When she disappeared beneath the water, he cried out in alarm and never forgot the scene.

His own conversion occurred as a teenager.

As I lay on the trundle bed on the night of March 3, 1877, I could not go to sleep. We had just had family prayers, and Father was reading and Mother was knitting. My younger brother had fallen asleep beside me; but I was in distress over my sins. In my desperation I began to talk in a whisper: "Lord Jesus, I do not know what to do. I have prayed, but get no relief. I read the Bible, but my sins are a burden on my soul. . . . If I am lost, I will go down trusting You." Then something happened. It seemed a great Presence filled the room and said to me almost in audible words: "My boy, I have been waiting for you to do what you have just done. You can count on Me to save you." I looked up to the old family clock on the mantel, and it was five minutes to eight o'clock.

Sampey didn't announce his conversion until July when he stepped forward in church, saying he now loved God and God's people as never before. The minister turned to the congregation and said: "Hereby we know that we have passed from death unto life, because we love the brethren."

That verse became Sampey's theme verse, for it impressed on him the mark of a Christian. Its words guided him for years to come, contributing greatly to his patient spirit and his willingness to serve. It became personified in him, and none who knew him doubted that he had passed from death to life, for he *did* love the brethren.

Today's Suggested Reading

1 John 3:13–24

We know that we have passed from death to life, because we love the brethren. He who does not love his brother abides in death. 1 John 3:14

December **21** A Gust of Praise

Medical technology has largely robbed us of the victorious deathbed scenes that end the biographies of many heroes of the Christian past. When the end comes now, we're often isolated, sedated, and connected to machines.

Not so John Fletcher, Wesley's associate. On Sunday, August 7, 1785, he began his sermon at church, but his countenance grew drawn and weak, his voice faltered, and he nearly fainted. Distressed murmurs ran through the congregation, and his wife Polly rushed to his side to dissuade him from continuing. But Fletcher sensed this was his last sermon, and he continued, mustering strength to discourse on the love and mercy of God. Afterward, he was helped home and took to his bed, "never again to walk in this world." He slept much after that, but during his lucid moments, Polly read and prayed with him.

She later wrote: *On Wednesday, he told me he had received such a manifestation of the full meaning of those words, "God is love," as he could never be able to express. "It fills my heart," said he, "every moment. O Polly, God is love! Shout, shout aloud! I want a gust to go to the ends of the earth."*

He then told her that, should speech fail, he would tap her twice with his finger to signify their testimony to each other of God's love.

The next day, his speech became befuddled, and Polly leaned over and whispered, "God is love." *Instantly, as if all his powers were awakened, he broke out in a rapture. "God is love! love! love! O for that gust of praise!"*

Polly remained by his side. He was hardly able to utter another word, but he kept tapping her with his finger. At last his lips moved again, and she heard him pray, "Head of the Church, be head of my wife!"

He sank quickly after that, yet frequently tapping Polly according to their sign, until "his precious soul entered into the joy of the Lord, without one struggle or groan, in the fifty-sixth year of his age."

Today's Suggested Reading

1 John 4:1–8

He who does not love does not know God, for God is love. 1 John 4:8

Cooling Blood

December **22**

It wasn't easy for Corrie ten Boom to forgive the Nazi captors who had tormented her at Ravensbruck. They had caused her to suffer horribly. Even worse, they had caused the death of her sister Betsy.

Ten years after her release, Corrie ran into a lady who wouldn't look her in the eyes. Asking about her, Corrie was told the woman had been a nurse at a concentration camp. Suddenly the memories flashed back. Corrie recalled taking Betsy to the infirmary to see this woman. Betsy's feet were paralyzed and she was dying. The nurse had been cruel and sharp-tongued.

Corrie's hatred now returned with vengeance. Her rage so boiled that she knew of but one thing to do. "Forgive me," she cried out to the Lord, "Forgive my hatred, O Lord. Teach me to love my enemies."

The blood of Jesus Christ seemed to suddenly cool her embittered heart, and Corrie felt the rage being displaced with a divine love she couldn't explain. She began praying for the woman, and one day shortly afterward she called the hospital where the nurse worked and invited the woman to a meeting at which she was speaking.

"What!" replied the nurse. "Do you want *me* to come?"

"Yes; that is why I called you."

"Then I'll come."

That evening the nurse listened carefully to Corrie's talk, and afterward Corrie sat down with her, opened her Bible, and explained 1 John 4:9: "In this the love of God was manifested toward us, that God has sent His only begotten Son into the world, that we might live through Him." The woman seemed to thirst for Corrie's quiet, confident words about God's love for us, His enemies. And that night, a former captive led her former captor to "a decision that made the angels sing."

God had taken Corrie's subconscious feelings of hatred, she later explained, and transformed them, using them as a window through which His light could shine into a darkened heart.

Today's Suggested Reading

1 John 4:9–16

In this the love of God was manifested toward us, that God has sent His only begotten Son into the world, that we might live through Him. 1 John 4:9

December **23** The Pearly Gate

William Tyndale was a brilliant, winsome scholar whose life was changed by finding today's verse in Erasmus' Greek New Testament. He called it *the pearly gate through which I entered the Kingdom. I used to think that salvation was not for me, since I did not love God; but those precious words showed me that God does not love us because we first loved Him. No, no; we love Him because He first loved us. It makes all the difference!*

Tyndale was born at a critical time. Christopher Columbus was discovering whole new worlds; the printing press was churning out books; and Luther's Reformation had rediscovered evangelical theology. As a young man, Tyndale felt the time was ripe to translate the Bible into the common languages, and began dreaming of rendering the Bible into English.

But his idea was poorly received by the British Church and State. Sir Thomas More was commissioned by Henry VIII to refute Tyndale, and the two carried on a war of words. In one of his early salvos, Tyndale published a letter in 1531 from Antwerp where he was in hiding. It began: *Our love and good works make not God first love us, nor change Him from hate to love. No, His love and deeds make us love, and change us from hate to love. For He loved us when we were evil, and His enemies; and chose us to make us good and to shew us love and to draw us to Him, that we should love again. If ye could see what is written in the first epistle of John, though all the other Scriptures were laid apart, ye should see all this. . . .*

Tyndale died at the stake at age 42, but he produced so accurate an English translation of Scripture that more than 90 percent of all his wordings appeared nearly 100 years later in the King James Version. He is called the "Father of the English Bible."

Today's Suggested Reading

1 John 4:12–19

We love Him because He first loved us. 1 John 4:19

The 66¢ Solution

Missionaries Dick Hillis and Margaret Humphrey were married on April 18, 1938, in a little house in Hankow, China. The only wedding music was the percussion of Japanese bombs in the distance. They moved into a drab, mud-brick house and settled into a flurry of missionary activity.

Seven months later, Margaret showed symptoms of fever. It rapidly worsened, and Dick anguished as it rose to 103 degrees, then to 105. With no doctor in the village and no adequate transportation to the distant hospital, he felt helpless. He prayed, but sensed no response from God. *Why? Why doesn't God answer? He couldn't take her from me. He knows I need her, not just for myself, but for the work also.*

As he knelt by Margaret's bed gripping her torrid hand, a sentence came to mind from a letter his father had written before his marriage: "Remember, Dick, if you are really in love, you will face the danger of loving the gift more than the Giver."

"Oh, God," Dick cried, "You have given me so much to love in Margaret. Is it possible I have loved her too much?" The closing words of 1 John flashed to mind: "Little children, keep yourselves from idols."

Knowing the Lord was working deeply in his heart, Dick knelt a long time, praying. "Lord, I give Margaret back to You. If You require it, I will walk to her grave, still trusting You. But if You will raise her up, I will always seek to put You first."

Peace came over him, allowing him to rest. The next morning when Margaret's temperature still hovered at 105 degrees, Dick decided to visit the local Chinese herb shop. The aged proprietor there found a small glass vial that a traveling medicine man had sold him two years previously. It was supposed to reduce fever. Dick purchased the solution for sixty-six cents, then hurried home and gave Margaret the injection. Her temperature began going down, and two weeks later she was good as new.*

Today's Suggested Reading
1 John 5:18–21

Little children, keep yourselves from idols. Amen. 1 John 5:21

*Adapted from Jan Winebrenner, *Steel in his Soul* (Chicago: Moody Press, 1985), pp. 60–62.

When He Came . . .

Jesus Christ came into the world with one thing in mind: To love us and wash us from our sins by His blood. He appeared for that reason a baby in Bethlehem, a lad in Nazareth, a preacher in Judea, a lamb on Calvary. In 1846, He reached out with that truth and touched a Scottish lad named James Geddie. And Geddie, wanting to touch others, left for the South Seas in 1848.

As his ship lumbered toward the New Hebrides, Geddie meditated on this verse, Revelation 1:5, writing in his journal: "My best enjoyments in time, and my prospects beyond the grave, center in the cross, which is the emblem of redeeming love."

Nothing could have prepared John for the evil he encountered while settling on the island of Aneityum. The inhabitants considered human flesh the most savory of foods, and cannibalism was rampant. Parents routinely killed and ate their own children. Violence, theft, and warfare were common. "If ever we win these benighted islanders," Geddie wrote, "we must draw them with cords of love. I know of no power that is adequate except the power of the living Christ who 'loved us and washed us from our sins by His own blood.'"

He combated the darkness by frequently preaching from Revelation 1:5: "Use no weapon but that which our Redeemer uses, the weapons of love. Let us constantly keep our hearts upon Him that loved us and washed us from our sins."

His journal for February 9, 1849 states: "In the darkness, degradation, and misery that surrounds me, I look forward in faith to the time when some of these poor islanders will unite in the triumphant song of ransomed souls, 'Unto Him that loved us and washed us from our sins in His own blood.'"

He lived to see it happen.

Geddie died just before Christmas, 1872, and a tablet was afterward installed in his island church: "In memory of John Geddie . . . Missionary from Nova Scotia to Aneityum for twenty-four years. When he landed in 1848, there were no Christians here, and when he left in 1872, there were no heathen."

Today's Suggested Reading
Revelation 1:1–8

To Him who loved us and washed us from our sins in His own blood. . . . Revelation 1:5

Stay of Death

At age 15, George T. B. Davis determined to give himself to the Lord's service; and, inspired by such mentors as D. L. Moody, R. A. Torrey, and Charles M. Alexander, he resolved to be a soul-winner. He promised himself to speak to someone each day about accepting Christ.

Sometimes I would forget to speak to someone during the day, and after I had retired would suddenly remember that I had not spoken to anyone that day about accepting Christ. I would get up and dress and go out on the streets. Perhaps the first person I met would be walking very rapidly and I would not speak to him, but presently I would find an opportunity and grasp it.

When World War I erupted, Davis began working among the soldiers under the auspices of the Pocket Testament League, distributing Bibles to those who would agree to carry them and read them.

While holding meetings in a military camp at Fort Matilda in Scotland, Davis met a Private Cairney who showed him a Pocket Testament League Bible that had saved his brother's life. The brother had kept it in the upper left-hand pocket of his jacket. Suddenly a sharp-nosed, steel-jacketed German bullet went straight for his heart, but struck the little Book instead. It plowed its way through page after page and finally stopped at Revelation 3:6, "He that hath an ear, let him hear what the Spirit saith unto the churches."

The soldier *did* listen and was thus spiritually prepared for death when, a month later, he was hit by shrapnel. Being in great pain, he groaned fearfully. A chum leaned over and said, "Jock, don't groan so."

He replied, "I know I'm groaning and I'm suffering, but think how the Savior suffered for us on Calvary."

Davis was given that little bullet-drilled New Testament, and he used it for the rest of the war to impress soldiers with the urgency of salvation, saying, "He who has an ear, let him hear."

Today's Suggested Reading
Revelation 3:1–6

He who has an ear, let him hear what the Spirit says to the churches.
Revelation 3:6

December **27**

And Songs before Unknown

Now that you've put away "Joy to the World" for another year, try some of Isaac Watts' other 600 hymns, such as "When I Survey the Wondrous Cross," "O God, Our Help in Ages Past," and "Jesus Shall Reign Wher'er the Sun." As you do, remember that Watts' very first hymn was based on Revelation 5.

The writing of hymns by an upstart teenager was a bold move, for in the years following the Reformation, Protestants were divided on the question of hymns. Lutherans and Moravians loved them. But most English churches, especially in the Calvinistic tradition, clung to the singing of Psalms alone.

One Sunday in 1692, Isaac Watts, 18, did not sing during church services. When his father rebuked him, Isaac retorted that the music wasn't worth singing, that the Psalms didn't rhyme, that they were wooden and awkward in form and phrase.

"Those hymns were good enough for your grandfather and father," said the senior Watts, "and they will have to be good enough for you."

"They will never do for me, Father, regardless of what you and your father thought of them."

"If you don't like the hymns we sing, then write better ones!"

"I have written better ones, Father, and if you will relax and listen, I will read one to you." Isaac told his father he had been studying the song of the angels in Revelation 5:6–10, and had rewritten it, giving it rhyme and rhythm.

Behold the glories of the Lamb / Amidst His Father's throne;
Prepare new honors for His name, / And songs before unknown.

His astonished father took his son's composition to the church, and the following Sunday the congregation loved it so much that Isaac was asked to bring another the next Sunday, and the next, and the next, for over 222 consecutive weeks.

Today Isaac Watts is called the father of modern English hymnody. He did indeed bring much joy to the world.

Today's Suggested Reading
Revelation 5:1–10

But one of the elders said to me, "Do not weep. Behold, the Lion of the tribe of Judah, the Root of David, has prevailed. . . . Revelation 5:5

Swarmed

December **28**

At Louisiana State University, Ricky McAlister acquired a small green New Testament from the Gideons, but stashed it away unread. Later, packing for a fishing trip, he tossed it into his gear for good luck. With two buddies, he drove through the night, arriving at their fishing spot early Monday morning. The weather was hot, the fish weren't biting, and Ricky got nothing but a blistering sunburn. Ditto Tuesday. Finally, the guys gave up and collapsed in their room with a chest of beer.

We were sitting there waiting for the weather to cool off, when my friend asked, "Have you got any sports magazines?" I said, "Yeah, out in the car, but I'm not going to get 'em. It's too hot." He said, "Well throw me that little green Bible."

He started thumbing through the Testament, then said, "Hey, listen to this." He was reading from Revelation. I had never heard of Revelation. He started reading about these giant locusts that were going to come and eat on people. The more he read, the more afraid I became. I sat there and put my beer down. All I could think about was something I hate worse than anything, for a spider or snake to crawl on me. I would have dreams sometimes of things crawling on me or biting me, and I would be terrified.

He kept reading, and I got so afraid I was shaking. All this time the Lord had been dealing with me and I had been rejecting and rejecting. Well, I got to thinking about those locusts and I said, "Why don't we go home?" While my friends went out to load the boat, I got that little Bible and started reading.

The next evening, Ricky attended a gospel service with his girlfriend, and there he gave his life to Christ. He later served the Lord in Bolivia, pastored in Louisiana, led one relative after another to Christ, and told audiences far and wide how he was driven to the Lord by a swarm of locusts.*

Today's Suggested Reading
Revelation 9:1–12

Then out of the smoke locusts came upon the earth. And to them was given power, as the scorpions of the earth have power. Revelation 9:3

*Adapted from "A Little Green Testament" by Ricky McAlister, in *Converted and Called* (Nashville: The Gideons International, n.d.), pp. 83–85.

December **29** Amen! and Alleluia!

Amen" and "Alleluia" are words that unite Christians around the world, for they are virtually the same in every language, as illustrated by a gripping story that Daniel Christiansen tells about a relative, a Romanian soldier in World War II, named Ana Gheorghe.

It was 1941, and Russian troops had overrun the Romanian region of Bessarabia and entered Moldavia. Ana and his comrades were badly frightened. Bullets whizzed around them, and mortar shells shook the earth. By day, Ana sought relief reading his Bible, but at night he could only crouch close to the earth and recall verses memorized in childhood.

One day during a spray of enemy fire, Ana was separated from his company. In a panic, he bolted deeper and deeper into the woods until, huddling at the base of a large tree, he fell asleep from exhaustion. The next day, trying to find his comrades, he moved cautiously toward the front, staying in the shadows of the trees, nibbling a crust of bread, drinking from streams. Hearing the battle closing in, he unslung his rifle, pulled the bolt, and watched for the enemy, his nerves near the breaking point. Twenty yards away, a Russian soldier suddenly appeared.

All my mental rehearsals of bravery served me nothing. I dropped my gun and fell to my knees, then buried my face in my sweating palms and began to pray. While praying, I waited for the cold touch of the Russian's rifle barrel against my head.

I felt a slight pressure on my shoulder close to my neck. I opened my eyes slowly. There was my enemy kneeling in front of me, his gun lying next to mine among the wildflowers. His eyes were closed in prayer. We did not understand a single word of the other's language, but we could pray. We ended our prayer with two words that need no translation: "Alleluia . . . Amen!"

Then, after a tearful embrace, we walked quickly to opposite sides of the clearing and disappeared beneath the trees.

Today's Suggested Reading
Revelation 19:1–8

And the twenty-four elders and the four living creatures fell down and worshiped God who sat on the throne, saying, "Amen! Alleluia!" Revelation 19:4

"One Last Time" December **30**

Prison Fellowship volunteer Bob McAlister found Rusty Woomer sitting in his cell motionless, face chalk-colored, dozens of roaches crawling over him. Bob tried talking with him, but the prisoner was unresponsive. "Rusty," said Bob at last, "just say the word 'Jesus.'" With much effort, Rusty pursed his lips together and whispered, "Jesus." When Bob asked Rusty if he wanted to trust Christ as Savior, tears came to his eyes and he nodded.

The following Monday, Bob was stunned by the difference. Rusty's cell was spotless, roaches and dirt gone. So was the pornography. "I spent all weekend cleaning my cell," said Rusty, "'cause I figured that's what Jesus wanted me to do."

For four years, the men enjoyed a deepening friendship, studying Scripture, praying, talking. Finally, Rusty's appeals were all denied and execution became certain.

On Rusty's last day on earth, he said an emotional goodbye to his father, sisters, and brother. Everyone was ushered out, and the two friends sat in quiet, somber fellowship, waiting for the end.

As Rusty's head and right leg were shaved he said, "Read me the Bible one last time." *I opened my Bible to Revelation 21. I read, ". . . and He shall wipe away every tear from their eyes; and there shall no longer be any death. . . ." A clump of Rusty's hair fell on my lap; another on my Bible. I looked up, and, with a half-shaven head, Rusty was smiling—a peaceful smile I have never seen on another human being.*

At 12:55 A.M. they came for Rusty. After reading him the death warrant, Warden George Martin asked, "Are you ready?"

"Let's go," he replied. I followed Rusty to the death chamber, and my final words to him were, "Rusty, look to Jesus." Rusty was strapped into the chair and a leather helmet attached to his head. I heard his last words: "I'm sorry. I claim Jesus Christ as my Savior. My only wish is that everyone in the world could feel the love I have felt from Him."

Five minutes later, Rusty was in heaven.*

Today's Suggested Reading
Revelation 21:1–5

Then I saw a new heaven and a new earth, for the first heaven and the first earth had passed away. Revelation 21:1

*Adapted from "Countdown to Paradise," by Bob McAlister in *Jubilee: The Monthly Newsletter of Prison Fellowship,* July, 1990, p. 1–5.

December **31** Whosoever Will

You might as well know the end of the story now. James Chalmers was eaten by cannibals on Goaribari Island in the South Seas on April 4, 1901. But his death matched his life—both were invested in passionately inviting benighted souls to come freely to Christ.

Chalmers had heard God's call to missionary service as a teen. His Scottish pastor had read a letter one Sunday from the Fiji Islands, telling of the gospel's power to transform cannibals, followed by an appeal for more workers. James resolved then and there to go.

James' conversion occurred three years later, at age eighteen, when a couple of Irish evangelists came into the area to preach. *It was raining hard, but I started; and on arriving at the bottom of the stairs, I listened whilst they sang "All People That on Earth Do Dwell" to the tune "Old Hundredth," and I thought I had never heard such singing before—so solemn, yet so joyful. I ascended the steps and entered. There was a large congregation intensely in earnest. The younger of the evangelists was the first to speak. He announced as his text these words: "Then the Spirit and the bride say, 'Come!' And let him who hears say, 'Come!' And let him who thirsts come. Whoever desires, let him take the water of life freely." He spoke directly to me. I felt it much; but at the close I hurried away back to town.*

James agonized over his spiritual condition for several days, describing himself as *pierced through and through, and lost beyond all hope of salvation.* The next morning, his minister, Rev. Gilbert Meikle, spoke to him of Christ's blood, assured him of God's love, and led him to the water of life.

Almost instantly James began preparing for the South Seas, never doubting his earlier call to missions. In time, he established 130 mission stations throughout New Guinea, and thousands came to Christ, including 64 men who became pastors, preachers, and missionaries.

Today's Suggested Reading
Revelation 22:12–21

Then the Spirit and the bride say, "Come!" And let him who hears say, "Come!" And let him who thirsts come. Whoever desires, let him take the water of life freely. Revelation 22:17

Index of Selected Illustrations

Robert J. Morgan, pastor of The Donelson Fellowship in Nashville, Tennessee, is the author of *On This Day* (Nelson), *Tiny Talks: A Book of Devotions for Young Children* (Nelson) and *Empowered Parenting* (LifeWay Press). He also served as General Editor of *The Children's Devotional Bible* (Nelson). He is a frequent contributor to magazines like *Leadership Journal* and conducts Bible conferences, parenting and marriage retreats, and leadership development seminars across the country. He is available through Cool Springs Artists & Speakers, Inc., at 615-771-6644, or visit the website at http://www.donelson.org.